Semiotics and Legal Theory

Semiotics and Legal Theory

Bernard S. Jackson

Professor of Law
University of Kent at Canterbury

Routledge & Kegan Paul
London, Boston, Melbourne and Henley

First published in 1985
by Routledge & Kegan Paul plc

14 Leicester Square, London WC2H 7PH, England

9 Park Street, Boston, Mass. 02108, USA

464 St Kilda Road, Melbourne,
Victoria 3004, Australia and

Broadway House, Newtown Road,
Henley on Thames, Oxon RG9 1EN, England

Printed in Great Britain by
Billing and Sons Ltd,
Worcester

Library of Congress Cataloging in Publication Data

Jackson, Bernard S.

Semiotics and legal theory.
Bibliography: p.
1. Semantics (Law) 2. Law—Philosophy. 3. Semiotics.
I. Title.
K213.J32 1985 340'.142 85-2467

ISBN 0-7100-9719-0

For Iain and Judith

CONTENTS

Contents

Part Three: Semiotic Presuppositions of Legal Theorists

Part Four: Conclusions

PREFACE

This book is an exercise in exposition, comparison, criticism and construction. I have taken two very different intellectual traditions, structuralist semiotics as represented by A.J. Greimas and modern (mainly positivist) legal theory as represented by Hart, MacCormick, Dworkin and Kelsen, and by juxtaposing them have sought to clarify and assess their respective semiotic presuppositions, in order to lay some foundations for a semiotically sensitive theory of law. This latter end could, no doubt, have been achieved without the weight of preceding exposition, which forms the bulk of Parts Two and Three. But that is not my style; I do not seek to conceal, as is common in some circles, the stimulation I receive from critical reflection upon the work of others. More important, I hope that this exercise in comparative theory will serve the cause of inter-disciplinary communication. The book is designed for both jurists and semioticians. To facilitate access across the disciplinary divide, I have included at the head of each chapter an abstract, which serves as both summary and conclusion to each section.

Semiotics and Legal Theory is the result of a project conceived in the late seventies. My interest in structuralism was first generated by a sense of dissatisfaction with the working methods and theoretical sensitivity of comparative legal history, a dissatisfaction which I expressed in some of my work on early Jewish Law (1975:ch.1, 1980c, 1980d). But I rapidly realised that the development of a structuralist methodology for legal history required an analysis of the structuralist contribution to legal theory. I offered a preliminary account of this as an overgrown paper to the 1979 conference of the (U.K.) Association for Legal and Social Philosophy at Durham. In

1980, I was awarded a Personal Research Grant by the Social Science Research Council, to develop this work further. It soon became apparent to me that 'structuralism' was as diverse as is 'legal theory', and that I must choose between a 'Cook's tour' of structuralism and a thorough presentation of one strand within it. The choice of the latter route, represented particularly by Part Two of this book, was facilitated by the availability from within that tradition of a 'pilot' application of its methods to a legal text. Through a critical exposition of this particular approach, I hope to reveal the major theoretical and methodological issues which arise throughout much of the structuralist tradition. At the same time, I have sought, particularly in the notes, to provide a broader indication of the range of work which is now available. Structuralism, if defined more loosely than is done in this book (where it is taken to mean the application of linguistic methods to units of discourse larger than a sentence) can be understood to include both Chomskian linguistics and Piagetian cognitive developmental psychology. But for reasons of both space and coherence, consideration of their relationship to legal studies has been excluded from the present work, and will appear elsewhere.

In the course of the last four years, my work has been greatly assisted by numerous institutions and individuals, from whom not only the present book but also the associated work in progress derives benefit. The project was conceived and executed in my years as Head of the Department of Law at Liverpool Polytechnic, and owes much to the tolerance and interest of my colleagues there. It received considerable impetus from a grant awarded by the SSRC, which made it possible for me to take six months' leave from my normal duties. Further travel and research assistance was generously provided by the British Academy in 1983, and by the British Council in 1984. The limitations of written discourse as a medium of communication are only too apparent to someone seeking to penetrate the arcana of a new discipline, and such progress as I have made would have been impossible without a wide range of personal contacts, and reactions to my lectures and conference papers. I am indebted to colleagues at the Law Schools of Osgoode Hall, Berkeley, Yale, Paris, Exeter and Cardiff, to the Comparative Literature Department at Beer Sheva, the Religious Studies Department at Lancaster, the Social

Studies Department at Liverpool Polytechnic, the Jean Piaget Centre at Manchester Polytechnic, and the School of Interdisciplinary Human Studies at the University of Bradford, for hosting seminars, and giving me the benefit of their reactions to various papers related to this book. Colleagues in America, France, Italy and Israel (where I spent a stimulating term as a Lady Davis Visiting Professor), as well as nearer to home, have kindly discussed various problems with me, and I should like to record my gratitude to them: Bruce Ackerman, Paul Amselek, **André-Jean Arnaud,** Anthony Beck, Hanina Ben Menahem, Danièle Bourcier, Albert Brimo, Massimo Brutti, Antonio and Gaetano Carcaterra, **Domenico Carzo,** Noam Chomsky, Amadeo Conte, Brenda Danet, Pierre Dauchy, **Mary Douglas,** Itamar Eben-Zoar, Yaron Ezrahi, Paolo Fabbri, Harel Fisch, Howard Gardner, Ruth Gavison, A.J. Greimas, **Peter Goodrich,** Donald Hermann, **Keekok Lee,** Alan Jenkins, **Mario Jori, Georges Kalinowski,** Duncan Kennedy, Frank Kermode, Stephan Körner, **Eric Landowski, Pierre Lerat,** Etienne Le Roy, Claude Lévi-Strauss, Mario Losano, Avishai Margalit, Antonio Anselmo Martino, **Stanley Paulson,** Menachem Perry, Massimo Piattelli-Palmarini, Shlomit Rimon, Ino Rossi, Natan Rotenstreich, Marina Sbisà, Uberto Scarpelli, David Schiff, Dimitri Segal, J.L. Sourioux, Dan Sperber, Sidney Strauss, Yan Thomas, Tuen Van Dijk, Helen Weinreich-Haste, Michel Villey.

A number of these colleagues (whose names are emboldened) have further assisted me by commenting on drafts of my work, as also have Roque Carrion-Wam, Michael Freeman, Neil MacCormick, Michael Moore, Iain Stewart and Tom Torrance. Above all, I must express my appreciation to two good friends: the semiotician Eric Landowski and the philosopher Stanley Paulson commented at various times on almost two full drafts of the present book.

Both my immediate colleagues and my family have rendered practical assistance going far beyond mere tolerance. I am especially indebted to my colleagues in the Liverpool Polytechnic Library, without whose ever-courteous and efficient operation of the Inter-Library Loans Service my research would have been impossible, and to my friend Roy Sharp, Head of the Department of Graphic Design, who kindly assisted with the diagrams. A huge amount of typing was undertaken by my father. The book is dedicated to my children - poor compensation for the hours of which they have been deprived. Nor was Judith terribly amused, at the time, by the contribution she unwittingly made to the analysis of black v. white (section 4.3).

PART ONE

Introduction

CHAPTER ONE

Mapping the Issues

(1.1) The range of legal and semiotic theories: Jurisprudential theories are often classified as naturalist, positivist or realist. Both naturalism and positivism see law as a reified system, but differ according to whether it is a matter only of human convention, or whether it includes (often rational) universals. Realism commonly rejects the reification of law, in favour of a view of legal rules related to human goals, practices and psychological states. Semiotic theories admit of similar classification. Chomsky stresses the universals of human language systems; structural semantics propose conventional systems of meaning; pragmatic theories often deny the autonomy of such systems, and view meaning in relation to the goals of human communication and the practices of its participants. Some exponents of linguistic realism criticise the formalist emphasis on 'langue' rather than 'parole' (Saussure) or 'competence' rather than 'performance' (Chomsky). **(1.2) Law as a Semiotic System:** The analysis of law involves the taking of positions on this range of legal and semiotic theories. Law may be regarded as a dual semiotic system, the language in which it is expressed and the discursive system expressed by that language. If so, choices still need to be made as to the type of semiotic analysis to be applied to the discursive system. The effect of differences between Peircian (pragmatic) and Saussurian (structuralist) semiotics are sketched in respect of the structure of semiosis (binary or triadic, representing different views of the status of the 'referent'), the classification of signs ('signals' or 'signs'), their processes (interpretation or decoding) and functions (communication, signification, connotation and the role of communicative intent). **(1.3) Law, Semiotics and Philosophy:** In legal philosophy Scandinavian legal realism has come closest to the view that language is central to the nature of law but in so doing it endorses a functionalist approach, akin to that of the 'speech act' tradition, viewing legal language primarily in terms of the goals and intentions of authors. European semiotics stresses the contribution of the language-system, of which the speaker may only be partly conscious. Both semiotics and legal theory offer attemps to mediate between these positions. Individualist and collectivist conceptions of action are reflected in the rival traditions.

1.1 THE RANGE OF LEGAL AND SEMIOTIC THEORIES

The question 'What is law ?' has many meanings, and its polysemicity is increasingly recognised in legal theory. It may mean: what universals, if any, are found in that phenomenon to which we attach the name 'law' ?; what are the origins of that phenomenon to which we attach the name 'law' ?; what do we seek to refer to when we use the word 'law' ?; what underlying concept is pre-supposed in our use of the word 'law' ?; what kind of objectivity, if any, corresponds to our concept 'law' ?; what empirical realities are to be observed in that to which we refer as 'law' ? Lurking behind all these questions is the further epistemological issue: why should our answer to any one - more likely, in practice, to any cluster of these questions - be regarded as significant ?

Legal theories may be crudely classified as naturalist, positivist or realist. Naturalists claim the existence of universals, often relating to the origins of law, and regard them as significant in contributing to the presence of an objective reality, the legal system. Positivists eschew such universals (at least for the purposes of legal theory), and, where they adopt criteria from the origins of law in order to construct an objective legal reality, their choice of origins reflect views on the significance of human action (individual or social). Realists eschew not only universals but also the claim to an objective legal reality, and instead regard as significant the empirical phenomena of the law, together with their causes and effects. Sometimes such realism extends to a scepticism of the very concept of normativity - a distinguishing feature of legal systems which is regarded as central by both naturalists and positivists.

Such fundamental issues as these have assumed a multitude of specific forms in the history of legal thought. This book addresses itself principally to the most prominent modern debates within positivism. The mold of classical legal positivism has, in the twentieth century, been cracking. Dworkin, while remaining at heart within the family of legal positivism, has offered criticisms inspired by both naturalism and realism; Kelsen, in his later period, made significant concessions to realism. These tensions within contemporary legal positivism are fully explored in Part Three, in terms of the semiotic presuppositions of some of its different versions. For the moment, it suffices to provide a basic account of the issues as they are presently debated.

Natural law theorists contend that human enactment is not the exclusive source of legal obligation; 'nature' is also such a source. A version of this approach goes back to the Stoic identification of nature with human reason. Sometimes it is claimed that this reason has been placed in human nature by God, but others in the rationalist tradition of natural law (and notably Grotius) see this further claim as inessential. Through this common human nature, mankind universally perceives the importance of certain basic norms. This leads, on the one hand, to an intuitive theory of morality, but more strongly to a theory of natural law: these basic norms are not merely fundamental rules which any system of human law **ought** to include; they are legal rules by their very nature.

Jurisprudential positivism rejects this approach. In terms of general philosophy, it claims that an 'ought' (whether moral or legal) cannot be derived from an 'is' (such as a human sentiment, albeit universal); in jurisprudential terms, it thus adheres to the view that there is no necessary connection between law and morality. Law is a matter exclusively of human choice, and where it incorporates elements of morality, that incorporation is contingent upon the exercise of such a choice within particular legal systems. The need to provide an account of law which does not commit the 'naturalistic fallacy' of deriving an 'ought' from an 'is' is taken most seriously by Hans Kelsen, who argues that the legal character of a norm depends exclusively upon its conformity with a superior norm within a hierarchical normative system, the apex of the system consisting of a 'basic norm' (**Grundnorm**) which is the logical presupposition on which the normative validity of the rest of the system depends. For Kelsen, any account of legal validity must be 'pure', in order to avoid the naturalistic fallacy; it must avoid any reductionism to such facts as are the subject matter of politics, psychology, sociology or economics.

Hart's version of positivism has many elements in common with that of Kelsen, but is less radical in its rejection of fact-reductionism, and departs from the Kelsenian view in the emphasis it places upon two particular 'central characteristics' of legal systems. For Hart, legal validity ultimately rests upon acceptance (a psychological fact) by officialdom of the normative character of the legal system. That system is characterised by the interaction of two distinct types of rules - 'primary' and 'secondary'. Primary rules concern the behaviour of the subjects of the system; secondary rules are chiefly concerned with the recognition and change of primary rules, and the manner of adjudication of disputes. It is a central characteristic of legal systems that its norms represent neither mere regularities of behaviour, nor responses to coercion, but rather are accepted from the 'internal point of view'. The legal systems of advanced societies rest upon acceptance, particularly by officialdom, of the view that one ought to follow primary rules because failure to do so would be breach of the secondary rules, and such failure would be a matter of reproach.

The secondary rules of the Hartian legal system thus depend upon convention, not nature. Their content, too, reflects the orientation of positivism towards an image of law based upon human choice. Whereas it might be conceptually possible within Hart's theory to envisage a legal system which adopts natural law (in the sense described above) as its criterion of recognition, what we actually find is the use of legal 'institutions' as the media through which such human choices are made. For these and other reasons, Hart holds strongly to the view that there is no necessary connection between law and morality. At the same time, he is very much concerned with the question of the morality of law: what rules law ought to contain as a matter of morality (his particular moral philosophy being constructed on utilitarian lines), even though he denies that any such arguments make the resulting norms legal.

Jurisprudential positivism, especially as represented by Hart, has been attacked by Ronald Dworkin on the grounds that no sufficient account of the workings of legal systems can be provided in terms of Hart's secondary rules. In particular, the central place of any 'ultimate' or 'master' rule of recognition is contested. The latter, Dworkin argues, can at best provide an account of but one component of the legal system - legal 'rules'. They cannot account for an equally important part of the legal system, namely 'legal principles'. Some critics of Dworkin have maintained that Hart's theory can readily accommodate this argument: that the distinction between 'rules' and 'principles', and the manner in which the two categories operate, is a matter of degree rather than a difference in kind, and that secondary rules of recognition can be formulated in such a manner as to include the workings of 'principles'. But there is more at stake in Dworkin's attack on positivism than the mere formulation of secondary rules of recognition. For Dworkin argues that the workings of 'principles' reflect a view of legal systems as not sufficiently accounted for by acts of human choice, but as including - at any moment of time - rational implications which have not yet been the subject of human choice. Thus, whereas the positivist views the legal system as a set of rules already established by acts of human choice (within the institutionalised legal system) combined with a discretion (authorised by the legal system) to decide new questions which have not yet been so determined, Dworkin rejects any such notion of discretion (which he labels 'strong'), and argues that it is necessary for the judge to act as if there already exists - before and independent of particular acts of will within the legal system - a privileged answer to any question which may arise for legal determination. But Dworkin distances himself from traditional theories of natural law in the following respect: the ultimate source of his (sometime) 'one correct answer' is not any universal morality or universal human reason, but rather the morality and political values of a particular human community.

Even within mainstream positivism, we encounter significant differences in defining the object 'law'. The nineteenth century English legal philosopher John Austin distinguished between 'law properly so called' and 'law strictly so called'. The former, the proper use of the term 'law', was any 'rule laid down for the guidance of an intelligent being by an intelligent being having power over him'; it included rules laid down by the members of a club, on pain of exclusion, and other imperatives which do not rely on state coercion. 'Laws strictly so called', on the other hand, were laid down in the context of sovereignty; these alone were 'positive law', and constituted the proper subject matter of jurisprudence. Even Hart, who rejects definitions (by way of necessary and sufficient conditions) of the complex concept 'law', accepts the distinction between 'paradigm' instances of law (such as a municipal legal system) and more remote instances, such as international law. Much depends upon the purpose of the classificatory exercise.

Within the class of realist theories of law, considerable diversity may also be found. Scandinavian realists have tended to reduce law to the psychological states of the participants - their feeling of obligation, mediated through language; American realists have stressed regularities of legal behaviour - what courts and others actually do - as forming the basis of predictions (predictions which might very well vary from official statements of the 'rule'). The difference between the two approaches reflects to some degree the battle-lines in psychology over behaviourism. The American research tends to view rules from an 'external viewpoint', rather than as a direct account of the attitudes of the participants. Others have taken a sociological rather than a psychological route, seeing law in terms of grand social movements, whether it be in the direction of a conservatively-oriented Historical Jurisprudence, which values legal evolution insofar as it preserves traditional values, or a liberal Sociology of Law devoted to maximising social engineering in aid of social democracy, or a Marxist Jurisprudence which sees the reality of the law as its reflection of causal (predominantly economic) processes leading inexorably to the socialist revolution. The Scandinavian realists have shown the greatest interest in legal language; their work forms an important bridge between traditional jurisprudence and the semiotics of law. The modern 'critical legal studies' movement has sometimes sought to integrate aspects of modern semiotics into its eclectic theoretical base. (1) Modern North American legal scholarship has begun to show an interest also in deconstruction (2) and hermeneutics (3).

The Range of Semiotic Theories

Semiotic theories display a comparable range of questions and approaches. Indeed, it would not be difficult to classify semiotic theories under the same rubrics of naturalist, positivist and realist.

Naturalism in semiotics is today most prominently represented by the philosophical claims which Chomsky takes to be implied by his account of linguistic, and particularly syntactic, structures. Chomsky seeks to provide an account of a universal linguistic competence, which in his view can best be explained in terms of the human genetic endowment. Like natural law theory, Chomsky relies heavily upon a form of rationalism, in his case that derived from Descartes. Opposition to such claims has come from two directions. On the one hand, there are those who approve of Chomsky's methods, and of the ontological presuppositions which they reflect, but who reject the naturalist conclusion. John Lyons, for example, accepts the feasibility of studying semantics 'as such', but rejects - or regards as unnecessary or unproven - such claims to innatism which Chomsky appears to make. By contrast Geoffrey Sampson rejects the whole notion that language may be studied 'as such', in the sense of a snapshot picture of a language system, rather than as an historical, changing phenomenon, to be viewed always in the context of its uses (e.g. 1980a:73f.). That latter viewpoint is more conventionally characterised in terms of the dominance of pragmatics over semantics.

The semiotic approach of the school of A.J. Greimas, which forms the principal focus of interest of Part Two of this book, may be characterised as predominantly (though by no means exclusively) positivist in this sense. It builds upon the tradition of structural semantics, which claims both the possibility and the desirability of a formal account of the system of meanings in a language, viewed synchronically. (4) That approach, derived from the tradition of Saussure, has its origin in linguistics. In common with other forms of structuralist theory, Greimasian semiotics then claims that units of language larger than the individual sentence - discursive units - are susceptible to the same methods of analysis as are applied in linguistics proper. The formal analysis of semantics thus becomes a model for the analysis of the underlying system which gives meaning to discourse. The subject matter of the analysis, at both the linguistic and discursive levels, is taken to be sufficiently identifiable and autonomous - the system of meanings of words on the one hand, the system of meanings in a given text on the other. **(5)**

Within positivist semiotics, we also find narrower and wider definitions of the proper subject matter. Sandor Hervey, in the Introduction to his excellent **Semiotic Perspectives,** classifies semiotic theories as having wide, medium or narrow scope (1982:3f.). **(6)** His categories are constructed in terms of two variables: whether semiotic theory should be restricted to communication taken as an intentional act (or whether it extends also to non-deliberate signification); and whether the conveying of meaning proceeds through a system or not. 'Wide' theories, exemplified for Hervey by Peirce and Morris, do not restrict the proper subject matter of semiotics in terms of either variable. 'Narrow' theories (e.g. Saussure) confine themselves to communication within a system, which is intended for such deliberate communication. 'Medium' theories adopt as a restriction only one of these variables: in the case of Speech Act theory (Austin, Searle), 'deliberate, conventional forms of communication' form the subject matter (whether the conventions amount to a 'system' or not), while for Barthes any form of communication (whether deliberate or not) falls within semiotics, provided that such communication occurs within a semiotic system. **(7)**

Modern linguistics has been dominated by the notion of language as a system, whether conceived in terms of the transformational grammar of Chomsky or the structural semantics derived from Saussure. Both manifestations of this view explicitly distinguish the study of language as a system from the study of particular manifestations of that sytem. Chomsky concerns himself primarily with linguistic 'competence' rather than linguistic 'performance'; Saussure distinguished the study of 'langue' (the language system) from that of 'parole' (speech: we might almost say the 'speech act', whether written or oral). Goodrich (1983,1984) compares such linguistic theories with legal positivism. Both construct an autonomous system as the object of their study, and exclude from their concerns the empirical manifestations of those systems (except insofar as the latter exemplify systemic features). Arguing instead for a form of Critical Theory, he condemns both legal and semiotic positivism as ideological mystifications. Even the notion of a conventional semantic 'core' (popularised amongst legal philosophers by Hart) is dismissed as the 'semantics of consensus'. Such systemic constructions serve only to divert attention from the real historical processes, and the power relations operating within them.

Goodrich's view may be taken to represent a form of linguistic realism, rejecting the reification of language-systems at the expense of attention to the actual operation of the language as a social and historical phenomenon. But linguistic realism, like legal realism, is not confined to one political view. The attack mounted by Sampson on the theories of Chomsky, an attack which extends to Chomsky's choice of 'competence' rather than 'performance' as the object of study, includes Chomsky's political as well as his linguistic views. Chomsky may count as a 'radical' in American terms, but he would hardly be found in any Marxist Pantheon; Sampson, however, stands more than a few discrete paces to the right of him. Between Sampson and Goodrich, there stands as large a chasm as that between Historical and Marxist Jurisprudence.

It has recently been suggested that the legal theory of Dworkin reflects an interest in 'performance' rather than 'competence', and in this sense is to be associated with realism rather than formalism in legal philosophy. Perrott bases this comparison upon Dworkin's claim that the operation of rules within a system (such as would be constituted by a positivist 'rule of recognition') fails to provide an adequate account of the empirical realities of law, particularly of the way judges reason in 'hard cases' (1980:12). Just as at the 'performance' level of a language, we encounter sentences which succeed in conveying meaning even though they are not 'well-formed' according to the rules of that language, so too we may find at the 'performance' level of law the actual use of rules and other phenomena (such as the Dworkinian principles) which are not formally valid in terms of the rules of recognition of the system. (8)

Dworkin undoubtedly does build upon the American Realist tradition in Jurisprudence. Like his predecessors, he argues that if one looks at the actual practice of legal reasoning, one finds the use of criteria for the recognition of law which are not sufficiently accounted for by the traditional positivist account. But Dworkin goes beyond his realist predecessors in important respects, in a manner such as to suggest that any parallel with linguistic theory cannot be restricted to the sphere of 'performance'. His 'legal principles' are not presented as in any way 'second-class' (a term which Perrott uses to describe the Chomskian conception of grammatically ill-formed but nevertheless acceptable sentences). Indeed, both Dworkin's legal principles and the hypothetical rules which they are likely to generate when activated by the judge are regarded as part and parcel of the legal system, even before they have been formulated. Here, Dworkin departs from positivism in the direction of natural law rather than realism. It is Hercules the supreme rationalist (Descartes transfigured) whom he puts in the driving seat. Chomsky, in accounting for ill-formed sentences, makes no comparable claims as to their membership of the language in question: such sentences themselves become part of the language (if not the language system) only once they are uttered and understood.

1.2 LAW AS A SEMIOTIC SYSTEM

When sentences are combined into larger units of discourse, the effect may be more than the simple accumulation of the atomic meanings of the individual sentences. The resultant discourse may have a 'meaning' of its own. That latter meaning is transmitted by a different 'code' than that of the language itself. Some semioticians claim that we have here the interaction of different semiotic systems.

The claim may be illustrated by reference to the example of literature. Not everyone in possession of the natural language 'English' can 'read' an English novel, even though the 'meaning' of each sentence or even paragraph may, in isolation, be clear to that reader. Semioticians would claim that this results from the fact that 'literature' involves the combination of a natural language with a further sign-system, - what might be called the 'language of literature'. The narratology of Greimas, to be considered in Chapter 3, is an example of such an approach. For him, natural languages 'develop within themselves secondary semiotic systems' (1982:301). Law is a further example of such a 'secondary semiotic system'. Indeed, we shall see that Greimas regards the 'deep' level of the meaning of a legal text as fully equivalent to that of a novel.

Such an approach has not gone without serious objection. It is argued, for example, that discourse beyond the level of the sentence is free from linguistic and semiotic constraints, and 'exclusively manifests the interaction of the speaker with his "situation in life" . . . (so that) speaking of the linguistic or structural laws which govern the creation of discourses is a contradiction in terms.' **(9)** A second objection relates to the notion of 'meaning' itself. Are we not using the word 'meaning' in different senses when we apply it to sentences on the one hand and a novel on the other ? **(10)** But the terminological argument may be conceded without surrendering the main ground. Even though the 'meaning' of a sentence may be a different thing from the 'meaning' of a novel, both may be regarded as within the subject matter of semiotics, in that both are forms (albeit very different forms) of signification. As to whether both forms of signification operate through structured systems (the first objection), the claim can hardly be excluded a priori; only time will tell whether the claims of the semiotician will prove sufficently plausible.

The analysis of law as a dual semiotic system may appear surprising to many legal philosophers. Those, in particular, who, like Hart, follow an 'ordinary language' approach, regard law as no more than the use of natural language for a particular purpose, in accordance perhaps with certain social (rather than semiotic) conventions. Yet 'dual semiotic' models are not entirely lacking from legal philosophy, despite the fact that they are not generally recognised as such. In varying degrees, rationalist conceptions of law approach such a dual semiotic view, whether rationality is applied at the level of justification and argument (Dworkin) or at that of the logic of norms. Such differences mirror, and to some degree reflect, internal debates regarding the nature of semiotics. Broadly, we may distinguish an 'American' school, inspired by Peirce and Morris, and oriented towards both pragmatics and logic **(11)**; on the other, we have a 'European' tradition descended from Saussure and Jakobson, and inspired by structuralism in general and structural semantics in particular. The differences between these two schools (neither of whose adherents can be defined in exclusively geographical terms) may be seen particularly in the divergence of their views on the structure and functions of semiosis. The present section explores these and related issues, not least because legal philosophy necessarily has to take a view on them. In Part Three, we shall find that modern legal positivism, particularly in its Hartian form, in important respects tacitly endorses the American rather than the European semiotic tradition.

The structure of semiosis: triadic or binary

Peirce viewed meaning as the interaction of elements in a triadic structure. The 'sign' (sometimes 'sign-vehicle' or 'representamen') mediated between an 'object' and its 'interpretant'. **(12)** In linguistics, the 'sign' might be a word. The word is used so that its meaning (the 'interpretant') may 'stand for' the object represented. A later version of this triadic relationship uses the term 'referent' of the object to which the sign refers **(13)**, and the terminology of 'referent' has now become commonplace.

In two respects, the semiotic theory of Peirce has been narrowed by adherents to the American semiotic tradition. First, Peirce's 'object' has been taken in a purely 'extensional' sense, contrary to what appears to have been Peirce's intentions (Eco 1976:60). An 'extensional' conception of the 'object' relates it exclusively to extra-linguistic phenomena, normally empirical phenomena in the outside world; an 'intensional' view, on the other hand, would view the object as part of the thought-system of language itself. We see the extensional view reflected in Morris's definition of semantics as 'the relation of signs to their designata and so to the objects which they may or do denote' (1971:35). Sampson relies upon such a conception in his argument against any 'rigorous scientific analysis of word-meanings', on the grounds that 'meaning' necessarily entails a relation of reference to the outside world, but that the outside world is constantly changing in unpredictable ways (1980a:60-4).

A second restriction is particularly associated with the 'analytical' tradition of 'linguistic philosophy' and 'speech act theory'. Meaning is seen not as the product of systemic semiotic relations, but rather of the intentions of its users. **(14)** A recent study notes that in Wittgenstein's view, 'to mean something' is grammatically equivalent to the expression 'to intend something', and this intention 'imparts a purpose or point to language use' (Brown 1974:118). In the influential theory of Strawson (1950), reference itself becomes a goal-oriented, pragmatic phenomenon. Speech act theory regards referring as 'an action that is performed in the utterance of an expression' (Searle 1971:7), and 'action' in this tradition is firmly identified with 'intentionality'. **(15)**

The European tradition, by contrast, conceives the structure of semiosis in terms of a binary opposition, the Saussurian **signifiant** and **signifié**, sometimes translated 'sound-image' **(16)** and 'mental image'. European semiotics holds both the **signifiant** and the **signifié** to be structured. In the case of language, Jakobson set forth the oppositional structures involved in phonology; Saussure laid the foundation for a comparable view of the **signifié**, wherein meanings were defined in terms of syntagmatic and paradigmatic axes - the relations between the words in the sequence of words actually uttered, and the choice of each word from within a linguistic structure defining those words which could be substituted for it. The precise status, for Saussure, of the **signifié** is not absolutely clear. **(17)** What is clear, is that European semiotics rejects the notion of 'referent', at least insofar as it is extensionally defined. **(18)** The referent, proclaims Landowski, is something 'about which the semiotician declines to speak' (1978:85). Would that this were so ! Greimas and Courtés explain their position thus: 'First, one needs to note that the extra-linguistic world (the world according to 'common sense') is given form by human beings and constituted by them as signification. Such a world, far from being the referent (i.e., the denotative signified of natural languages) is itself, on the contrary, a bi-planar language, a natural semiotics (or a semiotics of the physical World). The problem of the referent is then reduced to the question of the correlation between two semiotic systems (for example, natural languages and natural semiotics; pictural semiotics and natural semiotics). This is a problem of inter-semioticity (cf. intertextuality). Conceived thus as a natural semiotic system, the referent loses its need to exist as a linguistic concept.' **(19)** It would be wrong, however, to construct a total polarisation between the American and European semiotic traditions on this matter. **(20)** It has long been a commonpl ce of linguistics, from which the American semiotic tradition does not dissent, that all words do not have a referent. Indeed, there is increasing recognition within speech act theory that the meanings which the utterer intends to convey must necessarily make use of a conventional system, as may be seen from the continuation of Searle's definition of 'referring', which was only partially quoted above: referring is 'an action that is performed in the utterance of an expression with a particular sense provided by the rules for the use of the expression' (1971:7).

Conversely, European semiotics cannot and does not pretend that the outside world does not exist, or that the speaker may have intentions in relation to it when he makes an utterance. But for the European tradition, both the outside world and the utterer's intentions form part of the **semiotic function,** which is conceptually distinct from the sense of that which is uttered. Ducrot and Todorov comment on the Saussurian concept of the sign thus: 'This narrow definition of the sign obliges us to introduce other concepts in order to describe relationships that are similar and nonetheless different, customarily undifferentiated under the name 'signification' or 'sign.' Thus we will make a careful distinction (as almost all sign theorists have done) between signification and the referential function (sometimes called denotation) . . . denotation takes place not between a signifier and a signified but between the sign and the **referent,** that is, in the case that is the easiest to imagine, the real object: it is no longer the phonic or graphic sequence **apple** that is linked to the meaning 'apple'; rather the word (that is, the sign itself) **apple** is linked to real apples' (1979:101). They go on to argue that denotation is in fact less frequent than one might imagine, and to suggest that both Saussure and Peirce insisted on the marginal role of denotation in the definition of the sign. It seems clear, however, that the analytical tradition of linguistic philosophy rejects any conceptual distinction between signification regarded as a system of meaning and denotation viewed merely as a particular semiotic function.

The issue becomes important in considering the status of legal terminology. Law students have long been warned against viewing even the classifications of ordinary language as 'natural'. **(21)** Our classifications, even of natural objects, are constructed by men and retained through convention. A scientific terminology may have good reason to classify those same natural objects differently. For example, the

English language classifies a tomato as a vegetable, while botany classifies it as a fruit (Baldinger 1980:40). A legal system, too, is capable of constructing its own autonomous system of classification. It may, for example, choose to define 'cannabis' in a way which differs from both its botanical and its ordinary meaning sense. Greimas would claim that we have here a case of inter-semioticity. When the law uses the word 'cannabis', the legal meaning (as defined by the legal system) refers not to the natural object, but rather to the ordinary language sense attributed to that natural object. Analytical philosophy would deny the sufficiency of such an account, in the absence of consideration of the users' intentions.

Types of Sign: 'Signs' and 'Symbols'

Within semiotics, we encounter a variety of classifications of sign. The terminology is confusingly inconsistent from one writer to another. But beneath the terminological variations, there reside important philosophical differences, not unrelated to those which have just been discussed.

The starting point is Peirce's classification of signs as icons, indices or symbols. 'Icons' are defined as signs related to their objects by likeness, as in the case of a 'realist' painting; 'indices' are signs where there exists a factual link between the sign and its object, as where a part is taken to represent the whole or where a symptom is taken to indicate an illness, or in the gesture of pointing; 'symbols' exist where the relationship between sign and object can only be 'imputed', the result of a convention rather than nature. The predominant basis of the classification is thus the relation of sign (or 'representamen') to object.

Saussure preferred to reserve the term 'symbol' for the case where 'there is the rudiment of a natural bond between the signifier and the signified' (1966:68). He gave as an example the use of a pair of scales as a symbol of justice. The scales could not be replaced by just any other symbol, such as a chariot. There was a reason for the choice of the scales, presumably that of representing objectivity and even-handedness. Not all signs were of this character. In particular, Saussure stressed the 'arbitrary' (unmotivated) character of the linguistic sign. With the exception of cases of onomatopeia, there exists no connection whatsoever between the sound-image and the mental image which by convention it evokes. We can illustrate this through cross-linguistic comparison. The sound-image d-o-g evokes the mental image 'dog' in English but the same sound-image evokes the mental image 'fish' in Hebrew. There is no more reason for the association in the one language than in the other. (22)

For Peirce, an 'index' could serve as a sign even though constituted by factual, or natural events. (23) As noted already, signification for Peirce is an event in the mind of the receiver; it does not require a corresponding mental act on the part of an emitter. Others have sought to make a conceptual distinction between this type of process and that exemplified by conventional signs such as language. Eco distinguishes between a signal and a sign: 'A signal is a pertinent unit of a system that may be an expression system ordered to a content, but could also be a physical system without any semiotic purpose; as such it is studied by information theory in the stricter sense of the term. A signal can be a stimulus that does not mean anything but causes or elicits something; however, when used as the recognized **antecedent** of a foreseen **consequent** it may be viewed as a sign, inasmuch as it stands for its consequent (as far as the sender is concerned). On the other hand a sign is always an element of an **expression plane** conventionally correlated to one (or several) elements of a **content plane'** (1976:48). (24) As this indicates, the distinction involves consideration of the nature of the significatory process involved. In language, words typically (though not always) 'stand for' ('re-present') that which is signified. But a symptom of an illness (an example which is both an index in the sense of Peirce and Prieto, and a signal in the sense of Eco) cannot be said to 'stand for' the illness it signifies. It provides evidence, or information about that illness.

The distinction is important for the following reason. We have to ask whether signals are structured other than in the causal terms of the natural world, and if so whether they are structured on the model of the linguistic sign. It is a characteristic of structuralist semiotics to claim that the linguistic model is useful far beyond the linguistic sign itself. (25) The problem becomes acute when we consider discursive units larger than the sentence. Insofar as they provide information going beyond that contained in individual sentences, is that information conveyed on the model of 'signals' or 'signs'? For even structuralists increasingly concede that anything closely corresponding to the linguistic 'sign' disappears at this level. (26)

In France, the question of the semiotic processes involved in legal discourse was joined some years ago after the publication of Arnaud's study of the French Civil Code (1973). Arnaud sought to employ a Lévi-Straussian methodology to the Code, in order to show the meaning of the whole by reference to the inter-relation of its parts. (27) Lévi-Strauss had urged that we interpret 'society as a whole in terms of the theory of communication. This endeavor is possible on three levels, since the rules of kinship and marriage serve to ensure the circulation of women between groups, just as economic rules serve to ensure the circulation of goods and services, and linguistic rules the circulation of messages' (1968:83). In his analysis, Arnaud reconstructed the socio-economic implications of the rules of the Code, and argued that the egalitarian values proclaimed at the surface level of the Code are an ideology which conceals the survival of bourgeois values at the 'deep' (and here real) level. The linguist and semiotician Georges Mounin retorted that the 'meaning' of the legal Code could not be elicited as if it were a linguistic code; the Code might provide information regarding economic relations, values and ideologies, but if so it did so through 'indices' constructed for a different purpose (through 'signals' rather than signs). The decoding of signs involved the interpretation of the sign in terms of a code already known, whereas the interpretation of an index involved the use of that index for the reconstruction of a larger (unknown) system of signification (1973:177). Linguistic signification was manifested through a code; the non-linguistic signification of an index was not manifested by a code, but interpreted by a science (1974:16).

Process of semiosis: interpretation or decoding

The typology of signs puts in issue the psychological processes involved in their receipt. For Saussure the connection between the sound-image and the mental-image in the linguistic sign was arbitrary (1966:67-8). Today it is widely held that it is the very arbitrariness of the linguistic sign that explains its power to convey its message in a demonstrable fashion, and which at the same time shows the necessity of the presence of a system of difference with respect to other signs. **(28)** This is what Mounin implies as the process of semiosis involved in 'decoding'. He uses the following example to illustrate the difference in process involved as between an 'index' and a linguistic sign. He contrasts the proposition of Epicurus that 'blood is the sign of a wound' (index) with the use of the word 'blood' to signify that red viscous liquid which flows in our veins. When a Frenchman hears the word 'sang' he knows **immediately** the meaning of the word, since he is already in possession of a linguistic code which tells him. But when a Frenchman sees blood, he will not necessarily perceive immediately the connection between the blood and a wound; he may interpret the presence of the blood more or less exactly. Similarly, culture involves the use of 'indices'. It is not enough for a Frenchman to walk through the Parthenon in order to 'decode' the cultural significance of the Greek temple; he needs to study history and archaeology to do so. In order to interpret the significance of the French Civil Code, one needs to study sociology and economics; one cannot 'decode' it by linguistic methods (1974:15-6). **(29)**

But Mounin's argument is by no means conclusive. **(30)** Saussure himself recognised the relativity of arbitrariness as a semiotic phenomenon (1966:131ff.). He also explicitly recognised that customs and laws, as human institutions, were unlike language in being 'based in varying degrees on the natural relations of things' (1966:75). In general, semioticians are quite willing to concede that social signs are typically motivated (e.g. Guiraud 1971:107). But even though they may be socially motivated, they may still conventionally come to transmit a particular meaning without that kind of conscious ratiocination implied by Mounin's concept of 'interpretation by a science'.

An analogous problem is debated in modern legal theory. One of Dworkin's principal criticisms of contemporary positivism - arguably his most important point of criticism - is that positivism claims that recognition processes within law operate in a 'clearly demonstrable' fashion, while in fact they do not. The issue is fully explored in later chapters. Suffice it here to pose the issue in semiotic terms. A legal system provides processes by which we recognise certain propositions as 'legal rules'. What means does the legal system use in order to signify such membership ? In claiming that legal systems provide conclusive, clearly demonstrable tests of the existence of legal rules, positivism implies that the process of semiosis is through the use of 'signs'. In arguing, to the contrary, that the rights which exist within a legal system can only be ascertained through a cognitive, interpretative process, through first the identification and then the 'weighing' of 'principles', Dworkin suggests, at the very least, that there is more than one semiotic process involved in legal semiosis, and that something akin to 'signals' play an important part in it.

Semiotic Functions: communication and signification

Some semioticians, Mounin (e.g. 1970:11-5) being prominent amongst them, emphasise a distinction between **communication** and **signification.** 'Communication' involves the intentional use of a sign to convey a message; if the message that is conveyed was not intended by the user of the sign, we have at best 'signification'. In this, Mounin stands side by side with Buyssens as the more extreme exponents of the functionalist movement in semiotics (Hervey 1982:157-9). Not only do they insist upon a distinction between communication and signification; they seek to restrict the scope of semiotics to the former. Only phenomena displaying the three characteristics of conventionality, intention to communicate, and membership of a set may be regarded as semiotic (Hervey 1982:157). Semiotics, for Mounin, involves the use of linguistics as a model, and that in turn is taken to imply an intention to communicate. We may note that the first two of the three characteristics taken to define semiotic phenomena - conventionality and the intention to communicate - co-incide with the speech act tradition. It is only the third requirement, membership of a set, which indicates the historical relation to European semiotics. Hervey provides the following example to illustrate this third requirement: 'If I agree on a particular occasion with a particular friend that I will signal to him that the plan to rob a bank is on, by hanging my wig out of the window - a signal that will undoubtedly depend upon the convention agreed between the two of us, and that will undoubtedly manifest an intention to communicate - this phenomenon will fall outside the scope of semiotics . . . for the reason that there is no particular repertoire, set, or system of which this one-time signal forms a part.'

Mounin does not reject the notion of signification. But he regards the linguistic model as inappropriate to it. His criticism of Arnaud's study of the French Civil Code is directed not so much to what Arnaud does, as to Arnaud's description of what he does. Following Lévi-Strauss, Arnaud seeks to apply linguistic methods to the underlying socio-economic relations manifested by the code. For Mounin, such a claim is purely metaphorical, as is the purported use of Saussurian linguistics in the semiology of Barthes or the use of the linguistics of Hjelmslev in the narratology of Greimas.

In structuralist semiotics, a different view is taken. Intentional communication may be accepted as a particular species of semiotic phenomenon, but the existence of a significatory system is regarded as a necessary condition of such communication. Signification provides the means for the communicative end; it is necessary in order to account for how communication works. **(31)** Moreover, the structuralist tradition is reluctant to confine the notion of 'intention' to the sphere of consciousness. Human action may also reflect sub-conscious motivations; they may have an 'underlying significative intention'. **(32)**

Such arguments lead naturally to consideration of a further semiotic function, that of **connotation,** which has received particular attention in the work of Roland Barthes (1967:90ff.). Barthes defines connotation as 'a system of second-order meanings, which are so to speak parasitic on the language proper' (1967:30). Whereas 'denotation' arises from the referential level of language, 'connotation' belongs to the expressive sphere. For Barthes, following Hjelmslev, connotation is especially to be associated with 'complex systems of which language forms the first system' (and of which literature is cited as an example). **(33)** Barthes expresses the relationship between the systems thus: the first system, made up of linguistic signs, is a denotative system, but its signs may be grouped together in order to form connotators, or signifiers of connotation. Each such connotator, which may comprise large fragments of the discourse of denotation, refers to a signified in the same connotative system. But just as the signifier in this system is diffuse by comparison with the signifiers of the first (linguistic, denotative) system, so too the signified of connotation may be 'at once general, global and diffuse'. Barthes draws a close connection between the signifiers of connotation and 'rhetoric', and between the signifieds of connotation and 'ideology' (1967:89-92).

It is, perhaps, the rationalist tradition which inclines us to regard the denotative, linguistic model of communication as primary, and the connotative model as at best supplementary. For Barthes' own account indicates that, in terms of efficiency of communication (the maximum communicative effect for the minimum communicative effort), denotation is immensely superior to connotation. Denotation may, through the instrumentality of a single word or small group of words, convey a very specific meaning; connotation is apt to rely upon a larger combination of words or sentences, perhaps extending to 'the tone of a text, which is made up of numerous words, but which nevertheless refers to a single signified' (1967:91), and the message thereby conveyed is likely to be less specific. That is one reason why structuralist analyses are often regarded as trivial or banal: whereas a surface analysis relies upon the full significatory power of the language, and is capable of extracting meaning from the multiplicity of small units to be identified within it, a deep 'structural' analysis appears to reduce this specific detail to a few general themes. **(34)** But Barthes would reject the type of rationalist value thereby assumed. He would claim that the communication of moods, affective states, and value judgments are at least as powerful as the communication of specific messages. Frequently, he would argue, the connotations of a text operate at the subconscious level (both of author and reader) but they are no less powerful for that, much as we would like to view communication in an extreme rationalist mode: as limited to those messages which an individual human being consciously intends to transmit to another individual human being.

There is no doubt that law would fit into such a Barthesian framework. Just as literature consists, for Barthes, of a linguistic system (with its signifiers and its **denotata**) which, taken as a whole, manifests a (lesser number of) connotators which signify those feelings which it is the function of literature, as a separate semiotic system, to convey, so too he could argue that law consists of a surface language, whose signifiers denote the prescribed patterns of behaviour, but which may further reflect connotators (perhaps in the form of whole groups of norms) which signify the respective feelings regarding the social order which that particular legal semiotic conveys. Domenico Carzo has recently provided an example of such an analysis, in his study of the Italian law of succession (1981:91ff.). The difference between such an approach and those of more traditional stylistics and socio-linguistics (35) consists in the structuralist insistence on the relevance even here of a number of Saussurian concepts, such as the dependence of even connotative meaning upon structural relationships such as those involved in the syntagmatic / paradigmatic matrix. (36)

1.3 LAW, SEMIOTICS AND PHILOSOPHY

When legal theorists have from time to time turned their attention to legal language, the subject has not usually been viewed as central to legal philosophy itself; largely, it seems to have been assumed that the communication of law was a purely incidental and contingent concern, without significant effect on the central problems of jurisprudence. (37) Some forms of legal 'realism' have come closest to regarding language as integral to legal theory. This is the route chosen by Scandinavian realists like Olivecrona to indicate the source of those psychological states which they identify with law. It is language which induces the existence of such psychological states. The capacity of language to induce attitudes and feelings thus becomes central to legal philosophy. There is no objective reality to which the language so used corresponds. As Olivecrona put it: 'legal language....is not a veil hiding the true contents of the law, like clouds concealing the face of the earth to the eyes of an astronaut. It is an integral part of the legal system.' (38) Olivecrona's view has been endorsed in Britain by Williams: '"The law" is a collection of symbols capable of evoking ideas and emotions, together with the ideas and emotions so evoked' (1945:85f.).

Of course, the evocation of such ideas and emotions does not come about by chance. Legal language has human sources, and is used for a purpose, chiefly to serve as a particular instrument of social control. In the words of Olivecrona: 'the purpose of all legal enactments, judicial pronouncements, contracts, and other legal acts is to influence men's behavior and direct them in certain ways. The legal language must be viewed primarily as a means to this end. It is an instrument of social control and social intercourse.' (39)

In short, the Realist view endorses a functionalist conception of language, defined in terms of purposes and effects. Indeed, Olivecrona himself compared the approach of his predecessor Axel Hägerström to the speech act philosophy of J.L. Austin. (40) What characterises this functionalist approach is the assumption that man is the master of his language, rather than its servant. That is a view which we shall find to be shared by Hart, despite his identification of both law and language as social practices. (41) For Hart, as is argued below, interprets the role of law as a means of social control in terms of a communicational model, in which meaning is strictly defined as authorial intention.

European Semiotics has been far more sceptical regarding man's mastery over his language. This, indeed, has at the semi-popular level proved a central issue in debates concerning structuralism. (42) A legal philosophical symposium on the language of law published in France in 1974 shows a sensitivity to this issue. In the preface, Villey observes that 'law manifests itself to us only in forms of discourse . . . discourse subject to the laws of a language. Everything which jurists and the legislator utter is regulated, conditioned and channelled by this language. It is not sufficient to say that language is their instrument, without adding that this instrument, like all techniques, dominates them. Language is a 'servante-maîtresse', and in reality the language is itself knowledge; its vocabulary and syntax are a mode of thinking about the world, of carving out the structure of the world; of our science, our language constitutes the first half' (1974:1).

One could polarise the opposing viewpoints thus. Language is intelligible either by virtue of structures which dominate the messages which its users seek to convey, or by virtue of the intentions of its users and the context of its use. In short, the structural and functional approaches attach quite different values to the role played by the language itself in the communicational process. Clearly, the issue ought not to be thus polarised: the opposing viewpoints reflect signficant differences in emphasis, rather than contradictory propositions. Yet within linguistics the issue, often debated in terms of the dominance of semantic or pragmatic models (43), still arouses some heat. (44) The anthropologist Malinowski, for example, took the view that 'in its primitive uses, language . . is a mode of action and not an instrument of reflection' (1923:312). Sampson sees here an anticipation of Wittgenstein: 'words are tools, and the 'meaning' of a tool is its use: a view which Ludwig Wittgenstein acquired a considerable reputation by re-stating long after Malinowski had argued the point at length.' **(45)** Sampson finds this account inadequate. **(46)** Conversely, increasing attention within the Greimasian school of semiotics (representing a semantic approach) is being paid to the act of enunciation. **(47)**

Various attempts have been made to describe the relationship between semantics and pragmatics. Eco argues in effect that structural semantics provide parameters within which pragmatic choices are to be made (1976:95). Others are driven to metaphor in describing the nature of the compromise. Lyons tells us that 'the meaning of expressions and sentences is anchored by their characteristic use' (1981:168). Leech describes semantic structure 'not as a closed, rigid, conceptual system which tyrannizes over the thought processes of its users, but as an open-ended conceptual system, one which 'leaks', in the sense that it allows us to transcend its limitations by various types of semantic creativity' (1974:28). These same issues are reflected in contemporary legal philosophy, in discussions of the nature of legal concepts and the scope of judicial discretion - questions which loom large in Part Three.

The parallels noted in this chapter between debates in semiotic theory and in legal philosophy reflect not only the necessary implication of language in the legal process, but also a broad philosophical issue which is implicit equally in both. That issue is the tension between individualism and collectivism. Individualism suffuses the analytical philosophy of action, with its stress upon the volition of the individual actor. That characteristic is carried over into speech act theory, and indeed more generally into linguistic philosophy's endorsement of a concept of meaning defined in terms of authorial intention. **(48)** European semiotics, by contrast, implies a collectivist conception of language, rooted in Saussure's notion of the language-system as a social (or social psychological) fact. **(49)** More recently, Kristeva, Foucault and Derrida have sought to integrate semiotics into a theory of social action, within which stress is laid upon collective, unconscious motivations. (50) Eco, too, still holds that 'the subject is spoken by language', that 'as subjects, we are what the shape of the world produced by signs makes us become.' It is 'probably the collectivity of subjects' which activates the power of resegmentation of content of signs' (1984:45). The same tensions are reflected in legal theory: a spectrum can be constructed from the individualist conception of law manifested by Hart, particularly prominent in his account of 'meaning' (7.1), to the collectivist claims of Marxist jurisprudence.

PART TWO

Greimasian Semiotics and Law

CHAPTER TWO

Structural Semantics and Legal Language

(2.1) General Orientation of Greimasian Semiotics: Greimasian semiotics is related to classical structuralism in that it views discourse as a system modelled on language, and adopts an intensional view of the referent. **(2.2) The Constitution of the Legal Lexicon:** G/L take the legal lexicon to be constituted by the (discursive) act of naming in legislation, although that in itself creates only a **'univers juridique virtuel'**. **(2.3) Semantic Structure in Natural Language:** Greimas, in common with other versions of structural semantics, sees word meanings in natural languages as produced by rule-governed combinations of minimal semantic units (semes). **(2.4) Semantic Structure in Legal Language:** Multi-member sets and 'hyponymy' play an important part in the structure of the legal lexicon because of the latter's features of transitivity, nominalisation and hierarchical structure. Monosemicity also appears to be a feature of legal language, although its analysis requires the taking of positions on the conceptual problem of the distinction between 'meaning' and 'use'. The semantic structure of legal language renders it more readily susceptible to definition than is ordinary language. **(2.5) Clarity and Indeterminacy in Structural Semantics:** For Greimas, the semic core consists in the invariant semes of a lexeme, which in practice always combine with variable contextual semes to produce a sememe. His analysis is similar to Hart's distinction between 'core' and 'penumbra' but Hart's analysis, unlike that of Greimas, is not directed to a purely semantic (rather than pragmatic) question. **(2.6) The Autonomy of the Legal Lexicon:** The legal lexicon is autonomous in its constitution (G/L) and structure (Carcaterra, Thomas). Consideration of objections to this view, based on historical relations between the systems, shows the importance attached to tacit or subconscious choice by the structuralist tradition.

2.1 GENERAL ORIENTATION OF GREIMASIAN SEMIOTICS

The focus of Part Two is on the semiotic theory of A.J. Greimas and his Groupe de Recherches Sémio-Linguistiques (1), not least because of the application by Greimas and his collaborator Landowski of their approach to the analysis of legal discourse (1976:79-128).

Greimas stands firmly in the tradition of European semiotics, strongly influenced by structuralism. He develops and applies notions taken from Saussure, Jakobson, Hjelmslev and Lévi-Strauss. His object is not the interpretation of texts, but the explanation of the underlying structure of signification - that is, how the meaning in them is generated. Such a stance makes important philosophical assumptions, which are not universally shared. Principal amongst them is the claim that a text may have an autonomous meaning, which can be studied separately from the pragmatics of its enunciation. The study of such an autonomous text requires us to view it as a whole, in order to perceive the meaning which the various elements in it bear in relation to each other. (2) The Greimasian position on the basic semiotic issues introduced in Part One may be readily summarised. The analysis of discourse proceeds upon the same theoretical foundations as that developed in structural linguistics for the study of the sentence and the elements which compose it. There exists an underlying code, which it is the function of the semiotician (acting here as cryptanalyst rather than decoder) to crack. Semiotics includes the system of signification, and regards communicational intent (and a fortiori authorial intention) as separate matters. Language is not to be defined in terms of referring to the outside world, and should not be viewed merely as a neutral instrument in the hands of its users. The 'referent' of language is wholly internalised within it, as the mental image (cf. interpretant) which the signifier (or 'sign-vehicle') conveys. (3) The mental image evoked may itself serve as a signifier of a separate semiotic system.

2.2 THE CONSTITUTION OF THE LEGAL LEXICON

Two essential features of any natural language are a lexicon and a grammar. The former is the totality of words (or dictionary) recognised as belonging to that language; the latter combines a syntax (rules governing the combination of words in sentences, so as to produce sense) and a morphology (rules governing the formal variations of a word depending on its context). In this section, I consider the views of Greimas and Landowski (hereafter 'G/L') on the establishment of the 'lexicon' of legal discourse, this involving the transformation of lexical items from the natural language into a specifically legal lexicon (1976: esp. 87-93).

The impetus for this work came from an unusual source. In the late '60s, the Groupe was commissioned by the Paris Chamber of Commerce and Industry to write a report on the Company Law Statute of 1966 (Loi N. 66-537, 24th July 1966) as part of an inter-disciplinary programme. The results of this study were first presented publicly at a scholarly conference in 1970.

G/L use the phrase **production juridique** for the establishment of a semiotic object, or objects, bearing signification within legal discourse. Most commonly, this takes the form of transformation of elements from the natural language into the legal discourse. Thus, the **société commerciale** (hereafter 'SC') is constituted as a semiotic object within the legal discourse of the 1966 law. As constituted in that law, it becomes an object not only bearing signification, but also capable in turn of producing it.

The constitution of such semiotic objects as components of the legal discourse is accomplished through the act of naming them in legislation. G/L find it necessary to argue against the view that legislation merely makes use of terms which are already legal - a view which must be taken to evidence the survival power of natural law thinking in France. For G/L, it is the legislator who makes those terms legal. Of course, words which are used in legislation may have a prior non-legal existence and meaning; they may even constitute part of doctrinal or jurisprudential (in the English sense) discussion. At that stage, their status is that of **asémanticité juridique.** Their transformation to the status of **sémanticité juridique** requires their use by the legislator. It is only then that they become part of the 'referential level' of law (the legal lexicon), and are thus constituted as legal semiotic objects, the bearers of meaning **in law.**

Production juridique is viewed by G/L as a 'syntactic' process. The act of naming in legislation itself serves as a sign in legal discourse. The relations between that sign and the semiotic object thus named (itself a sign) are therefore syntactic (4), and form part of the 'legal grammar'.

Production juridique is the beginning but not the end of the process of creation of legal meaning. The conferment on a sign of the status of belonging to a particular semantic universe (here, that of law) does not in itself determine the meaning to be attached to that sign in that universe. The process of legal communication is incomplete at the stage of legislation. As G/L put it, **production juridique** takes a sign from the **discours non juridique,** and through using it (**production juridique**) place it on the **niveau référentiel** of law, which at that stage is merely a **univers juridique virtuel.** It remains **virtuel** until such time as the judge uses that term in the course of adjudication (**vérification juridique**).

In describing legislation as a **univers juridique virtuel,** G/L cannot be taken to mean that it lacks meaning as such, notwithstanding that a different meaning may be attached to it by further semiotic activities (such as that of the judge) at a later stage. What they appear to mean is that the meaning is incomplete for practical purposes. The legislative text may well constitute an independent discourse, with a meaning of its own; and clearly, it is the structure of precisely this meaning that G/L proceed to analyse in their study. The text, even if not read by anyone, would have a meaning. As discussed by G/L themselves, it is subjected to a further process of semiosis; similarly, when it is applied by the judge. We may compare the score of a musical work. It is produced by being inscribed according to a conventional musical notation. At that stage it has a meaning (not merely arbitrary marks on paper). It is 'actualised' in performance. But it may also be 'read' by someone who knows the musical notation, without being played. Equally, it may be studied without being played. By choosing judicial application as the form of 'actualisation' of the **'virtuel'** legislative discourse, G/L 'privilege' what may be regarded as just one possible form of semiotic activity by which the text may be 'actualised'.

It is **'vérification juridique'** which, for G/L, completes the process of communication. **Vérification juridique** is an activity of the judge. Taking the words or statements of the legislator, he converts them from potential communications of law into actual communications of law by verifying their status as law (or **grammaticalité juridique**) in the process of applying them. In applying the 'legislative discourse' to a case that comes before him, the judge is not only deciding what jurists might call a question of subsumption; he is also formally recognising the legislative status of the rule which he is applying. When he 're-states' (**re-dire**) the legislative rule, the judge confirms that it has been duly endowed with legal semioticity under those canonic rules which give the legislator this particular communicative power (1976:91-2).

2.3 SEMANTIC STRUCTURE IN NATURAL LANGUAGE

The modern tradition of structural linguistics commences with Saussure, notwithstanding the fact that he himself worked mostly in the tradition of 19th century comparative philology. But Saussure's influence today derives from his lecture notes, posthumously reconstructed and published as the **Cours de Linguistique Générale.** Lyons summarises the general claim of Saussure's teaching thus: '. . . every language is a unique relational structure, or system, and . . . the units which we identify, or postulate as theoretical constructs, in analysing the sentence of a particular language (sounds, words, meanings, etc.) derive both their essence and their existence from their relationships with other units in the same language-system. We cannot first identify the units and then, at a subsequent stage of the analysis, enquire what combinatorial or other relations hold between them: we simultaneously identify both the units and their interrelations. Linguistic units are but points in a system, or network, of relations; they are the terminals of these relations, and they have no prior and independent existence' (1977:231f.). The system, for Saussure, was a matrix with both syntagmatic and associative (or paradigmatic) axes. (5)

The development of phonology was to inject limitations into the idea of associative relations, which were lacking in Saussure's account. For although Saussure had himself stated the general principle that 'phonemes exist only as units of a system (and) that what matters in the working of language is not the **sound**, but the **opposition** of sounds . . . he had not attempted the actual description of phonological systems' (Lepschy 1970:61). In the course of elaborating the description of phonological systems, a number of limitations emerged. It was noted that not all differences in sound were distinctive, within a particular system, and that some combinations of distinctive sounds were excluded. Oppositional relations between distinctive sounds were bilateral (or binary) for some purposes, multilateral for others. (6) A common form of analysis of the sound features of different languages was developed, grouping the distinctive features into the classes of vocalic, consonantal and prosodic qualities (Lepschy 1970:59). An array of types of phonemic opposition ('privative, gradual, equipollent, etc.) was developed, each with its characteristic mode of functioning. In short, the sounds of language appeared to follow regular patterns of variation, rather than the kind of free association suggested by the Saussurian account.

The development of these notions is associated with the Prague Linguistic Circle, founded in 1926, and with the work of N.S. Trubetzkoy in particular. Both Roman Jakobson (like Trubetzkoy, a Russian who participated in the Prague circle) and Louis Hjelmslev are credited with having adapted this phonological structural model to semantics. As a result of their influence, the structural semantics of Greimas and contemporaries like Pottier and Coseriu appear much more formal and constrained than what, in outline, appeared to be suggested by Saussure.

Just as words may be broken into their component sounds, and these sounds identified as phonologically significant sound units (or phonemes), so too the meanings of words may be analysed as combinations of minimal semantically-significant units. The terminology to describe such units is not settled (7) but the most common terms nowadays appear to be 'semes' or 'semantic features'. (8) The identification of this unit is already a step on the road towards formalisation of semantics: the lexicon is viewed not as a limitless list of word-meanings, but as made up of the combination of a smaller, finite group of more general, basic units. The meanings of words can differ one from another according to a range of relational patterns. At one extreme, there may be **no** relationship between any of the component semes of word X and word Y; at the other, there may be found pairs of words which differ only in relation to one component seme. The relationships which may exist between semes are broadly categorised as 'oppositions', but within this a number of logical patterns (contraries, contradictories, marked, unmarked etc.) are discernible. (9) Sometimes, the opposition is described in terms of the positive or negative value of a particular seme. Despite the fact that these basic semantic units themselves take their meanings from the oppositional structures within which they are located, Ducrot and Todorov refer to them as 'semantic atoms' (1979:265), since they form the building blocks for larger units of meaning.

For an example of this kind of approach, one might take the words **man, woman, boy, girl** (Leech 1974:96f.). All of them involve semes (or semantic features) in respect of sex and age. These two semes will be represented as +male or -male (logically, equally +female or -female) and +adult or -adult (again, equally satisfactorily, +young or -young). The relationship between **man** and **boy** can then be represented in terms of a common +male seme, combined in the one case with a +adult seme and in the other with a -adult seme. Each term in this group of four will have one seme in common and one opposed seme in respect of two of the other three terms in the group. As regards the remaining relationships (**man** and **girl**; **woman** and **boy**), there is an opposition in **both** of the semes: **man** is a combination of +male and +adult, while **girl** is a combination of -male and -adult. This explains why the meaning of **man** appears to bear a more remote relationship to that of **girl**, than it does to either **woman** or **boy**. At the same time, we still have to explain why **girl** is perceived as a term with a closer meaning to **man** than is, for example, **train**. For one might argue that **train**, like **girl**, is also not adult and not male. The answer, in referential terms, is of course obvious: like a man, a girl but not a train is human. But when we seek to identify the mechanism by which the sense relations of the language (its intensional dimension) represent this distinction, there is more than one possibility. One such would be to say that there is a third seme involved in each of **man, woman, boy,** and **girl,** namely +human. **Train,** by contrast, would have an opposed seme -human. When one compares the relationship of **man** and **girl** with that between **man** and **train,** therefore, the former will be found to involve two oppositions, while the latter will involve three. Thus the meaning of **girl** seems to be closer to **man** than does **train.**

But this way of representing the situation might seem to lead to a system no less complex than one in which the basic unit of meaning is the word itself, so that every single word has to be learned without aid from a system of relationships. For there would seem to be no limit to the axes upon which each word would need to be assigned some positive or negative value. Rather, what is needed is a theory which tells one that a restricted set of semes is alone significant in the case of a particular word, just as in phonology only certain ranges of sound are regarded as distinctively different. In semantics, this function is performed by the theory of semantic fields. **(10)** In terms of the above example, +human or -human would not be an additional seme, alongside those relating to sex and age; rather, the words **man, woman, boy,** and **girl** would all belong to a single semantic field 'the human race'. It is by virtue of belonging to this particular semantic field that these words have semes which are distinctive in terms of sex and age. If one takes the word **train,** it would belong to some other semantic field (perhaps, vehicular object) within which semes relating to sex and age are not distinctive or relevant. That is not to say that one could not speak of **an old train.** But the very need to add the qualifying adjective **old** demonstrates the fact that there is no seme relevant to age within the semantic field to which the noun **train** belongs.

Semanticians have noted various special features in the structure of the lexicon of 'specialist' languages. For example, the elaboration of many-member lexical sets is said to be more typical of specialised taxonomies, and even when words of the ordinary language are incorporated into such specialised taxonomies, we often find a more rigid structure imposed on them than is characteristic of their use in everyday vocabulary (Lyons 1977:288). Such greater rigidity may take the form of 'unmarked' rather than 'marked' oppositions. **(11)** For example, in the opposition day/night, ordinary language can use day either as excluding night or as including it, depending on the context. It cannot, however, use night as including day, but only as opposed to it. In this sense, night is the marked, day the unmarked member of the oppositional pair. ('Man' is similarly unmarked in opposition to 'Woman'; feminists seek to alter this structure.) But in a specialist terminology, we might typically expect to find both day and night as unmarked, reflecting a relationship of contrariety. Further, a multi-member set may be structured serially in a specialist lexicon, even though the terms which compose the set are not so organised in the lexicon of ordinary usage. Trier examined the adjectives used for grouping examination candidates according to their performance. The examiners adopted a convention according to which candidates were to be classified in terms of the rank **excellent, good, average, fair, poor.** In that context, the adjectives formed a serially ordered set of incompatible terms, and the sense of each one was determined by its position in the rank (Lyons 1977:289).

2.4 SEMANTIC STRUCTURE IN LEGAL LANGUAGE

The structure of the legal lexicon exhibits these and other characteristics of technical language. Classification is clearly of the greatest importance for law, if it is to provide (or appear to provide) a finite set of general rules in order to regulate an infinite set of behaviours. Not surprisingly, therefore, we find a greater use of multi-member sets, rather than purely binary oppositions. Mutually exclusive multi-member sets provide a tighter and at the same time more flexible structure than overlapping (even unmarked) binary oppositions. The text studied by G/L may be taken as an example. There is no single 'contrary' term opposed to the SC; rather, the SC is constituted as one member of a set of mutually exclusive forms of legal personality.

Special interest attaches also to what linguists term 'hyponymy'. As Lyons puts it (1977:291):

> No less important than opposition and contrast as a paradigmatic relation of sense is the relation which holds between a more specific, or subordinate, lexeme and a more general or superordinate lexeme . . . there is no generally accepted term for this relation (or its converse). Recently, however, the term hyponymy . . .

> has been gaining currency; and it would seem to be more appropriate than such alternatives as 'inclusion' or 'subordination', which are also used in other senses in linguistics and logic. Let us say, then, that 'cow' is a hyponym of 'animal', 'rose' is a hyponym of 'flower', and so on; and further, that 'rose', 'tulip', 'daffodil', etc., since each is a hyponym of 'flower', are co-hyponyms (of the same lexeme).

Three features of hyponymy mentioned in Lyons' account appear to support the view that this is a sense relation crucially involved in the semantics of legal language. The first is his observation that 'hyponymy is a transitive relation. If **x** is a hyponym of **y** and **y** is a hyponym of **z**, then **x** is a hyponym of **z** . . for example, "cow" is a hyponym of "mammal" and "mammal" is a hyponym of "animal"; therefore "cow" is a hyponym of "animal" ' (1977: 292). We might indeed, invoke the notion of 'defeasibility' (**12**) in viewing such relations: legal concept **x** (e.g. the contract of employment), viewed as a hyponym of legal concept **y** (e.g. contract), will be subject to the rules attaching to the general concept as well as its own specific rules; but it is always open to the legislature or to authorised interpreters to exclude the applicability of a general rule of contract to a particular class of contract - as many examples show. Any difference between this example and that provided by Lyons is not related to the characteristics of hyponymy, but rather to the fact that his example uses a natural referent, while the (presumed) referent in the legal example is constructed.

A second characteristic of hyponymy is that 'verbs, adjectives, adverbs and other parts of speech cannot be inserted into the formula '**x** is a kind of **y**' without nominalization' (1977:294). Similarly, legal concepts are normally found to be nominalized; adjectival and adverbial forms, where they are found, tend not to be conceptualised.

Thirdly, Lyons observes that 'the relation of hyponymy imposes a hierarchical structure upon the vocabulary and upon particular fields within the vocabulary; and the hierarchical ordering of lexemes can be represented formally as a tree-diagram' (1977:295). The Common Lawyer is perhaps less receptive to this idea than his Civilian counterpart, but from at least the time of Blackstone it has been evident that English law, like Civilian systems, can readily be presented in this manner.

Hyponymy is a sense relation particularly well adapted to multiple taxonomy, typical of law. Within such multiple taxonomy, we may expect boundaries to be tight (Leech 1974:107). It does not, however, follow that binary opposition entails the absence of tight boundaries. Such may be true of marked oppositions (day/night) and polar oppositions (large/small) as used in ordinary language. But binary oppositions may also be constituted as contraries, wherein the presence of one unequivocally entails the absence of the other (alive/dead), what Leech terms a 'binary taxonomy' (1974:106-10).

In the light of the modern development of structural semantics, it is interesting to look at the presentation by Sourioux and Lerat of examples of French legal terminology (1976:32f.). Their work does not align itself to any particular theoretical position, although here they note the relevance of the Saussurian paradigmatic axis. They note that groups of legal terms (which may be substituted for each other along this axis) may be either 'closed' or 'open' (in the sense of admitting additions, which represent the development of legal institutions). It is notable that all their examples of 'closed' groups are binary pairs, and that most of them appear to be 'binary taxonomies' (with strict borders), in the sense of oppositions involving a contrast of direction, such as **acquéreur/vendeur, mandant/mandataire,** no doubt reflecting the transactional nature of many legal relations. The examples given of 'open groups', on the other hand, are almost invariably groups of three or more, representing 'multiple taxonomy' often within a relation of hyponymy. **(13)**

Monosemicity

Monosemicity is another noted feature of technical language in general. Technical terminology tends to be associated with one meaning only, as opposed to the commonly polysemic nature of ordinary language. **(14)** A study of the incidence of monosemicity in French legal terminology has been conducted by Sourioux and Lerat (1976:90-9). Of 144 legal terms beginning with the letter A, identified through dictionaries from the late 17th century which pay special attention to specialist terminology, they find that 98 have only one sense and one type of use. Fifteen more have one sense but several types of use. Twenty-six were polysemic, being usable in more than one sense at the same period of time, but of these only three are said to be 'juridically polysemic', as opposed to 'linguistically polysemic': only those which were 'juridically polysemic' could bear more than one meaning simultaneously **in law:** the others bore their additional meanings outside the law. A final category comprised five items, which had changed their (legal) meaning in the course of their history. If one assumes that there was a period in the history of each of these five terms in which the two legal meanings existed side by side, the total number of items exhibiting juridical polysemicity over the period of three hundred years remains only eight.

Two general features of this presentation may also be noted. First, polysemicity is not entirely excluded. At most, legal language exhibits a tendency against it (1976:35). Second, the distinction which Sourioux and Lerat use between the meaning **(sens)** and the manner of use **(emploi)** of the word itself implies a particular view of the relationship between semantics and pragmatics. The distinction between these concepts is not elaborated by the authors, but seems from the examples they use to be not incompatible with a theory of 'core' and 'context'. Thus **acte** is one of the rare examples of juridical polysemicity (1976:35,96), being associated with such very different notions as a formal written document on the one hand, and the manifestation of will designed to produce legal effects on the other. **(15)** By contrast the two examples discussed by Sourioux and Lerat of words with a single sense but several uses are 'increase' **(accroissement)** and 'assembly' **(assemblée)**. Here, the word appears to be used to evoke the same basic concept, but with a different set of technical associations in accordance with the particular context of law in which it is used. This differentiation of context is sometimes indicated by the use of different qualifying adjectives 'assemblée constituante', 'assemblée nationale', 'assemblée plénière', and sometimes by the general area of law (semantic field) in which it is used - 'accroissement' in the context of property (CC 556) or in the context of succession (CC 1044).

We may note, in conclusion, that all these features which distinguish the structure of the legal lexicon (as a 'technical' language) from that of the lexicon of the ordinary language are such as to render legal lexemes more rather than less definable than their ordinary language counterparts. Whereas in the typical binary oppositional structure, the semantic focus is on the 'core' of each element of the opposition, rather than the boundaries, the opposite is true for non-binary, and particularly multi-member sets. Within binary oppositions, the apparent preference of law for contraries rather than marked or polar oppositions would point in the same direction. So, obviously, does the greater incidence of monosemicity. For the moment, we may regard these features as consequent upon such institutional control over the lexicon as is reflected in G/L's account (2.2 above). That institutional control may be thought to extend also to semantic change (Carzo 1981:88). Whereas semantic change in natural language can be regarded as a matter of gradual drift, change in the meaning of legal terms may occur in an institutionalised setting overnight, at a quite identifiable moment in time. The semantic theory of Humpty Dumpty, on this account, needs supplementation. Not only does the ability to define words entail power; institutional power is itself required, in legal discourse, to define words. **(16)**

2.5 CLARITY AND INDETERMINACY IN STRUCTURAL SEMANTICS

Structural semantics have moved in an increasingly formal direction, such as to emphasise the manner in which meanings are rendered determinate. By the time we reach Greimas, consideration of semantic indeterminacy is virtually set aside. How, then, does the notion of a 'semic core' (with which Hart's 'core of settled meaning' might appear to converge) fit into the system of oppositional semes proposed by structural semantics ? The idea of meaning as a function of relationships within pairs might seem to run contrary to a conception of the meaning of a word as represented by the image of its core and penumbra. If **boy** is to be represented in terms of a combination of +male and -adult, located within a classeme **(17)** +human (this last also taking its meaning from its relation with other classemes), where does one locate the semic core of the word ?

The answer is that the semic core is represented by **both** +male and -adult, since these are invariant units of meaning whenever **boy** is used. However, the use of a word is never fully represented by the semic core. There are, in addition, contextual semes which become relevant in particular contexts. Thus, in practice the semic core never appears in isolation, but rather in the form of 'sememes', wich combine the semic core with the relevant contextual semes. **(18)** Presumably, this would involve regarding the lexeme **boy** in such a question as 'what is the semic core of **boy**?' as a sememe consisting of the semic core (+male and -adult) together with a contextual seme '-other contextual semes', this negative contextual seme being invoked from the fact that the context of the question is the search for the semic core only !

The existence of some invariant element in the meaning of words is commonly regarded as a necessary condition of the functioning of natural languages. As Jakobson puts it: 'But variations cannot be acknowledged without the existence of invariants. On the level of meaning as well as of sound, the problem of the invariants is pivotal for the analysis of a given language at a given stage. These invariants, puzzling for the cyrptanalyst, are familiar to the habitual decoder who listens to a new context and nevertheless knows beforehand what its words mean, granted he belongs to the same speech community and is not a pathological case' (1953:19). Translated into the more technical account of Greimas, this means that it is the semic core which renders the use of words in new contexts intelligible. The semic core has also been seen as underlying the phenomenon of polysemy (Nida 1979: 11f), but the kind of contribution it can here make seems to be irregular (Palmer 1981: 105), and examples of its use seem to owe as much to the more traditional historical approach of comparative philology than to structural semantics. But, more generally, as a method of analysis of the semantic structure of words, the Greimasian account in terms of a semic core and variable contextual semes is not regarded as unusual (Culler 1975: 77f.).

Before proceeding any further, it may be as well to distinguish a number of different questions which may be posed in relation to the meaning of a word. First, we may ask whether a word, when used in a new context, has any meaning at all. That, I take it, is the point of Jakobson's remark quoted above: he seeks to explain how a word used in a new context will immediately and regularly (amongst members of a particular speech community) be understood (decoded) in an overlapping fashion. That claim does not, however, represent an affirmative answer to a second, distinguishable question: Does the existence of an invariant semic core mean that users of the word regularly attribute the same contours or borderlines to its use ? Here we might say, applying the Hartian terminology, that the presence of a core of settled meaning does not imply the absence of a penumbra of doubt (7.2-3). Such a penumbra results not only from the involvement of variable contextual semes, but also from the notion of a seme itself, as conceived in structural semantics. Since semes receive their meaning by their relation to other semes, this relationship being conceived by Greimas predominantly in terms of binary opposition, the focus of each seme is at its centre rather than its periphery (Baldinger 1980:31). That is not to say that the periphery is variable in content (as are the contextual semes), but rather that it is less sharply defined and therefore more susceptible to variations in interpretation. The image of a penumbra of doubt may thus be entirely appropriate, even at the semantic level, and should not be regarded as a feature peculiar to 'general terms' - as Hart might appear to suggest (1961:123). All linguistic terms, in the absence of accompanying deictic expressions and with the exception of proper names, are 'general'. However, the conformity of the Hartian analysis to the semantician's answer to our second question should not conceal the fact that Hart's conceptualisation appears to be a response **not** to that second question, but rather to a third, also distinguishable issue: what factors are involved in adjudication ? **(19)** Adjudication takes us beyond the range of pure semantics. Baldinger points to one side of the dilemma: '. . . we should pity jurists, who, making use of ordinary language, have to draw precise borders. From the viewpoint of language theory, this is impossible; yet, juridically, punishment, and even the alternative **guilty-innocent** depends on such a limiting of reality.' **(20)** But this is only one part of the dilemma. It would be possible to reduce the use of ordinary language to a minimum, and substitute a purely formal language (as is attempted in some forms of legal informatics). But then the value of (apparent) intelligibility to the public would be lost. Nor does the dilemma end there. Given what is at stake in the context of legal adjudication, a need to re-define the 'core' may arise. Adjudication may prove difficult precisely because the language of the law is clear but its clarity does not lead to a desirable result. (21)

2.6 THE AUTONOMY OF THE LEGAL LEXICON

Arguments are sometimes advanced that legal language is 'autonomous' of the natural language. It is necessary, however, to distinguish a number of different aspects.

First, it may be seen very clearly that for G/L the legal lexicon is autonomously **constituted,** that is to say, there is a specific process, requiring the participation of a legal institution, by which semiotic objects enter the legal lexicon. At least as far as legislative discourse is concerned, the act of naming in legislation is a necessary requirement. We have seen that this is regarded by G/L as a syntactic process, the relation between one sign and another. It gives the legislative discourse, thus constituted, ' a certain autonomy'. (22) A different type of claim to the autonomy of legal language is made in terms of the semantic relations within the lexicon, once constituted. A. Carcaterra argues that the specificity of legal language cannot be identified by the presence in it of particular 'technical terms'. Following Saussure, he takes specificity to reside in the system, rather than the elements which make it up (1979:106f.); the independence of legal language is in principle total (1968:222f.). The language of law represents an entire universe of legal meanings, the choice of any one of which, in a particular utterance, reflects the exclusion or absence of the other available legal meanings (1972). Within legislative discourse, there exists moreover elements which may be regarded as legal 'primitives', which reflect the preceptive (normative) character of the discourse (1979:109f.). Thomas formulates the argument in terms of a 'metalanguage' of law, which defines the terms which are available for use in the language of law (1974:110f.). In effect, these arguments reflect an application of the Saussurian (or post-Saussurian) view of the 'paradigmatic' axis of semantic relations, the fact that there is a system which defines what terms may meaningfully be substituted for what, in the context of a particular system of law. The meaning of a legal utterance depends on what is absent just as much as on what is present. (23) The paradigmatic axis of the legal lexicon is typically organised in 'classe es' or 'semantic fields'. (24)

Examples given of such 'classemes' are 'person', 'thing', 'duty', 'power', 'capacity', and 'conformity'. We may note that it is a list which includes, but goes beyond, deontic operators.

Thus far, the argument has proceeded from linguistic principles. Given the way the legal lexicon is constituted, and the nature of any semantic relations (according to the European semiotic tradition), then legal language, having a lexicon constituted in a manner different from that of the ordinary language, and involving terms related to each other in ways different from those of the ordinary language, must be autonomous of the ordinary language. Such an argument does not exclude the possibility of substantial historical influence from ordinary to legal language, or of considerable factual correspondence. Such historical and factual considerations are sometimes invoked as an argument against the principle of autonomy. Some variations on this theme may be briefly considered.

The first argument relates to intelligibility. Mounin, while conceding that the language of law has both lexical and syntactic peculiarities, notes that it needs to draw upon the whole resources of the natural language for its intelligibilty. Quoting Stalin's argument against 'class languages', he notes that although some social group or class may have a specific lexicon, and even particular phonological and syntactic characteristics of its own, the essential bases of the natural language - the same phonology, the same general lexicon, the same morphology and the same syntax - are still found in it. Without them, there could be no understanding whatsoever between lawyers and non-lawyers of the same natural language group. Those features which do distinguish class or legal language are therefore to be regarded as socio-linguistic phenomena, and not questions of language proper. **(25)** But Mounin's argument explains only cases of **apparent** intelligibility of legal language to the layman. The layman reads legal language as if it were natural language; he may be quite oblivious to those systemic differences which give the same words a different meaning to the lawyer. Equally, we have to account for the occurrence of incomprehension of legal language even amongst those who have a sophisticated knowledge of the natural language concerned. Kurt Baldinger is a linguist who has paid particular attention to legal language (1980:42-61). In the course of his discussion, he quotes a paragraph of the German Manual of Fiscal Law, and comments: 'I am perfectly happy if you understand none of that, because I cannot understand it in German either.' It is lack of knowledge of the system, rather than lack of knowledge of individual lexical items, which produces this effect.

A second objection to the 'autonomy' argument is sometimes made in terms of the invocation of ordinary language meaning by judges in the course of legal interpretation. This is a phenomenon which is particularly well-known in the Common Law world, and applies both to the development of law through precedent and to statutory interpretation. Does this not show that the legal system itself recognises its dependence upon the semantics of ordinary language ?

Even if the answer is affirmative, the claim to the principle of the autonomy of legal language would not thereby be prejudiced. For if ordinary language meanings are admitted, it is solely by virtue of the choice made within the legal system to admit such meanings. (A useful analogy is to be found in loan words, taken from one natural language to another. Such words are no less words of the recipient language by virtue of the fact that their historical origin lies in some other natural language.) Despite the theoretical possibility of constructing objective criteria to determine when ordinary language interpretation should and should not be used (such as by making the presumption in its favour conclusive, in the absence of explicit legal definition), such studies as are available suggest that the ordinary language argument is in fact deployed arbitrarily by Common Law Judges. **(26)** It appears to be a phenomenon belonging primarily to the rhetoric of legal argument. It does not provide evidence on the semantic question of the relation between legal and natural language.

The notion of 'choice' has here been given a wide meaning, in accordance with the structuralist approach. Legal systems often exempt officials from the need to make conscious choices by providing them with presumptions and 'closure rules', to regulate situations where conscious choices are not made. An example is to be found in the rule of interpretation, adopted in some legal systems, according to which it is presumed that a term bears its meaning in the ordinary language unless there has been an act of imposition of legal meaning (e.g. Wroblewski 1960:273), a view described by Thomas (1974:118) as 'le principe d'un renvoi au sens commun en l'absence de toute définition explicite du législateur'. But this view is to be rejected for a number of reasons. It ignores the possibility that interpretation in the absence of explicit legal definition may not be by reference to the concepts of ordinary language, but rather to the (there unstated) legal concepts which form the system within which legal language takes its meaning. This approach is adopted by A. Carcaterra (1970) in his analysis of the notion of good faith (**bona fides**) in Roman law. That concept was not to be labelled 'moral', and interpreted by reference to its historical roots in the writings of the Stoics. By being used in the juristic texts, the concept had become legal, and bore a legal meaning given to it within the system of legal semantics established by those texts. This places in a new light such legal concepts as beloved of the lawyer as the 'reasonable man'. **(27)** Such concepts do not represent a direct link between the law and the cultural values of a particular society, as Sourioux and Lerat maintain. Rather, any such social or cultural values to which the common terminology refers are institutionalised and perhaps inevitably transformed by the fact of legal encoding. **(28)** Yet the common terminology is not without its importance. For certainly, it creates the appearance of a direct reference by law to contemporary socio-cultural values. As such, it may be regarded, depending on one's ideological viewpoint, either as a necessary and legitimate instrument directed towards social cohesion, or a means of legitimation of an alien, oppressive system. The terminological link thus becomes important for the pragmatics, rather than the semantics, of law.

The argument between structuralists and functionalists over the autonomy of legal language may thus be seen to reflect philosophical differences regarding the nature of human choice - an issue which, as we have seen (1.3), underlies much of the common problematics of semiotics and legal theory. The fact that a word may have one sense in legal language and another in ordinary language might be taken to indicate the linguistic means by which law is, to use the phrase of Sourioux and Lerat (1976:35), 'soumis aux interférences de la morale, de l'Histoire, de facteurs sociaux et culturels multiples'. One sees here the difference between a descriptive, historical account of semantic relationships and the more formal approach of Carcaterra and Thomas. The non-legal sense of a word adopted into the legal lexicon provides the jurist with the source of one possible choice as to its particular meaning in law. (29) But the choice, as Carcaterra and Thomas would argue, can only be made from within the legal system, and does not occur automatically as a result of the semantic pull of the non-legal meaning. 'Choice' in this context is not to be taken in an exclusively psychological, positive and conscious sense. The toleration of an historical influence from non-legal to legal meaning would also count, for these purposes, as choice. The same issue arises in respect of the relation between ideology and legal language. G/L speak of specialised discourse as possessing a certain degree of autonomy (1976:83), and Carrion-Wam stresses, in this context, the transference of ideological elements from the semantic universe of the ordinary language to that of the legal language (5.2 below). Such a position of semi-autonomy can be conceptualised in terms of the differing roles of historical and formal/structural elements.

CHAPTER THREE

The Syntagmatic Level of Legal Discourse

(3.1) General Characteristics: Greimas combines the structuralist use of a linguistic model for analysis of discourse with the formalist tradition in folklore analysis. Narrative is the level of any text, rather than a genre. G/L attempt a narrative analysis, distinguishing syntagmatic and paradigmatic levels, of both the legal content and legal grammar which appear in the level of manifestation of the text. The purpose is the analysis of the means by which any meaning is conveyed, not the choice of particular meanings (interpretation). **(3.2) 'Actants':** The minimal unit of narrative grammar corresponding to the nominal phrase is the **'actant'**, which is organised in a matrix of the categories sender/receiver, subject/object, helper/opponent. The **société commerciale** of the 1966 Loi is identified as an **actant collectif**, performing the role of **actant-sujet.** This structure entails a dominance of objects over persons in the constitution of the SC. The power relations within the SC, in which management is dominant over the general assembly, also reflect actantial structure, and mirror the different relation between person and object found in the rules regarding directors' shareholdings. **(3.3) 'Fonctions':** 'Functions' along with 'attributions' and 'qualifications' are the equivalents in narrative grammar of predicates in linguistics. They tell us what the **actant** does or is. The attribution of a collective will to the SC involves the same relations between units (of will) and collectivities as constitute the SC in terms of capital. Legality is also an attribute which has to be constructed for the SC. The SC receives a message from the legislator as to how it may express a particular will and under what conditions it will be accorded the attribute of legality. Where the economic aims of the SC have been performed, distribution of profits (or loss) or investment (or borrowing) reflect the narrative function 'gift'. **(3.4) The Narrative Syntagm:** The **actants** and **fonctions** combine in the elements of an overall narrative syntagm, expressed in one version as 'manipulation, competence, performance, recognition'. The different **actants** have distinctive roles at various stages of the narrative syntagm and different kinds of objects (including modal objects) also have their particular places. Patterns of legal behaviour manifest this same narrative algorithm, which can be expressed both in the abstract terms of the narrative syntagm or in the anthropomorphic vocabulary based on folklore analysis.

3.1 GENERAL CHARACTERISTICS

Greimas is a semiotician. He wants to know how meaning is constructed. He assumes that there exists an underlying process, wherein small units combine in regular ways, such as admits of something like scientific description. The same kind of process through which the meaning of sememes is constructed is taken to account also for the construction of the meaning of sentences and larger discursive units. As Culler puts it, Greimas poses the question 'how far is it possible to account for meaning in literature on the hypothesis that minimal semantic features combine in law-governed ways to produce large-scale semantic effects' (1975:76). In literature, the minimal semantic units are **actants** and their **fonctions.** The units of this 'actantial model' combine in regular ways along both syntagmatic and paradigmatic axes. The syntagmatic axis provides the structure of the plot, while the paradigmatic axis imposes semiotic constraints upon the choice of elements in the syntagmatic axis, these constraints deriving from a quasi-logical construction - the 'semiotic square'. The syntagmatic axis is itself a formalisation of the plot of any actual story, and the constraints in the model indicate that their exists a finite repertoire of plot structures which will convey meaning. **(1)**

The Syntagmatic Level of Legal Discourse

But while Greimas advocates the use of linguistic methods in pursuit of narrative grammar, he stresses a difference in level between the deep narrative grammar and its (linguistic or non-linguistic) manifestations. 'Narrative structures are distinct from linguistic structures because they can be revealed by languages other than the natural languages (in cinema, dreams, etc.)' (1971:793); nevertheless, 'the linguist . . will not fail to take note that narrative structures present characteristics which are remarkably **recurrent,** that these recurrences allow for the recording of distinguishable **regularities,** and that they thus lead to the construction of a **narrative grammar.** In this case it is evident that he will utilize the concept of grammar in its most general and non-metaphorical sense, understanding such a grammar to consist in a limited number of principles of structural organization of narrative units, complete with rules for the combination and functioning of these units, leading to the production of narrative objects' (1971:794).

Greimasian narrative structure combines the tradition of structural linguistics with the formalist tradition in folklore analysis, descending from Vladimir Propp. The latter claimed that the Russian folktale is analysable within thirty-one 'functions'; these are further reduced to six by Greimas, who in effect compensates for this reduction by postulating something equivalent to transformational rules, deriving from the logical or paradigmatic axis. This combination of Russian formalism and structural linguistics, which has shaped the orientation of Greimas, is one which he shares with Lévi-Strauss. There is also convergence between Greimas and Lévi-Strauss in respect of the type of data which they have studied: without excluding other types of material, both have attended primarily to narrative texts (in the case of Lévi-Strauss, oral narrative or myth; for Greimas, primarily written texts). Greimas has in fact also studied with Lévi-Strauss, and the two stand together as representing a distinct form of structuralism, characterised by more universalistic and 'scientific' claims than the forms encountered in the words of Barthes, Foucault, Derrida and others.

Law and literature are sometimes presented as standing at opposite poles of a spectrum - the one characterised by literalism and constraint, the other by imagery and creativity. If so, the attempt to apply a 'narrative model' to law would appear idiosyncratic. (2) But

Greimas conceives of narrative as a universal level of discourse, not a particular genre. Literature too is subject to semiotic constraints, and at the deepest level these constraints are universal features of discourse - whether literary or legal. In fact, it is a particular form of logic which for Greimas represents common ground between semantics, literature and law. Narrative grammar is conceived as a general form of articulation of any kind of content, an articulation which is anterior to the manifestation of that content (whether in language or not) and which one might consider as a 'forme d'organisation de l'imaginaire humain' (1976:94). Narrative structures can appear either explicitly or implicitly in the reports (**récits**) of the discourse; while the discourse might thus appear as a more or less spontaneous production, the narrative structures in reality are recurrent from one text to another, from one form of semiotics to another, indeed from one culture to another.

Greimas and Rastier distinguish three levels of structure in narrative (1968:87; cf. 1970:135f.):

> - **deep structures,** which define the fundamental mode of existence of an individual or a society, and subsequently the conditions of existence of semiotic objects. As far as we know, the elementary constituants of deep structures have a definable logical status.
> - **superficial structures** constitute a semiotic grammar which arranges into discursive forms the contents susceptible of manifestation. The products of this grammar system are independent of the expression which reveals them, in as far as they can theoretically appear in any substance, and, in the case of linguistic objects, in any language.
> - **the structures of manifestation** produce and organize the significances. Although they can include quasi-universals, they remain particular to any given language (or more precisely they define the particular characteristics of languages), or to any given material. They are studied by the superficial stylistics of morphemes, shapes, colors, etc.

The 'superficial structures' are thus not to be equated with the level of manifestation of the narrative itself (in later work more commonly referred to as the discursive level). Elsewhere Greimas calls the level of deep structures the 'semiological' level; that of the 'superficial structures' the 'semantic' level. The former relates to the paradigmatic axis, and is essentially logical in character, developing the use of binary oppositional structures of Lévi-Strauss. The latter relates to the 'syntagmatic' or 'anthropomorphic' level, and represents a formalisation of the work of Propp and Souriau.

'Narrative grammar' is thus conceived as the interrelation of the 'deep structures' (3) and 'superficial structures'. It is independent of the particular forms in which particular narratives are expressed: the narrative grammar of a particular story would not differ according to whether the story was told in language (whether oral or written), mime, pictographs, film, or some other genre. Of course, each of these different genres might have its own set of structures, each distinct in some way from the others (as, for example, arbitrariness is taken to be a particular characteristic of the linguistic sign). But when used as forms of expression of narrative, each of these different genres will reflect (though not reflect only) the same narrative grammar. Literature is thus regarded, by Greimas and his associates, as a dual semiotic system, wherein the structures of signification of both the normally linguistically-expressed level of manifestation, and the deep level of immanence of narrative, require separate consideration.

This chapter is concerned with the level of the 'superficial structures', a level variously described as 'anthropomorphic' and 'syntagmatic' - for reasons which will appear. 'Superficial' is not used in any derogatory sense (Greimas 1972:166), but only to indicate that this level is intermediate between that of manifestation on the one hand, and that of the **'grammaire fondamentale'** with its logical relations on the other (Bremond 1975:365). It is 'anthropomorphic' in the sense that it uses the figures of human actors (depersonalised as **actants**) accomplishing tasks, submitting to tests, and achieving ends. It is very much a goal-directed level, where human action takes the centre of the stage. It involves following through the various **fonctions** of the accomplishment of those goals, and thus is based on the syntagmatic axis of the narrative: the sequence of events which the level of manifestation discloses, rather than alternatives which the logic of signification might have substituted.

We see in all this the particular character of the Greimasian argument. It is structuralist not only in its claim that narrative grammar is a transference of the grammar of the sentence (particularly the relations between its nominal phrases and predicates) to discursive units larger than the sentence, but also in its attention to the relations between nature and culture (4.2 below) and its emphasis upon the centrality of binary oppositional relationships within the structure of signification. It is semiotic in its attention to the appearances which the text creates, and the manner in which it creates them. What is present in the text must be understood in terms of what is absent, and in this respect the Greimasian account is particularly interesting in the role which it attributes to the legislator as an **actant** itself operating at the same syntagmatic level as the SC. Emphasis upon the semiotic appearance is a prominent feature of G/L's account of the **'grammaire juridique'** (5.1). Indeed, G/L distinguish **'grammaire juridique'** and **'grammaire narrative'** not as different parts of the legal discourse (corresponding to distinctions like 'procedural' and 'substantive' law, or to that between 'secondary' and 'primary' rules), but rather as different levels of analysis appertaining to the same legal material. In short, legal procedures themselves are amenable to analysis in terms of narrative grammar (1976:95).

Despite the use of the alternative terminology 'semantic' to refer to the syntagmatic (or 'anthropomorphic' or 'superficial') level of the deep structure of the text, Greimasian semiotics does not attempt 'interpretation'. The purpose is not to identify the means of arriving at any 'right' meaning, or any criteria for preferring one meaning to another. It is rather to discover what conditions must be satisfied in order to attribute any meaning at all to the discourse. (4) What Sturrock writes of Barthes applies equally to Greimas: '. . . he shifts the critic's responsibility in respect of meaning by attending not to the product but to the system whereby it is produced: not to significance but to the process of signification. Barthes would like us to understand **how** texts mean before we start worrying about **what** they mean' (1979:58). Calloud similarly distinguishes between 'analysis' and 'interpretation', with reference to the structural semiotics of Greimas (1979:57f.,65). Interpretation, for Greimas, is an **activity** of the receiver of a message, a **faire interpretatif** which forms the converse of the **faire persuasif** of the emitter of the message (1976:36). We may thus say that both persuasion and interpretation are activities of the users of the message, and belong to the pragmatics of discourse; the structural semiotics of Greimas, on the other hand, seek the conditions necessary for the **message itself** to bear signification.

This methodological objective must be borne in mind in considering G/L's analysis of the 1966 law. Moreover, they do not seek to provide a comprehensive account of the meaning structures of the text. The 'pilot' nature of their study is indicated by the working hypothesis which they propose: if we recognise narrative properties in **some** sequences of legal discourse, we may be justified in the use of general narrative models to account for the organisation of entire legal discourses. Here, only parts of the 1966 law (which in fact extends to 509 articles taking up 68 columns of J.O.) are analysed. (5) Yet the pilot character of the study should not divert us from the substantial claims which are made. It follows from the nature of the Greimasian conception of narrativity that it should be applicable to non-literary as well as literary discourses on human action: and its selectivity in the detail to which it attends is a straightforward extension of the method as applied to literature, not a reflection of the authors' lack of legal training. If Greimasian narratology is not designed to provide an interpretation of the surface manifestation of a literary text, we should not expect it to provide an interpretation of the surface manifestation of a legal text either.

3.2 'ACTANTS'

The minimal units of the narrative grammar are **actants** and **fonctions** (sometimes, **qualifications**), corresponding respectively to nominal phrases and predicates of the sentence (Culler 1975: 82).

The notion of an **actant** is firmly distinguished from that of a 'character' in the narrative plot. In part, this represents the deliberate avoidance of a psychological orientation. As Chatman puts it: 'The structuralists wish to base their analyses strictly on what characters DO in a story, not what they ARE - by some outside psychological measure' (1972:57). Indeed, Calloud goes so far as to say that 'the illusion of a personage with a stable identity which is reinforced by the power of the proper name is nothing but a 'narrative effect' ' (1976:19). The underlying reason for this stance is that actions admit of formalisation, in structural terms, while 'character' is less readily structurable: 'A "personage" . . . is only a more or less ephemeral "flower" blooming on the narrative branch for the joy and edification of the reader. Of course, it is for the flower or the fruit that one takes patient care of the plant. Far from existing primarily for themselves, as real beings which are secondarily in relationship with each other, the actors of a narrative are above all in relationship with each other. The unstable "figures" created through this interrelationship are for them the sole horizon of existence' (Calloud 1976:20).

An **actant** is therefore more like a role which a person may play in relation to another person, rather than a character. It follows that a character in the plot may exemplify a number of different **actants,** and that conversely a single **actant** may be variously represented in the plot by different characters. **(6)** Thus the **actants** are not directly identifiable from the 'level of manifestation' of the narrative; rather, they are generated and defined by the deep structure of the narrative (Hawkes 1977:89).

Examples of **actants** are 'subject' and 'object' and 'sender' and 'receiver'. Greimas analyses the narrative statement:

Eve gives an apple to Adam

in the following way: Eve represents the **actant** subject in relation to the apple (which represents the **actant** object), while at the same time representing the **actant** sender in relation to Adam, who represents the **actant** receiver. Developing the research of Propp and Souriau, Greimas claims that three actantial categories - subject/object, sender/receiver and helper/opponent - form the units (corresponding to nominal phrases) which in combination with narrative functions are capable of accounting for the construction of meaning in narrative (1966:176-80).

The six **actants** are organised in a matrix, or actantial model. Greimas' analysis of 'Eve gives an apple to Adam' (above) reveals part, but not all, of the scheme. The full statement is: (7)

Sender ----→	Object ----→	Receiver
	↑	
Helper ----→	Subject ←----	Opponent

More recently, Greimasian semiotics has tended to view the category helper/opponent not as actantial, but rather as modal values which may affect the subject in his capacity to fulfil the task he has in hand. **(8)**

Thus far we have been concerned only with the **actants.** We have yet to add what it is in the narrative statement that the **actants** do. In other words, we have yet to consider the F of the Greimasian formula **EN = F(A),** which takes the typical narrative statement to be the relationship between an **actant** and a **fonction.** But before we turn to **fonctions** (3.3), we must note that the very notion of an actantial role implies some form of activity as between the opposed pairs of each actantial category. Greimas sees this relationship in **modal** terms (1966:132f.). The three interlinked axes represent relationships of communication (sender/receiver), volition (subject/object), and power (helper/opponent), the last including the modalities of capacity and knowledge. **(9)** It is within this network of relations that each **actant** is to be defined. In the case of 'subject' and 'object', the definition must take account of the interaction of two different axes of the matrix: the object is defined in terms of both what the subject wills and what the sender communicates; the subject in terms of both what the helper assists (and the opponent obstructs) and the objects desired. **(10)**

The definition of the **actants** in terms of each other gives the scheme a syntactic character, and indeed the term **actant** was taken from the study of syntactic structure by the linguist Tesnière. **(11)**

In their account of the 1966 Loi G/L identify the **société commerciale** (hereafter SC) as an **actant,** and in particular as an **actant-sujet.** We attribute legal personality to it, and thereby invest it with the capacity to perform legal acts. Although the SC which appears in the 1966 law is not a particular, historical entity, it is still treated by G/L as an **acteur,** comparable to the character or person who appears at the 'surface' level of a novel. Semiotic analysis then seeks to identify such an **acteur** with the actantial (cf. nominal) category of narrative grammar which it reflects, i.e. its status as an **actant.** There is, however, an important difference between a class of legal persons instituted by a legislative text, and a character in a novel, who may have no semiotic function outside that text.

G/L apply the Saussurian distinction between 'syntagmatic' and 'paradigmatic' to the **actant collectif** (97). The **actant syntagmatique** would be defined exclusively in terms of its functions, the potential programme of action which it is capable of performing. G/L give the example of a car manufacturer, conceived as an **actant syntagmatique,** within whose single programme different **acteurs** (such as engineers, management, specialised workers, etc.) take their turns in contributing to the single production programme. But one can also distinguish a form of **actant collectif paradigmatique:** such as the first class of a **lycée,** or a recognized social group within a society. Here, the **actant collectif** is characterised not by the possibility of integrating its individual **acteurs** into a single programme of action, but rather by its place in a system of hierarchical classification: the class or social group belongs to a larger and hierarchically superior collectivity, the (whole) **lycée,** or the (whole) national community; but the **acteurs** which make up this **actant collectif paradigmatique** have in common a functional field or specific qualifications which distinguish them from other **actants collectifs** belonging to the same hierarchical classification. Nevertheless, one **actant collectif** may be substituted for another within the particular meaning-system of that hierarchy. The SC of the 1966 Loi is identified as such an **actant collectif.** In relation to other **actants collectifs** recognised by the law, it is an **actant collectif paradigmatique;** in relation to its functioning in relation to other **actants** within the text, it is an **actant collectif syntagmatique.**

Semantic Investment of the 'actant collectif paradigmatique'

The formal structure of the **actant collectif paradigmatique** is analysed by G/L in terms of the opposition between units **(U)** and totality **(T)**, combined with the attributes of units and totalities in terms of the opposition between integral **(i)** and partitive **(p)** characteristics. (12) The **actant collectif** is a partitive totality **(Tp)**, that is a whole within which distinct parts are recognised. Its opposite is a collection of units each conceived only in relation to itself **(Ui)**. This reflects, at the discursive level, the semic form of analysis which we have considered in the context of structural semantics (section 2.3). G/L here seek to identify the minimal conceptual units which in combination make up the formal structure of (at this stage, any) **actant collectif.** **T** and **p** may be regarded as the semic components of the **actant collectif.**

This formal analysis would apply to the construction of any **actant collectif paradigmatique.** G/L then go on to discuss the semantic features which this legal discourse (the 1966 law) attribute to the **actant collectif,** which distinguish it specifically as an SC. They identify the semantic specificity of the SC with a particular semantic investment of **p,** the partitive character of the totality (99). This partitive character, which is substituted for the integrity of the individual **(i)** and which confines his role to that of participation in the new totality, is conceived as a **'qualification'** which is attached to an **actant.** Greimasian narratology distinguishes two types of **qualification,** the one being permanent and characterised by the relationship of attribution, the other being temporary and possessive in character. What characterises commercial law is the almost exclusive use of temporary possessive attributions. Specifically, a participant in an SC ceases to be conceived as an individual person with an integral character **(i)** and is defined exclusively as the possessor of a portion of capital **(p).** He is identified, for these purposes, not by what he 'is' but by what he 'has' (99f.).

However, the identification of the partitive character of the **actant collectif** as, in the case of the SC, the possessor of a portion of capital, itself invites analysis in terms of narrative grammar. We have a qualification **(q)** of an **actant (A)** to whom an object of value **(O)** is attributed.

This can be expressed in the formula of an **énoncé qualificatif:**

Q (A: O)

But this formula could be invested in three different ways. If Q is invested as 'possesses', then both **A** and **O** can remain relatively uninvested (In G/L's terminology, they can remain as **'cases vides'**: 100). **A** need be invested only as 'someone' and **O** as 'something', but the attributive statement that **A** possesses **O** will still be communicated through the semantic investment of **Q.** A second possibility is to invest **A** as 'possessor', leaving Q invested merely as 'of' and **O** as 'something'. Third, **O** may be invested as 'the thing possessed', and this will logically (if not linguistically) imply the semantic investment of Q as a relationship of possession and **A** as the person who possesses. These three ways of investing the semantic formula differ in that in the first there is no relation of dominance between **A** and **O** implied; in the second **A** is dominant over **O:** and in the third **O** is dominant over **A.** If **A** is chosen as dominant, then the discursive world is presented as one of proprietors (**actants**) where objects are defined in terms of their capacity to be possessed; if **O** is dominant, the world is conceived in terms of objects of value, in search of possessors. There is thus a difference in world view implied in the choice between different forms of semantic investment of the formula. Different discourses may invest this formula of attribution in different ways. But for the purpose of investing the **actant collectif,** G/L suggest (102), only one of these three possibilities is available, namely the third - in which it is **O** which is dominant. Only this form will serve to represent the logical operation of implication from **Up** to **Tp. (13)** In syntagmatic terms, this is the process by which the different units become conjoined in the totality. This process is achieved by the transfer of any object of value, and requires the participant to be conceived as under the dominance of the object: the object remains the same while the **actant** is transformed by virtue of his joining with others as sharers of the capital. **Whoever** possesses that portion of capital is a part of the new totality; it is by virtue of that, rather than by virtue of his personality, that the individual is incorporated. That is not to say that the **SC** is represented merely by the totality of the capital **(O).**

Participants in the **SC** are regarded semiotically as **relations** between **O** and **A** (a characteristically structuralist stance). But in the particular relationship which flows from the semiotic constraints imposed by the need to invest an **actant collectif,** the relation is one in which **O** is dominant over **A.**

The Power Structure within the SC

The distribution of power within the organs of the SC is also taken to reflect actantial structure (113). Two distinct **actants** are envisaged by the legislator as the instruments of exercise of social power within the SC, and thus as the means which it is given (its **pouvoir-faire**) to perform the will with which it has been invested. These two **actants** are the **actant décisionnaire** (the general assembly) and the **actant gestionnaire** (management). These two types of **actant** have their respective syntactic and semantic structures, which define and differentiate them.

The general assembly of the SC, as the decision-making **actant,** is the sovereign possessor of social power within the SC, in conformity with law. It is made up of the mass of participants in the company defined in terms of the relationship of possession. But each participant is characterised by the dominance of the 'object possessed'; he takes part in the meetings not in any personal capacity, but as the holder for the time being of a section of capital. Nevertheless, the legal discourse seeks to attach value to the term 'possessor' - at least symbolically - by requiring his physical presence, and in setting out rules for the convening and regularity of meetings for the purposes of taking decisions. The **pouvoir-faire** which is accorded to the general assembly by the text is not, however, the power directly to turn a mere project into an actualized programme (in narrative terms, to perform the contract). Rather, we have here an interpolated syntagm which stands between the **pouvoir-faire** and the performative act itself, since the power of the general assembly is merely a power of decision, the exercise of which leads only to decisions and not to their implementation.

G/L seek to suggest that the general assembly is not the real residue of the SC's **pouvoir-faire,** but nevertheless are concerned to explicate its semiotic function (114f.). The taking of votes in the general assembly merely makes explicit the balance of social power which is already in the assembly, but the very taking of the vote removes antagonistic groupings, by a conflict which determines (and legitimates?) the victory of one group of protagonists. What happens here is both formal, in that it does not in itself generate action, and conventional, in that it operates through the rules of a game. Moreover, the kinds of power entrusted to the general assembly, and the modes of their exercise, show that the power of decision entrusted to the general assembly represents a narrowly defined functional field. It comprises decision on the very existence of the collective subject (modifications of status, dissolution and merger of companies), decisions on the quantitative dimensions of the collective **actant** (additions to and reductions of its capital), and decisions on the object of desire of the collective subject (the distribution of dividends). With the exception of this last, the power of decision is exercised essentially at the level of the existence (**être**) of the SC, and not in respect of its activity (**faire**). Correspondingly, G/L suggest that the matters subject to decision by the assembly are limited and prescribed, whereas the power of implementation (**pouvoir-faire**) of the SC is stated by the law in terms of what the management is not prohibited from doing. Indeed, the most important decision of the general assembly appears to be the delegation of its power to a new receiver-**actant,** which is the true subject of the SC's action, namely the **actant gestionnaire.**

The power of the **actant gestionnaire** has a number of distinct characteristics. First, it possesses an integral character, in that it is delegated as a whole, and not submitted to arbitrary division. Secondly, it is a residual power, limited only negatively by the areas reserved for the **actant décisionnaire** on the one hand and by explicit prohibitions (of the law) which regulate any manifestations of 'savage' social interest on the other. By implication, the powers of the **actant décisionnaire** are different: they are conferred piecemeal (by the law itself), and exist only in so far as they are explicity stated. The limitations placed upon the power of the **actant gestionnaire** are accorded a special significance. The fact that the **actant gestionnaire** cannot change the size of the SC, nor decide to disband it, combined with the powers which are actually given to the **actant gestionnaire,** produce an equivalence between the SC and the **actant gestionnaire** itself. The **actant gestionnaire** is a subject of action distinct from the SC, but at the same time co-extensive with it. In this way, the SC can itself monitor the exercise of its powers, and the performance of its tasks. The 1966 law itself pays little attention to the actual performance of these economic tasks. It is only the consequences of these performances which are represented in the text, in the form of the acquisition of objects of value and their return to the sender (as distribution of dividends).

The participants in the **actant gestionnaire** are also conceived differently from those in the **actant décisionnaire.** Whereas the latter appear under the dominance of the object possessed (as representatives of portions of capital), the former are defined as permanent possessors of shares. The directors must personally own a minimum number of shares, and may not alienate them while remaining as directors (116, citing article 95). Here, then, shares must follow persons, the thing possessed therefore being under the dominance of the possesor. The internal distribution of power within the **société** thus appears as a structure of relationships between two terms, where the anonymous power represented by the shares is counterbalanced by the personal power of the managing directors.

Thus far, we have been dealing with the **actant sujet.** What of the **actant objet** ? According to the 'canonical formulae' of narrative grammar, the initial 'desire' of the subject is based upon a 'lack' (here, a 'lack of gain'). The action of the subject is therefore the liquidation of this lack, accomplished through the transfer of an object of value to the **société** where this lack was manifested. The objects of value which the **société** is 'contracted' to acquire therefore perform the role of **actant-objet.**

3.3 'FONCTIONS'

We turn now to the second narrative structure, the **fonction.** In his analysis of one hundred Russian folktales, Propp had identified thirty-one recurrent 'functions', understood as the action of a person defined by its significance in the unravelling of the plot. **(14)** For Propp, these were the minimal units of the narrative, and the 'morphology' of the folktale consisted in the laws which govern their combination. Two such laws were identified.

First, there was a correlation between functions and the seven character types or spheres of action which Propp also identified. These latter, from which the Greimasian **actant** was to be developed, were the villain, the donor, the helper, the princess and her father, the despatcher, the hero, and the false hero. The thirty-one functions were distributed amongst these characters in such a way that the same functions were always carried out by the same characters. Secondly, there existed a non-reversible sequence of functions. Some of them (e.g. villainy, lack) represented initial states; others were intermediate moves in the narrative (e.g. struggle); while others represented terminal states (e.g. marriage, gain, escape).

Greimas followed Lévi-Strauss in regarding Propp's scheme as insufficiently formalised (Hawkes 1977:93). Just as the seven characters or spheres of action became three binary oppositional pairs for Greimas, so too the functions are reorganised in a much smaller, but more highly structured group of binary oppositions (Greimas 1966:194ff.). The effect is to free Propp's morphology of its second law. The functions no longer have to appear in a fixed order of succession (Galland 1973: 40). The structure of the folktale is no longer conceived purely in terms of syntagmatic succession (Greimas 1966:195). Instead, the logic of binary oppositions is brought to bear. For example, the function violation is no longer conceived as separate from, and necessarily subsequent in the narrative to, the function of prohibition; instead, the two presuppose each other in a single binary oppositional relationship. **(15)** This again serves to attribute to the minimal narrative units their places in both the logical and syntagmatic axes. On the one hand, combinations of functions generate the syntagmatic axis; on the other, these combinations reflect logical relationships which integrate the oppositions with their negations. As Culler puts it, in contrasting Propp with Lévi-Strauss and Greimas: ' . . a set of thirty-one functions cannot but seem an arbitrary array, and it is structurally much more satisfying to the analyst if he can make them transformations of three or four basic elements' (1975:213).

'Functions' are the predicates of narrative statements which have attracted the greatest attention. But Greimasian analysis does not regard them as the only type of predicate. Two other types may be distinguished: 'attributions' or 'qualifications'. They correspond to sentences which tell us not what the subject does but what he is. What the subject 'is' will ultimately determine what he does or fails to do: 'competence' precedes 'performance' in the narrative syntagm (section 3.4 below). The importance which this kind of predicate has for law will be obvious. Semiotic and legal theory converge in the centrality they attach to the concept 'power' ('pouvoir'). For G/L, the SC is invested with specific syntactic functions, which make it an **actant-sujet.** As such, it is an **actant** which has been invested with the modality of will, **vouloir,** such as to make it capable of formulating a goal, and attaining, through the performance of functions, an 'object'. The text of the 1966 law itself talks about the **'objet'** of the company; in semiotic terms, too, the identification of the SC as a **sujet** entails the attribution to it of desire for an **objet** (105).

The identification of the SC as a **sujet collectif** entails the attribution to it of a **vouloir collectif.** The semiotician seeks to analyse the conditions required to construct such a **vouloir collectif,** and to identify the specific object of the SC's desire. G/L apply the same model constructed to account for the structure of the **actant collectif.** (**16**) This is done by suggesting that the individuals (**Ui**) who are transformed into participants (**Up**) bring with them not only their portions of capital (**valeurs objectives**), but also their will (conceived as **valeurs subjectives**). This will can be regarded as partitive (**p**) in so far as it is regarded as a partial and specific desire, which conforms to the particular object envisaged, and not as the totality of desires which one normally finds within an individual. It is the putting together of these partial wills which allows us to conceive of the attribution of a **vouloir social** to the **actant collectif** which is constituted in parallel fashion by the overall acquisition of capital.

The SC must also be accorded the attribute of legality. The process revealed by the text, according to G/L, is analogous to that whereby a new-born child has its birth and integration into society recognised. The SC must be named, its seat and possible duration fixed, and its existence entered in the commercial register. These processes of recognition of the SC as a legal entity belong to the syntagmatic level of narrative grammar.

At this level, the establishment of a goal is conceived in terms of the narrative syntagm 'contract' (used more broadly than in its legal sense, as G/L observe), within which the actantial pairs subject-object and sender-receiver are both involved. Thus, 'contract' involves the transmission of a **vouloir faire** by a sender to a receiver who accepts it. The 'sender' here is the mass of participants in the company, who charge it with a collective will and a particular task, and who thereby invests the company as a **sujet collectif** (106). But at this stage the **sujet collectif** is 'savage' (natural, non-legal); without more, it may perform its tasks in an excessive and disorderly fashion. It therefore requires to be 'civilised' through being incorporated by the legislator in the legal order. This process follows the same path as does the recognition of the legal status of the SC as **actant collectif.** The **vouloir collectif** which at this stage exists only on the referential level of law becomes the receiver of a second contract, the sender on this occasion being the legislator himself. This second contract lays down the permitted forms of behaviour of the SC and the sanctions for their breach, thus partially transforming a **vouloir-faire** into a **devoir-faire.** In this way, a savage will is transformed into a cultural duty (106f.). Both the management and the general assembly have their particular **fonctions.** Whereas that of the management is liquidation of the lack of gain (acquisition of profit), the function of the general assembly is to distribute the gains. But this leads to a problem in terms of the constitution of the **société** as an **'actant collectif'.** The allocation of the gains is not made to the **société** as instituted in the form of an **actant collectif,** but rather to the individual actors in their (personal) quality as participants. Thus the **société** appears to be dissolved symbolically every time the profits are distributed. G/L note that where performance of economic activity results not in profit but rather in loss, it is not the general assembly which is made responsible, but rather management which has to account, and which ultimately may be disqualified. This reminds them of the story of the little prince who takes only the praise, while his little friend the beggar takes the punishment.

In a third possible case, that of non-distribution of profits, which are devoted to the self-financing of the company (profits ploughed back into investment), the narrative function of 'gift' is fulfilled to the advantage of the **société** itself as an **actant collectif,** rather than for the advantage of the participants as individuals.

Gift is a function considered in narrative structure as the reaffirmation of the contract through the transfer of an object of value. But the identities of both the sender and receiver of this 'gift' will differ in cases of profit and loss (117f.). Where there is a profit, it is the general assembly (the **actant décisionnaire**) which sends the object of value (profits) to the participants in the company. But where a loss is incurred, it is the management (**actant gestionnaire**) which sends the object of value (here negative) to the **société**, here conceived as an **actant collectif.** In this latter case, one assumes this to take the form of the presentation of deficit accounts to the general assembly. Indeed, G/L see these relationships as reflecting a dual conception of the **société** as sender, in that sometimes it appears as a temporary semiotic object which is symbolically dismembered by the periodic fulfilment of its objectives (in the form of distribution of profits), while at the same time continuing as a permanent **actant collectif,** a social entity which it is sought always to enrich and enlarge.

3.4 THE NARRATIVE SYNTAGM

We are now in a position to consider how the minimal semantic units of the discourse combine together at the syntagmatic level. The Greimasian analysis commences from a systematisation of the thirty-one functions of Propp. Of the latter, 'prohibition', 'violation' and 'test' (**épreuve**) are particularly important. Greimas retains such anthropomorphic notions, but combines 'prohibition' and 'violation' in the notion of 'contract', and distinguishes three different types of 'test', through which a large number of other Proppian functions can be integrated. The subject has to be both instituted as such and qualified to act. In the formal analysis of narrative, he is subjected to a 'qualifying test'. Thereafter, he seeks to perform the goal for which he has been instituted as subject: the 'principal test' or 'performance' of the 'contract'. Finally, there is a 'glorifying test', a 'glorification of the hero', which serves to show recognition that the task has been performed, through receipt of some 'object' which results in the removal of the initial misfortune or lack which the 'contract' sought to remedy. **(17)**

Such formulations remain close to the terms of Propp's analysis of the Russian folktales. More recently, however, the overall narrative syntagm has come to be expressed more abstractly. For example, the formulation of the syntagm is expressed by Calloud in terms of a 'narrative algorithm' according to which 'the trajectory which explores the fullest potentialities of the narrative structure is one with four phases or stages: manipulation, competence, performance, recognition'. **(18)** Here, 'contract' has become 'manipulation'. It is the process by which the subject is made to do (**faire faire**) something - the process wherein the goal which he will pursue in the story is established. This goal is set by the communication to the subject of either a volition (**vouloir-faire**) or an obligation to do something (**devoir-faire**). 'Competence' is an abstraction of the Proppian 'qualifying test'. It is the process whereby the subject of the action is qualified to achieve his objective. This too involves the communication of an object of value, but this time what is communicated is a modal value, the power to act (**pouvoir-faire**) or knowledge of how to act (**savoir-faire**). 'Performance' is an abstraction from the 'principal test', through which the initial state is transformed into the final state. Finally, the term 'sanction' is used to abstract from the 'glorifying test', wherein recognition is given to the true state of affairs that has now been achieved in the story (Calloud 1979:63).

Within this overall narrative syntagm, a sequence of individual narrative syntagms can be identified, corresponding broadly to the phases of the 'narrative algorithm'. These distinct narrative syntagms are particularly important, since it is within them that the minimal narrative units, the **actants** and **fonctions,** can be seen to operate in law-governed combinations. **(19)** The different **actants** have distinct roles in the various syntagms. The sender and receiver are involved in the establishment of the contract; the process involves the communication of a goal by someone to someone else. In the qualifying test, the subject finds himself beset within the **actant** helper/opponent: as in the 'qualifying test' of Propp, he must struggle to establish his credentials. Performance involves the acquisition by the subject of the object. **(20)** The final phase - in Greimasian terminology, 'sanction' - again involves the sender/receiver, in that the message of recognition is communicated. This corresponds to the function 'attribution' in Propp (Calloud 1976:27).

There is also a correlation between different kinds of

object of value and the syntagms which form different parts of the overall narrative statement. Calloud distinguishes between modal objects (volition/obligation or power/cognition) which are brought into play in 'manipulation' and 'competence'; value objects on which 'performance' centres; and 'cognition objects' which are communicated in 'sanction'. **(21)** This classification of objects also generates a typology of narrative statements which may be made about them. The formula

$$\mathbf{EN = F(A)}$$

assumes the dominance of action (**faire**), and can be applied most typically to the 'performance' syntagm, which forms the characteristic action of the plot. But both 'manipulation' and 'competence' involve the transference (or communication) of **modal** objects, and typically generate modal statements. Similarly, 'sanction' involves recognition of the final state of the narrative, in which the subject **has** the object, or a state of affairs has come into **being.** The narrative must therefore use 'attributive statements' in relation to them. Thus, alongside **énoncés performatifs,** there exist **énoncés modaux** and **énoncés attributifs** (Galland 1973:47). In classifications of the different types of **énoncé narratif, performatifs** and **attributifs** are sometimes placed under the general category of **énoncés descriptifs,** in opposition to **énoncés modaux** (Bremond 1972:368).

Patterns of legal behaviour are described by G/L as **micro-récits juridiques,** and are taken to be manifestations of general narrative algorithms. For example, the constitution of the SC and the procedures which establish it correspond to the narrative sequence of the establishment of contract and the granting of a performative will to the subject. Similarly, social agents or organs must receive the modalities of power and knowledge. The auditing of accounts provides an example of the 'anthropomorphic' level of the narrative grammar: through it, one achieves the 'glorification of the hero' (if the accounts are sound) or the 'unmasking of the traitor' (if the books are cooked). The SC passes through a series of 'tests', which are both anthropomorphic (in that they represent the sequence of human action) and which provide models of what the legal system requires.

The SC receives its 'contract' through the merger of

individual wills into a collective will (3.2 above). It is endowed with its legal power to act by receiving the appropriate modal values from the legislator. At the 'performance' stage of the narrative syntagm, the SC is charged with the activity of acquisition (1976:107). This leads to a 'narrativisation' of economic life, which thus appears in the legal discourse as a closed field of foreseeable confrontations of subjects endowed with will, each one representing his own interests. One might then consider those subjects who pursue their legitimate interests as **'sujets-héros'**, and those whose interests are illegitimate as **'anti-sujets-traîtres'**. This would generate a typology of legal performances (or 'tests'), in which one might predict two types of conflict: (a) a subject who represents legitimate social interest might enter the lists against an anti-subject, the incarnation of personal interest (for example, a partner accused of abuse of power); (b) a subject representing the general interest (thus including third parties) might conflict with an anti-subject who acts in the name of the 'savage' social interest (thus contrary to the rights of third parties). We would thus have a basic syntax of legal conflicts, characterised by the interchangeability of the roles of subject and anti-subject which properly belongs to any system of syntax: when the **société** defends its legitimate interests, it assumes the role of 'hero'; when it exceeds its powers, it is changed into a 'traitor'.

The final state of the narrative syntagm is termed 'sanction' by Greimas, 'recognition' by Calloud. It corresponds, in anthropomorphic terms, to the 'glorification of the hero'. In the 1966 law, it takes the form of the management report back to the general meeting, a **micro-récit juridique** in which there is a transference of the modal value of knowledge, **savoir,** from the **actant gestionnaire** to the **actant décisionnaire.** This is the stage at which the actions of management are assessed in terms of their implementation of the desired course of action. From the viewpoint of the **actant décisionnaire,** this stage of knowledge about the action represents a syntactic equivalence with the transfer of power to the management which was made before the performance of its economic activity; management now transfers to the assembly a knowledge as to how this power has been used (116). Here, we may note, the legislator enables the SC to monitor the performance of its own tasks. This monitoring constitutes a form of 'recognition', but it is not recognition confined to, or primarily directed towards, the legal status of the acts which have been performed, but rather to their economic implications.

CHAPTER FOUR

The Paradigmatic Level of Legal Discourse

(4.1) The 'Semiotic Square': The Greimasian semiotic square, wherein relations between contraries and contradictories are formalised, is applied by Greimas not only to the analysis of semes in structural semantics but also to the units and sequences of narrative grammar; it is claimed that these logical relations receive 'polemic' representation at the superficial level. **(4.2) Applications to Legal Discourse:** Examination of G/L's analysis of the structure of the SC in terms of the semiotic square and its polemic representation indicates a willingness to expand the account to correlated contraries without contradictories, thus going beyond the strictly logical model. The square is similarly used to analyse the institution of the SC as a legal person with the role of **actant collectif,** and to the classifications of the interests which it may seek. The latter example shows the superimposition of squares, correlating the classification of interests with the modalities of their regulation and the institutional level at which this regulation is achieved (the legislature, instituting the legal culture). **(4.3) Semiotics and Logic:** Blanché develops a hexagon from the classical square of propositional logic, and Greimas regards the semiotic square, applicable equally to semic categories and narrative grammar, as isomorphic with it. But the semiotic square diverges in important respects from the logical model - differences explicable in terms of the subject-matter of the analyses, their objectives and intellectual origins. **(4.4) Modalities:** Modalities have a special place in Greimasian semiotics, through their role at the syntagmatic level as 'modal values' which may and often must be transferred in order to activate the narrative algorithm. Analyses of modalities in terms of the square here tend to conform to the model of the classical square as used to illustrate the propositions of deontic and aletheic logic. By superimposition and inversion of squares, Greimas seeks to find which combinations of modalities are compatible, so that they may appear together in the same narrative syntagm. The analysis complements the claim of deonticians as to the interdefinability of duty and permission, and suggests that 'power' in the legal sense can be accounted for as a special semantic investment of the same modal relationships.

4.1 THE 'SEMIOTIC SQUARE'

Both structural semantics and narrative grammar involve, for Greimas, quasi-logical operations which he formalises in the 'semiotic square'. This is an attempt to explain how the 'paradigmatic' axis of the Saussurian language system works. Culler describes the Greimasian (and Lévi-Straussian) approach thus: 'They argue that the basic structure of a story is that of a four-term homology in which A is to B as C is to D. In the clearest statement of this position, Greimas argues that to grasp a story as a whole is to organize it according to a structure of this kind so that the initial situation is to the final situation as a problem is to its resolution' (1975a: 131). This is formally expressed as:

A : B :: C : D

so that, for example, acceptance (A) of a mandate (B) in the contractual syntagm of the story may be regarded as homologous to recognition (C) of performance (D) in the 'glorifying test' or 'sanction'.

The model, thus stated, tells us more about the syntagmatic than the paradigmatic axis. **A : B** is at the beginning of the story, **C : D** at the end. On this account, we are not told what value is placed upon the **:** - in other words what the actual relationship between A and B, C and D is. It is when we explore the relations within the pairs that we encounter the 'logical' claims of the model, and its relationship to the paradigmatic axis.

This latter relation is sometimes expressed as:

$$A : B :: -A : -B$$

so that the relationship between the two elements in a binary opposition is homologous to that between the negations of those elements. The logical relationship between the elements in a binary opposition are universal and formal, not dependent upon their particular semantic or narrative investment. The latter depends upon an analysis of the narrative as a whole, thus upon the syntagmatic axis, since it will particularly be influenced by the semantic investment of the corresponding homologue. Thus one has to analyse the narrative as a whole in order to know what A and B are (partly by reference to the similarly decodable C and D), but one knows in advance what the logical relation between A and B will be. This type of analysis is seen as an extension of structural semantics in that the narrative unit (**A : B**) is like a sememe composed of semes in a regular relation, whose structure is oppositional. In both cases, one has the interaction of semantic values, defined in oppositional terms, and their negations (as in 'boy' analysed as +male and -adult, 2.3 above).

The relations within a binary opposition are described in terms of the 'working model' (Calloud 1979:71) of the 'semiotic square', based upon relations of contrariety (opposition) and contradiction (negation) as in the logical square descended from Aristotle. (1) In this, the relations involved in a binary opposition like black v. white are represented as in figure 1, the relationship between the opposed terms themselves (s1 and s2) involving a double operation, of negation and presupposition. Black is the opposite of white because it falls within non-white; conversely, white may be the opposite of black in so far as white is included within the class of non-black. It may readily be seen from this that the relationship of contradiction establishes a class within which it is a necessary condition that the opposed term must fall. But this relationship of presupposition does not form a sufficient condition for the generation of the opposite: black is not the only category which falls within non-white, etc. It is this choice of the presupposition of the contradiction which requires further semantic investment from the syntagmatic axis. (2)

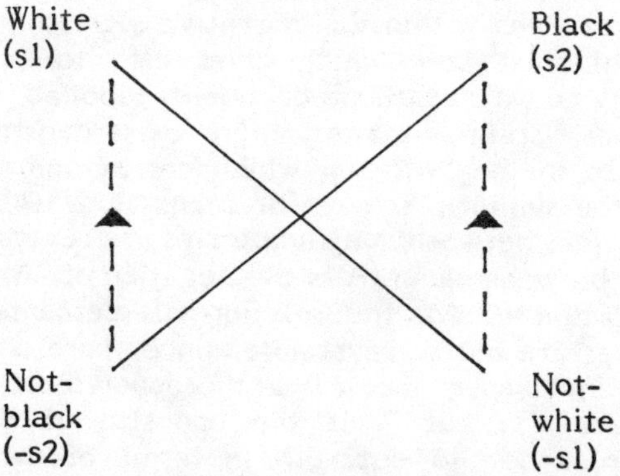

(Figure 1)

The square, as thus described, represents relationships of meaning in a static mode, but the model seeks also to represent the process of creation of meanings. (3) One of the formal properties claimed for the model is that 'using each of the four terms as point of departure, one can obtain the three others by the two operations: by taking the contradictory and by taking the contrary'. (4) In this sense, every time any one of the four values is manifested, the other three are present in potential. We thus see the projections of each term which give it its meaning, but also the constraints which govern the choice of elements in the syntagm at any point in the syntagmatic axis. Contraries are 'incompatible from the point of view of their realization in discourse' (Calloud 1979:55, 68f.).

Thus far, we have been considering the relations between semic categories. One can apply such analysis in a relatively straightforward fashion to semic categories particularly characteristic of law, such as modalities (4.4), and indeed to combinations of semic categories. But Greimas takes the argument two significant steps further. First, he applies it at the level of narrative grammar to the minimal units of literary (and legal) discourse, the **actants** and **fonctions**, in order to show their structure. For example, we find G/L analysing the 'actantial structure' of the SC in this manner (4.2). Secondly, and more controversially, he seeks to apply the same analysis to sequences within the various narrative syntagms, and indeed to the relations within the 'narrative algorithm' as a whole. It is this last step which gives rise to the four-term homology on which Calloud comments (above).

Thus, Greimas claims, there exist constraints on the sequences in the syntagm, which correspond to operations within the semiotic square (Bremond 1972:364f.). Whereas the relations between contradictories are reversible, with no tertium between them (A is the negation of -A, just as -A is the negation of A), the relation of elements within the contraries are not so reversible, since there is a (different) tertium involved in them: B is the opposite of A, in that it presuposes -A; but A is the opposite of B in that it presupposes not -A but -B. In terms of the square, we cannot move directly along the horizontal axes, either between contraries or subcontraries, nor can we move down the vertical axes but only up them.

This further application of the semiotic square to the syntagmatic relations at the level of narrative grammar is expressed in terms of an equivalence between the logical relation of contradiction and its 'polemic' representation in the narrative in terms of domination (McKnight 1978:173f.). The 'taxonomic model' of the semiotic square is regarded as a statement of elements (contraries and contradictories) on which 'operations' can be performed only in certain directions (Bremond 1972:364f.). The relation of negation is regarded as a reversible syntactic operation: s1 may thus be transformed into -s1, or -s1 to s1. The effect of this operation is said to produce a disjunction (which can readily be translated into anthropomorphic terms, once the 'polemic' character of the model is accepted). As between the negation of a term and its opposite, there exists an operation of presupposition (which conjoins), but this operation can be performed only in one direction (up but not down the vertical axes of the square). This unidirectionality within the square has its counterpart at the superficial level: the story has the temporal attributes of history - irreversibility and choice. And this in turn reflects the activity of man in history, which is irreversible, free and responsible (Greimas 1966:211). The model is thus characterised by the interplay of constraints and choices. (5)

The precise nature of the relation between the 'logical'

and 'syntagmatic' levels of the narrative grammar appears thus far to have eluded conceptualisation. Greimas speaks of 'isotopy', and writes of the combination of syntagmatic sequences at the superficial level as 'only anthropomorphic representations of these (basic, logical) operations' (McKnight 1978:158, 178), and Calloud describes the relationship as 'one of secret complicity rather than one of open points of contact' (1979:72). Bremond suggests that the concepts of Greimasian narrative grammar receive an 'incarnation' at the level of superficial grammar; human or humanised beings come to personify the concepts of narrative grammar and their transformations, so that a 'faire anthropomorphe' in the superficial grammar corresponds to the conceptual operations of the semiotic square (1972:366).

In the formula of narrative statements **EN = F(A),** both **F** and **A** are seen as projecting contradictories (and their 'polemic' representations) which in turn imply contraries. Thus each is susceptible to 'carrification' (representation as a semiotic square). The two squares are superimposed on each other, but with the contradictory of **F1** being imposed upon the contrary of **A1.** This implies the dominance of **s1** and **s2,** and from this superimposition further operations can be worked out which will take account of the reciprocal constraints of the two interacting squares. Galland seeks a threefold correspondence between the two levels, with 'confrontation', 'domination' and 'attribution' representing at the superficial level the logical relations of reversibility (in contradiction), negation and affirmation (1973:46). The details of the account differ from one author to another, even within the Greimasian school, and criticism of the whole enterprise has not been lacking. What matters for present purposes is the nature of the attempt, to view human will and action in terms of logical operations.

The narrative syntagms of the superficial level are taken to represent correlated sets of binary oppositions, each set exhibiting the formal properties of the square and capable of sustaining its operations. Indeed, it is the superimposition of different binary oppositional squares that generates the sequence of the story. 'Prohibition' is the 'negative transformation' of 'command', and 'violation' is the 'negative transformation' of 'acceptance'. But it is the syntagmatic sequence which represents the establishment of contract, and the conjunction of 'prohibition' and 'violation' which represents the rupture of that contract, the restoration of which may then be indicated. The two binary pairs thus correlated retain the logical qualities of their respective squares, from which Greimas thus deduces the formula: **if** acceptance of command results in the establishment of contract, **then** violation of a prohibition results in the rupture of that contract. (6)

4.2 APPLICATIONS TO LEGAL DISCOURSE

In G/L's analysis of the 1966 Loi, the semiotic square is used to account for the semiotic relations involved in the constitution of the legal **actant** and the performance of its tasks. The economic activities of the SC are 'narrativised' in terms of lack and acquisition, which are related to conjunctive and disjunctive relationships within the semiotic square.

The SC has the actantial role of **'actant-sujet'**, but as an **actant** it is constituted with particular characteristics: it is an **actant collectif.** G/L (98f.) formalise the relations between the semes which constitute that notion (unit v. totality; integral v. partitive relations: section 3.2 above) in the form of a semiotic square (figure 2):

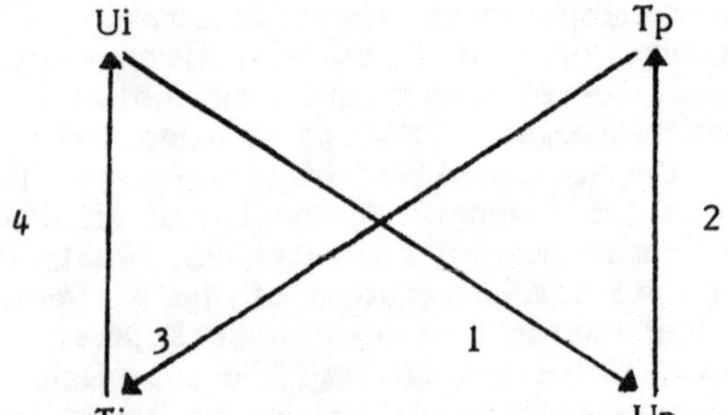

(Figure 2)

In order to proceed from a collection of individuals (situated at point **Ui,** at the top left) to a new collective entity **(Tp,** at the top right), the following operations are required: (1) first the transformation of **Ui** into **Up,** by the negation of the integrity of the individual and the assertion of his partitive character; (2) then the implication (or presupposition) from **Up** into **Tp** by the conjunction of the individuals to whom a partitive character has now been attributed from discrete units into a single totality. There is a disjunction of the independence of the individuals (**Ui**) representing the contradiction, and a conjunction of such (now partitive) individuals into a partitive totality, representing the implication.

If this analysis is sound, it represents an illustration of the interaction between logical and syntagmatic levels in Greimasian analysis. However, some serious questions remain unresolved. Is the square here conceived simply as a representation of the logical structure of a single opposition, such that the formula may be represented as **A : B : : -A : -B** or is it supposed to represent the interrelation of two opposed pairs, such that **A : B : : C : D**? If it is the former, then **Up** must be conceived as the negation of **Ui**, and **Ti** as the negation of **Tp.** But it is difficult to conceive of the relationships in this way, other than at a highly metaphoric, or perhaps even anthropomorphic, level. In proceeding from **Ui** to **Up,** G/L do indeed call the 'transformation' a 'negation' of the integrity of the individual unit, and the assertion of its partitive character. This can be understood at the anthropomorphic level in terms of a 'disjunction' of the hitherto united elements of the unit. But in logical terms, 'partitive' is not the negation (contradiction) of 'integral', but rather its opposite (contrary). Indeed, in describing this operation, G/L refer to two separate logical operations, the **negation** of the integrity of the individual unit, and the **assertion** of its partitive character. Again, it is difficult to understand **Ti** as the negation of **Tp:** not only is **i** the opposite rather than the negation of **p:** here, there is not even a disjunctive anthropomorphic operation, but rather the reverse - what was previously partitive is now 'conjoined' into something integral. Thus it would seem that G/L cannot here intend the model to manifest the relations **A : B : : -A : -B.**

What of the alternative? The problem here identified in regarding **i** and **p** as reversible negations is avoided if we regard them instead as opposites, as indeed is suggested by G/L's description of the transformation from **Ui** to **Up** in terms of negation and assertion. Perhaps, then, we should view **p** and **i** as the **C** and **D** of the formula **A : B : : C : D** ? This would be possible, even given the notion of semiotic constraints which flow from the superimposition of one square upon another, such that the contradictory relationship of one square is imposed upon the contrary relation of the other. According to this argument, **i** and **p** can be regarded as contraries, rather than contradictories. However, this argument too must necessarily fail, since if **i** is superimposed upon **U, p** would have to be superimposed upon **-U,** and this is not what is claimed by G/L. Indeed, their logical analysis of the **actant collectif** seems to fail upon one very simple objection: nowhere in their account is there any genuine contradictory. **(7)** This is one application of the semiotic square which departs fundamentally from the classical square of the logicians. Such a departure from a strict logical model does not, however, unduly perturb the Greimasian school. Semiotics does not purport to be pure logic, but rather to provide an account of those 'logical' relations which actually underlie our language and its discourses. **(8)**

Thus far, we have accounted only for the constitution of the SC as an **actant collectif.** Further steps are necessary to incorporate this **actant collectif** into the 'legal' culture. We have seen how G/L view this process at the syntagmatic ('anthropomorphic') level, in terms of the formal acts required by the **Loi** for the recognition of the SC. These steps too are taken to reflect the operations of the semiotic square, specifically those operations numbered 3 and 4 in Figure 2.

Operation 3 is the transformation of the **actant collectif** conceived as a totality made up of parts **(Tp)** by conferring on it the status of an individualized **acteur (Ti,** a totality which acts as an integral unit). This is reflected in the syntax of surface grammar according to which the company is granted its legal name. It thereby becomes temporarily an **acteur juridique.** A final operation, from Ti to Ui, is needed to integrate this new legal person into the class of legal personality which is the SC, giving it a recognised legal role - an **actant juridique.** But the presentation of the logical relations here involved must again be regarded as sketchy. We are told that operation 4 involves a conjunction integrating the particular company into the class of commercial companies recognised by law. But this is surely a description of the discursive effect of the process, not an account of the logical operation through which it is achieved. It is difficult to conceive of the transformation of **T** into **U** as a conjunction (104), when the reverse operation, from **U** to **T**, has already been described as a conjunction in the context of Operation 2.

Thus far, the existence of the SC has been defined in terms of a semiotic object qualified by the relation of possession. Within the narrative syntagm, it is invested with a will. But this must be a will to do (**faire**) something, and this something is acquisition. Viewed as a static semiotic object, the SC thus is a subject which possesses an object; in terms of the dynamism of the narrative syntagm, it is a subject which seeks to perform the goal of acquisition (107).

This will to acquire is termed **'intérêt'**. G/L argue that the taxonomy of different kinds of interests can be represented in terms of a square, arranged in such a way as to show transformations from interests classified as 'savage' (pertaining to nature) to interests classified as pertaining to culture. This square correlates with the logical analysis of legislative rules (prescriptions or prohibitions) pertaining to the behaviour which may realise such interests, and which qualify them as legal or illegal (figure 3).

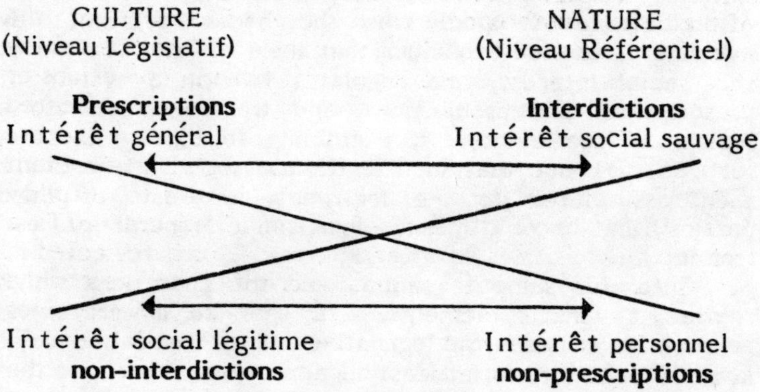

(Figure 3)

In setting out the operations represented by this taxonomy, G/L appear to imply a set of constraints on the sequences or kinds of transformation which may be effected at the syntagmatic level (again, impliedly reflecting the relationship they proclaim between 'logical' and superficial levels). Thus, one starts at the top left, with a 'physical person', conceived as **not yet** having formed the desire to participate in a collective enterprise (of acquisition), and who thus has the status of a 'third party' (vis-à-vis the SC). However, he forms part of the wider national group, and his 'legitimate interests' are protected to the extent that they conform to those of the 'general interest'. This 'general interest' belonging to the wider national group is itself a cultural construction. Next, this person may come to express a desire to acquire new property through participation in a collective enterprise. (One must assume that he has received a 'contract' to this effect.) But this will to appropriate is not (yet or completely) governed by rules: there are no applicable prescriptions. It is termed 'personal interest' (bottom right), and belongs to 'nature' in that it is not (yet or completely) subject to social regulation. The first step in the socialization of this individual will to acquire consists in its collocation with similar personal interests of other individuals. Since all of them are still not yet or completely subject to social control, so that their exercise may result in what society would regard as excessive appropriation, they remain 'savage', pertaining to nature (top right), and are the subject of prohibitions. It is only when they become legitimate by avoiding prohibited behaviour that the legislator recognises this social interest, and regulates it with a system of prescriptions and prohibitions, and transforms it into a legitimate social interest, pertaining to culture (bottom left). (9) G/L add that such legitimate social interests are then 'assimilated to the legitimate interests of third parties', and become masked in a single 'general interest' (top left).

Into this same taxonomy, and the operations which relate its various elements, G/L seek to integrate the relationship between the legislative and referential levels of law (109). Culture (or at least 'legal culture') is here created at the legislative level, while the 'referential level' reflects 'nature' (individual or social interest, unregulated by law). But there are semiotic constraints upon the manner in which the legislator may seek to effect the desired transformations, resulting from the superimposition of correlated squares. In particular, 'savage' social interest is subject to prohibitions, but when these savage social interests are transformed into legitimate social interests, the prohibitions are negated (in a relationship of contradiction) and transformed into non-prohibitions. Those social interests which are thus recognised as legitimate belong to a vast undefined field of non-prohibited behaviour, expressed in terms of liberties which are not constrained by express prohibitions. But non-prohibited behaviour does not mean non-regulated behaviour. Culture operates at the legislative level through prescriptions, not prohibitions. Legal existence itself only comes about through naming at the legislative level (2.2), and thus the creation of legitimate social or general interests requires **prescriptive** rules which will specify the behaviour required in order to institute the necessary semiotic objects. That, it seems, is why the last operation around the square is required, from bottom left to top left. The legitimate social interest, characterised by non-prohibitions (the negation of nature), requires to be implicated in the class opposed to nature, characterised by institutive prescriptions.

One can understand the roles attributed to prescription and prohibition by G/L in terms of the semiotics of the text under study. The text is primarily concerned with what should be done in order to achieve certain goals, from the institution of the SC as a legal person, to its use of those powers which are conferred by the law and which in turn define the area of legitimate action of the SC. One could conceive of a company law without any prohibitions, based upon the assumption that any action which fell outside the range of the stated prescriptions could result only in a legal nullity. That would provide some semiotic justification for the respective roles here attributed to prescriptions and prohibitions, and would not be affected either by the consideration that the model could hardly be applied equally to criminal law texts, or by the existence in a separate document of penal provisions concerning companies. In fact, however, that kind of semiotic justification of G/L's argument is not fully borne out by the text of the 1966 law. After a preliminary chapter of a general character (articles 1-9), the text is divided into three titles, the first designated 'Règles de fonctionnement des diverses sociétés commerciales' (articles 10-422), the second 'Dispositions Pénales' (articles 423-489), and the third 'Dispositions diverses et transitoires' (articles 490-509). While the first title is very much longer than the second, the prominence which the text itself gives to the distinction between prescriptions and prohibitions - and its presentation of the latter as a major unit of organisation - can hardly be ignored by the semiotician. G/L fail to address themselves to this fact, and one can only speculate on what their response would be. Could it be that they would focus upon the form in which these penal provisions are expressed, each one commencing with the formula 'Seront punis . . . ', and argue that the duty to punish in the circumstances stated represents a prescription which in semiotic terms takes precedence over the behaviour which is prohibited only in the sense that punishment is to be attached to it ? Again, one might note, there are echoes of Kelsen in the structure of the norm which such an analysis might suggest.

The correlation of prescriptions and prohibitions (and their negations) with the taxonomy of interests in G/L's formalisation is perhaps designed, more even than the series of operations round the square, starting and finishing with top left, to manifest the logical level of narrative grammar. Non-prescription is the negation (contradiction) of prescription; prohibition is the opposite of prescription (or its contrary). 'Prescription' can thus stand as **A**; 'interdiction' as **B**; 'non-prescription' as **-A**; and non-interdiction as **-B**. But G/L wish further to stress the capacity of this formalisation to express also the anthropomorphic level. Thus they suggest that the 'interests' can be considered as represented by subjects endowed with economic will (109f.).

4.3 SEMIOTICS AND LOGIC

Greimas has claimed that his semiotic square is 'isomorphic' to the logical hexagon of Blanché. **(10)** The meaning of that claim is explored in this section: the elaboration of the ancient logical square by Blanché is recounted; the differences between the logical and semiotic squares are identified; some explanations of those differences are noted and appraised and a broad assessment of the issues concludes the discussion.

The Logical Square and the Hexagon of Blanché

It all begins with the propositional logic of Aristotle, the representation of that logic in the form of a square by

Apuleius, and the exploration of the relations within that square by the scholastics. **(11)** Aristotle was concerned with propositions related in terms of quantity and/or quality. To take an ancient example, 'All desire is good' is a proposition in which 'good' is a 'quality' attributed to the subject 'desire' in the quantity 'all'. The contrary proposition 'No desire is good' opposes 'all' with 'no'. Such contraries cannot both be true, although they can both be false. Both the quality and the quantity are capable of being negated by a contradictory, as well as opposed by a contrary. The variables generate the following four propositions, which are examples of types to which scholastic logic applied the symbols A, E, I, O:

A: All desire is good

E: No desire is good

I: Some desire is good

O: Some desire is not good.

A stands to O in a relationship of contradiction: if A is true, O must be false (and the reverse); conversely, if A is false, O must be true. E stands to I in the same relationship of contradiction. A third logical relationship (subalternation) links A with I, E with O. Both cannot be false, although both need not be true. If A is true, I must also be true (but not vice versa); if E is true, O must be true (but not vice versa). It is this last relationship which is involved in the famous Aristotelian syllogism:

(1) All desire is good

(2) Ambition is a desire

(3) Therefore ambition is good

The reason why the minor premise (2) leads to the conclusion (3) is that if the major premise (1) is true, then we have a proposition of type A, and therefore it must also be true that a proposition of type I generated by A must also be true. The minor premise (2) qualifies the conclusion (3) as I, an instance of A. The same can be done with the negative forms E and O. Conversely, if I is false, A must also be false (but not vice versa); if O is false, E must also be false (but not vice versa).

Apuleius depicted these relationships in the form of a square (figure 4):

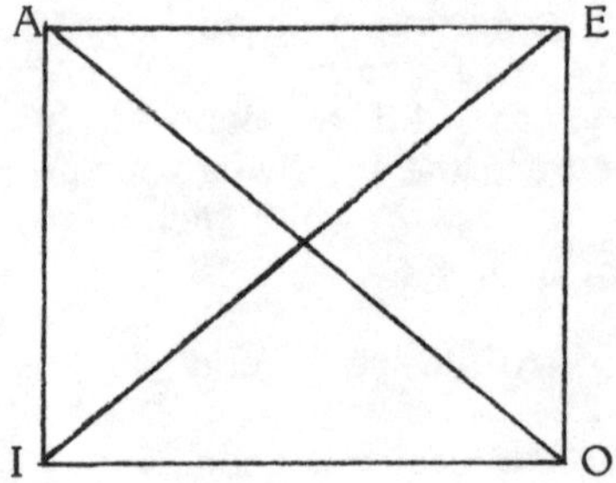

(Figure 4)

Here the diagonals represent the contradictory relationships, and the vertical sides of the square, read downwards, involve relationships of inclusion: A includes I, E includes O. However, the scholastics realised that the two horizontal sides of the square were not logically equivalent: I and O can simultaneously be true, while A and E cannot. The relationship between I and O came to be known as 'subcontrariety', that between A and E as 'contrariety'. The name 'subalternation' has become the technical designation of the relationship of inclusion represented by the horizontal sides of the square.

The distinctions between the four relationships can be understood in terms of the operation of two variables: exclusivity and reversibility. Contradiction is an exclusive form of negation, in the sense that no further possibilities exist: if A is true, there is no possibility other than that O is false. Conversely, if A is false, there is no possibility other than that O is true. In other words, we have here a relationship of logical entailment: A entails -O; -A entails O. **(12)** But the same does not apply in relation to contraries. Their relationship is not exclusive, in that both A and E may be false, while a third term (here, either I or O) may be true. (The quantities 'all' and 'none' may both be false, while still leaving it possible that 'some').

	Exclusivity	Reversibility
Contrariety	-	+
Contradiction	+	+
Subcontrariety	-	-
Subalternation	+	-

In the case of subcontrariety, it is possible to affirm both I and O simultaneously, through a third possibility which combines them: some desires may be good, while others may not be good; both I and O can be true, provided only that the 'some' in both propositions does not refer to the same desire. But this relationship is not reversible. If we negate both I and O (external negations), we arrive at their contradictories: A and E, which cannot stand together compatibly within a third term, but can only admit of mediation by a neutral third term (neither A nor E). In the case of subalternation, we do have exclusivity in one direction: A does entail I (without any third possibility); E similarly entails O. However, I does not entail A, nor does O entail E. I can still be true while A is false; O can still be true while E is false. In other words, A is a sufficient but not a necessary condition of I. In terms of symbolic logic, we can say

A I (T11 of Kalinowski 1972a:166)

but not

A I.

The external negation of I similarly entails the external negation of A (T12), but not vice versa. The same relationships obtain between E and O and their external negations (T13-14).

From the above, it can be seen that the relationship

between contraries differs from that between subcontraries. This was appreciated by the scholastic commentators upon the classical square. Their account implies the existence of two further points, one negating both contraries, the other a point which combines both contraries. Blanché has sought to make explicit these implicit understandings of the relationships between contraries and contradictories, by converting the square into a hexagon, with the addition of Y as the neutral point, and U as the compound (sometimes, 'complex') point. This last may appear difficult to understand. If A and E are contraries, such that E entails the negation of A (**13**), how can we combine these two contraries into a compound term (U) ? Blanché justifies this move by showing that U is in the same (triadic) opposition to the subcontraries, I and O, as the neutral term, Y, is in relation to the contraries, A and E. We can represent the argument thus far as shown in figure 5:

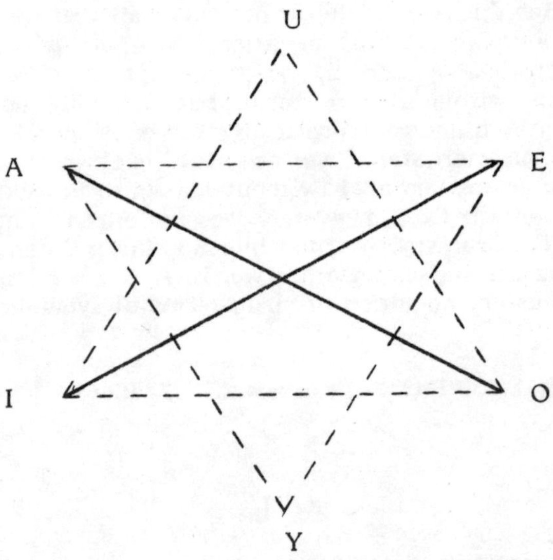

(Figure 5)

It might be objected that while this shows that there is a difference between contraries and subcontraries, in that contraries stand in a triadic opposition of which Y is the third term, while subcontraries stand in a triadic opposition whose third term is U, it does seem to imply that the relationship between the two contraries is the same as the relationship between the two subcontraries, and this is clearly not the case. The parallel between the two triadic oppositions is, indeed, demonstrated when one compares the theorems of contrariety (T1-T6) with the theorems of subcontrariety (T19-T24) as stated by Kalinowski (1972a: 165f). But Blanché is not yet finished. The difference between the contraries and the subcontraries is shown when we add the relationships between the contraries and U (which is **not** the third term of the triadic opposition to which the contraries belong) and the relationships between the subcontraries and Y (which is **not** the third term of the opposition to which the subcontraries belong). Here, we must add two further relations: conjunction and disjunction. The matter may become clearer when we take account of one further vital innovation introduced by Blanché. He shows that these relationships obtain not merely in the kind of logic derived from the Aristotelian tradition (involving homonymic propositions with a common subject and predicate), but also to simple propositions asserting a quality, such as 'it is cold'. **(14)** Blanché adds that this extension transforms the theory of propositional opposition into an instrument by which we may study the opposition between concepts (1966:31); Greimas, as we have observed, goes further in abandoning the propositional form altogether, and by applying the scheme to semic oppositions and their narrative analogues. **(15)**

We can now add to the diagram (Figure 6) those elements which complete Blanché's presentation: a line of contradiction between U and Y (cf. Kalinowski's T33-6, 1972a:166); the relations between the contraries (A and E) and U; and those between the subcontraries (I and O) and Y. (Unbroken lines here represent contradictions, broken lines subalternation, and dotted lines triadic oppositions.) We shall give A the semantic value 'white', and E the semantic value 'black', here following Greimas, in order to provide examples of the operation of the hexagon (figure 6). We can readily see that whereas Y, the neutral term in opposition to both of the contraries, **includes** both of the subcontraries, U, the compound term, generated by the triadic opposition between the subcontraries, cannot

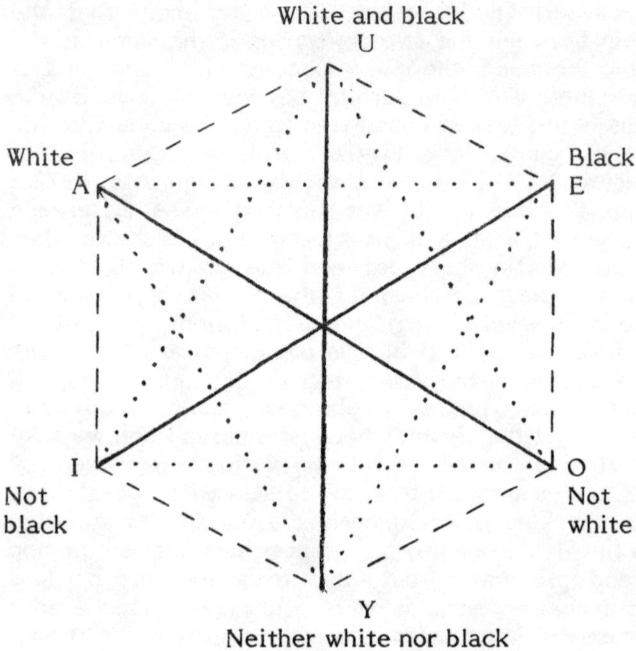

(Figure 6 (**16**))

simultaneously include the two contraries (which here are mutually exclusive). If we have a class of objects which are neither white nor black (Y), some of them may be 'not black' (I) while others may be 'not white' (O). But we can have no such class of objects which are all 'white and black' (U), such that some of them are (only) 'white' (A) while others are (only) 'black' (E). Since I and O are not mutually exclusive, they can be conjoined through simultaneous conjunctive relations with Y. But since A and E are mutually exclusive, they cannot be mutually conjoined within U; rather, U represents a form of disjunction between them, in that U may be generated only through the abandonment by A of its exclusivity of E, or by the abandonment by E of its exclusivity of A. Such an account of the difference between Y and U, in terms of conjunction and disjunction, is suggested by Blanché. (17) But Kalinowski's statement of the theorems implicit in Blanché's system (1972a:165f.) indicates that these relations of conjunction and disjunction are in fact relations of subalternation (comparable to those between A and I and between E and O). That is why they have here been represented by unbroken lines in Figure 6. We have seen that such relations of subalternation are characterised by exclusivity (the one term entails some value, whether positive or negative, of the other term, there being no third possibility) and lack of reversibility. Thus white (A) entails non-black (I); something which is white cannot be black (T11), while I does not entail A (something which is not black need not be white); something which is not not-black (thus, is black) cannot be white (Kalinowski T12: -I ⊃ -A), but it does not follow that something which is not white (-A) cannot be black (-I).

From Kalinowski's demonstration, it can be seen that the same relations of subalternation apply between Y and I (T7-8), between Y and O (T9-10), between A and U (T15-16) and between E and U (T17-18). But there is a difference between the roles of Y and U in these relations of subalternation. We saw above the relationship between subalternation and the syllogism. The syllogism is based upon the assumption of a logical relationship of subalternation between the major premise and the conclusion. Assuming the truth of the minor premise (which asserts the subsumption of the conclusion in the major premise), if the major premise is true, then the conclusion must also be true; if the conclusion is false, then the major premise must also be false. At the same time, the truth of the conclusion does not entail the truth of the major premise, nor does the falsity of the major premise entail the falsity of the conclusion. Even though we are no longer dealing with propositions regarding quality and quantity, we can still mark one term in a relationship of subalternation as dominant over the other, in that its positive value entails the positive value of the other, but not vice versa. If we continue to call such a dominant term the 'major premise', we can say that in the relations of subalternation involving Y and U, Y stands to both I and O as the major premise in the relations of subalternation (Kalinowski's T7-10), while U always stands as the minor premise in its relations of subalternation with A and E (Kalinowski's T15-18).

The final addition entailed by the refinement of the

square into a hexagon is the relationship of contradiction between Y and U. This is said to follow the laws of duality of de Morgan, whereby the negation of a conjunction is equivalent to the disjunction between the negation of each of the terms of that conjunction. Here, the conjunction is Y, its terms I and O. The negations of those two terms are E and A respectively. The disjunction between A and E is U. U is therefore the negation (here meaning 'external negation', or contradiction) of Y. The exclusivity and reversibility of this relationship of contradiction is expressed in Kalinowski's T33-36 (1972a:166). If something is not 'not black or white' (i.e. neither the one alternative nor the other), it must be white and black: the negation of Y entails U (T35); if something is not white and black, it must be neither black nor white: the negation of U entails the affirmation of Y (T36), etc.

Blanché and Greimas Compared

The relation between the logical square of Blanché and the semiotic square of Greimas has attracted some comment in France in recent years. **(18)** Amongst the principal points of distinction **(19)**, the following are particularly noteworthy:

(1) It is immediately apparent that the relations between the contraries in the logical square (quite apart from the refinements of Blanché) are not equivalent to the relations between the subcontraries. To the scholastics, the contraries were 'incongruae' whereas the subcontraries were 'subpares' (de Libera 1976:30). Today, we can contrast them in terms of Kalinowski's T1-6 on the one hand and 19-24 on the other: whereas the theorems for contraries are constructed by taking the positive value of one contrary and stating its entailment in terms of the negative value of one of the other contraries, the theorems for subcontraries are constructed by taking the negative value of one subcontrary and stating its entailment in terms of the positive value of some other subcontrary. Yet the logic of Greimasian semiotics is based upon formulae such as:

$$A : B :: C : D$$

and

$$A : B :: -A : -B$$

If, in fact, -A is conceived as a contradictory of A, and -B is conceived as a contradictory of B, then according to the logical square -A must stand to -B in the relationship of subcontrariety, and that relationship differs from the relationship between A and B, which is contrariety. We must conclude either that Greimas is dealing with contradictories, in which case the logic of the semiotic square **may** approach that of the logical square, but the formula **A : B : : -A : -B** is wrong, or that he is not dealing with contradictories (in the relations between A and -A, B and -B), in which case the semiotic square does not approach the logical square, but the formula may be right (or at least meaningful). In examining the other differences between the semiotic and logical squares, we may encounter some evidence as to which of these two hypotheses is correct.

(2) The semiotic square is highly selective in the logical operations which it regards as significant (perhaps even possible). Although the semiotic square seems to make use of exclusive negations which are in theory reversible (as between s1 and -s1 in figure 1 above), in practice no use is made of this reversibility in the operations which are performed upon the square. One always begins from the positive value, not the negative. This might be taken to indicate that these relations are not true contradictories, thus supporting the second hypothesis suggested above. A similar point may be made in relation to the relationships which the logician terms subalternation. In the logical square, operations may be performed upon either of the terms in a relationship of subalternation. We may have recourse once again to Kalinowski's analysis for a demonstration: even without adding the neutral and compound points of Blanché, T11-14 indicate that we may go either up or down the vertical sides of the square. If we go down, we start with a positive value and conclude with a positive value; if we go up, we start with a negative value and conclude with a negative value. But Greimas goes only up. He has no use to make of the relationship for the purposes of syllogistic deduction (going down, - the starting point of the Aristotelian analysis). If, then, the relationship between s1 and -s2 (or between A and -B) is one of subalternation, Greimas makes only very partial use of it (cf. Kalinowski 1981:6).

(3) It was observed above (4.1) that the relationship which Greimas calls presupposition - sometimes, 'implication' (20) - is not a sufficient condition of the generation of a contrary from the subcontrary which is the contradictory of the other contrary. Again, the difference can be seen by reference to Kalinowski's theorems. They show that where a subcontrary (I or O) forms the protasis of a theorem, with a contrary (A or E respectively) as the apodosis, that theorem is always expressed in terms of a negative value of the subcontrary (T12 and T14; similarly where U is introduced into the protasis, T16 and T18). Greimas, on the other hand, starts with a positive value of the subcontrary: if -s1 or -s2 is **true**, whereas Kalinowski's theorems begin with: if I (or O) is **false.** Since Greimas starts with this positive value of the subcontrary, he cannot establish a relationship of entailment. That is why there is nothing corresponding to his 'presupposition' represented in Kalinowski's theorems. Of course, Greimas does not claim to establish any such relationship of entailment, and this is precisely one of the differences between the logical and the semiotic square. What Greimas and Rastier do claim is a relationship of 'inclusion': -s2 includes s1, -s1 includes s2 (1968:90). That claim **could** be expressed in terms of entailment, in the form of a theorem: 'if -s2 is false, then s1 must also be false' (cf. Kalinowski's T12 and T14). But Greimas chooses not to express himself in this way, for reasons which may become apparent in the next sub-section.

Greimas and Rastier (1968) use the language of semantics, rather than that of logic, to express the relationship of presupposition: s1 + -s2 is for them a 'semic structure', whose 'structural dimensions' are described as a 'deixis', and similarly with s2 + -s1. But if this amounts to a (typically structuralist) claim that linguistics may be directly applied to this 'deep logical' level, it is a claim which others have sought strongly to deny. Bremond (1972:374) insists that such operations of presupposition as may be represented in an analysis of narrative are organised according to rules which are independent of the linguistic manifestation of the narrative, and cannot themselves be linguistic. He insists that the relationship which Greimas is claiming turns out to be a system of choices and constraints which is specifically semiotic, and neither logical nor linguistic.

(4) Despite the claim of Greimas and Rastier that the semiotic square is isomorphic to Blanché's hexagon, some have suggested that the semiotic square could **not** admit of the totality of Blanché's refinements, even though these may be claimed merely to make explicit what was implicit in the classical square. Doubts have been expressed, in particular, regarding the compatibility of the compound term, U, with the semiotic square. It has been pointed out that whereas the subcontraries are not incompatible, and thus may both be included within a neutral term (Y), the contraries are incompatible, and cannot be (as they are not claimed to be) included within the compound term U. Rather, the contraries have a disjunctive relationship with U, reflecting their mutual incongruity. But incongruity is not logical incompatibility. The contraries form part of a (triadic) opposition, not a contradiction. It is thus logically possible for them to be given a relationship in a compound term such as U. For the semiotician, matters stand differently. He seeks to represent the logic of discursive manifestations. Such oppositions as black and white cannot be compounded, if the discourse is to remain intelligible; it is out of such systems of **différence** that meaning is constructed. The semiotician may be able to mediate between the opposition by having it apply to different phenomena, or aspects of a phenomenon, or different stages in the development of the narrative. But such a mediation would be neither required nor permitted by the logician. Thus it has been argued that the semiotic square cannot become a hexagon: 'A single thing cannot be said to be white and black at the same time and in the same way' (in Galland 1976:25).

Some Explanations of the Differences

These differences are substantial. They are best explained in terms of the total enterprises in which logicians and semioticians (21) are involved. One such difference relates to subject-matter. We have noted that Aristotle and Apuleius were concerned with propositions dealing with quantities and qualities, and that Blanché radically extended the applicability of the classical square which was so derived. Ricoeur (1980:30) suggests that despite that extension, the subject-matter of Greimasian semiotics is still different. Blanché may have extended the square to concepts serving as predicates, but the concern of Greimas is with semes, the basic units of meaning - whether of lexical items, as in traditional semantics, or in larger discursive formations such as are found in narrative. This indicates that the relations between 'black' and 'white' might differ according to whether those terms are used as conceptual predicates (Blanché) or semes (Greimas). Similarly, Nef observes that Blanché's scheme is partly based on lexicalised forms, which means that he bases his scheme on logical opposition and not on a semantic axis of semes (1976:13). Greimas certainly accepts that the semiotic square represents a semantic axis (1968:41). Kalinowski makes a similar distinction between logic and semiotics when he writes that logic is not concerned with relations between expressions (syntactic relations), relations between expressions and what they signify or designate (semantic relations) or relations between expressions and their users (pragmatic relations), but rather with relations between states of being **(états de choses)**, and between propositions (about them) which are substitutable in their content (1976:11).

The differences between Greimas and Blanché reflect differing historical influences, which themselves embody differing objectives. There is a large measure of consensus regarding the nature of their respective historical orientations. As Nef observes (1976:13), Greimas himself accepts that the semiotic square is based on the Saussurian thesis of **différence** as applied to phonological binarism (Jakobson), and on the use by Lévi-Strauss of oppositions in the study of myth. Landowski concedes that one difference between American semiotics (descended from Peirce) and European semiotics as represented by the Parisian school is that the former has never broken its links with logic (the tradition of Frege, Quine, Tarski, Montague, Kripke), while European semiotics is conscious of the 'deviant' character of the logic it uses, which has a more anthropological inspiration (1982:9f).

There is also a degree of commonality in the perception of the differences in objectives of the two schools (cf. Kalinowski 1981:7). Ricoeur stresses the claim of the semiotic square to represent the elementary structures of signification (1980:7): if something signifies, that is not because the person to whom it signifies has some intuition of what it signifies, but rather because he is able (presumably, unconsciously) to deploy a basic system of relations - those of contrariety, contradiction and presupposition. But that in itself might not tell us very much about such sequences of meaning as are contained in discursive structures. Ricoeur sees the 1968 and later versions of Greimasian theory as representing a significant advance in this direction. Greimas too has recognised a distinction between the functions or objectives of his 1968 and 1969 versions (in Nef 1976:22). For him, the 1968 version seeks to account for the way meaning is articulated in order to be **apprehended** as signification; the 1969 version, on the other hand, represents how signification is **produced** by a series of operations which are creative of differentiated positions. One sees from this that Greimas is willing to distinguish between the way in which meaning is produced, and the way in which it is understood. Both concerns, however, seem to locate semiotics somewhere on the interface between linguistics, psychology and epistemology, rather than in the domain of logic or philosophy. Many of the differences identified in this section are understandable in the light of such a diversity of objectives.

Conclusion

The semiotic square has been criticised as both too weak and too strong (Combet 1981:32). Kalinowski wonders whether the semiotic square must always diverge from the form which generates the hexagon; if not, he challenges the semioticians to explain the incidence of the divergence (1981:7f). Ricoeur, on the other hand, finds the semiotic square too strong to explain narrative formations; it supposes that the semiotic constraints are greater than they are, and in practice the model often has to be weakened in order to serve as an aid to interpretation (1980:9). Greimas in fact appears to take some comfort from being caught in these opposing cross-currents. Such structures as the semiotic square allow us to provide an account of an increasingly large number of semiotic objects (in Nef 1976:26). In short, he claims, the system works; semiotics is primarily a praxis.

4.4 MODALITIES

An important aspect of the Greimasian analysis of the syntagmatic level is the claim that 'modal objects' (such as knowledge, power, will) may be transferred, in the same way as objects of economic value or messages. This proves particularly significant in the 'competence' syntagm of the narrative algorithm. The subject, for whom a task has been instituted by contract, must have or obtain a competence in order to perform that task. In this sense, a 'hierarchy of modal values' is said to be basic to the syntagmatic series: performance requires the ability to perform; the ability to perform requires knowledge how to perform; knowledge how to perform requires the desire to perform (McKnight 1978:177). This generates a taxonomy of modal values, such as volition, knowledge, power and indeed obligation. The items in this taxonomy are susceptible to carrification, as in figure 7:

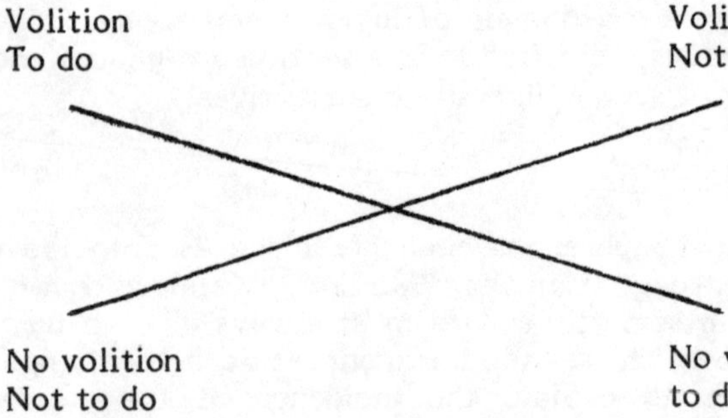

(Figure 7)

(In this and subsequent graphic representations, the square will be represented by diagonals.) Similarly with 'obligation to do', 'knowledge how to do', 'power to do', etc. Calloud points out that each square draws attention to four different possibilities of the subject, and that we can superimpose the squares of several modalities (1979:74f).

In a symposium published in issue number 43 of the Journal **Langages**, both Kalinowski and Greimas contribute articles on modalities. We see in them reflections of both parallels and differences between logicians and semioticians, as explored in the last section. Kalinowski (1976) seeks to demonstrate the inter-definability of obligation, prohibition and permission, through the use of the hexagon of Blanché. **(22)** Greimas' concern is with the modalities underlying discourse, - that is, underlying the utterances we actually find in texts. His starting point is the identification of structures of signification comparable (within units of discourse) to the semic structures of semantics. He starts, therefore, with the most basic types of predicate: being (**être**) and doing (**faire**), which can thus generate two basic forms of statement: 'Utterances of doing' (**énoncés de faire**) and 'utterances of state' (**énoncés d'état**) (1976a:91, 1982:193f.). Greimas then considers combinations of these modalities, conceiving them as pairs of modal subjects and modal predicates. The four possible combinations characterise the four elements in the narrative algorithm (1976a:92-5, 1982:194). Thus: **(23)**

Faire-être	Doing Modalizing Being	Performance
Etre du faire	Being Modalizing Doing	Competence
Etre d'être	Being Modalizing Being	Verediction
Faire faire	Doing Modalizing Doing	'Manipulation'

Putting the matter less technically, 'performance' involves making some state of affairs come about; 'competence' involves being in a state to act; 'verediction' involves establishing that a state of affairs does exist; 'manipulation' involves making someone do something. The latter pair differ from the former in that the subject of the modal operator and the subject of the modality which is the predicate can be different: X can recognise the existence of state Y, X can make Y act. (Such modalities are called 'translative'.) We see from the Greimasian analysis that these four relations belong to a common semic structure. We see the full list of possibilities (permutations) from which law has made its choice. We are assisted in understanding the choice by seeing the range from which it is made.

The nature of the semiotic square is well illustrated by the account Greimas gives (1976a:93f.) of **être** as the modal predicate of the modal structure 'verediction' (figure 8):

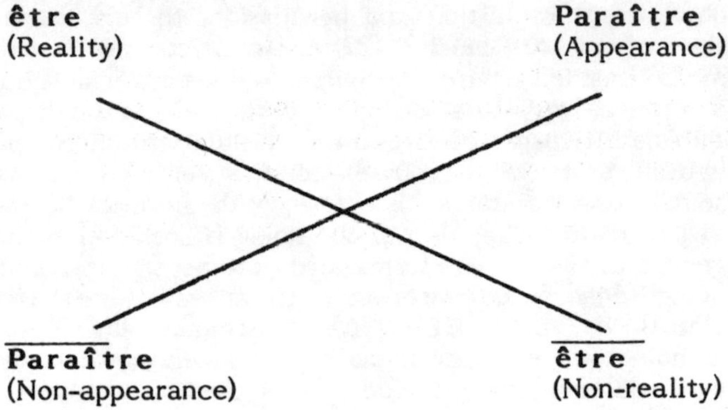

(Figure 8)

Why, one might ask, should 'reality' (**être**) be understood as an element in a binary opposition of which the other term is 'appearance' (**paraître**)? This, after all, is not logically entailed. We might conceive of alternatives, for example reality v. possibility. (24) Greimas claims that the starting point for semiotics, unlike logic, is not an a priori axiom, but rather a large number of analyses of the organisation of actual discourse, wherein it is shown that this particular opposition plays a signifying role (1982:194). He then goes on to describe the various relationships of the square not in terms of the logical categories of contrariety, contradiction and subalternation, but rather as schemas (the diagonal lines of the square), axes (the horizontals), and deixes (the verticals). Thus, the relationship between reality and non-reality is a schema called 'immanence'; that between appearance and non-appearance is a schema called 'manifestation'. The axis of the contraries is called 'truth', that of the sub-contraries is called 'falsity'; the 'positive deixis' (reality plus non-appearance) is called 'secret'; the 'negative deixis' (lack of reality plus appearance) is called 'lie'. We see from this presentation of the modalities of '**être**' (in opposition to **paraître**) that it generates a structure of meaning, wherein the relations of the notions of truth and falsity, secrecy and lie (or should it be 'illusion'?) are set forth through the deployment of binary oppositions on the one hand and semic combinations on the other.

The combination **faire faire** is for Greimas only one example of 'factitive' relations. One can also have **faire savoir, faire croire,** etc. They often appear to be kinds of reported imperatives (1976a:95), but the function of this relation can equally involve the concepts of communication, representation, delegation, etc. Greimas comments that a deeper study would probably make this modal category appear as one of the universals which allow us to account for numerous signifying human practices (1976a:95).

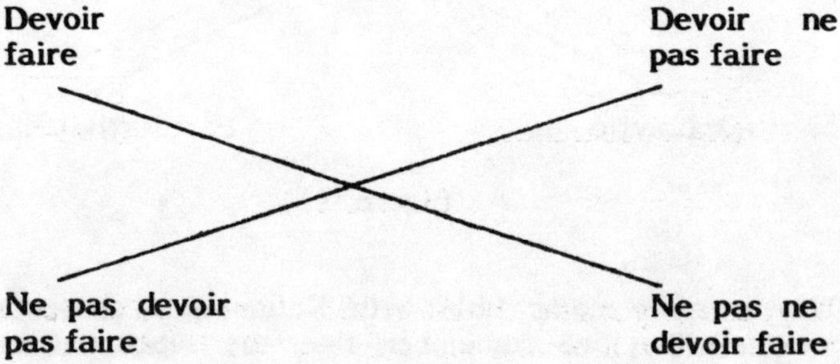

(Figure 9)

Thus far, the Greimasian account may seem to have had little in common with the concerns of deontic logicians regarding modalities. **(25)** Its concern has been with the modalities of existence and action, and their relation to narrative structures (1976a:96,99). But deontic modalities soon become relevant. Greimas suggests that 'competence' is a state of being which itself may be subject to modalisation, and offers a provisional list of four **'surmodalisations'** of it: **vouloir, devoir, pouvoir, savoir.** The competence to act may be constituted by investing the subject with a will to do, a duty to do, a power to do or knowledge of how to do (or, presumably, of some combination of the four). Since such **'surmodalisations'** are modifications of the basic structure of competence (**être du faire**), Greimas (1976a:97) offers a semiotic square where **devoir** is substituted for **être** (figure 9).

We can see already how closely this is beginning to approach the logical representation of deontic modalities (**26**) and Greimas goes on to translate the four terms of this square into the traditional language of deontic modalities (figure 10):

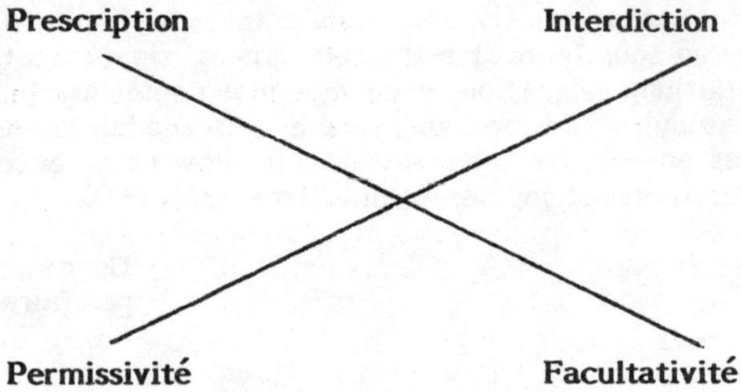

(Figure 10)

This is quite compatible with Kalinowski's presentation, provided that we remember that the subcontraries are unilateral forms of permission. But Greimas points to two differences betwen the semiotic and the logical approaches. First, he observes that while the semiotician tends to interpret **devoir** as the will of the sender (of a message), the logician tends rather to see 'will' in terms of a self-impelled duty (1976a:97). This, perhaps, may serve as a nice illustration of the proposition that the orientation of the semiotician is towards narrative roles and interpersonal communication, while that of the logician is towards deontic concepts. Second, Greimas comments upon the process of nominalisation effected between the first version of the square (**devoir faire**, etc.) and the second (**prescription**, etc.). For the logician, this may be no more than a procedure of denomination, attaching a different (arbitrary) name to the same process. For the semiotician, on the other hand, it signifies the conversion of a modal predicate into a modal value. We have seen already the important role which such modal values play in the theory of Greimas. They, like objects of value, are forms of message which are transferred from one party to another. This is a vital step required to reduce all aspects of human culture to a communicational (semiotic) model. If 'obligation' is a modal value which is transferred from one party to another, much as a (legal) contract may have the effect of transferring property from one party to another, then at one single blow law becomes susceptible to analysis in terms of language (or at least semiotics), and the distinction between 'is' and 'ought' is transcended. Of course, one might ask on what grounds 'competence' is said to be subject to these particular four modalities (and modal values). Again, the answer is quite simply that this is a form of analysis which has been found to work (1982:194).

Not only does the Greimasian analysis suggest a reduction of the distinction between modal and other values, it also suggests a reduction of the different types of modalities (1976a:98f.). Thus far, we have considered only **devoir faire.** Greimas goes on to show the same modal structure for **devoir être** (figure 11), again in nominalised form:

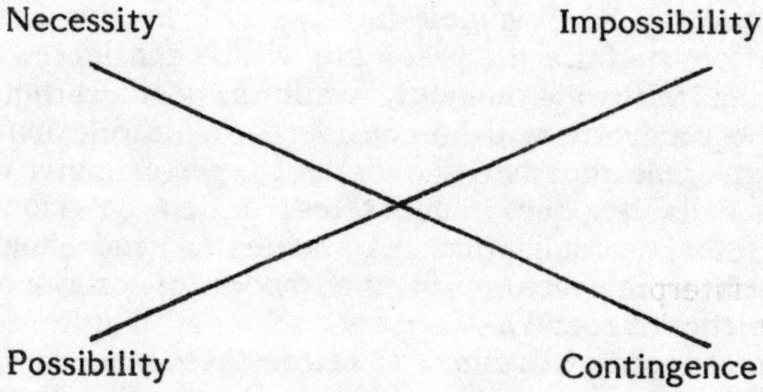

(Figure 11)

The result, he suggests, is a set of aletheic modalities (**27**), which are seen to have the same modal structure as deontic modalities. But one can go further. The structure of these **'surmodalisations'** is that they are a combination of one of **vouloir, devoir, pouvoir, savoir** with one of **faire** and **être.** If one represents the former list by the common symbol **m** (modal statement), one can represent the square in terms which are common to the various combinations, by signifying the respective internal and external negations (figure 12, where the superimposed bar denotes negation). Here, the left hand square represents the possible modalisations of **faire,** the right hand the possible modalisations of **être.** At least eight forms of possible logic can be foreseen. Deontic logic rests on **devoir-faire**, but one could foresee a **'logique volitive'** (or **'boulestique'**), based upon the operations which may be performed within a

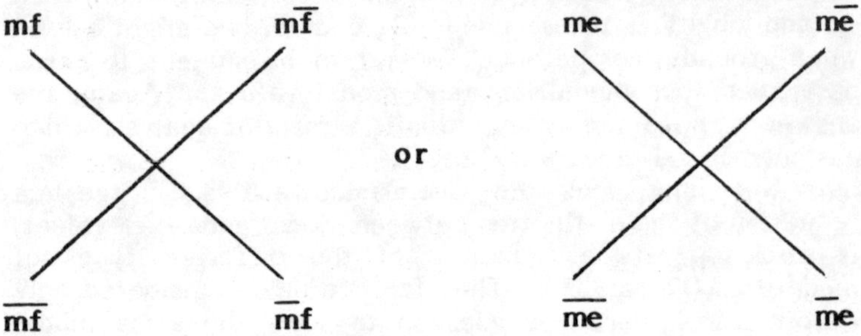

(Figure 12)

square starting with **vouloir-faire**, etc. In the case of modalisations of **faire** the predicate will be considered in its relationship with the subject, while in modalisations of **être**, the predicate will be considered in its relation with the object. One thus has two distinct types of logic, which Greimas calls **'logiques subjectives'**, which describe and regulate the modalisation of subjects, and **'logiques objectives'**, which deal with the modes of existence of stated objects (1976a:99).

The concern of Greimas to relate these possible logics of modalities to the syntagmatic level of narrative discourse evokes a classification of modalities in terms of their possible functions at the syntagmatic level (1976a:99f.). He sees this presentation as suggested both by a long philosophical tradition and by its apparent conformity with the canonic schemes of narrative structure (if not always with the level of manifestation of narrative itself). Thus, the establishment of the subject is marked by the appearance of the modalities of **devoir-faire** and/or **vouloir-faire**; the subject is someone to whom the modal value of the obligation to act or the will to act is transferred. On the other hand, the qualification of the subject (giving him the capacity to perform the act which he has been established as subject to do) is marked by the modal combinations of **pouvoir-faire** and/or **savoir-faire.** Greimas uses the term 'competence' to include both of these groups (**28**), whereas in our earlier presentation (3.4) 'competence' was reserved (following Calloud) for the second syntagm in the narrative algorithm. It is, in fact, a feature of this recent article of Greimas that he presents the syntagm 'contract' in far less clear-cut a manner than hitherto. This, perhaps, is a result of his observation that at the level of manifestation one sometimes finds that the subject can be endowed with **pouvoir-faire** without possessing the **vouloir-faire** which ought to have preceded it (1976a:100).

In order further to test the system of relationships obtaining between the different **surmodaliations** of competence, Greimas effects a series of superimpositions of the semiotic squares, by retaining one in a static form and superimposing upon it another in which, progressively, the axes (contraries and subcontraries), schemas (contradictories) and deixes (subalternations) are inverted. The object is to ascertain what compatibilities and incompatibilities emerge. He proceeds in this way through **devoir être** and **pouvoir être, devoir-faire** and **vouloir-faire,** and **devoir-faire** and **savoir-faire** (1976a:101-7). From the jurisprudential point of view, this is particularly interesting for any light it might cast upon the relations of duty and power (typically, **devoir-faire** and **pouvoir-faire,** although this is not one of the pairs chosen for the exercise in superimposition). Greimas notes that when the axes of the modal structure of **pouvoir être** are inverted upon the

A Duty to be **E Duty not to be**
I No power not to be **O No power to be**

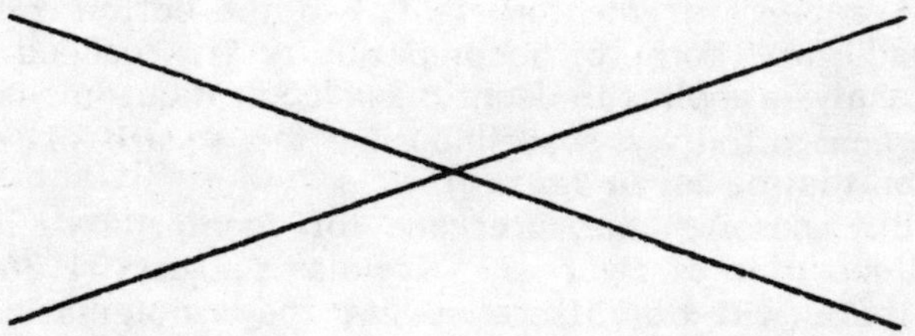

I No duty not to be **O No duty to be**
A Power to be **E Power not to be**

(Figure 13)

modal structure of **devoir être,** a conformity is produced (figure 13). But in fact, Greimas here does nothing which is not common amongst logicians. This is merely one way of representing the interdefinability of the aletheic modalities of necessity and possibility (figure 11); if **faire** is substituted for **être** in both squares, we may similarly represent the interdefinability of duty and permission (cf. figures 9-10). It would be wrong, of course, to deduce from this that power and duty (as understood in jurisprudence) are interdefinable. **'Pouvoir faire'** here must be taken in the sense of 'permission' rather than 'power', and thus the conformity which Greimas here observes might be regarded as no more than a systematization of his own earlier denomination of **'ne pas devoir ne pas faire'** as **'permissivité'**. But Greimas is not finished. The superimposition represented in figure 13 is only the first of four possible homologations. In it, the relationship of subcontrariety of the **pouvoir être** square is superimposed upon that of contrariety of the **devoir être** square, as is seen by the addition of the conventional alphabetical symbols. The result is 'conformity', a strong form of compatibility (in fact, a logical entailment): if a person has a duty to be X, he cannot have a 'power' (= permission) not to be X, etc. A weaker form of compatibility, termed 'complementarity' is produced by superimposing the contraries of the second square on those of the first. The other two inversions produce incompatibility. Where the schemas of the second modality are inverted (so that **A** appears at the bottom right, **O** at the top left, etc.), an incompatibility termed 'contrariety' is produced between the two squares; where it is the deixes which are inverted (so that **A** appears at the top right, **I** at the bottom right), a 'contradictory' form of incompatibility is produced. The same analysis applies to deontic and 'boulestique' modalities, as demonstrated by superimposing the square of **vouloir faire** on that of **devoir faire.**

But despite the presence of 'conformity' in the superimposition of figure 13, Greimas suggests (1976a:103) that there will be differences at the syntagmatic level according to whether necessity is generated by the one **'surmodalisation'** (**devoir être**) or by the other (**ne pas pouvoir ne pas être**). These modal structures do not, according to Greimas, determine the unfolding of the modalities at the syntagmatic level. He sees the syntagmatic sequence as between **devoir-faire** and **vouloir-faire** as giving rise to a classification of two different types of 'contract'. Where **devoir-faire** leads to **vouloir-faire** (the duty to act producing a will to act), we have a **'contract injonctif'**; where the **vouloir-faire** precedes the **devoir-faire** (the will to act producing a duty to act), we have a **contrat permissif** (1976a:105). The difference between injunction and permission is seen in terms of the place accorded to will, in relation to duty, at the syntagmatic level.

In introducing the superimposition of **devoir-faire** and **savoir-faire,** Greimas notes that it may be considered as a model of the functioning of social codes, in relation to the competence of the subjects to which those codes apply. In this context, he notes that the juxtaposition of **devoir-faire** with **pouvoir-faire** would also be suggestive (1976a:105). He gives the rules of a system of law as an explicit example of the social codes which this particular confrontation might be taken to represent (1976a:107). Here, too, the inversions produce a set of relations (figure 14):

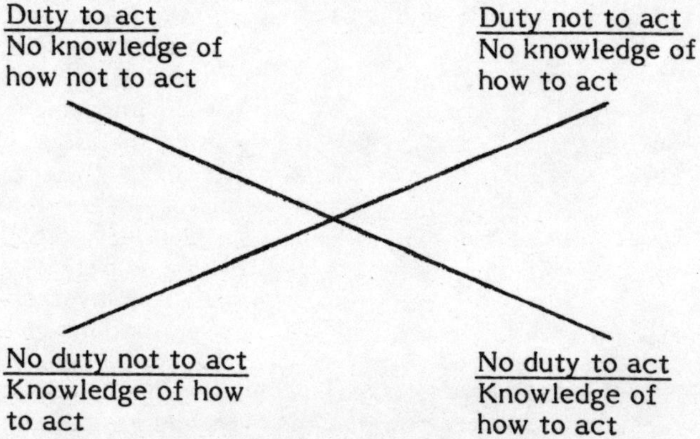

(Figure 14)

The compatibilities might well appear more plausible if one were to substitute 'power' for 'knowledge'. But here again, one would be dealing with 'permission' and not with 'power' in the jurisprudential sense. Neither the logical nor the semiotic analyses which we have considered appear explicitly to deal with that latter form of relation.

We may speculate upon the reason. 'Power' may be analysed as a special form of 'permission', a permission to do a particular kind of thing. It is a permission not simply to perform an ordinary act (a 'brute fact' or 'hard fact', we may say), but rather to perform an act which changes the legal situation. It is, indeed, a permission to perform an 'institutive act'. In other words, the **'faire'** refers not merely to an act, but to the creation of an instance of an institution of a particular cultural system, an instance which (as the example of the SC shows) is itself constituted as a semiotic object, capable of performing the role of **actant sujet** and of creating further signification. It is this specific investment of the modal value **faire** in **pouvoir faire** which distinguishes a power from a permission. **(29)** The distinction between them must be sought at the purely linguistic level, as different semantic investments of the same semiotic form. **(30)**

CHAPTER FIVE

The 'Legal Grammar'

(5.1) The Legal Grammar of G/L: The legislative text contains its own account of the generation of legal meaning, in the appearance of the legislator, the record of his performative utterance and the messages he communicates to the SC (and the absence of his own legitimation). The structure and activity of the legislator reflects the same narrative grammar described in chapters 3-4. The legislator incorporates semiotic phenomena in the referential world of law but leaves them there as virtual until they are performed and verified in legal practice. **(5.2) The Legal Grammar of Carrion-Wam:** Carrion-Wam sees the legal grammar in purely syntagmatic terms, and identifies the litigant rather than the judge as receiver. The judge has his own autonomous discourse, separate from that of the legislator. There is a hierarchical relationship between legislator and judge, though both are authorities transforming one form of discourse into another. Carrion-Wam takes a more traditional view than G/L of legal modalities, and regards the judge as having a choice between alternative semantic methodologies.

5.1 THE LEGAL GRAMMAR OF G/L

One of the most significant aspects of G/L's analysis is their account of what they call the 'legal grammar' (**la grammaire juridique**). Here, the methods and perspectives of Greimasian narrative grammar are directed in turn to the activities of the legislator and judge themselves, as they appear in the legal discourse of the 1966 Loi. In chapter 2, we considered only the effect of their activities on the objects of those activities - the incorporation of legal terminology, its recognition as legal in the act of application. But Greimasian semiotics would reject any non-semiotic account of the legislator and judge themselves. They do not appear in the legal discourse as dei ex machina; they too are part of a communicational process. They have actantial roles and structures. We have to analyse the legal discourse to see what part it presents them as playing in the legal story.

Such talk of 'the legal story' might strike legal philosophers as metaphorical. (1) Roque Carrion-Wam, a Peruvian legal philosopher at the University of Carabobo, Venezuela, seeks to build a model of legal discourse based in part upon Greimasian semiotic perspectives, but without using the approach of narrative grammar. This chapter expounds and compares the two approaches.

G/L do not themselves set out to provide a fresh start for legal philosophy. Their concern is the analysis of a particular text, viewed as a specimen of legal discourse. As semioticians, however, they are particularly sensitive to the communicational force of the form of the message, as well as its content. And in its form, the Loi of 1966 is 'standard'. For this reason, the semiotic analysis of a particular legal text may be generalised in terms of that particular genre of legal discourse - the discourse of the legislator. That, of course, should not be equated with the semiotic analysis of 'law'. What we conventionally describe as the legal system contains many different genres of text, each one of which requires independent semiotic analysis, not least for such explicit and implicit cross-referencing to other forms of legal discourse. (2) Nevertheless, G/L's analysis does frequently impinge upon the concerns of legal philosophy. In chapter one, a summary account was provided of the principal approaches encountered in legal philosophy: positivism, naturalism and realism. G/L's analysis provides significant parallels to all three. The next chapter considers those parallels more systematically, under these three conventional headings. I argue that, far from reflecting an incoherent eclecticism, these parallels may be made to add up to an integrated theory, which gives proper place to the most enduring insights of the various traditions of legal philosophy, and indeed of the general philosophical traditions from which they emerge. (3) In short, we have a

bricolage in the best sense of the term.

Our account of the construction of the legal lexicon in chapter 2 might have given the impression that G/L simply adopt a conventional view of the 'given' legal status and roles of the legislator and judge. Not so. The starting point of their analysis is their reading of the semiotic characteristics of the text itself. There, they observe, one immediately notices a difference between legal and other semiotic systems. Whereas the grammar of social semiotics usually remains implicit, underlying the discourse which it produces (as in the example of the code of table manners), the legal grammar seeks to be explicit and to make its rules public (87f.). It is a deliberately constructed grammar (unlike that of a natural language), and presents itself as such. G/L attach particular significance to the presence at the head of the Loi of the enactment formula: 'Le Président de la République promulgue la loi dont la teneur suit'. This tells us not merely that the law is the expression of a collective will; it records an act of enunciation, and accords legal status - 'in the manner of a divine fiat' - to the whole collection of legal utterances which follow. Such utterances would not claim their legal character without this original performative act. What is significant, for G/L, is the fact that this performative act is itself recorded in the discourse. They do not have to infer its existence, or go outside the discourse for the context of its enunciation. The performative act is itself a part of the discourse of the 1966 law.

It follows that explicit statement in the law is the criterion of existence of legal (or at least legislative) statements. If something is not said in the law, then it does not exist for the purposes of the law. G/L see the legal concept 'nullity' in these terms. If people purport to set up a company which does not conform to the legislative model, they do not 'violate' the law; they simply fail to create anything which exists for the purposes of that legal discourse (89). This is why **production juridique** is defined in terms of naming in legislation (2.2 above).

The legislator appears explicitly in the legal discourse. But this in itself is not sufficient for G/L to account for the semiotic status of the legislator. He is not simply another word used in legal discourse; he has actantial roles and functions. These roles and functions reflect the structures of narrative grammar.

Take first the actantial structure of the legislator. Given the performative act recorded in the discourse, one of his roles is that of 'sender'. He has to be instituted as an **actant.** G/L take the view that he is an **actant collectif,** like the SC itself, and structured in a similar fashion (3.2, 4.2 above). That implies the existence of operations which result in the receipt by the legislator of its semiotic characteristics from other sources. The legislator is presented as the expression of the 'national will', and thus as the syntactic exponent of the social **actant** which is the national community (111). Its activity is to 'speak', but its role so to speak comes through the mediation of all the elements which make up the structure of this **actant collectif.** Ultimately this leads to a last receiver, who is installed as the subject of the speech act (**sujet de l'énonciation**) of the legal discourse - the legislator himself. This legal discourse is the global statement (**énoncé**) of the legislator, something which he himself sends on as a message.

The legislator, thus instituted, may now be the subject of narrative statements. It is the equivalent, as we have seen, at the narrative level of a nominal phrase in the sentence. Two basic kinds of predicate are available, telling us what the **actant** is (according to the formula **E (A),** where **E** stands for 'ê t r e') or what he does (according to the formula **F (A),** where **F** stands for 'faire').

Significantly, perhaps, G/L have nothing to say about discursive statements of a type E(A), where A is the legislator. This contrasts with the position as regards the rules which the law contains. They are instituted with the attribute of legality by being explicitly mentioned by the legislator in the discourse. But there are no comparable statements such as to institute the legislator as legal - none, that is, if we follow one of the postulates of Greimasian semiotics, and confine our attention to the contours of the discourse itself. (4) We shall presently have to consider the implications of this 'absence' for legal philosophy.

The matter is different when we turn to the alternative formula of the narrative syntagm, F(A). We do know from the discourse what the legislator does. The legislator is present in the legal text as a receiver-subject of the legal will to act. It acts through the utterance of discourse. This discourse both establishes and maintains a certain 'legal culture', characterised as 'legal good manners' and compared with table manners, conventions of conversation, etc. G/L suggest a parallel between the establishment of these legal conventions and the initiation rituals and qualifying tests of popular folklore. All of them represent rites of passage from nature to culture (111f.).

The legislator acts in the text not only as the provider of the capacity of the SC, the installer of its will (as **actant-instaurateur**), but also as an **actant-controleur** which seeks to verify the competence of the subject (here the SC) and its continuing adherence to the conventions. The legislator thus assumes multiple roles in the legal discourse itself; he becomes conceived as not merely a simple **actant**, but as an **'architecture actantielle complexe'** (113). G/L suggest that the legislator communicates as a double sender with 'hierarchically inferior semiotic objects' - SC's conceived as receivers, in that they receive from the legislator both a knowledge (**savoir**) which provides their capacity to perform these duties, and the status of a collective subject endowed with a **'devoir-faire'** (duty to act) (113). (5) This **devoir-faire** is both imperative and restrictive: it restricts the range of goals which are recognised as legally legitimate, and prescribes the manner in which the legitimate goals may be achieved. This, perhaps, allows us to resolve in semiotic terms a problem which has often troubled legal theorists. We may institute an entity with legal personality, giving it powers defined in advance. We may then seek to impose criminal liability to it, should it commit certain offences (which involve acts beyond its legal powers). But since its personality is defined in terms of what it has legal power to do, how can we punish it for what it lacks legal personality to do ? A Greimasian analysis would be capable of regarding the same company as fulfilling different actantial roles when it acts legally and criminally. In the latter case, it acts as 'opponent', in anthropomorphic terms as 'anti-hero' (110).

Of course, G/L recognise that even the performative act of the legislator as recorded in the discourse does not in itself affect the world outside the discourse. It merely communicates the message that the content of the discourse is regarded as legal. Words previously belonging only to the natural language are now incorporated into another discursive system: they are endowed with **sémanticité juridique. Production juridique** thus transforms semiotic objects previously characterised by **asémanticité juridique** into semiotic objects possessing **sémanticité juridique** (92).

When we look further, beyond the legislative discourse, to legal practice, we find another peculiar characteristic of law as a semiotic system. Law, unlike other semiotic systems, possesses a 'recurrent procedure of verification'. A grammar is (as Chomsky stresses) capable of generating an unlimited number of utterances. We may be in possession of a code whereby we can recognise such utterances as well-formed or not. But there exists no procedure for verification of such conclusions. In law, the matter stands differently. Legal language derives much of its force from the fact that it constantly anticipates and practises such procedures of verification. (**6**) Law is able to achieve this through its particular structure of delegation of power, wherein the original sender of the legal messages (the legislator) is substituted by a supplementary sender who is called upon to re-state the law (the judge). In 'applying' the law, the judge thus both verifies (confirms) the legal status of utterances within the legislative discourse, and transforms them from general legislative messages into more specific judicial messages, which can be interjected into social life itself. The 'virtual' is then made 'actual'. Through this restatement and redirection of the message, the judge may play a part in the story of the lives of the litigants; he may send them a 'contract', by communicating to them a particular duty-to-act (**devoir-faire** - a modal value). In this sense, legal practice too involves 'production of law', in the form not only of potentially new rules but also of communications of (new and specific) legal messages (91). But the legal meaning of events in the world, or the legal status of normative statements made outside the legislative discourse, can only be incorporated within the legal discourse by verification of their grammatical conformity with the canonical statements of the legislative discourse itself, and this task falls to the practice of the courts (92). Thus, while **production juridique** results in the institution of certain statements as possessing **sémanticité juridique, vérification juridique** tests the conformity of other statements and events by what is impliedly a syntactic process (the relation of signs to signs), so as to determine whether these other statements or events possess legal **grammaticalité**.

G/L represent these processes as in figure 15 (93). It is by no means clear that G/L themselves claim this representation to have the properties of a semiotic square.

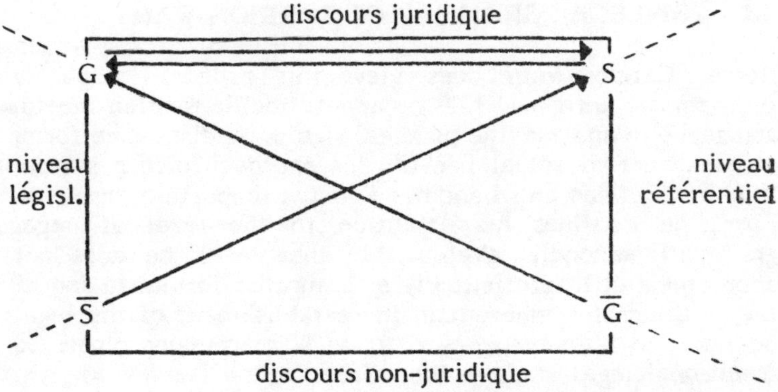

(Figure 15)

Certainly, if it is viewed as such, it is an example of a square which deviates from the logical model. It is, perhaps, best to view the processes it encapsulates in syntagmatic terms. We start at the bottom left with a semiotic object (perhaps, a normative proposition) characterised by **asémanticité juridique.** By naming it in legislation (diagonal left to right), the legislator effects **production juridique,** thus endowing the object with **sémanticité juridique.** It now exists on the 'referential level' of law (top right). But it has not yet been verified or applied. We have reached the right side of the diagram. Through the process **vérification juridique** (diagonal right to left), the status of that statement is both verified, and some other statement or event is incorporated into the legal discourse, by having its status verified as possessing **grammaticalité juridique** through comparison with the semiotic object endowed with **sémanticité juridique** at the referential level. We are now at the top left of the diagram, with the statements of the judge having been endowed with both **sémanticité juridique** and **grammaticalité juridique.** The difficulty with G/L's schema is that one can account meaningfully for three sides of it, but not for the fourth. They describe the left hand side as the 'legislative level', characterised by the presence of legal grammar, but without content. It is not immediately apparent what this means.

5.2 THE LEGAL GRAMMAR OF CARRION-WAM

Roque Carrion-Wam does view this process in purely syntagmatic terms. While he adopts the Saussurian motto, and seeks to analyse 'the juridical sign in its discursive form, in the heart of social life' (7), his approach diverges from that of Greimas and Landowski in two important respects. First, he confines his attention to the level of 'legal grammar'; secondly, even within that level, he does not adopt their characteristically structuralist formalization of the relationships inherent in the establishment of the legal lexicon. In both respects, Carrion-Wam remains closer to traditional legal analysis than Greimas and Landowski. On the one hand, he confines his attention to the level at which the specificity of law is claimed to be located, and excludes the level where law reflects more general structures; on the other, his view of the specific semiotics of law takes more account of the normative hierarchy of law than does that of his Parisian colleagues. Carrion-Wam adds a further requirement to G/L's notion of **production juridique.** It is not any use of a term in legislation that results in **production juridique.** The semantic universe of law is not as wide as the semantic universe of the natural language from which legal terms are drawn. Legal propositions involve the use (at both 'deep' and 'surface' levels) of a small group of 'modal operators', wherein X is prohibited, permitted, or required. In more conventional terminology, legal propositions are normative, not descriptive. Thus, Carrion-Wam would argue, terms used in purely descriptive statements do not become endowed with **sémanticité juridique** even when those descriptive statements occur in legislation.

Moreover, Carrion-Wam declines to view **production juridique** as a sufficient act of legal communication. For him, it is not sufficient that the legislator might be 'sending' a **'devoir-faire'** to the SC, conceived as a semiotic object with an actantial role. Confining himself to the surface level, Carrion-Wam regards the addressee (receiver) of the legal message sent by the legislator not as the judge but rather as the ultimate subject to whom the permission/prohibition/requirement applies, the judge being merely an intermediary. Only when the judge applies the legislative message can one say that there is a real 'sender' (the legislator) and 'receiver' (the subject). Before that stage, the sender of the message is a mere 'linguistic construction' while the receiver is 'an empty space, an eventuality that will be realised and defined . . . ' only when the judicial discourse is itself communicated to him.

But the lawyer might well wish to qualify such a view. He would contest the assumption that the role of the judge is essential, as unnecessarily presupposing 'contentious' business. Even without judicial intervention, he might argue, the placing of the term within legislation does endow it with some meaning. That meaning may well not be authoritatively certain, but the citizen who reads the legislation will not be entitled to say: 'this is a legal word, but no meaning has yet been attached to it, and therefore I am at liberty to attach any meaning I desire.' At the very least, the meaning will be (for him) subject to such semantic constraints as would attach to it in the natural language, these constraints being endowed with presumptive legal status by the fact that it is the natural language from which the legislator has taken the term. Similarly, the intervention of the judge is not a necessary condition for the creation of an effective act of legal communication. Acts of Parliament are bought, read and acted upon by citizens regularly on the day of promulgation, as are musical scores (before any public performance) and various other types of mass communication which can involve both public and private manifestations. Nevertheless, the semiotic analysis does suggest two important conclusions for legal theory. First, whatever the presumptive status of the semantic constraints from natural language, the judge (at least) has the formal freedom in law to endow a word inserted by the legislator into the legal lexicon with whatever meaning he wishes. Secondly, a distinction is to be drawn between unimplemented norms and those made effective through action.

Carrion-Wam attaches greater significance than G/L to the autonomy of judicial discourse, although this difference in emphasis may well reflect little more than the fact that the prime focus of G/L is a legislative text. At any rate, for Carrion-Wam there are **three** languages to be considered: natural language, 'juridical legislative discourse' (JLD), and 'juridical jurisprudential discourse' (JJD). Of these, the second is legislation in its linguistic expression, the third is the judgments (or formal statements of decision: the 'sentences' of Civil Law Systems), in their linguistic expression. These three languages may all refer to the same (signifying) 'social events', but they do so in different ways. Thus, the languages are described as 'isotopic' but not 'isomorphic'. The three languages are conceived as independent semiotics, **each** with both a grammar and a semantics of its own. Carrion-Wam is clear that **production juridique** is not merely the establishment of a word by transference from the lexicon of the natural language to the lexicon of the legal language, but also the transference of some part at least of its meaning. In particular, Carrion-Wam emphasises the ideological component of natural language. (8) Natural language is at one and the same time a reflection of the social world, and a means of organising it. Natural language is 'ideological' in the sense that a language 'structures the universe of values that predominates in society'. It expresses a certain type of meaning attached to the phenomena of the social world; it is 'an ideologically oriented instrument of communication'. Since, for Carrion-Wam as for G/L, **production juridique** involves a transference from natural language into legal discourse, it follows, at least for him, that the 'semantic ideological universe' of the natural language is itself projected into the JLD in the course of transference. Since the legislative discourse for Carrion-Wam is the origin of at least one of the two possible forms of the semantics of judicial discourse (below), it follows that the ideological component of the natural language is, to this extent, carried through also to the latter.

Carrion-Wam differs from G/L in two further respects, both of which appear to indicate a greater sympathy with the traditional hierarchical view of the legal systems. For Carrion-Wam dispenses with representation of these relationships in the form of the square, and explicitly speaks of the judge as a 'secondary authority' in relation to the 'primary authority' who is the legislator. But the significance of 'primary' and 'secondary' remains unclear. For the roles of legislator and judge are presented in terms of semiotic rather than normative functions, namely in effecting transformations between the three independent semiotic systems which Carrion-Wam has identified. It is the legislator who effects a transformation of the discourse of natural language into legislation (JLD), and it is the judge who is the authority who transforms legislation (JLD) into judicial decisions (JJD). From this it is clear that the authority of the judge is 'secondary' in the sense that without the activity of the legislator, he would have nothing to transform. That, however, does not answer the question whether the judge's authority, or semiotic capacity to effect such transformations, is dependent upon the legislator, or rather derives directly from the meta-language in virtue of which the roles of both legislator and judge are instituted. There are, however, other aspects of Carrion-Wam's presentation which appear to favour the latter interpretation.

In describing the process of production of legislative discourse, Carrion-Wam requires the intervention of 'an authority (A1) provided of a change-maker (CM)'. It is this authority who transforms natural language into the language of law, thereby producing legislative discourse. A1 is defined as 'the institution of Congress (Parliament) that by virtue of the **power** that is invested in it (by an original law called the Constitution) promulgates (dictates a law) a discourse (a linguistic organization) that will be called **law**'. Whereas G/L take a semiotic view of the status of legislation, Carrion-Wam here seems to adopt a more conventional juristic analysis, in terms of powers conferred under a normative order.

The involvement in the transformation process of a 'change-maker' is less unfamiliar to lawyers than its terminology might suggest. Carrion-Wam defines it as the 'transforming action' that is represented by the legislator (A1) when he transforms natural language into legislative discourse, or by the judge (A2) when he transforms legislative into judicial discourse. The nature of this 'transforming action' is perhaps better expressed by G/L. As we have seen, they describe the formula 'Le Président de la République promulgue la loi dont la teneur suit' as a 'performative act' by virtue of which the norms that follow are endowed with their legal quality (1976:88).

Modalities, once again, are taken by Carrion-Wam to distinguish the grammar of the artificial languages of legislative and judicial discourse from that of the natural language. The former are characterised by 'a modal network whose operators (called deontics in modal logic) orient' the legal discourse in such a way as to give the semantic universe of a natural language, with its ideological overtones, a specific form. It is such a modal network, expressed in terms like 'prohibited', 'permitted', 'required', which characterise such 'qualifying statements' and 'functional statements' (in Greimasian terms, **E(A)** and **F(A)**) as are found in these two types of legal discourse. It is noticeable that here too Carrion-Wam is prepared to give a more specific, normative appropriation to concepts which G/L regard as general modal objects. Here too, Carrion-Wam stands closer to both conventional legal analysis and the tradition of deontic logic.

Carrion-Wam differs from G/L also in the relationship he perceives between the semantics of legislative discourse and those of judicial discourse. For G/L, this question hardly arises. Judicial language has no independent semantics; it merely uses that which has received **sémanticité juridique** through the activity of the legislator termed **production juridique.** But for Carrion-Wam, this is only one of two possible alternatives. The judge may choose either to combine the semantics of JLD with those of the 'social event' (of the natural language) which arises from adjudication, or to adopt a different semantic of his own. These two possibilities are not elaborated by Carrion-Wam. However, it seems that the first possibility corresponds to that of G/L and may in terms of legal logic be regarded as an act of subsumption, while the latter involves the 'creation' (Carrion-Wam's word) of a new semantic component that is thereby incorporated into the legislative discourse. Like Kelsen, Carrion-Wam provides the judge with alternatives: he may decide either inside or outside the frame of the semantics of legal discourse. **(9)**

Chapter Six

Preliminary Conclusions for Legal Theory

(6.1) Semiotics and Legal Positivism: Although the semiotic account of law appears to endorse a substantive form of positivism, characterised by the doctrine of incorporation, in reality it is only describing the claims it sees as made by the text: it is the text which claims that the legal universe is constituted by statement (a form of positing) in legislation. Semiotic theory regards both the normative hierarchy and the notion of validity as part of the message of the text. But semiotics does endorse a radical form of positivism in defining the object of study. **(6.2) Semiotics and Jurisprudential Naturalism:** The 'naturalist' contribution of semiotics to jurisprudence is largely methodological, in directing attention to the need to identify those structures of signification which allow us to incorporate and understand law as a semiotic universe of legal culture. Greimasian semiotics claims that narrative grammar explains not only how legal texts assert the specificity of legal discourse but also how those texts communicate meaning at all. It does so partly by virtue of its tacit incorporation of a theory of all human action (literary, legal, etc.). **(6.3) Semiotics and Legal Realism:** Despite attacks on its formalism and lack of a socio-economic or historical dimension, Greimasian semiotics shares important perspectives with jurisprudential realism. It is sceptical of the ontological claims of positivism, and regards the self-image of the legal system merely as an appearance whose truth-claims the text (often tacitly) communicates. The role and dominance of legislation is part of that message, conveyed by aspects of the legislative form that we all too readily take for granted.

6.1 SEMIOTICS AND LEGAL POSITIVISM

The legal grammar which G/L's analysis of the legal discourse reveals is, not unsurprisingly, uncompromisingly positivistic. This, after all, is the dominant philosophy of legal practice, and pre-eminently that of legislators. For positivism, in its various forms (1), is a philosophy of law as laid down from above.

The legal grammar consists, as we have seen, in the complementary processes of **production juridique** and **vérification juridique.** Both require clearly identifiable acts, that of the legislator in 'speaking', that of the judge in referring to the legislation. It is this classical positivistic process, whereby recognition of a phenomenon as belonging to a particular system is determined by procedural tests, that is reflected in the very construction of the legal lexicon: for G/L, it is the act of naming in legislation which institutes a word as legal. G/L do not themselves, however, go on to claim the autonomy of legal semantics, and Carrion-Wam stresses the inter-relatedness of the semantics of the natural language with that of the legal language. It might seem that the effect of **production juridique** for G/L is merely the institution of an autonomous set of **signifiants,** without any necessary implication as to the autonomy of the **signifiés** which will be (arbitrarily) related to the **signifiants** in the system of legal semantics. But this is an unlikely **argumentum e silentio.** Carcaterra and Thomas (2.6) are more explicit on this issue. Their view of the autonomy of legal semantics extends to the system of meanings of words, as well as the words themselves. If ordinary language meanings are admitted into the legal system, they argue, it is solely by virtue of a choice made within the legal system to admit such meanings. We may note that this argument is closely connected with the positivist view of the working of moral standards within the legal system. Such moral standards enter the legal system often through the use of words from ordinary language, which imply reference to the standards of the ordinary man in the street. Thus, the law does not claim that it has its own autonomous conception of 'reasonableness', 'fairness', 'good faith'. When such expressions are used within the legal system, they often require more precise definitions than those required in the contexts of ordinary usage. Nevertheless, such terms are customarily viewed as referring to 'non-legal' standards, and the latter are therefore taken as constraints upon the meaning attached to those terms when used even in law. Yet the very choice of those terms for use within the legal system implies a decision taken from within the legal system so to use them. Hart, in particular, has deployed such arguments regarding the relationship between law and morality. It is always open to a legal system to incorporate moral standards, whether in the form of rights entrenched in constitutions, or as standards of conduct to be applied by judges. But such moral standards enter the law solely by virtue of incorporation - a choice made from within the legal system itself; the standards do not inhere within the legal system because they are moral. Thus the presence of both moral standards and ordinary language terminology within the legal system is no argument against the positivist thesis that law is defined by institutional means. **(2)**

Some add a further requirement to this semiotic version of positivism. It is not sufficient that a word be 'named' in legislation for it to belong to the legal lexicon. Carrion-Wam insists that it must be used within a normative utterance, one characterised by the presence of a legal primitive, one of the deontic operators. There has been a similar debate in the Italian literature concerning the nature of technical legal terms. Martino argues (against Scarpelli) that concepts cannot be 'normative' until and unless they are used in normative utterances, that is, in the context of a whole legal utterance (1975:55). That is tantamount to saying that specificity cannot reside at the level of the content of law, but only at that of its form. The technical term is a semantic unit of the ordinary language, and becomes normative only when used within the structure of a norm. Both Thomas and Martino seem to reflect the classical positivist concept of incorporation: there are no such things as inherently legal meanings, but meanings may be made legal by an act of will recognised for that purpose by the legal system. The difference between Thomas and Martino appears to be that the latter recognises only the utterance of the term within a complete legal norm as the mode of incorporation, while Thomas takes a wider view, one which admits of legal meanings outside legal utterances, once the relevant (but by him undefined) process of incorporation has taken place.

Despite their view of the legal system as a process of the communication of messages, from legislator to SC and to judge, from judge to litigants, and so on, there is a faint hint in G/L's account of the type of hierarchical relationship which positivists typically see in the legal system. The positivist has to give an account of the legal validity of the authority which both legislator and judge exercise. Otherwise, their utterances cannot be distinguished from any other commands backed by force. The positivist answer consists in the claim that there exist legal rules, or norms of competence, which grant such authority to legislator and judge. Typically, it is the constitution (whether written or unwritten) which is the source of such authority. There then arises the question of the legal validity of the constitution itself. The latter has to be based upon something other than the authority of legislator and judge. Positivists answer the riddle in different ways, Kelsen through the presupposition of a further norm, the **Grundnorm,** Hart through the identification in the constitution of a rule or rules of recognition, whose validity rest upon their acceptance by the officials.

G/L might seem to have a similar problem. It is not a matter of legal competence which concerns them, but rather the question of semiotic competence. Both legislator and judge are clearly instituted in the legal discourse as 'semiotic objects', institutions capable of creating and transmitting meaning within the particular universe of legal discourse. How do they receive such competence ? They cannot create it themselves. Rather, they receive such 'competence' (as the term is used in the narrative algorithm) through discursive statements which attribute that competence to them, **'énoncés qualificatifs'.** It is such utterances which establish both legislator and judge as semiotic objects. That in itself might not imply any 'hierarchical' relationship. When the legislator institutes the SC as a semiotic object, he is simply a 'sender' transferring a collection of 'modal values' (which taken together represent 'competence') to the SC, viewed as 'receiver'. As a result, the acts of the SC will have meaning within the universe of legal discourse. But when G/L come to describe the activity of the judge (1976:91), they regard him as possessing a 'metalanguage' with which to test the propositions that come before him. (3)

There is a clear structural similarity between metalanguage/language and constitution/legislation. But the lawyer would be wrong to read the semiotic account in too legal a manner. Neither 'validity', nor the normative hierarchy which the lawyer often sees as required to account for it, figure in the semioticians' argument. Rather, the semiotician is concerned with the fact that only certain terms of the natural language are regarded as bearing meaning in law; he seeks to explain the rules which men have constructed in order to produce such meaning. The choice of 'use in legislation' is a sign of the fact that a term belongs to the legal language. Since there is, for G/L, no alternative to this particular sign, it follows that any other **être sémiotique** must be created through the agency of the legislator, if it is to bear meaning in law. But it should be noted that the legislator uses exactly the same techniques, **énoncés qualificatifs** and **énoncés fonctionels,** in the creation of other **êtres sémiotiques** in law as were used in order to constitute the legislator himself as such an **être sémiotique.** Naming in legislation is an **arbitrary** sign for the semiotician, and does not imply either legal/political 'powers' or legal/political legitimation.

Thus far, we have been concerned with the extent to which the legal discourse presents the image of a positivistic legal system. G/L do not thereby commit themselves to any truth-claims (4) for such an account; their orientation on the substantive issues of legal theory is far closer to that of the realists (6.3). The real convergence between G/L and legal positivism resides at the methodological level. In their definition of the object of enquiry, G/L adopt a radically positivistic stance - more radical, indeed, than that of most positivists in legal philosophy. G/L start and finish with a particular text. (5) Their methodology is even 'purer' than that of Kelsen - if adherence to the model of the natural sciences is regarded as the yardstick. The object of G/L's enquiry is not a reified concept, 'law', or a diffuse institutional structure, the 'legal system', or even a discrete metaphysical entity, 'a law'. Rather, their object of enquiry is precisely that which was presented to them by the Paris Chamber of Commerce and Industry: Loi n.66-537 - no more and no less. Neither 'law' nor 'the legal system' nor 'a law' can be brought into the semiotic laboratory for examination; Loi n.66-537 - the text, that is, whatever the nature of the messages it happens to contain - can indeed be put under the semiotic microscope. This methodological restriction necessarily puts in doubt the positivist conception of the unity of the legal system. Significantly, perhaps, G/L entitle their study 'Analyse sémiotique d'**un** discours juridique'; whether the text studied is typical of legislative discourse, not to say legal discourse in general, is a matter for comparative investigation, not for tacit assumption. In this respect, the semiotic approach stands at the opposite end of the spectrum to Kelsen. The 'Pure Theory' starts with the assumption - Kelsen claims, the 'experience' - of the unity of the legal system (understood as the system of objectively valid legal norms), and is thus forced to invent a single 'basic norm' (**Grundnorm**) as the source of all normative authorisation within the system. In methodological terms, the semiotic viewpoint is even more positivistic than that of Kelsen.

Kelsen also claimed that through, and only through, a process of authorisation proceeding down a hierarchical normative order could acts performed in the legal system be interpreted as having the 'objective' meaning of legal validity (1967:2-4). (6) For Kelsen, 'meaning' is the interpretation placed upon events by human minds. Different persons may attach different interpretations to the event; hence, the meanings they attach will be 'subjective'. The legal meaning attached to events is not of this character. It does not vary from individual to individual, nor does it depend upon the interpretation of a norm as legal by the parties involved. Since the phenomenon law is understood as possessing this characteristic of 'objective meaning', any account of law cannot depend upon factual psychological states which will vary from individual to individual. It is in order to account for this attribute of law that Kelsen finds it necessary to construct a hierarchy of norms.

The semiotician would go only a small part of the way with this analysis. He would agree that we have here the transformation of natural events into events of a particular cultural significance (that of law), by the attribution of a particular meaning to them. Beyond that the semiotician is apt to diverge. First, the 'natural events' are not always regarded as a passive 'referent', to which the constructed meaning is applied. Carrion-Wam endorses the idea of a 'natural' semioticity, so that the process of transformation into legal meaning involves the relationship between a natural and a constructed semiotic system, a form of 'intersemioticity'. More important, the attachment of the particular form of meaning which we call legal to these events would not be regarded by the semiotician as involving any notion such as the 'objective meaning' postulated by Kelsen. How, then, would the semiotician account for the phenomena which Kelsen seeks to explain in terms of 'objective meaning' ? He would do so by claiming that such objective meaning is part of the semiotic **appearance** of law, part of the specific message which its form conveys. What will interest the semiotician is not the truth or falsity of the claims made by the discourse (7), but rather **how** any appearance of objectivity is created and communicated. It is at this point that the semiotician will, indeed, have recourse to logical relationships akin to those which Kelsen himself deploys.

The semiotician's lack of commitment to the concept of an objective, normative order, other than as forming the content of a message which is communicated, stems from his scepticism not only at the positivist conception of 'objectivity' but also at the radical separation of fact and norm which underlies the conception of a 'normative order'. (8) One does not have to ascend to the level of the **'Grundnorm'** in order to see the difference between Kelsen and the semioticians. For the latter do not endorse the strict differentiation between 'is' and 'ought', insisted on by Kelsen (1967:5ff.). Even at the more mundane levels of the interpretation by a judge of a particular 'social event' as falling within the legal universe, or the production of legislative discourse in conformity with the **énoncés qualificatifs** and **énoncés fonctionnels** which establish the legislator as an authority possessing that power, the semiotician adheres to an analysis which accords to the rules or norms no status different from that of any other communicative statements. Such norms, rules or conventions are descriptions of statements reflecting the desires of their authors, or the collective wishes of a society. Any parallel drawn between the semioticians' meta-language and the Kelsenian hierarchy of norms must be viewed in the light of this basic philosophical difference. Even the rules of a legal meta-language are not 'norms' in Kelsen's sense.

In another respect, however, the positivist methodologies of G/L and Kelsen lead them in a similar direction. Kelsen seeks to maintain his normative theory 'pure' of non-normative factors, such as psychologism. Although cognitive processes are accepted as a necessary part of the interpretation processes inherent in the creation and application of norms, the objective meaning which characterises legal validity is not, and cannot be for Kelsen, dependent upon such cognitive states. Such cognitive factors exist in the realm of 'is', while the relations between norms can exist only in the realm of 'ought'; it is logically impermissible to derive the latter from the former.

Semioticians also seek to avoid psychologism, but for entirely different reasons. The normative element in Kelsen's theory is reduced by them to a communicational process - the visible transfer of messages, not merely the psychological states of the authors and receivers of those messages. **(9)** Similarly, the cognitive processes which Kelsen accepts as necessarily involved in interpretation are discounted by semioticians of the school of Greimas except in so far as they appear in the communicational process, as part of the perceptible discourse. The semiotic approach of Greimas and his school can thus also be labelled a 'pure' theory of law. But it seeks to be a purely communicational, not a purely normative theory.

6.2 SEMIOTICS AND JURISPRUDENTIAL NATURALISM

If the positivism of G/L is to be located at the methodological level, and particularly in the definition of the object of study, their 'naturalism' emerges in the universalistic claims they make for the underlying semiotic structures, those of the 'narrative grammar', which make the discourse meaningful at all. For here, we come closest to the structuralism of Lévi-Strauss, in seeking to identify 'Les structures élémentaires de la signification'. **(10)** The search for such basic, universal structures of signification can be viewed as a manifestation of the naturalist tradition, insofar as it locates such universals within human nature itself. **(11)** Thus, G/L describe the narrative structures as 'presenting themselves in the form of explicit or implicit reports (récits) which, while appearing as if more or less spontaneously produced, do in fact recur from one text to another, from one semiotic to another, from one culture to another. Despite important structural and functional differences, these recurrent narratives appear as subject to a system of organisational regulation, so that they can be assessed in terms of a general narrative grammar.' That general narrative grammar 'may be considered as a form of organisation of the human spirit' (une forme d'organisation de l'imaginaire humain). (12)

Narrative grammar is organised through binary oppositional structures, which combine in regular fashion along both syntagmatic and paradigmatic axes. These structures, however, do not determine the level of manifestation of the text. Rather, they impose 'semiotic constraints', within which historical factors, such as ideology, may influence the choice of what is possible. They 'provide a grid opening new possibilities of interpretation that the 'naive' reader could have overlooked and eliminating others because they are not coherent with the text system' (Bastide). It is these same structures which underlie the meaningfulness of modal statements, wherein 'modal values' are communicated and transferred. Narrative grammar thus imposes 'semiotic constraints' on all types of discourse. That does not mean that it itself generates or requires any particular kind of discourse, nor does it imply that such constraints as go back to 'l'imaginaire humain' are the only operative constraints. Indeed, there is no need to see here any opposition between individualistic and social conceptions of the human spirit. (13) Greimasian semiotics thus has no quarrel with legal positivism in respect of the claim of the latter that the sources of law are social, i.e. that law emanates from human beings in society through the use of the institutions human beings have set up for those purposes. (14) For example, Carrion-Wam affirms that the problem for the semiotician is how the linguistically expressed appearance of the legal phenomenon is produced 'in our own social and institutional experience' of the language. The point of divergence is rather the analysis of the institutions used to recognise the law. The positivist legal philosopher insists on giving a normative account of them; the semiotician views the institutions as he finds them in the discourse, as communicational instruments.

In the light of this, it may be argued that any 'naturalist' claims of Greimasian narrative grammar are irrelevant to legal philosophy. The latter seeks to analyse the 'nature' of law by locating it within a particular genus of phenomena, and by differentiating it from other species of that genus. Hart, while he objects to definition per genus et differentiam as a method of legal philosophy, nevertheless seeks to elucidate the central characteristics of law by first locating legal rules as a species of social rules (and analysing the latter), and then by differentiating legal rules from other types of social rules. Even at the level of the genus, it may be argued, there is no place for structuralist naturalism, in that our conception of 'social rules' is not generated by the universals of human nature, but may be culturally contingent. The positivist could even concede the claims of Greimasian narrative grammar, but still claim its irrelevance to legal philosophy. The legal philosopher, he might argue, does not purport to provide an account of everything that contributes to the workings of a legal system. If he did, then legal philosophy would have to incorporate virtually every science known to man. For there would be no human law without human biology, no human law without the laws of thermodynamics, etc., given that the workings of the legal system presupposes the existence of men and of the material world in which they live. At a more mundane level, they might claim, there is no need to incorporate Chomskian syntactic structures within legal philosophy, just because law uses instruments which include syntactically well-formed sentences. On the same argument, narrative grammar may or may not contribute to the generation of legal texts, but it has nothing to do with what makes those texts legal.

To this line of argument, there are two types of reply. The first is that such a legal philosopher himself constructs both the specificity of his object of study, and attaches an implicit value to it. Whether we operate at the level of 'Law', 'the legal system', or 'a law', the claim to the kind of specificity which the positivist legal philosopher speaks (normativity, objectivity, as discussed in the last section) rests purely and simply on what that legal philosopher wants to find. In short, the autonomy of the legal object is a product of values and ideology. The fact that this appears to many to be a surprising and radical proposition only attests to the success of legal ideology in making a particular cultural form appear natural.

A second response involves further consideration of the relationship between 'narrative grammar' and what G/L call 'legal grammar'. In introducing the former concept, they observe that 'legal grammar' is not the only grammar which regulates legal discourse and that we encounter, side by side with it, numerous manifestations of narrative grammar (94). That might still seem to leave the door open to an argument that it is the legal grammar, representing a particular legal culture, which make this discourse recognisable as legal. But that is hardly the effect of G/L's analysis. As we have seen, what they describe as the 'legal grammar' is part of the message which the text seeks to convey. The discourse claims the existence of a metalanguage, for example, with which the judge is able to effect **vérification juridique**; that implies no factual prediction that this is indeed the set of rules which the judge will apply. Moreover, the 'legal grammar', as part of the content of the text, is itself made intelligible through the workings of narrative grammar. We have seen several important examples: the manner in which both legislator and judge, like the SC itself, are constituted as semiotic objects, and the roles which they variously play in the narrative algorithm.

In short, narrative grammar contributes to our understanding of how legal discourse works. If we adopt a truly positivist methodology in defining the object of study, we have to conclude that legal philosophy is nothing other than the study of legal discourse. Universal semiotic constraints may not provide a sufficient account of how the text works, but they provide a necessary part of that account. G/L do not themselves attempt to tell us why it is necessary. (Perhaps that was not part of their mandate from the Paris Chamber of Commerce and Industry.) But two preliminary suggestions may here be made. First, the formalisation of the paradigmatic level in terms of combinations of binary oppositions, and the analysis of those binary oppositions, can assist materially in identifying the place of legal discourse as between the traditions of 'logic' and 'rhetoric'. **(15)** Here, indeed, we have a parallel to Hart's type of quest. Secondly, the universals proposed at the syntagmatic level of narrative grammar provide us with the germs of an alternative philosophy of action to that of contemporary analytical philosophy, with which contemporary positivism increasingly aligns itself. **(16)** It would hardly be far-fetched to construct such an alternative philosophy of action on the basis of the narrative algorithm, and to apply it to the individual human action and not merely to such sequences of action as make up a 'story' or 'plot'. Such an alternative philosophy of action would be more comprehensive than that of analytical philosophy. It would stress the essential places of goal-formation, competence and recognition of past action (through retrospection - whether institutionalised or not), as well as the decision to act on a goal and the performance of the act. It would attend also to both the unconscious sources of human action, and its underlying constraints.

Thus, 'recognition' is a vital element in the semiotic model. In narrative, attention is directed not merely to the setting-up of goals, the achieving of the competence to perform those goals, and the acts which constitute their acievement, but also to the recognition of those acts as having achieved those goals. The same is true of law. Narrative, economics and law may all have their different internal forms of recognition (or verification). In the context of the SC, more than one form may be involved: the recognition of the achievement of economic objectives, and the recognition of their achievement as legal. But the structure of recognition, and its place in the narrative algorithm, are the same. Of course, 'rules of recognition' play a crucial role in the legal theory of Hart. But the Hartian class of 'rules of recognition' includes some rather varying phenomena, which semiotic analysis, with its emphasis upon different communicative roles, may assist us to distinguish.

G/L stress that recognition 'as law' is to be understood as the verification of the incorporation into a particular cultural sub-system of phenomena which were not previously recognised as belonging to it. Here the influence of Lévi-Strauss is apparent. The general process of the appropriation of natural phenomena into human culture, by the communication of messages about them, here receives a particular application. General human culture, including its economic activity, is now regarded as 'nature' ('savage' in that it is not subject to the conventions of the particular legal culture); the legal discourse is concerned with the transformation of such 'nature' into (legal) 'culture' through the communication of particular forms of message about it. Those messages contain the 'rites of initiation' of the general culture into legal culture. They may well be (but need not necessarily be) socially contingent. But they are meaningful in virtue of universal structures of signification, of which we may be only partly conscious.

To accept that these are the directions in which a semiotic naturalism may contribute to legal philosophy does not necessarily entail endorsement of the details of G/L's analysis. The approach may require significant refinement, at both the syntagmatic and paradigmatic levels. Criticism of the Greimasian approach has not been lacking, not least from those associated, to a greater or lesser degree, with French structuralism. Yet at the end of the day, one is left with the impression that something like Greimasian narrative grammar does have a place in the analysis of law, whatever the strength of the criticisms of it as applied to literature. **(17)**

The logical level of Greimasian narrative grammar is a ready target for criticism as a gratuitous metaphysical invention. Bremond suggests that it reflects a 'nostalgie platonicienne', and sees it as redundant (1972:370f.), and Barthes is quoted as having compared the attempt to develop a narrative structure with the activity of 'Buddhists whose aesthetic practices enable them to see a whole landscape in a bean' (McKnight 1978:178f.). But the status of the logical structures as a postulate is not denied by the Greimasian school. In order to understand the procedures of construction and organisation of discourse, Greimas claims that we can and must postulate such logical presuppositions, partly on the basis of analysis of actual discourse, partly from our appreciation of the conditions under which discourse can exist and be produced (1976:12). Calloud similarly speaks of order and form as 'postulated at a deep level' (1979:77).

Legal philosophers are not unfamiliar with such epistemological postulates: Kelsen claimed such a status for his **Grundnorm. (18)** But the postulate is not conceived as immune from scientific testing. Patte writes that the narrative structure 'is common to all narratives in all cultures and is also presupposed by anyone able to recognize meaningful narratives - that is, any human being. A verification of this postulate is a matter of scientific research' (in Calloud 1976:xi). Such 'verification', of course, can hardly involve Popperian falsification. Like Chomskian linguistics, it involves rather the search for the scientifically most powerful explanation, that which will explain the greatest amount of phenomena by means of the simplest possible explanatory structure.

Alternative explanations are not lacking. Ricoeur, for example, seeks to explain the importance of modalities in the narrative sequence as reflecting phenomenological categories, rather than the semiotic square (1980:15). Moreover, the square by its nature is applicable only to semantic units which are at least sufficiently defined to admit of semic analysis. Eco points out that it therefore excludes applicability to the 'fuzzy concepts' studied by Lakoff (Eco 1976:82f.). He contrasts, for this purpose, a statement like 'one sells what one owns and buys what one needs' (no fuzzy concepts), with one like 'anyone who buys receives something while anyone who sells gives something'. Here, however, law may have an advantage over both ordinary language and narrative. We have noted the apparent implication of 'hyponymy' (2.4) as a prominent feature of at least one level of legal semantics, that of its technical terminology. Here, we are unlikely to encounter even that form of 'fuzziness' which is implicit in ordinary binary oppositional structure. It may be necessary to refine the 'logical' level, as applied to law, to take account of that phenomenon.

At the syntagmatic level, there is a common complaint that Greimasian narratology loses the sense of temporality of the narrative; that it reduced it to a taxonomy operating on an achronic matrix. Barthes notes that this is nothing new. Aristotle himself, in his contrast between tragedy and historical narrative, was already giving primacy to the logical over the chronological (citing **Poetics** 1459a). Contemporary researchers like Lévi-Strauss, Greimas, Bremond and Todorov are accused of doing the same, in line with the Lévi-Straussian proposition that 'the order of chronological succession is absorbed in an atemporal matrix structure' (Barthes 1977:98). Ricoeur seeks, by contrast to Greimas, to 're-establish the primacy of plot over structure', accusing Greimas of having used narrative structure to deprive plot of its 'master role' in narrative (Ricoeur 1981:280). For Ricoeur, alternative action and the possibility of failure are as essential to the narrative as the actual action. Whereas for Greimas competence and performance are merely median points in the narrative algorithm between the beginning of the story and its end, for Ricoeur it is the quest which is central. The quest cannot be reduced to finite atemporal states, and this shows that the diachronic cannot be absorbed into an achronic reading (1981:285). This illustrates nicely the difference between an approach based on structural semantics, and one reflecting a psychologically-oriented action theory. **(19)** Greimasian narratology is not insensitive to this kind of criticism, and Greimas has himself suggested that narrative is susceptible to a 'double interpretation', on the one hand atemporal and reflecting the logical model, on the other hand diachronic, reflecting the succession of human actions in the text-sequence. **(20)** But it is unclear whether this alternative interpretation is regarded as independent of the 'superficial level', and of the implication of that level with the logical structure. **(21)**

One theme that runs through many of the criticisms of Greimasian semiotics is a rejection of any conception of the 'prison-house of language' (Jameson 1972). The autonomy of the text, and the semiotic constraints which operate through it, are perceived as unacceptable restraints on human liberty, an intolerable form of determinism. The offence is all the more great when applied to an activity (literature) which is taken to epitomise human creativity. Thus Bremond stoutly denies that liberty, truth and beauty are illusions created by the narrative which serve only to mask the play of semiotic constraints. If there is a game, he argues, it is not subject to, but rather operates upon those constraints. Literature can thus be a liberating experience which exploits and surmounts literary rules (1972:381f.). But when we turn to law, we are confronted with forms of social organisation, not of individual artistic expression. Traditional legal theory has its own version already of the structural constraints which define the system. If we substitute a semiotic for a normative ontology, we may still find that something like the Greimasian semiotic structures have a vital role to play in explaining how the system works.

6.3 SEMIOTICS AND LEGAL REALISM

Some have taken the Greimasian methodological restriction to the text as the object of study, together with his highly formal account of its underlying semiotic processes, as standing in the way of a 'realist' view of any discourse, whether it be legal or narrative. Eco expresses this view with particular reference to the isolation of the Greimasian functions from the socio-cultural context of the text: 'The functions of plot acquire value only when measured against the value systems of a given group. A fact cannot be defined as "unexpected" if we do not know the **systems of expectation** of the addressee. Thus even the researchers into the structure of narration refer to a socio-historical definition of semantic structures' (1976:145 n.10). In other words, the oppositional structure need not necessarily be a universal of the human mind or, on a different level, a peculiarity of a particular text; it may reflect social rules or conventions which are extra-textual (if not extra-linguistic in character). Greimas, however, does claim that the narrative model uses categories derived from social structure: 'The fact of defining the narrative **énoncé** and narrative as a whole as a network of relations between **actants** allows for the interpretation of the narrative model at the epistemological level as one of the fundamental forms of the **organization of the imaginary** (cf. psychoanalysis, mythology), whose generality rests, moreover, on the utilization of basic categories derived from social structure (production and exchange, especially)' (1971:799). Recent developments in semiotics, associated particularly with Chabrol and Parret, point towards a **'socio-sémantique discursive'**, which seeks a more integrated view of narrative grammar and socio-linguistics (Landowski 1981:127 col. 2). Carzo, too, sees in 'semio-sociology' a tool for the demystification of the power of normative discourse (1983:65).

Others offer a more fundamental objection. Benveniste takes the view that discourse beyond the level of the sentence is free from linguistic and semiotic constraints, and 'exclusively manifests the interaction of the speaker with his "situation in life" . . (so that) speaking of the linguistic or structural laws which govern the creation of discourses is a contradiction in terms.' **(22)** However, treating the text as an autonomous semiotic unit does not exclude - either in theory or in practice - consideration of the non-linguistic dimensions of the text, on the socio-linguistic, ideological, historical or personal levels. Indeed, the concern of the semiotician is in large part with **how** these factors are communicated, or - what may be equally significant - how they are concealed in the discourse. To those who argue that socio-economic realities may not be inscribed in the discourse, the Greimasian response would be couched in methodological terms. If it is not inscribed in this particular discourse, it may be inscribed in another.

Preliminary Conclusions for Legal Theory

The range of discourse which may be the subject of semiotic study is not necessarily limited to formal legal documents. That such documents are 'formal' and 'legal' is precisely part of the message which their form conveys. Greimasian semiotics would therefore require socio-economic realities to be revealed by some object or other of semiotic study. It is here that its reductionism is most open to question. Since all human culture (including, following Lévi-Strauss, systems of kinship and exchange) are to be viewed as systems of communication, any socio-economic realities which are not so communicated fail even to be considered. But following a 'pure' positivist methodology (6.1), it might be argued that if such 'realities' fail to be manifested (even through structural analysis), we are hardly entitled to assert their existence. **(23)** In making such an assertion, are we not falling into exactly the same trap as that which reifies 'Law', 'the legal system' or even 'a law' ? **(24)**

When we turn back to G/L's account of what is happening in the text (rather than why it is happening) we find much in common with 'realist' approaches in legal philosophy. We find a similar scepticism about the ontological claims of positivism, the existence of a separate 'normative' universe, characterised by its own particular form of truth - legal validity. The approach of semiotics, however, is not to dismiss the normative sphere as either fiction or mystification, but rather to analyse what kind of message is thereby being communicated. **(25)** As we have seen, G/L regard prescriptive language not as a separate language-form but rather as the transference of a particular kind of semiotic object, the modal value (section 4.4 above). In this context, even forms of competence take their place in the narrative algorithm. It is simply a question of who conveys what particular modal values (power, knowledge) to whom. The discourse may indeed establish a particular syntax for the creation of objects which convey meaning within law: in this sense 'use in legislation' is from the semiotic point of view a purely arbitrary sign that what has been named belongs to the legal system; it creates no 'normative' entity on that account. Similarly, in the case of duties and restrictions on powers. When the 1966 Loi lays down the limits of the legal competence of the SC, it does not create a particular normative entity, but rather appears in the discourse as sending a particular message to the SC, which provides the latter with its 'contract'. The semiotician does not suggest that the SC, viewed as receiver, has the capacity to decline the 'contract' sent to him by the legislator. This latter contract is not merely a contract of adhesion; it is an offer which the SC cannot refuse. Nevertheless, the semiotician avoids a hierarchical presentation, in that he sees the law, in the shape of the legislator, as itself an **actant** participating in the actantial model at the same syntagmatic level as the **sujet** which is to be invested with (legally legitimate) goals. If 'will' is transformed into 'duty', this is conceived by the semiotician as a process of communication, and not as a process of imputation. The semiotician may regard the claims of the positivist as the semiotic appearance which it is his task to explain. But he seeks to explain it in a different frame of reference. In this, he stands shoulder to shoulder with legal realists and sociologists of law, and in opposition to 'pure', normative or deontic theories. The independence of 'ought' from 'is' is itself a semiotic appearance.

Such a denial of positivist ontological claims has been a feature of Scandinavian legal realism in particular; so too has an interest in legal language. **(26)** The American approach, by contrast, has been more concerned with the realities of legal practice. Here too, comparison may be made with G/L's analysis. Even though their concern is purely with a legislative text, they acknowledge that the legislative discourse remains 'virtual' until actualised by judicial application. Similarly, the American Realist Gray argued that legislation was not itself law, but only a source of law **(27)** - a view which Kelsen set out to contest, but which ultimately even he seems forced to concede. **(28)** The merit of this particular argument need not unduly concern us; legislation may well in fact be acted upon as law quite outside the judicial process. Even so, G/L's insistence that the process of application of law involves the institution of a separate semiotic object, the judge, and the activity of that semiotic object in **vérification juridique,** provides a semiotic version of the argument that there is no necessary connection between what the judge actually recognises and that which the legislator communicates to him.

Throughout their account, G/L stress the appearance which the text conveys. Legislation claims a dominance over social life. For example, it is in the form as constituted by the text, and only in that form, that the company will function in social life. The fact that this claim may require substantial qualification when tested against the empirical data of social life does not detract from the importance of the claim which the text is making. Like legal realism and legal sociology, legal semiotics is highly sensitive to the potential divide between appearance and reality. But unlike some forms of legal realism and legal sociology, it avoids the mistake of dismissing the claim in so far as it falls short of reality. The claim itself is important, and may have its own effects in social life. The semiotician is therefore particularly interested in **how** the claim is communicated. **(29)**

In various ways, the form of the legislative discourse also communicates claims about the legal system. The use of a performative speech act which installs a conventional and explicit world order, the use of prescriptive and prohibitory rules in order to limit the precise functions of the entities which the discourse calls into existence - all this creates the appearance of a solid, immobile structure; the immutability of law is thus communicated as one of the principal connotations of the text (1976:90f.). Again, the fact that the legislation uses words which have their origin in the natural language, without (for the most part) explicitly defining them, conceals the function of the legislator in constructing the legal lexicon; it reinforces the conventional view (whose background lies in jurisprudential naturalism) that legal language exists prior to and independent of legislation, while legislation merely organises that language and chooses the specific messages it will convey. Legal language, in reality a cultural construction, is itself made to appear natural, self-evident. The adoption of 'explicit statement' as the arbitrary sign of membership of a legal system (the syntactic rule of the legal grammar) produces the appearance of a system characterised by public knowledge and lack of ambiguity; the grammar of other social semiotic systems, by contrast, remains implicit, underlying the discourse which it produces. **(30)** The explicit character of the legal grammar itself involves a claim that the law is not only known to all, but also that as the product of a well-formed grammar, it leaves no place for ambiguity (1976:87f.). Explicitness also conveys the impression of comprehensiveness: **production juridique** implies the exclusive existence of a **univers juridique présent,** a 'positive' set of legal terms and concepts

(87), so that that which is not said does not exist (89). This, once again, is part of the appearance the text conveys; G/L imply no endorsement of the truth-claims of the message.

G/L's remarks regarding the illusion of the pre-existence of legal terminology, by contrast with the fact of its construction by the legislator, go beyond the issue of the mere installation of sound-images (**signifiants**) as part of the legal lexicon. Also involved is the vexed theoretical question of the status of the referent. This turns out to be more than a theoretical question for general linguistics; a particular view of the referent - specifically, the extensional view - is communicated by the language. The appearance is created that the phenomena named within the text possess a natural (or social) reality, which it is the role of law only to organise. But as far as the universe of legal meaning is concerned, it is by the explicit act of naming alone that the legislator brings the company into existence. The law does not 'refer' to phenomena existing outside it. Despite the impression which it creates, that it transforms a situation of unregulated outside phenomena (nature) into a state of regulated outside phenomena (culture), it is the legal discourse itself which creates the phenomena from above. At best, the legislative discourse may refer to other types of discourse, both conventionally called legal and non-legal. But the appearance of a direct reference from one set of discourse to the external world is an illusion. For Greimas, semiotic relations do not work in this way.

The very monosemicity of the legal language (**31**) is itself regarded by Greimas as a form of discourse, which, by presenting the appearance of scientific hardness, performs a rhetorical function (1976:36f.).

The form of the legislative discourse also conveys messages regarding the nature of the judicial function. The rules contained in the statute are presented as self-evidently legal, by virtue of the fact that they follow an explicit performative act, the enactment formula. It follows that the acceptance of them by the judge as legal is merely 'verification' of their self-evident, pre-existent legal status. This, once again, is the appearance or claim which the legislative discourse makes; we are not required to endorse that claim.

A similar argument may be made in respect of judicial interpretation of the legislative rules. Their appearance as unambiguous and comprehensive implies a mechanical or deductive process on the part of the judge. To use the terminology of Hart, most cases will fall within the 'core of settled meaning', and thus be 'easy' (32); they will not therefore involve the exercise by the judge of a discretion. Such assumptions have long been challenged by Realists. (33)

6.4 CONCLUSION

Greimasian semiotics points the way towards a satisfactory integration of positivist, naturalist, and realist viewpoints. But from those traditions, it deploys a highly selective group of insights, assigning to each a role (or function) in its own model of a theory of law. From positivism, it takes the methodological restriction of the object of enquiry - a text, or collection of texts; from naturalism it derives an epistemological model, the postulation of universal categories of signification; from realism, it derives a scepticism regarding the ontological claims (traditional in both positivism and naturalism) of constructed semiotic objects, together with a concern to describe (without endorsing) that which it finds in the communicational process which makes up the law. But these three functions do not directly generate each other. The 'realist' views noted in 6.3 do not flow directly from the epistemological claims of 'narrative grammar' (6.2); they derive largely from the 'surface' characteristics of the text, and would be endorsed by many who regard as an irrelevance the formalisation of semiotic universals. Nevertheless, 'narrative grammar' does direct our attention to facets of the text which may otherwise lie unnoticed - for example, the fact of concealment of the institution of goals - and may in this way serve to broaden the horizons of legal philosophy by bringing it into contact with a more comprehensive model of action than that which much currently legal philosophy tacitly endorses.

PART THREE

Semiotic Presuppositions of Legal Theorists

CHAPTER SEVEN

Hart and the Semiotics of Legal Rules

(7.1) Hart's Philosophy of Language: An early definition of 'meaning' by Hart (anticipating Grice) shows his emphasis on the communication of authorial/speaker's intention. The referent of legal language is that to which the speaker intends to refer. It is a referent in the outside world, thus allowing Hart also to endorse a theory of truth-conditions. The Preface to **The Concept of Law** illustrates the tensions in Hart's thought between truth-conditions and a conception of meaning more influenced by pragmatics. Here, ordinary usage and social situation appear primarily as constituting the subject-matter to which analytical jurisprudence is to address itself. **(7.2) The Core of Settled Meaning:** Hart's account of the 'core of settled meaning', despite its formulation, is predominantly pragmatic rather than semantic in character: it assumes as its context the activity of interpretation in particular cases. The distribution and strength of the core derive from social values, not linguistics. Ross points the way to a better integration of linguistic system and interpretative context, which indiates the 'choice' made even when context is taken for grant. **(7.3) The Penumbra of Uncertainty and Hart's Communicational Model:** Hart places his conception of meaning within a communicational model, which takes account of different communicational contexts. This allows him to regard some forms of indeterminacy as themselves reflecting authorial intention, in the light of particular circumstances. Where indeterminacy results from a purely linguistic penumbra, Hart (unlike MacCormick) regards it as representing a 'crisis in communication', not a resource for the judge.

7.1 HART'S PHILOSOPHY OF LANGUAGE

Amongst contemporary positivist legal philosophers, H.L.A. Hart has dealt most explicitly with questions relating to the nature of law as a semiotic system. But he approaches the matter not from the perspectives of general linguistics (much less semiotics), but rather from those of the philosophy of language, particularly those strands associated with Wittgenstein (1) and J.L. Austin. His treatment of the language of law is selective, oriented towards the questions posed in the philosophical tradition from which he stems. He is noted for his analysis of two issues in particular. First, he opposes the use of 'definition' as a form of enquiry into the theory of law; second, he adopts a semantic theory, wherein general terms display in their use a 'core of settled meaning' surrounded by a 'penumbra of uncertainty', together with what I here describe as a 'communicational model' of law, tied to the purposes of the users of language. These two issues reflect, respectively, a Wittgensteinian view of semantics - invoked by Hart when he opposes 'definition' in the name of Wittgensteinian 'family resemblances' (2) - and that philosophy of action reflected by the 'speech act' tradition of J.L. Austin. (3)

The linguistic philosophy deployed by Hart stands in some important respects at the opposite end of the spectrum of semiotic theories from that of Greimas. He is interested in communication, viewed as a consciously intentional act, and not in signification. He adopts ordinary language assumptions regarding the relationship between words and external referents. He regards the contexts of language use as integral to the understanding of 'meaning'. He attributes no autonomy to the legal text, or to the legal lexicon which it establishes. He is unconcerned with the semiotic presuppositions of the communication of meaning. In short, he sees no reason to go beyond the 'surface' level of the way people actually think and talk about the law, and every reason not to do so. The actions of people, inspired by their intentions, are what count.

Yet Hart would not and could not deny the presence of a linguistic 'system' which the actors need to use in order to achieve their communicational ends. Mere individualistic willing and acting would not be sufficient; the ends may be achieved only through adhering to the rules of a system (like those of a game) which provide the means by which the ends may be achieved. Hart accepts that language operates like other forms of social rule, instituted by convention. But beyond this, he pays relatively little attention to the nature of the system which is employed. Like law itself, the language of law is conceived as a purely neutral tool, which may be more or less efficient, but which can otherwise be valued only in terms of the objectives of those who use it.

Hart does not put forward an explicit and systematic philosophy of language. But he does take some strong positions on some of the crucial issues which are needed to construct such a philosophy. In particular, he gives a very particular account of 'meaning', implies a position on the relations between semantics and pragmatics, takes a conventional view of 'reference', and identifies the specificity of a certain class of legal concepts, while at the same time according a privileged place to the evidence of 'ordinary language' in elucidating the central concepts of jurisprudence. A full account of Hart's philosophy of language would attend to the place of each of these contributions in the general development of his thought, and in the intellectual context of the particular debates in which they were generated. Here, it is proposed instead to take a synoptic view, notwithstanding the underlying tensions which need to be resolved if a systematic philosophy of language is to be constructed from them. **(4)**

Meaning

For Hart 'meaning' entails the communication of not merely that which the speaker intends, but also the fact that he intends it. This was stated as early as 1952, in a review of John Holloway's **Language and Intelligence:**

> Before we speak of a person meaning something by a statement, it must be true not merely (i) that he uttered noises and those were in fact interpreted as signs and not merely (ii) that he intended the noises to be interpreted as signs, but that he should intend the listener not merely to believe or to do something but to recognise from the utterance that **he intended** the listener to believe or do something. Thus two notions

> are essential to an analysis of the meaning and understanding of words though irrelevant to a similar analysis of signs. The first is that of the listener recognising from the speaker's utterance the speaker's **intention** that he should respond (e.g. believe or do something) in certain ways, **but recognising it without necessarily responding in these ways;** the second is that of the speaker intending when he uses words that the listener should **thus** recognise his intention. (5)

We may note in this that Hart impliedly equates what is meant when 'we speak of a **person meaning** something by a statement' with 'an analysis of the meaning and understanding of words'. There is here a refusal to detach the meaning of the words from the act (and intention) of the person uttering those words. Hart thus anticipates by five years the well-known theory of Grice (1957) to this effect; and in **The Concept of Law** (1961:235) he cites both Grice and his own earlier article in support of the necessity, in accounting for an imperative utterance, that 'the speaker should intend the person addressed to recognize that this is his purpose in speaking and to be influenced thereby to act as the speaker desires.' (6)

Such an account of 'meaning' has not been universally approved, even within linguistic philosophy itself. As long ago as 1958, Alf Ross criticised attempts to interpret statutory language in terms of legislative purpose: 'in legal rules concerning our central legal institutions, deeply rooted in cultural tradition, it often seems impossible to discern any purpose . . . The fact is that the fundamental legal institutions exist as cultural postulates of their own right, and not because they serve any social purpose' (147). Strawson has similarly concluded that the Gricean analysis becomes ever more inappropriate as one enters the region of institutionalised procedures, because of the difficulty of isolating the audience to whom the utterer is to be taken to intend to address his message (1964:455). Searle too seeks to develop and refine J.L. Austin's account of the notion of an illocutionary act in terms of Grice's analysis of meaning. (7) He goes further than Strawson, in questioning whether even 'such basic illocutionary notions as statement, request, promise, etc.' can be explicated without employing such notions as rule or convention, but employing only the concepts of intention, response, procedure, etc. (1971:9).

This argument, of course, goes beyond the mere claim that the language we use in communicating our intentions is rule-governed, in the sense that its semantics are structured **(8)**; it maintains that it is not only the semantics of the words used in the utterance which are rule-governed, but also their pragmatics - in the form of the institutionalisation of the speech act itself. Significantly, Hervey sees a parallel here with the notion of 'notificative indication' of Luis Prieto. **(9)** We are dealing, he observes, with a typical 'I-know-that-you-know' situation: 'each must be aware that they are "playing the same game" according to the same constitutive rules, with the aim of communicating - unless this intention is clear to both parties, a deliberate act of reference cannot be made' (1982:116).

Despite the fact that law involves the use of the most institutionalised forms of speech act, Hart himself says little to qualify his intention-response conception of meaning; indeed, he even explains interpretation in 'plain' cases in terms of 'general agreement in judgments as to the applicability of the classifying terms' (1961:123) - agreement here being the convergence of the wills of the judges, rather than underlying conventions.

The intention-response conception of meaning leads to a purely extensional view of the referent of legal language, as a function of the intention of the utterer, not of the words themselves. **(10)** It is this view which underlies Hart's description of the difficulties of defining abstract legal concepts, through the traditional process **per genus et differentiam.** The latter is available only where there exists a clear external referent. Thus, an elephant can be defined as a 'quadruped (the **genus**) distinguished from others by its possession of a thick skin, tusks and trunk' and a triangle can be defined as a 'three-sided rectilinear figure . . the supposition that a general expression can be defined in this way rests on the tacit assumption that all the instances of **what is to be defined** as triangles and elephants have common characteristics which are signified by the expression defined' (1961:15, emphasis supplied). By contrast, 'the first efforts to define words like "corporation" "right" or "duty" reveal that these do not have the straightforward connexion with counterparts in the world of fact which most ordinary words have and to which we appeal in our definition of ordinary words. There is nothing which simply "corresponds" to these legal words . . .' **(11)** But in fact the constructed nature of the referent is not unfamiliar to semanticians (Baldinger 1980:39), and is less atypical of ordinary language than Hart supposes. More important, Hart notes that 'whereas the definitional question "what is a corporation ?" leads only to philosophical perplexities, we are quite able to describe the use of the concept of corporation embodied in a complete legal (normative) utterance" (1953:17-21). We can do so by 'specifying the conditions under which such statements are true and the manner in which they are used' (1953:21).

The extensional conception of the referent is clear from this. It is possible to specify the conditions under which a statement is true only by reference to the outside world; truth-claims, by contrast, have no part to play in purely intensional conceptions of language, such as that represented by Greimasian semiotics. Moreover, it is clear that when Hart talks about the manner in which the statements are used, he has in mind the goals of the speakers in relation to action in the outside world. But it is difficult to marry such a truth-conditions conception of meaning with one based upon authorial intention. The conditions under which the statements are true may simply not correspond to the manner in which they are used. **(12)** This same tension is reflected in Hart's brief statement of his methodology, in the much-discussed Preface to **The Concept of Law.**

Ordinary Language, Analytical Jurisprudence and Descriptive Sociology

A clue to Hart's resolution of this tension may be found in the structure of the Preface to **The Concept of Law,** a statement whose brevity is in inverse proportion to the commentary which it has attracted. **(13)** Within the general aim of furthering 'the understanding of law, coercion, and morality as different but related social phenomena', Hart distinguishes (in separate paragraphs) two distinct enterprises. 'The lawyer will regard the book as an essay in analytical jurisprudence, for it is concerned with the clarification of the general framework of legal thought.' The next paragraph commences: 'Notwithstanding its concern with analysis the book may also be regarded as an essay in descriptive sociology.' It is in the latter context that ordinary language method is to be invoked: 'Many important distinctions, which are not immediately obvious, between types of social situation or relationships may best be brought to light by an examination of the standard uses of the relevant expressions and of the way in which these depend on a social context, itself often left unstated. In this field of study it is particularly true that we may use, as Professor J.L. Austin said, "a sharpened awareness of words to sharpen our perception of the phenomena" ' (1961:vii). There seems, then, to be a clear methodological distinction: analytical method is to be used in order to clarify the general framework of legal thought (jurisprudence), while ordinary language method is to be used to throw light on the types of social situation involved (descriptive sociology).

This simple reading of the Preface is challenged by one disturbing fact. What is commonly regarded as one of the leading examples of the use of Hartian ordinary language method - the distinction between 'being obliged' and 'having an obligation' - is adduced in the Preface not in the paragraph on descriptive sociology, but in the context of the analytical endeavour. But when we look at the structure of the argument in this first paragraph, we find that that linguistic distinction is offered not as a means for the clarification of something else (whether analytical or social), but rather as one of a number of 'questions which may well be said to be about the meanings of words'. The linguistic distinction is part of the problem, not the method of its solution. And later in this same paragraph, Hart points to his distinction between 'internal' and 'external' statements about social rules as one of the central themes of the book, and by implication the key to the solution of the linguistic problems listed earlier in the paragraph.

How are these two discrete methods to be integrated within the general aim of the book, as quoted above ? The short answer would appear to be that ordinary linguistic usage provides evidence of distinctions in social situations which are popularly conceived to be significant; and that analytical philosophy can provide (independent) reasons to believe that such popular distinctions are philosophically well-grounded. The privileged status thus given to the ordinary world-view is, in practice, qualified in important respects. First, even if ordinary language is regarded as a legitimate source of hypotheses for analytical jurisprudence, it is certainly not regarded as the exclusive source. Secondly, the distinctions drawn in ordinary language have, at best, a presumptive force, but any such presumption is clearly rebuttable on analytical grounds. Hacker notes and exemplifies both qualifications: 'It is noteworthy that adopting methods of "linguistic analysis" in no way precludes stipulative introduction of technical terminology where necessary (e.g. "primary and secondary rules"), nor explication which intentionally strays from ordinary or even technical-legal use where such explication is justified by its illuminative power (e.g. "legal power", "power conferring rules")' (1977:2). Similarly, the treatment of 'a legal right' in Hart's inaugural lecture is already entirely analytical in character (1953:16f.).

The role which Hart assigns to linguistic analysis is to bring to light important distinctions between types of social situation, such as may not be immediately obvious. This is to be achieved through an examination not only of 'the standard uses of the relevant expressions' but also of 'the way in which these depend on a social context, itself often left unstated'. The conjunction between these two methodological postulates is ambiguous, and the ambiguity reflects the same underlying problem of locating Hart's position on meaning as has been noted already. The ambiguity is revealed by asking whether Hart recommends one method or a choice of two. Must the 'examination of the standard uses of the relevant expressions' always be accompanied by examination 'of the way in which these depend on a social context' (implying a denial of any notion of standard meaning independent of context), or is the study of the social context of linguistic usage merely an optional addition to the examination of the standard uses of the relevant expressions ? **(14)**

The first of these alternatives, which insists that ordinary linguistic usage can itself only be understood by reference to the social context in which it is used, appears to be falsified by Hart's very first use of the method in **The Concept of Law.** He uses ordinary usage in order to negate any equation of the existence of a rule with the mere fact that people generally behave in accordance with it. 'Mere convergence in behaviour between members of a social group may exist (all may regularly drink tea at breakfast or go weekly to the cinema) and yet there may be no rule **requiring** it. The difference between the two social situations of mere convergent behaviour and the existence of a social rule shows itself linguistically. In describing the latter we may, though we need not, make use of certain words which would be misleading if we meant only to assert the former. These are the words 'must', 'should', and 'ought to', which in spite of differences share certain common functions in indicating the presence of a rule requiring certain conduct' (1961:9). This use of the method readily exemplifies the principles recommended in the Preface: 'mere convergent behaviour' and 'the existence of a social rule' are regarded as distinct social situations, the difference between which is important for analytical purposes. Linguistic usage, in the form of modal verbs which may be used where there is a rule but not where there is mere convergent behaviour, provides evidence of the existence of that distinction at the level of social psychology. But Hart does not go on to provide any further account of the 'social context' in which that language is (even ordinarily) used. Moreover, we may note that when he specifies 'the crucial difference between merely convergent habitual behaviour in a social group and the existence of a rule of which the words "must", "should", and "ought to" are often a sign' **(15)**, it is to the opinions of legal theorists that he turns. The distinctions between different types of social situation are thus shown to be 'important' in analytical terms, and not merely because they represent a distinction endorsed by linguistic usage, thereby reflecting a world-view which prevails in a particular linguistic culture.

7.2 THE CORE OF SETTLED MEANING

When he turns to the problems of interpretation, Hart attempts to steer a middle course between 'formalism' on the one hand and 'scepticism' or 'realism' on the other. Interpretation in law ought to involve neither a 'mechanical jurisprudence', which calls for no human choices (1961:125), nor an absence of communication of intelligible general standards, which would amount to anarchy (1961:121). Some middle way is desirable. **(16)** Happily, such a middle way is available to us, and forms an almost inevitable feature of legal interpretation. The 'core of settled meaning' of general terms provides us with the necessary stability and order; their 'penumbra of uncertainty' saves us from the perils of formalism.

Thus stated, it sounds as if Hart is endorsing a highly traditional semantic theory, and that, contrary to his general approach, he is resorting to the characteristics of a **language-system**, rather than to those of **language-use.** There will, he tells us, 'indeed be plain cases constantly recurring in similar contexts to which general expressions are clearly applicable' (1961:123). The very terminology of the 'core' reminds us of the **noyau sémique** of structural semantics, although this is not the source from which Hart took it. (17) Indeed, Hart's views might appear not to conflict with critical comments on the 'speech act' approach to the problem of literal meaning, recently made by Hervey: 'The situation is only aggravated by those exponents of "speech act theory" who, turning things upside-down, insist on seeing the "pragmatic" aspects of semiotic acts (propositional acts, locutionary acts, perlocutionary acts) as being basic to "literal" meanings, and not vice versa' (1982:112). In fact, Hart has been criticised for having adopted 'a naive theory of language in which meaning is a fixed entity with central and peripheral clarity, independent of the context of language and the use of concepts' (Broekman 1975:40).

But such criticism is largely misdirected. Hart does present us with a theory of legal pragmatics, but it is dressed up in semantic clothing. But before this can be shown, it is important to stress a distinction which is reflected in the organisation of Hart's **Concept,** but is only later made explicit. (18) Hart's critical comments on the use of definition, reproducing part of the argument of his inaugural lecture, occur in the first, methodological chapter, concerned with analysis of the question 'What is Law ?' The methodology is taken up again, in particular, in the final chapter, devoted to international law. Most of the book is concerned with this question, which we may call a 'question of meaning': we do use the term 'law' to refer to a widely divergent group of phenomena, all of which reflect the 'complex concept' - 'law'. From the linguistic point of view, Hart's problem is to explain how we unselfconsciously use the term 'law' of those different phenomena. We know the range of external phenomena to which the word can be used to refer. We have the code, but we want to know how it works. Definition **per genus et differentiam** will not help us (19); we have to employ (a version of) the Wittgensteinian notion of 'family resemblance'. We start from the 'paradigm' case of law - the municipal legal system - and identify its central characteristics. We then consider which of these central characteristics are taken away in the non-paradigm cases (such as 'international law') and look at the reasons why, notwithstanding, our code still has us unselfconsciously use the same word.

In Chapter VII of **Concept,** on the other hand, Hart is no longer enquiring into the structures of meaning of an existing code. He is not analysing a pre-existent set of usages of words; rather, he is enquiring into the process of production of a (possibly new) meaning of a word. What I shall call the 'question of interpretation' does not refer to a usage which is already established by convention. The question of interpretation presents itself in a different form from the question of meaning. We are asking not 'what is the meaning of expression/concept X ?' but rather 'does/ought expression X apply to situation Y ?'. We do not know in advance that it does; the question is whether we should make it do so. Notwithstanding this difference, Hart implies in **The Concept of Law** that our problem consists in coping with the distinction between paradigm and non-paradigm cases. He describes difficult cases as those whose 'fact-situations . . . possess only some of the features of the plain cases but others which they lack' (1961:123). **(20)** Such formulations should not, however, lead us to conclude that Hart endorsed any notion that words have an 'inherent' rather than a purely conventional meaning. Where there exists a 'core of undisputed meaning', it is precisely because the meaning has not been disputed. As Lyons has put it: 'Although we may reject the straightforward identification of meaning and use . . . we may yet wish to maintain that the meaning of expressions and sentences is anchored by their characteristic use' (1981:168). Hart takes the same view of judicial interpretation in easy cases: 'The plain case, where the general terms seem to need no interpretation and where the recognition of instances seems unproblematic or "automatic", are only the familar ones, constantly recurring in similar contexts, where there is general agreement in judgments as to the applicability of the classifying terms.' **(21)**

It is in the light of the 'question of interpretation' that Hart seeks both to justify the existence of the 'core' and at the same time deny its absolute character. The existence of a core of settled meaning is based by Hart upon observation of the workings of the legal system: 'Its successful operation over vast areas of social life depends on a widely diffused capacity to recognize particular acts, things, and circumstances as instances of the general classifications that the law makes' (1961:121). MacCormick expresses the point more forcibly: 'For all rules (except very badly drafted ones) there are some clear cases, and for some there are many clear cases. If that were not so, the possibility of any legal system existing anywhere as any sort of guidance of anyone's conduct for any purpose would be nil. Common experience however reveals not merely the possibility but the actuality of legal guidance of behaviour' (1981:125). Here, indeed, the semantic character of legal language is being expressed as a conclusion of the perceived manner in which the language is used, rather than in terms of inherent qualities. It is this same perception of the workings of the legal system which results in the further claim, that the 'core' is in fact dominant over the 'penumbra': '. . . in the vast majority of cases there is very little doubt . . . the life of the law consists to a very large extent in the guidance both of officials and private individuals by determinate rules which, unlike the applications of variable standards, do **not** require from them a fresh judgment from case to case. This salient fact of social life remains true, even though uncertainties may break out as to the applicability of any rule (whether written or communicated by precedent) to a concrete case. Here at the margin of rules and in the fields left open by the theory of precedents, the courts perform a rule-producing function . . ' (22).

Not only is the general need for a 'core' explained in pragmatic terms; so too is its distribution and substantive meaning. Hart notes that different types of use of legal language reflect different social needs: 'the need for certain rules which can, over great areas of conduct, safely be applied by private individuals to themselves without fresh official guidance or weighing up of social issues, and the need to leave open, for later settlement by an informed, official choice, issues which can only be properly appreciated and settled when they arise in a concrete case' (1961:127). Where the need for clear rules is recognised, their content will be clear, not as a contingent effect of the use of certain language, but because the intentions of the authors of those rules are clear. 'Paradigm, clear cases' reflect the extent to which 'our aim in legislating is so far determinate because we have made a certain choice'; the penumbra, on the other hand, reflects the degree to which our aim is (for whatever reason) indeterminate (1961:125f.).

Yet even so, Hart clearly recognises that the core is not absolute, given the nature of the activity of interpretation:

> Legal rules may have a central core of undisputed meaning, and in some cases it may be difficult to imagine a dispute as to the meaning of a rule breaking out. The provision of s.9 of the Wills Act 1837 that there must be two witnesses to a will may not seem likely to raise problems of interpretation. Yet all rules have a penumbra of uncertainty where the judge must choose between alternatives. Even the meaning of the innocent-seeming provision of the Wills Act that the testator must **sign** the will may prove doubtful in certain circumstances. What if the testator used a pseudonym ? Or if his hand was guided by another ? Or if he wrote his initials only ? Or if he put his full, correct, name unaided, but at the top of the first page instead of at the bottom of the last ? Would all these cases be 'signing' within the meaning of the legal rule ? (1961:12)

In this passage, Hart comes close to identifying the 'core' with 'meaning' and the 'penumbra' with 'interpretation' as distinguished above. **(23)** In this sense, it is clear that all rules have a penumbra of doubt; but the core of settled meaning appears to be presented as a practical possibility, rather than a conceptual inevitability. Some unforeseen situation may arise which may render doubtful the application of something whose meaning had hitherto been regarded as settled. For the purposes of interpretation, therefore, there is no conceptual inevitability about the notion of a 'settled core'. That would not prevent the semantician from regarding the meaning of those very words as remaining settled, notwithstanding the problem that may have arisen as regards interpretation.

In some areas of the legal system, however, the 'core' may be given a special dominance; it may be taken to override such special contextual features as may arise in particular problems of interpretation. Even there, for Hart, the capacity of legal language to override context is not a property inherent in that language, but rather the result of acts of will on the part of its users (again, a matter of pragmatics). He speaks of administrative regulation on the one hand and the use of very general standards on the other as two techniques consideration of which 'throws into relief the characteristics of those wide areas of conduct which are successfully controlled **ab initio** by rule, requiring specific actions, with only a fringe of open texture, instead of a variable standard. They are characterized by the fact that certain distinguishable actions, events, or states of affairs **are of such practical importance to us,** as things either to avert or bring about, that very few concomitant circumstances **incline us to regard them differently**' (1961:130, emphasis supplied).

Hart was later to confess to some difficulty in accounting for 'what makes a "clear case" clear or makes a general rule obviously and uniquely applicable to a particular case'. (24) But already in 1958, Ross had perhaps pointed the way towards an integration of structural semantics into a predominantly pragmatic account of interpretation. Context and situation were not the only factors determining meaning, even though they may be the most important. There also existed the 'synonymic or systematic plane'. (25) This means that the meaning of the word is determined more precisely if it is compared with other words which can occupy the same place in a sentence and which afford a more comprehensive 'field of meaning' (1958:118). This, clearly, is the Saussurian 'paradigmatic' axis. As for the legal context, Ross rejects the view that 'statutory interpretation can or must take as its starting point the ordinary meaning of the words as warranted by usage . . . Only the context and the desire to find a "good" or "reasonable" meaning in relation to a given situation determines the meaning of the individual words. But the function of the context is often so taken for granted that it escapes attention' (1958:117f.). In other words, there exists in legal interpretation a semantic penetration of the language-system of ordinary language - a penetration which, as Carrion-Wam stresses (5.2 above), necessarily carries an ideological content with it. But when the judge actually applies the plain, 'ordinary', meaning (notwithstanding any presumption that he should do so), it is he who decides on that action, and it is he who is responsible for it. Once again, we see here the underlying tension between the philosophy of action of the analytical school and that of structuralist semiotics. The fact that the judge takes the context for granted, or regards the application of the general term in that context as 'automatic', would not from the viewpoint of a structuralist semiotics negate the claim that the judge had 'decided' to take that view, or that he was (in a sense which Hart, above all, would probably not accept) 'responsible' for that decision. **(26)**

7.3 THE PENUMBRA OF UNCERTAINTY AND HART'S COMMUNICATIONAL MODEL

In chapter VII of **The Concept of Law,** if not elsewhere, a communicational model is prominent. **(27)** The section on 'open texture' commences thus:

> In any large group general rules, standards, and principles must be the main instrument of social control, and not particular directions given to each individual separately. If it were not possible to communicate general standards of conduct, which multitudes of individuals could understand, without further direction, as requiring from them certain conduct when occasion arose, nothing that we now recognize as law could exist . . . Two principal devices, at first sight very different from each other, have been used for the communication of such standards of conduct in advance of the successive occasions on which they are to be applied. One of them makes a maximal and the other a minimal use of general classifying words. The first is typified by what we call legislation and the second by precedent. (1961:121)

When, a little later, Hart comes to explore the particular indeterminacies which characterise precedent, he again describes the problem in terms of a communicational model, 'the communication of general rules by authoritative examples' (1961:131).

The possibility of communicating general standards 'which multitudes of individuals could understand, without further direction' is elsewhere connected directly with the distinction between core and penumbra: **(28)**

> If we are to communicate with each other at all, and if, as in the most elementary form of law, we are to express our intentions that a certain type of behaviour

> be regulated by rules, then the general words we use . . must have some standard instance in which no doubts are felt about their application. There must be a core of settled meaning, but there will be, as well, a penumbra of debatable cases in which words are neither obviously applicable nor obviously ruled out.

Those latter, penumbral cases precipitate

> 'something in the nature of a crisis in communication . . . there are reasons both for and against our use of a general term, and no firm convention or general agreement dictates its use, or, on the other hand, its rejection by the person concerned to classify. If in such cases doubts are to be resolved, something in the nature of a choice between open alternatives must be made by whoever is to resolve them' (1961:123f.)

The notion of communication of general standards involves, for Hart, the transference of the meanings intended to apply to those standards by their originators. **(29)** The use of language of which the sense is determinate (albeit that that determinacy is conventional) reflects that degree of determinacy in the intention of the originators of the rule:

> When we are bold enough to frame some general rule of conduct (e.g. a rule that no vehicle may be taken into the park), the language used in this context fixes necessary conditions **(30)** which anything must satisfy if it is to be within its scope, and certain clear examples of what is certainly within its scope may be present to our minds. They are the paradigm, clear cases (the motor car, the bus, the motor-cycle); and our aim in legislating is so far determinate because we have made a certain choice. We have initially settled the question that peace and quiet in the park is to be maintained at the cost, at any rate, of the exclusion of these things. (1961:125f.)

Hart continues his analysis of the use of general words, by reference to the example of a rule that 'no vehicle may be taken into the park', by noting the inevitable indeterminacy - what we may call 'linguistic indeterminacy' - which attaches to the penumbra of such general words:

> On the other hand, until we have put the general aim of peace in the park into conjunction with those cases which we did not, or perhaps could not, initially envisage (perhaps a toy motor-car electrically propelled) our aim is, in this direction, indeterminate. We have not settled, because we have not anticipated, the question which will be raised by the unenvisaged case when it occurs: whether some degree of peace in the park is to be sacrificed to, or defended against, those children whose pleasure or interest it is to use these things. When the unenvisaged case does arise, we confront the issues at stake and can settle the question by choosing between the competing interests in the way which best satisfies us. In doing so we shall have rendered more determinate our initial aim, and shall incidentally have settled a question as to the meaning, for the purposes of this rule, of a general word. (1961:126)

Here, we may observe some slippage from the strict sense of 'meaning' adopted by Hart in 1952. For here, in the case where authorial intention is absent, 'meaning' becomes something which may be attributed by the receiver.

Such cases of 'linguistic indeterminacy' may be regarded as unmotivated. But this is not merely because the new cases which have arisen were unenvisaged by the original authors; rather, it is because the authors did not adopt this general language **with a view to** the determination of the unenvisaged cases which they anticipated would occur. **(31)** It is this last feature which distinguishes Hart's discussion of such phrases as 'fair rate', 'safe system of work', and the standard of due care in cases of negligence:

> Sometimes the sphere to be legally controlled is recognized from the start as one in which the features of individual cases will vary so much in socially important but unpredictable respects, that uniform rules to be applied from case to case without further official direction cannot usefully be framed by the legislature in advance. Accordingly, to regulate such a sphere the legislature sets up very general standards

> and then delegates to an administrative, rule-making body acquainted with the varying types of case, the task of fashioning rules adapted to their special needs. Thus the legislature may require an industry to maintain certain standards: to charge only a **fair rate** or to provide **safe systems** of work . . . A second similar technique is used where the sphere to be controlled is such that it is impossible to identify a class of specific actions to be uniformly done or foreborne and to make them the subject of a simple rule, yet the range of circumstances, though very varied, covers familiar features of common experience. Here common judgments of what is 'reasonable' can be used by the law. This technique leaves to individuals, subject to correction by a court, the task of weighing up and striking a reasonable balance between the social claims which arise in various unanticipatable forms. (1961:127ff.)

Both of these techniques represent decisions made by the originators of the rules that it is appropriate for them to defer judgment on the cases which they know they themselves are unable to anticipate, but which they realise will (as a general class) occur (1961:127). Here, then, what is communicated is a very limited semantic constraint, plus the intention that the detail should be filled in by others. The two techniques differ only as regards the identity of the person to whom delegated authority is given. In the first technique, it is to some expert administrative agency, which will formulate detailed rules and communicate them on to those subject to the rules; in the second, discretion is said by Hart to be left to the individuals subject to the rules, but subject to subsequent correction by a court. We can distinguish these cases from those of 'linguistic indeterminacy' by calling them 'motivated indeterminacy'.

The role of 'motivated indeterminacy' has been widely recognised, and not in the Common Law world alone. Ejam Mackaay, of the Law Faculty of Montreal, writes that one has the impression that 'normes vagues' which employ terms like 'bonne foi', 'bonnes moeurs', 'ordre public', etc., have been chosen deliberately in order to allow the courts to introduce factors whose nature can only be described in advance in a general manner and which receive their precision only in the concrete context of social life

(1979:35). (32) That such cases are indeed 'motivated' seems to be supported by the particular nature of the linguistic ambiguity which they utilize. Linguistic ambiguity is of two kinds, lexical and syntactic (Palmer 1981:106f.). But the indeterminacy of which Hart here speaks is always lexical, never syntactic. When we encounter a case of syntactic ambiguity, we invariably categorize the case as one of defective drafting; we do not put it down to 'motivated indeterminacy'. (33) .

If a case is to be made for the desirability of 'linguistic indeterminacy', it must be made on entirely different grounds. It is this 'linguistic indeterminacy' which MacCormick seeks to exploit, for the purposes of creative legal argument in 'hard cases':

> (O)ne has to stress that this activity of distinguishing and reconciling ostensibly or potentially conflicting rules takes place within a wider argumentative context which is concerned **inter alia** with values and principles and other standards of conduct. That shows that the Hartian distinction between a rule's 'core of certainty' and 'penumbra of doubt' is by no means an inert and invariant 'given' arising from the purely linguistic properties of rules formulated in ordinary legal language. The possibility of ambiguity in rules is a **resource** available to the judge, who may sometimes have reason to squeeze the 'core' down to the absolute indistinguishable and unavoidable minimum, and at other times in other contexts may have reason to give a broad and liberal reading of the rule so that it captures matters within even its remotest penumbra. (1981:127)

Now this represents a considerable advance on the approach of Hart. For him, 'linguistic indeterminacy' is quite different from 'motivated indeterminacy'. The latter represents a conscious technique, a choice to exploit a particular structural characteristic of language, one might almost say a speech act. But the former is presented by Hart as a limitation, which is inherent in the (unavoidable) use of general terms; he does not associate it with the standards other than rules which he claims operate in the legal system (34), and which MacCormick sees as entering legal argument through the open door of the penumbra.

Linguistic indeterminacy is thus unmotivated, and when MacCormick advocates its exploitation in the course of legal argument, he is advocating a creative use of language in 'interpretation', which has no connection with 'meaning' in the Hartian sense.

The cases of 'motivated indeterminacy' are fully compatible with Hart's communicational model; MacCormick's reinterpretation of the cases of 'linguistic indeterminacy' is not. It is precisely at this point, where MacCormick departs from Hart, that the difference may be seen between communicational and hermeneutic models. **(35)** A communicational model looks at the use made of language (including its 'meaning') from the viewpoint of the author's intention; the hermeneutic approach looks at this use from the viewpoint of the interpreter. **(36)** Both approaches, of course, are used in law, and authorial intention is not necessarily given the primacy in interpretation which Hart's analysis might suggest (cf. Twining and Miers 1982:200f.). But the issue is not merely one of descriptive accuracy. Much turns, for legal theory, on the respective places assigned to 'meaning' and 'interpretation'. Further consideration of these issues is reserved for Part Four.

CHAPTER EIGHT

MacCormick and the Semiotics of Legal Doctrine

(8.1) Legal Institutions and Narrative Syntagms: The temporal and transformative features of MacCormick's institutional rules parallel the Greimasian syntagmatic level of narrative grammar, in respect of 'competence', 'performance' and 'recognition', but differ in the absence of the institution of goals, in viewing recognition in normative rather than descriptive terms, and in a different relationship between competence, performance and recognition. **(8.2) Semiotics and 'Institutional Fact':** MacCormick's notion of 'institutional fact', derived from Searle, should not be understood as a reduction of law to fact. But it does require satisfaction of empirical conditions - patterns of behaviour and groups attributing meaning to them - which Greimasian semiotics would question. The difference is illustrated by reference to impossible or absurd laws. Despite endorsing a Platonic ontology for legal institutions, MacCormick rejects necessary and sufficient conditions for their existence. His dilemma stems from a failure to distinguish legislative and judicial discourse, the former being a formalistic system of meaning, the latter an open system of interpretation. **(8.3) The Semiotic Function of Legal Concepts:** MacCormick regards the semiotic function of legal concepts as primarily doctrinal, forming a convenient method of exposition, which reduces the number and complexity of individual rules which would otherwise need to be stated separately. Such concepts serve the convenience of 'lawyers'. But MacCormick wrongly regards the cognitive and semiotic demands of practitioners and jurists as equivalent. Moreover, the use of classificatory terms may have connotations which go beyond the logical properties which facilitate exposition.

8.1 LEGAL INSTITUTIONS AND NARRATIVE SYNTAGMS

For MacCormick, legal institutions form an essential part of the structure of the legal system. They consist of **sets** of rules, which are respectively institutive, consequential and terminative (1973:5-7). Examples are contracts, rights of ownership, corporations, and marriages - what are more commonly termed 'legal concepts'. But the designation 'legal concepts' does not do justice to the interrelationship of the sets of rules which structure such concepts, sets of rules which (we might say, in pursuing the semiotic parallel) admit of the communication of meaning as legal concepts. Thus, 'the law lays down that on the occurrence of a certain (perhaps complex) act or event a specific instance of the institution in question comes into existence'; those requirements form the 'institutive rule' of the legal concept concerned. Once the legal concept has thus been instituted, it has consequences in law: 'It is possible to consider the law, in so far as it provides for these consequences in relation to any one such institution, as comprising a set of rules', which MacCormick terms 'consequential rules'. Finally, the law must also provide rules governing the termination of the institution at some point in time; such rules are 'terminative rules'.

It is perhaps not insignificant that MacCormick sets out the three classes of rule which make up the institution in this sequence: institutive, consequential, terminative. In so doing, he is following the temporal sequence which necessarily represents the life-history of an instance of the institution (a particular contract, etc.) in practice. The temporal dimension is one which MacCormick himself emphasises: 'Contracts, rights of ownership, corporations, and marriages have temporal, though not spatial existence; they are set up, or as we might say 'instituted', by the performance of some act or the occurrence of some event and they continue in existence until the moment of some further act or event' (1973:5). This parallels the temporal sequence of the syntagmatic level of Greimasian narrative grammar and its application by G/L themselves to the life-history of the SC. The parallel is significant. Like the relations of narrative grammar represented at the syntagmatic level, the sequence institutive-consequential-terminative could have been represented otherwise; specifically, this triad is logically reducible to two classes, since the terminative rules are functionally (and sometimes also in terms of content) no more than the negation of the institutive rules. In his account of legal institutions, MacCormick thus opts for a temporal rather than a logical presentation. (1)

The type of picture of the legal system represented by this view of law as (importantly, if not exclusively) institutional fact also resembles the general character of the syntagmatic level of Greimasian narrative grammar. Narrative is there conceived as a genre which represents life in terms of a sequence of states and transformations. (2) There exist semiotic constraints upon the range of possible states, and the manner in which they may be transformed, these constraints themselves representing the construction of human culture out of nature. So too, within the particular universe of law, legal subjects may be conceived as proceeding through a life-history represented by different legal states and the transformations between them. The 'states' are the various sets of consequential rules, the 'transformations' are the institutive/terminative sets of rules which apply to those states. Each legal institution may be compared to a single 'narrative syntagm', these various narrative syntagms being linked in an overall narrative algorithm. MacCormick sees a similar process of interlocking of institutions in complex chains ('almost like biological molecules': 1973:21). He gives as an example the case of a right of ownership of a piece of land. A person may be instituted as owner. A consequence (the state of ownership) is that he has a power to create a security over that land. Without further acts on his part, he does not exercise the power. But if he does act in the manner prescribed by the institutive rules of the legal institution of security over land, he transforms his position (and that of others) into the new state represented by the consequences of the legal institution of security over land.

This comparison of the narrative grammarian's states and transformations with MacCormick's institutive, terminative and consequential rules illustrates a proposition ventured already earlier, in the light of some of the common criticisms of Greimasian narratology (6.2), namely that the Greimasian approach may be more appropriately applied to law than to literature. Some of the criticisms of Greimasian narratology as over-formalistic appear less telling when applied in the context of law. For whereas the characterisation of life in human culture generally in terms of states and transformations may appear to do less than justice to the diversity and affectivity of human life and personality, it is commonly believed amongst legal philosophers that the characterisation of life in legal culture is indeed a matter of determining whether a particular facet of ordinary life falls inside or outside any number of determinate legal states. **(3)**

When we look at MacCormick's account of 'institutive conditions' (the conditions laid down by the institutive rules in order to establish an instance of the legal institution concerned, with the various legal consequences that entails), we find more specific parallels to the syntagmatic level of Greimasian narratology. These institutive conditions involve 'the types of acts which must be performed, the classes of persons who have 'capacity' to perform them, the procedural formalities if any which must be observed, and the circumstances which are essential to validity of the act together indeed with the circumstances such as duress or error whose presence will vitiate an ostensibly valid act' (1973:13). In the case of institutive rules which give rise to legal powers, they 'must specify what class of people has capacity, or what specifically denominated or appointed person or group has competence, in respect of the institution in question; (it) must specify the requisite act, and any procedural formalities by which it is to be attended; and it must specify the circumstances whose presence is essential to the validity of the act, and any vitiating circumstances whose presence will result in the invalidity of the act. To express it formulaically, the general form of an institutive rule which gives rise to a legal power is: If a person having qualifications **q** performs act **a** by procedure **p** then if the circumstances are **c**, then a valid instance of the institution **i** exists' (1973:19f). **(4)** We see immediately the presupposition that transformations from one legal state to another must be performed by **acts;** comparison may be made with the basic formula of narrative grammar: **F(A).** Further, the person performing the act must be qualified (have 'competence' - a term used both by MacCormick and

Calloud), so that the possession of **q** is a necessary part of the satisfaction of the institutive rules. Here, we are very close to the qualificatory statements of Greimasian narrative grammar, and the notion that the acquisition of competence (in the form of transfer of the modal values of power and/or knowledge) is an essential part of the narrative algorithm. (5) In short, MacCormick's account of legal institutions provides clear parallels to the narrative syntagm's 'competence' and 'performance'.

The final syntagm of the Greimasian narrative algorithm also finds a parallel in MacCormick's account, though less directly. Hart had identified the central characteristics of a legal system as including the 'union of primary and secondary rules'. (6) Amongst those 'secondary rules', Hart gave special prominence to 'rules of recognition'. Such a rule states 'some feature or features possession of which by a suggested rule is taken as a conclusive affirmative indication that it is a rule of the group to be supported by the social pressure it exerts' (1961:92). Rules of recognition thus provide an 'authoritative mark' of the membership of another rule of a 'legal system'. It thus serves, in semiotic terms, like a badge of identity, although for positivist legal theory it has further functions in supporting purely normative conclusions, namely the legal 'validity' of the rule in question.

MacCormick prefers to construe the distinction between primary and secondary rules in terms of that between consequential and institutive/terminative rules (1973:20-2). An important effect of such a view is to relate 'rules of recognition' to the institutive and terminative syntagms of what I may call MacCormick's institutional algorithm. As G/L's account of the 'legal grammar' shows, this has special application in law, where the recognition processes are institutionalised (their **vérification juridique**). The institutive/terminative conditions provide criteria for the recognition of instances of that institution as having that legal status. Not only do they define the modal values which must be transferred in order to create the institutional consequences ('contract' or 'competence'; in anthropomorphic terms, the 'qualifying test'); equally they provide for subsequent authoritative recognition (as by a court) that the acts performed do indeed qualify as instances of the legal institution in question (the Greimasian 'sanction' or 'recognition'; in anthropomorphic terms, the 'glorifying test').

We may use G/L's own example, the **société commerciale** of the 1966 Loi, in order to illustrate this parallel between institutional theory and Greimasian narratology. Such a company would count for MacCormick as a legal institution. The 1966 law creates it as an institution; the actions of people in society create, through their acts ('brute facts'), instances of that institution; and those 'brute facts', understood in the light of the institutional rules, are what MacCormick calls 'institutional fact'. The statute provides both institutive and terminative rules of the legal institution, which state the conditions of its creation and its termination. The institutive rules both define and confer upon an instance of the institution its legal capacity to do that which the law empowers it to do, obliges it to do, or both. But such institutive and terminative rules have another function also. If a dispute arises subsequently regarding the activity of an instance of the institution, a particular SC, then these rules will be used to determine whether the acts of the SC were legally valid. They will serve as an 'authoritative mark' of the character of those acts, a means by which we may recognise whether those acts are legally 'valid' or not. This illustrates, incidentally, a particular mark of positivism itself, in that the legal 'validity' of an institution is defined exclusively in terms of such membership rules, laid down by authority.

G/L's account runs along similar lines. The legislator endows the SC with a competence to act, by the transfer to it of modal values, particularly **pouvoir-faire** and **savoir-faire.** The SC is thereby instituted to act in a way which counts according to the meaning-system of the Law. Subsequently, the judge may be called upon to recognise whether the acts performed by the SC do in fact count within such a meaning-system, through **vérification juridique.** What is missing from G/L's presentation - a very significant 'absence' - is any account of 'validity' as a normative rather than a semiotic characteristic. Normative validity is simply one of the claims made by the text, as is the implication that the institutive rules stated in the law are the exclusive means of creating that semiotic object.

There are also deeper levels of dissimilarity between MacCormick's institutionalism and Greimasian semiotics.

One of the difficulties observed in Hart's theory is the apparent lack of distinction between the use of secondary rules in order to qualify both rules of the system (public law) and acts of legal persons subsumed under those rules (private law). It is, in part, this difficulty which leads MacCormick to seek to re-interpret Hart's 'secondary rules' in institutional terms. MacCormick would say that public law and private law institutions have the same structure, but merely a different content. For example, 'legislation' is a public law institution, the institutive rules for which are provided by the constitution. A contract or a company, by contrast, is a private law institution, the institutive rules of which are provided by legislation or some other recognised source of legal rules. This enables MacCormick, as also Kelsen (7), to adopt a semiotically-sensitive analysis of legal phenomena, while at the same time retaining the notion of a normative hierarchy. If we were to ask MacCormick why the institutive rules of the SC are 'legal', he would refer us to the legal institution 'legislation', of which the 1966 Loi is taken to be an instance. He would say, in other words, that the legal character of the institution is based on a separate set of rules, found outside the text of the legislation itself. By contrast, as we have seen, Greimasian semiotics requires us to view each text as an autonomous unit, making its own claims. For G/L, the legal character of the SC is a claim being made within the text itself, in the enactment formula. Semiotics is unconcerned with the truth of that claim; the only question is whether an instance of the SC will bear the authoritative marks of membership of that particular meaning-system, not any further characterisation of that system as legally 'valid'. Of course, such claims may well be made, and may call for semiotic analysis, in other documents - whether they be overtly political/ideological documents (such as a Declaration of Independence), or apparently 'legal' ones (such as a constitution).

In one respect, however, G/L do not appear to adhere completely to their own methodological postulates. It is in their section on 'legal practice' (1976:90-3) that they provide their general account of **vérification juridique.** It seems to follow from this that the process of verification lies in the hands of the judge, when faced with particular instances of the legal institution SC. In the case of MacCormick, such an analysis raises no theoretical problems. The linguistic presuppositions of the speech act tradition allow for extra-textual reference, so that there is no problem in regarding the attribution of meaning to real acts and events in terms of a set of rules provided in a particular text as a single semiotic process. But Greimas, as we have seen, rejects the notion of an external referent. It is therefore difficult to understand how the qualification of real acts and events by the judge can count as part of the same semiotic process as that contained in the statute. The statute itself may, of course, provide for or indeed require judicial 'verification' of the acts of the SC. But if so, that is simply part of the narrative algorithm of the legislative discourse. Its relationship to judicial discourse on the one hand, and to distinct forms of both legal and non-legal discourse on the other, should count simply as a form of 'inter-semioticity'. In principle, the relationship between that legislative discourse and events in the world should be no different, for G/L, from the relationship between a piece of historical writing and the events which that writing describes (the latter being, for Greimas, a form of 'natural semioticity'), or even between the story in a novel and the activities of people in real life who might choose to 'act out' its story. **(8)**

There does, however, seem to be one important difference between the operation of the narrative algorithm in law and literature. In the latter, the object of 'recognition' is the 'performance'. The task of performing some goal was instituted at the start of the narrative, and at its conclusion there is a need to verify whether that task has indeed been accomplished. The competence of the subject may be a necessary condition of performance of the task, but in narrative it is not a sufficient condition. The subject may have been endowed with competence, but yet fail to achieve the task; conversely, once the task is performed, competence to perform it is presupposed (Bastide). The legal version of the narrative algorithm, which we have modelled upon MacCormick's analysis of legal institutions, is different. Since 'competence' is identified with the satisfaction of institutive/terminative rules, the acquisition of 'competence' is both a necessary and a sufficient condition of the performance of the task. That follows from the normative relationship between the institutive/terminative rules and the consequential rules. It follows, therefore, that 'recognition' may here be directed to the acquisition of that competence (as here broadly defined). Therein may lie one facet of the specificity of law. It is this, in fact, which may provide a semiotic account of the specific normative character which the text claims for its messages.

A more radical difference between law and literature appears to reside in the apparent absence in law of an analogue to the first member of the narrative algorithm: 'manipulation' or 'contract'. This is the stage of the narrative at which goals are set, the task to be performed is defined. Its apparent absence from the analysis of legal institutions is not altogether surprising. MacCormick takes the traditional view of law as a means to an end. The end is not itself a matter of law; it is generated outside the legal system. In fact, this distinction correlates closely with that drawn by MacCormick between the functions of legal and social institutions; the latter function to set goals; their role is in relation to the end, not the means. This provides another clue as to why 'recognition' in law is directed towards 'competence' rather than 'performance'. 'Competence' is a matter of legal means; recognition in law is concerned with the legality of the means, not the legitimacy of the end.

Of course, this distinction between means and end, as expressed by the absence in law of an equivalent to the first member of the narrative algorithm **(9)**, is a matter of the semiotic appearance of law, the message which legal discourse seeks to convey. The very absence **(10)** from the legal discourse of the process of setting the goals is part of the message to be conveyed, that law is a technical instrument, conceptually unrelated to the aims and objectives of the users of the system, the people who set its goals. The absence of 'manipulation' from the text is a powerful means of communication. **(11)**

8.2 SEMIOTICS AND 'INSTITUTIONAL FACT'

One of MacCormick's objectives is to present a view on the proper relationship between legal philosophy and the sociology of law (1973:1). Hence, the emphasis not merely upon 'institutions', but upon 'institutional fact'. Indeed, he goes so far as to claim that 'every legal philosopher and jurisprudent is concerned to see law as fact, although only one, Olivecrona, gave that title to a book' (1973:2). But what are 'institutional facts' ? The concept is taken from Searle, and, as applied by MacCormick to law, it is opposed to 'brute fact' on the one hand and 'social institutions' on the other. (12)

'Brute facts', as argued by Searle, 'share the feature that the concepts which make up the knowledge are essentially physical, or, in its dualistic version, either physical or mental. The model for systematic knowledge of this kind is the natural sciences, and the basis for a knowledge of this kind is generally supposed to be simple empirical observations recording sense experiences.' (13) But much of our language cannot be accounted for in this way:

> It is obvious that large tracts of apparently fact-stating language do not consist of concepts which are part of this picture . . . there are many kinds of facts, and facts which obviously are objective facts and not matters of opinion or sentiment or emotion at all (as statements in ethics and aesthetics might be regarded), which are hard, if not impossible, to assimilate to this picture . . . a marriage ceremony, a baseball game, a trial, and a legislative action involve a variety of physical movements, states, and raw feels, but a specification of one of these events only in such terms is not so far a specification of it as a marriage ceremony, baseball game, a trial, or a legislative action. The physical events and raw feels only count as part of such events given certain other conditions and against a background of certain kinds of institutions. Such facts . . . I propose to call **institutional facts.** They are indeed facts; but their existence, unlike the existence of brute facts, presupposes the existence of certain human institutions. It is only given the institution of marriage that certain forms of behavior constitute Mr. Smith's marrying Miss Jones. (1969:50f.)

This lengthy quotation from Searle serves to highlight the implications of MacCormick's thesis, that law should be seen not merely as a set of 'legal institutions', but rather as 'institutional fact'. Just as Searle is concerned with the status of linguistic propositions which apparently state facts of an objective character, even though they cannot be verified with the methodology of the natural sciences, so too MacCormick is interested in the status of 'a proposition whose truth depends not merely upon the occurrence of acts or events in the world but also upon the application of rules to such acts or events' (1973:4). He too is concerned to explain the fact that certain kinds of proposition of law have an objectively verifiable status, irrespective of the knowledge or opinion of the participants (1973:3), and despite the absence of a natural science methodology. MacCormick's example is on the same plane as Searle's discussion of Mr. Smith's marriage to Miss Jones: 'The existence of a contract is, in a philosophical sense, a matter of institutional fact' (1973:4). By this, he means not that the legal institution 'contract', or the rules which constitute it, are a matter of fact, but rather that Mr. Smith's contract is a fact of a particular kind, namely one which can be meaningfully described only on the basis of an understanding of the legal institution 'contract'. Whether Mr. Smith's actions (the brute facts) constitute a contract or not can in principle be objectively tested, by asking whether they can truthfully be regarded as instances of those model acts or events which are 'ordinarily necessary' and 'presumptively sufficient' (1973:24-7) in terms of the 'institutive rules' of the legal institution 'contract'.

MacCormick is thus very far from reducing 'law' to 'fact'. His concern, at this stage at least of the argument, is **only** with this type of legal proposition, relating to the meaning of specified acts of human behaviour. So far from representing a factual or sociological approach to law, MacCormick is here saying nothing which would offend the Pure Theory of Hans Kelsen, who also distinguished between 'An act or series of acts - a happening . . perceived by our senses: an external manifestation of human conduct' and 'the legal meaning of this act' (1967:2). For Kelsen, too, the meaning of the act, taken 'as an external fact' (Searle would say: a 'brute fact'), could be determined either subjectively or objectively. The legal (objective) meaning of the act was to be determined by interpreting that act in the light of a legal norm: 'The external fact whose objective meaning is a legal or illegal act is always an event that can be perceived by the senses . . however, this event as such, . . is not an object of legal cognition. What turns this event into a legal or illegal act is not its physical existence . . but the objective meaning resulting from its interpretation. The specifically legal meaning of this act is derived from a 'norm' whose content refers to the act; this norm confers legal meaning to the act, so that it may be interpreted according to this norm. The norm functions as a scheme of interpretation'. (14) MacCormick may well dissent from the views of Kelsen regarding the internal structure of norms and the manner of their interrelationship within a legal system. But in his conception of the relation between fact and law, he differs from Kelsen only in the manner of his formulation. Even for Kelsen, a proposition about facts which interpreted those facts objectively (legally) would count as a proposition of law, which could be correct or incorrect (Kelsen would avoid 'true or false'), 'authentic' or 'inauthentic' (valid or invalid), depending on the identity of the person uttering that statement.

The normative purity of MacCormick's 'institutional fact' receives confirmation from the distinction he stresses between 'legal institutions' and 'social institutions'. By the latter, he means 'certain types of social system or sub-system, such as universities, schools, hospitals, orphanages, libraries, sporting organisations, and the like . . these are organisations of people which retain their organisational identity through time even though their personnel may change, because they are getting on with some job, and getting on with it in an organised way' (1973:9). Such social institutions are often of great importance for law, since 'law is in various ways made, sustained, enforced and elaborated by an interacting set of social institutions' (1973:10). Such social institutions may thus generate legal institutions on the historical plane, and secure their implementation in practice. But conceptually, they are distinct: social institutions may themselves be regulated by legal institutions, and any shortfall in their behaviour from those legal standards will thus be a 'ground for serious and justified criticism' (1973:10). It is these social institutions which may, for MacCormick, supply at least one of the missing parts of the narrative algorithm (7.1): they may be the source of the goal of legal action, thus representing 'contract' (or 'manipulation'). MacCormick impliedly endorses the view of law as a piece of social engineering; it functions as the means to achieve certain goals, these goals being set by those who operate the machinery. MacCormick's attempt to marry a variety of the truth-conditions conception of meaning with a pragmatic, conventionalist understanding of language in terms of its uses, is particularly striking. As already noted, he sees institutional fact as capable of generating 'a proposition whose truth depends not merely upon the occurrence of acts or events in the world but also upon the application of rules to such acts or events'. **(15)** We must look further at his understanding of both these empirical acts or events in the world, and the rules whose application to those acts or events generate institutional meaning.

MacCormick's view of law as institutional fact implies that law cannot exist in the absence of two empirical conditions: first, the existence of patterns of behaviour which are capable of being regarded as instances of the legal institutions of the particular system; second, the existence of some group which actually does attribute meaning to the brute facts in accordance with the legal institutions of that system. **(16)** But Greimasian semiotics might well, in my estimation, question both of these empirical conditions, and strong arguments can independently be advanced against them. The semiotician would put the objection in terms of the autonomy of the communicative processes of the text: they may make **claims** regarding the existence of behaviour patterns, and of groups who are likely to interpret those patterns in a certain manner. But those claims are simply the messages which the text communicates; no implication follows with regard to their truth.

The two empirical conditions may also be questioned on independent, jurisprudential grounds. Suppose that Parliament took a flight of fancy, and enacted a scheme of welfare benefits for those above the age of two hundred. Failing the return of Methuselah, brute facts could not occur such as would satisfy the institutive rules of the legal institution represented by that scheme. Would we say, nonetheless, that such a legal institution did not exist ? The example may be extreme, but the notion of 'ideal laws' **(17)** has considerable historical support. Again, suppose our fanciful legislature enacted rules which were not impossible, but only absurd, so absurd indeed that neither the population at large regarded them as standards for the regulation of actual behaviour, nor did the officials regard them as appropriate for enforcement. Suppose, for example, that Parliament enacted a law making it a criminal offence, punishable by a fine of two hundred pounds, for anyone to walk on the gaps between paving stones (in line with the popular children's game) but that no-one (outside the legislature, at least) really does regard the brute fact of stepping on such a gap as an institutional fact such as should lead to the consequence of the two hundred pound fine. Are we to say, in both these cases, that there is no law, since the conditions of an institutional fact are not fulfilled ? **(18)** What matters, surely, is the **claim** made by the law itself that institutional facts may arise under it, irrespective of the truth or falsity of that claim. And that, I take it, would be the approach of the semiotician. More often than not, the claim may in fact be true, in that the two empirical conditions will be satisfied. That is the standard case, to which alone MacCormick attends. But the fact that it is the standard case does not mean that the two empirical conditions are conceptually necessary.

Whereas MacCormick seeks to view law as 'institutional fact', the semiotician may be said to view law as merely one species of 'semiological fact'. For the former (as also for Kelsen) fact and law, behaviour and rule, are essentially distinct categories. The relationship between them is that the behaviour is here interpreted in the light of the rule. For the semiotician, the matter stands differently. The fact is not the behaviour which is to be regulated by the rule, but rather the communication process itself. It is a fact that the legislator communicates certain messages; the fact that the content of those messages is a set of rules does not involve the interpretation of the communicative fact in any different fashion. The content of the message could be facts, stories, music or visual images, just as well as rules. It is the semiotician, rather than MacCormick (1973:2), who can more justifiably claim that we are all 'realists' now.

MacCormick's view of the role of legal institutions in mediating between the 'brute facts' (the first empirical condition) and the meaning attributed to those facts (by a group whose existence constitutes the second empirical condition) leads him to consider the ontological status of the legal institutions themselves. The institutional concept must be logically prior to any factual instance of it (1973:9). The institution is reified 'by naming it'. **(19)** With some embarrassment, MacCormick endows the institution with a Platonic form of ontology: '. . . Plato thought that the idea of beds was logically prior to the existence of any particular bed; that has always seemed to me a singularly implausible view in relation to brute facts; but at least the world of legal institutions is a world safe for Platonists;

whether that is good or bad publicity for the world of legal institutions I should not care to say, but it is clear that the institution as a concept is logically prior to the existence of any instance of it.' It would not, however, be difficult to rescue MacCormick from his Platonic shipwreck. Kelsen took an exactly parallel route, with somewhat less peril. For him, the norm served as a 'schema of interpretation'. In this, he regarded himself as applying a Kantian epistemology, rather than a Platonic ontology. **(20)**

Given this understanding of the objectivity of institutional fact, based upon a natural science model, it is with some surprise that we find MacCormick arguing, in the third section of his lecture, for the open texture, if not defeasibility, of institutive/terminative rules. Such rules do not provide 'necessary and sufficient' conditions for the existence of an instance of the institution in question; at best, they provide what MacCormick describes as ordinarily necessary and presumptively sufficient conditions. The argument here seeks to incorporate substantial aspects of the Hartian understanding of legal language. **(21)** Like Hart, MacCormick seeks to distance himself from what he describes as formalism ('a formalistic heaven of institutions', 1973:22). Following Hart, a solution is to be found in the open texture of the language of the rules. That language provides a sufficient consensus as to how one goes about creating instances of the legal institution, while at the same time leaving a degree of flexibility. Institutive rules too, we may say, have their 'core of settled meaning' surrounded by their 'penumbra of doubt' (7.2-3). But this is no mere consequence of the use of natural language in law. MacCormick does not confine his objection to necessary and sufficient conditions to the presence of language which, whether so intended or not, is indeterminate. In a manner reminiscent of Hart's notion of 'defeasibility' **(22)**, he argues that these conditions both are and should be indeterminate, in the sense that they should always be open to exceptions which have not been previously defined: 'it thus appears that no formulation, however detailed, of the institutive rule of an institution, can be taken as giving a complete list of sufficient conditions for the validity of a purported instance of the institution, any more than as stating conditions each of which is in all cases necessary. Any such formulation of a rule has to be read as subject to possible further exceptions, has to be read, if we would be realistic, in the light of relevant legal principles already established and of possible new ones based on conceptions of the purpose of the institution in the context of changing social conditions and values' (1973:27).

This argument, however, is open to serious objection. It neglects the distinction between 'meaning' and 'interpretation' which was found useful in accounting for Hart's own views (7.2); it fails to attach sufficient weight to the communicative model within which Hart himself locates a theory of interpretation. Consider again the French 1966 Loi. It signifies the existence within the legislative discourse of, inter alia, a legal institution called the SC. There can hardly be any doubt that the legislative discourse presents the SC as a legal institution, whose creation is defined in terms of necessary and sufficient conditions. That is precisely the 'formalist' appearance which the legislative discourse seeks to convey. If we look at the legislative discourse alone, and ask what is its meaning, we can produce an answer in that determinate form. It is only when we go outside the text, and ask how the legislative discourse is to be applied, through the interpretation of particular facts and events as instances of that institution, that the qualifications which MacCormick seeks to make become relevant. Their relevance belongs to a different form of legal discourse. We may have necessary and sufficent conditions in the legislative discourse, while at the same time those very conditions may be no more than ordinarily necessary and presumptively sufficient in judicial discourse. Formalism and objectivity (or at least its appearance) belong to the legislative form of discourse; flexibility (or its appearance) to judicial discourse. MacCormick, by contrast, takes a referential view of the meaning of the legislative discourse (8.1), and seeks to produce a unified picture of the legal system, characterised at one and the same time by formalism and the existence of truth-conditions and by flexibility allied to the purposes of the users of the messages. **(23)**

The argument that these elements will not combine has itself received a number of expressions. Hart's notion of defeasibility has been attacked on philosophical grounds. Strawson has argued that the Gricean model of meaning, based upon authorial intention, is not applicable to types of illocutionary acts which are essentially conventional, that is, whose meaning is regulated by a system of rules. More recently, Hervey has gone further, in suggesting that it may be appropriate to draw the border line between 'semiotic acts' and other significative acts of a non-semiotic nature precisely in terms of the presence in the former of Searle's 'constitutive conventions'. Searle's 'speech act' is a semiotic act by virtue of the fact that it is governed by such conventions (1982:110). Most significant, perhaps, is a recent analysis by Sbisà and Fabbri of two different models of speech acts, the first (and most commonly presupposed) stressing communicative intention and setting necessary and sufficient conditions for force-indicating devices, the second locating speech acts within a theory of interaction which looks to participant construction and which for that reason rejects necessary and sufficient conditions. **(24)**

Here as elsewhere, Ross was ahead of his time. His notion of 'systematic concepts' bears close comparison to MacCormick's legal institutions. But it was 'scientific language' which was characterised by a tendency to cultivate the pure formation of systematic concepts and in this way to make itself independent of context and situation (1958:119). He contrasted the 'synonymic-systematic method' with that to be found in judicial interpretation. The latter employed context and situation as its fundamental aids, since legal directives were 'preponderantly' couched in the terminology of everyday language.

8.3 THE SEMIOTIC FUNCTION OF LEGAL CONCEPTS

Despite the role which we see legal institutions as playing in the creation of the institutional meaning of acts and events in everyday social life, MacCormick recognises that institutional concepts fulfil a particular semiotic function in the exposition of the law by legal writers, and in its operation by lawyers: 'We can show that and show how they do use institutional concepts to organise their material and subdivide it into manageable units' (1973:16). Here and elsewhere, MacCormick suggests that legal institutions are an essential epistemological device for the communication of a complex body of rules. In Greimasian terms, they may lay claim to the status of 'les structures élémentaires de la signification du droit'.

This notion of the epistemological role of legal institutions in the hands of both legal writers and legal practitioners leads MacCormick to criticise the claim of

Hart that the distinction between power-conferring and duty-imposing rules, and by extension the generality of legal concepts, are endorsed by the perceptions and language of the average citizen (1973:16f.). Rather, MacCormick insists, the institutional facts to which he refers operate 'only within the legal universe of discourse' (1973:5), and this universe of discourse is for the most part of interest primarily to lawyers. For example, every time a passenger pays his fare on the Edinburgh bus, an institutional fact (the establishment of a contract) is created, even though few people other than lawyers would know (or care) about it; it is only when there is a crash and a passenger is injured or his property damaged that the brute fact of the passing of the coins becomes regarded by the passenger as the institutional fact of the establishment of a contract with the Edinburgh Corporation (1973:3). 'From his point of view, all the talk of contracts may be no more than a set of impenetrable legal equations worked out **ex post facto** by his lawyers as steps to proving **quod est demonstrandum** for him, namely that he is entitled to compensation. The present legal frame of reference imposes upon lawyers the necessity to present matters in that way, but who knows how their clients perceive such matters ? For them, our legal techniques may be no more than part of a process of mystification' (1973:17). Here, MacCormick begins to approach the conception of law as a semiological fact. Not only does he show an awareness of the restricted group within which this communication is designed to operate; he also hints (through the supposed viewpoint of his cynical Morningside commuter) that the rules of the law of contract may not after all have an objective meaning, but may rather be the means used by lawyers to achieve the ends which their clients seek.

The doctrinal function of institutional concepts also emerges from MacCormick's response to a famous argument of Ross. The latter had argued that such concepts are logically and semiotically redundant. In his famous article 'Tu-Tu' (1957), Ross argues that 'systematic' legal concepts such as 'right', 'duty', 'ownership', 'territory', etc., have no independent semantic reference whatsoever, other than being link-words which can mediate between legally defined conditions and legally defined consequences. The usefulness of such terms resides (only) in the assistance they provide us in presenting the law in a clear and systematic fashion. Just as a simple society can logically dispense with the diagnosis of certain acts as 'Tu-Tu', and link the consequences of being 'Tu-Tu' with the conditions which give rise to that diagnosis, so too may it be argued, MacCormick observes, that whole sets of institutive and consequential rules are logically related in the same way, and render logically superfluous the diagnosis of the link between them in terms of a legal institution or concept (1973:12, using contract as an example).

It may be worth noting that the logical objection can and should be taken much further, if the objective is to reconstruct the legal system in a fashion which (whatever its cognitive inconvenience) dispenses with a maximum of logical redundancies. MacCormick puts the argument thus (1973:12):

> The objection can be given concrete form, again using contract as an example, in the following way: the supposed institutive rule of contract has some such form as 'If two or more parties made an agreement of a certain kind, and provided that a number of required circumstances obtains, then a valid contract exists between them'. It is further supposed that there are consequential rules making such provision as that 'If a valid contract exists (between certain parties), then each of the parties has a duty to do what he has agreed to do, subject to any agreed conditions'. But since inspection of these postulated rules reveals that precisely the same terms ('a valid contract exists') function as consequence in the first and as condition in the second, we can by the simplest of logical operations delete these terms from each of the rules and render the whole into a single rule of the form 'If two or more parties make an agreement of a certain kind, and provided that a number of circumstances obtains, then each of the parties has a duty to do what he has agreed to do, subject to any agreed conditions'.

But although MacCormick has here eliminated the 'diagnosis' in terms of a 'legal institution' ('a valid contract exists'), he has not in fact eliminated the **assumption** of the existence of a single institution from his formula. For it is only on the basis of such an assumption that he can reconstruct 'the supposed institutive rule' and the consequential rules, conceived as a single set. In other words, the very classification of conditions as an 'institutive rule' and of the consequential rules as a single set itself represents a concession to cognitive convenience, and is redundant on a strictly logical analysis. What, then, would an analysis of the law of contract rid of such redundant classification look like ? The complete answer would consist of a set of norms each one of which was completely independent logically from any other. That would involve a great deal of repetition, in that every single variable would have to appear in every individual norm, and the set of norms needed to represent the whole law of contract would require to be of a size such that each variable would generate a set of norms in which all possible combinations of the other variables was included.

Let us take a formalisation of a highly simplified version of the law of contract in order to illustrate this point. Suppose that there are only three institutive conditions of a valid contract, which we shall call A, B and C. Suppose also that there are only three possible legally recognised consequences of a valid contract, which we shall call X, Y and Z. Let us call the institution of contract 'I'. MacCormick's argument, quoted above, merely urges the convenience of reducing:

(1) If A and B and C, then I
and (2) If I, then X and Y and Z
to (3) If A and B and C, then X and Y and Z.

However, this presupposes the logical necessity of classifying A, B, and C as a single set of institutive rules, and X, Y and Z as a single set of consequences. If we abandon this assumption, we require to do the following to represent this very basic version of the law of contract:-

(4) If A and B and C, then X
(5) If A and -B and C, then -X
(6) If A and B and -C, then -X
(7) If A and -B and -C, then -X
(8) If -A and B and C, then -X
(9) If -A and -B and C, then -X
(10) If -A and B and -C, then -X
(11) If -A and -B and -C, then -X

This, of course, is only the start. It does not represent a full statement of the variations where A (treated positively or negatively) is the base. We need sixteen further norms, the first eight of which will be identical to (4) - (11) except that Y/-Y will be substituted for X/-X, and a further eight in which Z/-Z is substituted for X/-X. Without the classificatory assumptions of the institution, we require not two norms, but twenty-four. The two-norm version which MacCormick reconstructs from Ross itself represents a significant concession towards the needs of cognition and communication. It is true, of course, that my twenty-four norms can be reduced to MacCormick's two by a simple logical process, namely the use in the conditions of 'if and only if' and the use in the consequences of conjunctive 'ors'. But the addition of such operators is merely a logical representation of the classificatory presuppositions, based on the theory of institutions, which represent the issue under debate.

There are, in fact, two distinct logical facets of the structure of legal institutions which MacCormick sets out. The first is the normative relationship between conditions and consequences: 'if . . then legally . . ', what Kelsen calls the relationship of imputation. Secondly, there is the classification of conditions and the classification of consequences. The above demonstration in terms of a simple version of the law of contract shows that the real difference which the introduction of 'institutions' makes is in relation to the cognition and communicaton of the latter, not the former. The normative relationship between conditions and consequences remains constant in all the formulae, (1) - (11). Despite MacCormick's apparent claim that institutions are the link between institutive, consequential and terminative rules, they in fact represent no more than a classification of the various sets of institutive, consequential and terminative rules. The links between institutive, consequential and terminative rules are inherent in the structure of the norm itself. **(25)**

MacCormick's response to Ross's argument is termed by him 'practical' in character, and the practical needs he has in mind are of a cognitive and communicative (hence semiotic) character. 'Lawyers and legal writers' do deploy such legal institutions and concepts, and do so because of the complexity of the relationships between whole sets of institutive, consequential and terminative rules

(1973:13). **(26)** Here MacCormick dissents from the view of Hart, for whom ordinary language shows that such conceptions as the distinction between power-conferring rules and duty-imposing rules are perceived by the average citizen (1973:16f). But for what purposes do lawyers use legal institutions ? MacCormick mentions both the legal practitioner and the legal writer. He implies that the cognitive and communicative needs of the two of them are equivalent. He states these needs thus: ' . . Institutional terms as used by lawyers can only be understood as the organising and connecting terms between complex sets of institutive consequential and terminative rules. Moreover, the very complexity of the subject-matter suggests a compelling practical justification for the continued use of such terminology . . . for simplicity, at any rate relative simplicity, in expounding or operating with law, we need to break the whole mass of legal material into simple but patently interrelated unitary rules; our institutional terms make this possible, each within its own range' (1973:13,15).

But the forms of legal literature with which we are familiar belie MacCormick's equivalence of the needs of the practitioner and the legal scholar or scientist. **(27)** MacCormick himself notes the closeness between Searle's philosophical conception of an institution and the traditional legal usage of the term, as exemplified by the titles of Buckland's **The Main Institutions of Roman Private Law** or Renner's **The Institutions of Private Law and their Social Functions** (1973:4). In fact, legal institutions in this sense go back to the 'institutional' books of Roman legal literature. Large passages of the **Institutiones** of Gaius are arranged in a manner which reflects just this kind of conception. The passage in Book I, paragraphs 52-141, examines systematically first the manner in which various forms of personal status are created (their institutive rules) and then are terminated (their terminative rules). This kind of arrangement is particularly pronounced in books of a predominantly pedagogic character; indeed, that genre of Roman legal literature which was written as introductory books for students is called the 'institutional writings'. It forms the model also for the development of legal textbooks for students in the modern period. Its strength is that it allows the student to see the place of particular rules in the legal system as a whole: to see the wood for the trees. As MacCormick puts it, 'We can break down complex bodies of legal material into comparatively simple sets of interrelated rules; and yet on the other hand we can treat large bodies of law in an organised and generalised way, not just as a mass of bits and pieces' (1973:7).

But the practitioner may very well be interested only in one bit of the law; its place in some aesthetic or didactic structure may, to him, be quite irrelevant. Hence, forms of legal literature designed for practitioners have often departed radically from the model we have been considering. One need think only of the traditional English Abridgements, often arranged in a purely alphabetic manner. Of some interest, in this connection, is the arrangement of one widely-used monthly updating service in English law, **Current Law.** Here, the material is presented under an alphabetically-arranged series of headings. Some of these headings would count as 'legal institutions' as defined by MacCormick, and indeed some of them represent the same broad institutional concepts as are used in teaching the general principles of English law: Contract, Tort, etc. But others are different, being of a primarily functional character: 'Agriculture', 'Aliens', 'Animals', 'Aviation', 'Banking'. This suits the practitioner, since his work may very well reflect such practical, rather than pedagogical divisions. **Current Law** also includes an intermediate type of entry, legal concepts of a more specific and specialised kind than the general headings of 'Contract' and 'Tort', but which nevertheless can be represented as having a clear, internal institutional structure: 'Agency', 'Copyright', etc., classifications which could well be taken either in a conceptual or a functional sense. Today's legal practitioner, it seems, needs to operate with concepts of all three types, and not merely with the broad legal institutions such as are familiar to the law student. **Current Law** may very well here reflect different stages of cognitive development of the legal system, from purely functional to low-level conceptual classification, and ultimately to more integrating forms of conceptual classification. But equally, it shows that the cognitive and communicative techniques of earlier stages are not necessarily to be discarded later on. The broad, integrating conceptual jurisprudence (whose immediate sources lie in German Pandektenrecht, and its appropriation in England, not least by John Austin) may presently dominate legal education, and thus create the impression of being the normal, or even inevitable, modes of expression of complex systems of law. But in fact, this approach is not inevitable even for legal education, and some recent developments in England in the teaching of law to business students (who are not to be initiated into the fraternity of the legal profession) suggests the pedagogical utility of the more functional schemes.

The semiotic function of legal classification has not escaped the attention of legal historians and sociologists of law. Take the following norm of the biblical law of homicide, discussed by Daube **(28)**: 'But if he struck him down with an instrument of iron, so that he died, he is a murderer; the murderer shall be put to death' (Numbers 35:16). This norm (with Ross) can be formalised as 'When x = y and y ⊃ z, then x ⊃ z', y here being represented not by 'Tu-Tu' or 'ownership' but by 'murderer'. Other norms of the biblical law of murder do dispense with the linking systematic concept, and are thus comparable to Ross's reduction of:

(1) If a person has eaten of the chief's food he is **Tu-Tu**

(2) If a person is **Tu-Tu** he shall be subjected to a ceremony of purification

to the more direct form:

(3) If a person has eaten of the chief's food he shall be subjected to a ceremony of purification.

Daube suggests that the form in Numbers 35:16 may have its origin in ancient medical texts, and labels it the 'diagnosis' form. Its incidence occurs where conventional boundaries are challenged, here representing an expansion of the traditional conceptions of causation and/or intention. **(29)** In this case, the motive for the logically redundant clause 'he is a murderer' is not to simplify an otherwise overly complex construction. The sentence would be shorter, and no less clear, if 'is a murderer; the murderer' were omitted; the phrase, we might say, is linguistically and cognitively redundant, as well as logically so. Apart from the function of the phrase as a response to an implied, conventional view that such a person should not be put to death as a murderer, the clause also has a second semiotic function, in relation to the identity of the utterer. This is the legislator speaking, and a divine legislator at that: from him, the very assertion that the accused is to be classified as a murderer is itself a speech act akin to naming which constitutes the homicide as a form of murder. **(30)** Categorical statement is the mode of rhetoric of the person with authority, the legislator. Where classification is used by the legal writer, it requires rational (or other) justification; it will not stand, as a rhetorical device, on its own.

In the biblical example, it is clear that the semiotic function of the logically redundant systematic term is connected with the connotations of its use in the ordinary language: although this may not be your image of a murderer, I, God, say it is. Such connections are not restricted to ancient law. The meaning which such terms possess in popular language, however legally inaccurate at a particular time, may be thought to exert some pull or influence on the manner in which they are used in the legal system. Fletcher (1976, 1978) has cast revealing light on the history of the Common Law of Larceny by attending to the 'collective image of acting like a thief'. Nor should we accept, for historical purposes, any claim that systematic legal concepts operate as purely neutral link-words in the construction of normative propositions. Modern sociological theory is sensitive to the properties of 'labelling'.

CHAPTER NINE

DWORKIN AND THE SEMIOTICS OF LEGAL ARGUMENT

(9.1) The Semiotic Character of Dworkinian Logic: Dworkin seeks to contest the claims of positivism to the existence of 'logical spaces' in the legal system. On Dworkin's account, positivists claim that spaces exist both between dispositive concepts that have been laid down and in the absence of the laying down of such concepts. But the first of these claims is inessential to positivism. Dworkin's logical arguments, though compatible with the methods and assumptions of the semiotic square of Greimas, are inconsistent with the logical square as developed by Blanché and formalised by Kalinowski. This casts light on the true character of Dworkin's argument as providing an account of legal discourse, not of the logic of norms. **(9.2) Interpretation in Law and Literature:** Dworkin supports his argument against 'no right answer' by adducing literary criticism as an analogue to legal interpretation. In both, rational arguments may be constructed about matters neither stated in the text nor necessarily to be inferred from it. Such arguments are judged according to their 'fit' with the text. Dworkin here describes an interpretative practice. He concedes that even such criteria may fail to produce a best solution - a form of 'logical space' which in general he seeks to deny. But he argues that such cases will, as a matter of practice, be virtually excluded in modern, complex legal systems. **(9.3) Demonstrability and the Semiotic Processes of Legal Argument:** Dworkin rightly sees demonstrability as a central claim of positivism. But he argues that law may exist without being demonstrable just as there are non-demonstrable but existent 'facts of narrative consistency'. Dworkin's argument can be made without entailing extravagant ontological claims, as an account of the conventions of the participants in legal construction. The concept of demonstrability also evokes comparison with the manner in which linguistics and semiotics conceive significatory systems to work. Modern semiotics parallel the movement away from mechanical demonstrability. But the parallel also suggests that Dworkin has not injected sufficient realism into the jurisprudential account of how signification works in law. **(9.4) A Characterisation of Dworkinian Semiotics:** The methodology of interpretation which Dworkin advocates is fiercely systemic in character, as shown by its prescriptions on the corpus for interpretation, the theory of mistakes, and the preference for principle above policy. Argument is conducted through non-arbitrary signs. But it is a system more appropriate to the lecture theatre than the courtroom.

9.1 DWORKIN'S ARGUMENT FOR A SEMIOTIC FORM OF LOGIC

One of the principal, and most controversial, claims made by Ronald Dworkin is that there is nearly always a right answer to a legal problem, even before it has been decided. He opposes the positivist claim that at least in 'hard cases' (where there is no clearly applicable rule) there exists in principle no legally right answer, until such time as the issue is authoritatively determined by a court or other authorised legal organ. In an essay published in 1977, Dworkin attacked the positivist view on logical grounds. The positivists argue that there exists within any legal system at any given time areas of 'logical space' between the easy (determined) cases; in such areas the judge creates rather than applies law. Dworkin seeks to deny that any such logical space exists.

He presents the following example. 'Suppose the legislature has passed a statute stipulating that "sacrilegious contracts shall henceforth be invalid." The community is divided as to whether a contract signed on Sunday is, for that reason alone, sacrilegious. It is known that very few of the legislators had that question in mind when they voted, and that they are now equally divided on the question of whether it should be so interpreted. Tom and Tim have signed a contract on Sunday, and Tom now sues Tim to enforce the terms of the contract, whose validity Tim contests. Shall we say that there is a right answer to the question of whether Tom's contract is valid, even though the community is deeply divided about what the right answer is ? Or is it more realistic to say that there simply is no right answer to that question ?' (1977:58). The positivist, according to Dworkin, may argue that there is no right answer on either or both of two grounds: (1) That the choice between 'Tom's contract is valid' and 'Tom's contract is not valid' does not exhaust the logical possibilities of the range of dispositions which may be available; in logic, if not in previously settled law, there may be further alternatives. (2) Even if the two dispositions quoted above do exhaust the logical space, neither of them may be true, precisely because the case has not yet been determined. Dworkin formalises the argument in the following manner:

> Let (**-p**) be defined as the logical negation of (**p**), so that if (**p**) is false (**-p**) is true, and if (**-p**) is false (**p**) is true. Let the proposition that Tom's contract is valid be represented by **'p'** and the proposition that his contract is not valid as **'non-p'**. The unpopular theory both versions of the thesis oppose holds that the question about Tom's contract must have a right answer, even if we are not sure what it is, because (**non-p**) is identical with (**-p**) and either (**p**) is true or (**-p**) is true because ((**p**) or (**-p**)) is necessarily true. The first version argues that the supposition that (**non-p**) is identical to (**-p**) is a mistake; (**non-p**) should be represented as a proposition (**r**) that is not the logical negation of (**p**) . . . the second version, on the other hand, does not deny that (**non-p**) is identical to (**-p**); instead it holds that in some cases neither (**p**) nor (**-p**) is true, that is, that in some cases bivalence does not hold. (1977:61)

Dworkin's 'logical negation' is clearly a contradictory, characterised by exclusivity and reversibility (4.3); the proposition that Tom's contract is not valid (**'non-p'**) is in fact a contrary, although this is not expressed clearly in the present passage.

The logic of dispositive concepts

The first positivist argument which Dworkin rejects is that the range of dispositions available in Tom's case is not limited to 'Tim is liable' and 'Tim is exempt'. Dworkin concedes that these two possible dispositions are related to each other only as contraries **(p)** and **(non-p)**. But he argues that **(non-p)** is identical with **(-p)**, the contradictory of **(p)**. As applied to the example, the positivist might argue that there is 'a third possibility, which is that an exchange of promises may constitute neither a valid contract, such that judges have a duty to enforce the exchange, nor a contract that is not valid, with the consequences that judges have a duty not to enforce it, but something else that might be called, for example, an "inchoate" contract' (1977:60). Positivists suppose, according to Dworkin, that contrary dispositions in a legal system are not exclusive, even if we have no name for the logical space between them; they suppose 'that there is space between a dispositive concept and its apparent negation **(1)** that is occupied by a distinct concept, like the concept of an inchoate contract, though, as it happens, we do not have a separate name for that distinct concept' (1977:62). Such a position, for Dworkin, 'obscures the interesting and distinctive role of dispositive concepts in legal argument. These concepts provide a special kind of bridge between certain sorts of events and the conclusory claims about rights and duties that hold if these events can be demonstrated to have occurred. They both designate tests for conclusory claims and insist that if the tests they designate are not met, then the opposite conclusory claim, not simply the denial of the first, holds instead' (1977:65).

The position which Dworkin seeks to oppose can be represented in terms of the hexagon (4.3). If we invest A as 'Tim is liable', E will then be invested as 'Tim is exempt', O as 'Tim is not liable', I as 'Tim is not exempt', and Y as 'Tim is neither exempt nor liable' (figure 16). Dworkin is thus attributing to the positivists the claim that A and E are not exclusive, but rather exist within a triadic opposition, which includes the neutral term Y. In Dworkin's terms, A is **(p)**, E is **(non-p)** and Y is his 'third possibility'. If it is not the case that 'Tim is liable' (A), it does not necessarily follow that 'Tim is exempt' (E), since it remains possible that 'Tim is neither exempt nor liable' (Y). But Dworkin rejects this view. He claims an identity between (**non-p**) and (**-p**), thus

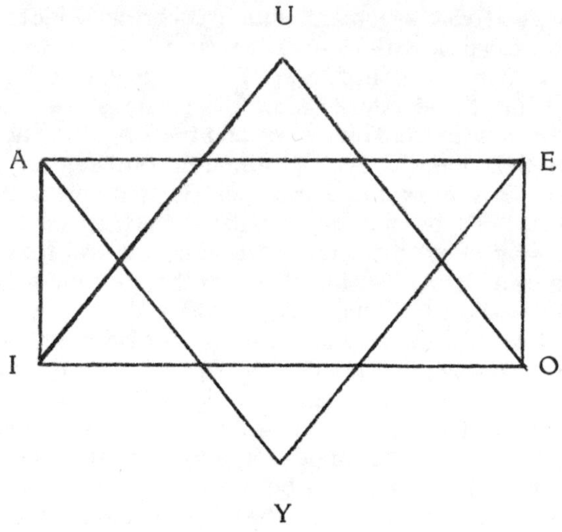

(Figure 16)

an identity between A's contrary, E, and its contradictory, O. His denial of the third possibility, combined with his claim to the practical identity of the contrary and the

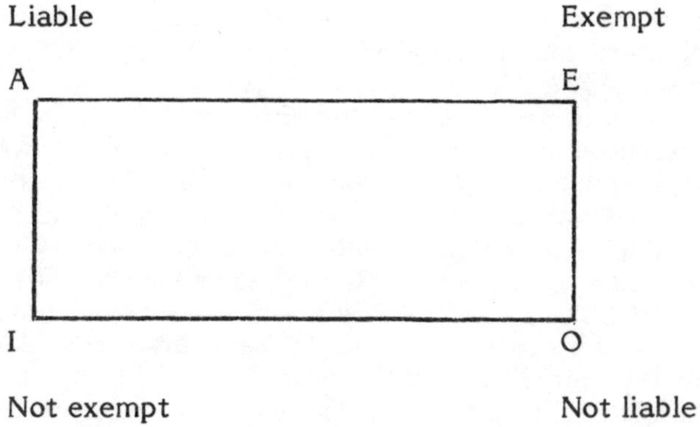

(Figure 17)

contradictory, represents an endorsement of the superiority of the semiotic over the logical square, as an account of the choices available within the range of dispositive concepts (Figure 17). Dworkin's argument is that if it is not the case that 'Tim is liable' (A), it must be the case that 'Tim is exempt' (E). But this is **not** supported by the logic of the classical square. We can use Kalinowski's formalisation of the relevant operations round the logical model (1972a:165f.) by way of illustration. (1) If it is true that Tim is liable, then it must be false that he is not liable (Kalinowski T25: $A \supset -O$); (2) If it is false that he is not liable, it must be false that he is exempt, assuming 'exempt' to be a particular case of 'not liable' (T14: $-O \supset -E$). We can then eliminate the common -O as the consequence in T25 and the condition in T14 and combine the two formulae into $A \supset -E$. The same process can be repeated in reverse, starting with the positive value of E: $E \supset -I$ (T29); $-I \supset -A$ (T12); $E \supset -A$ (T2). But this formalises only one aspect of the relationship of contrariety: affirmation of one contrary entails negation of the other. What Dworkin seeks to show, in common with Greimasian semiotics, is the converse: that negation of one contrary entails affirmation of the other (thus to the exclusion of any third possibility). But here the logical square cannot assist. If we start with negation of one contrary, we reach only the affirmation of its contradictory: if it is false that Tim is liable, it must be true that he is not liable ($-A \supset O$, T27). But from the truth of O, we cannot logically infer the truth of E. There is no formula $O \supset E$. That is the relationship of 'presupposition' or 'implication' which requires, as we have seen, a non-logical choice (4.3). That choice is made by investing the square with semic categories (liable v. exempt) rather than with the internal and external negations of propositions, so that A = it is true that Tim is liable; E = it is true that Tim is not liable; O = it is not true that Tim is liable; I = it is not true that Tim is not liable (**2**). When we adopt the latter model, as extended into the hexagon, we find a triadic relationship wherein the negation of one contrary entails the affirmation of either the other contrary or the third possibility: $-A \supset (E$ or $Y)$, $-E \supset (A$ or $Y)$. The exclusion of the third possibility is thus **not** a logical claim, despite Dworkin. The choice of Greimas to ignore Y is made on semiotic, not logical grounds.

In fact, it is far from clear that positivists do claim

the existence of the 'third possibility' in the manner in which Dworkin suggests. He cites no positivist who actually holds to this first version. Let us then put a positivist into the position of adjudicating between Tom and Tim. Suppose that he were to conclude that Tom and Tim had entered into an 'inchoate contract', the consequences of which differ from both **(p)** and **(non-p)**. In other words, neither the normal consequences of contractual liability, nor the normal consequences of contractual exemption apply; the case is to be decided, for example, on the basis of restitution principles. Surely the positivist would there say that the judges are making **two** decisions, in both of which they decide between two possibilities. First, they decide that there is no valid contract, hence there is no contractual liability (put otherwise: there is contractual exemption); second, they decide that the circumstances found a claim in restitution, hence there is restitution liability (and not restitution exemption). On this point, the positivist too is adopting a semiotic rather than a logical analysis. He is claiming that if Tim is not contractually liable, he is contractually exempt (**-p** = **non-p**), although there is no logical theorem which supports that view. Applying MacCormick's theory of legal institutions, the judge is likely to ask himself first whether the institutive rules of contract apply, and on coming to a negative conclusion will ask whether the institutive rules of restitution apply.

There is, in fact, very little difference between Dworkin and positivism on this issue. **(3)** In so far as a tension does here exist between the logical and the semiotic accounts, it is to be resolved in exactly the same way as that between Greimas and Blanché, in terms of the differing objectives of the enterprise (4.3). Thus, a logician like Kalinowski might affirm that a third possibility (Blanché's Y) does exist, but at the level of the logic of norms, not that of conscious judicial argument. But Dworkin claims repeatedly that his account is superior in that it represents the way in which lawyers actually talk and argue (e.g. 1977:59). His argument, therefore, is directed not against logicians but rather against alternative accounts of linguistic usage amongst lawyers. This alone can explain why Hart (rather than Kelsen) is his prime target. **(4)**

The logic of law creation

The second version of the 'no right answer' thesis introduces new, perhaps more significant, considerations. Here Dworkin is concerned not with the internal negation of legal propositions (whether in the form of contraries, **non-p,** or contradictories, **-p**) but with their external negation. The issue now becomes whether there exists a logical space between the legal propositions 'it is true (in law) that **p**' and 'it is not true (in law) that **p.**' (For these purposes, **p** and **non-p** are substitutable.) Here, there is indeed a real difference between Dworkin and the positivists, as a recent article by Alexander and Bayles makes clear. They note that (according to Dworkin) 'positivists hold that legal propositions are true if and only if some set of facts obtains such as the sovereign having commanded that certain types of contracts are valid' (1980:268). Alexander and Bayles represent this positivist position by the formula:

$$S(p) \supset p$$

meaning that legal proposition **p** is true if and only if the sovereign has commanded it (or whatever other facts are required to obtain). That proposition, however, may be negated either internally or externally. The positivist would certainly agree that if **S(p)** is internally negated **-p** must follow:

$$S(-p) \supset -p$$

meaning that **-p** is a true legal proposition if the sovereign has commanded **-p.** However, the positivist would not necessarily accept that the same applies to an external negation. He is not committed to:

$$-S(p) \supset -p$$

since here the sovereign has not commanded anything. This is the place where the positivist is taken to affirm a logical space which Dworkin denies. Unless a particular legal system has adopted a closure rule such as:

$$-S(p) \supset -p$$

then the position is indeterminate, and the judge has a discretion to create a new rule. If, on the other hand, the legal system does adopt such a closure rule, the result will be no. 13 of Alexander and Bayles (1980:271), namely:

$$[-S(p) \vee S(-p)] \equiv -p$$

meaning that legal proposition **-p** is true if and only if either the sovereign has not commanded **p** or the sovereign has commanded **-p**. But for Dworkin (1977:70-6), legal systems do assume closure rules, even if they have not been laid down.

This issue too can usefully be represented by contrasting the operations of Blanché's hexagon with those of Greimas' semiotic square. This time, we shall invest the hexagon (Figure 5) thus:

A	**S(p)**	(command to do **p**)
E	**S(-p)**	(command not to do **p**)
O	**-S(p)**	(no command to do **p**)
I	**-S(-p)**	(no command not to do **p**)
Y	**-S((p) v (-p))**	(no command either to do **p** or not to do **p**)
U	**S((p) + (-p))**	(command to do **p** and not to do **p**)

For any practical purposes, U may be ignored, as explained earlier (4.3). Here, the logical space claimed to exist by the positivists is (despite Dworkin) logically coherent, since A and E form only two parts of a triadic opposition, which admits of a third term, Y. If the positivist does not assume the existence of a closure rule, then **Y** represents a logical space left vacant by the failure to **S** on the one hand and the absence of such a closure rule on the other; this is where judicial discretion operates. Dworkin prefers a semiotic version of the logical relations, and one which would invest them in terms of the duty of the judge. Alexander and Bayles adopt **Oj(q)** as representing 'the judge is obligated to enforce the contract' (1980:269). This would generate, with Dworkin, the following investment of the semiotic square:

A	**Oj(q)**	'The judge is obligated to enforce the contract'
E	**Oj(-q)**	'The judge is obligated not to enforce the contract'
O	**-Oj(q)**	'The judge is not obligated to enforce the contract'
I	**-Oj(-q)**	'The judge is not obligated not to enforce the contract'

From this point, the same arguments apply as in our analysis of Dworkin's account of the first version of the 'no right answer' thesis. We can say that the square generates a movement from O to E, in so far as the negation of O presupposes or implies the negation of E. But that in itself does not imply that the judge is always under some duty. For we can only move from O to E by virtue of the fact that O is a contradictory of A (where the judge is under a duty to act). In other words, we can reach **A** from **E** (via **I**), or **E** from **A** (via **O**), in both cases ending up with a duty upon the judge to act in a certain way. But **A** and **E** are not in logic our only possible starting points. In logic, the very presence of **A** and **E** entails the existence of the neutral term **Y** - the location, as we have seen, of the 'third possibility'. Dworkin's model, here represented by the square, adopts as a semiotic constraint the closure rule, whose absence from the logical model is signified by the presence there of **Y**.

Here too, we can intepret the difference in terms of the respective orientations of logic and semiotics. Dworkin appeals again to ordinary experience of the working of legal systems, as evidenced by the way informed people talk about it. To them, either **A** or **E** are intelligible, but **Y** is not. Positivists, on the other hand, do find **Y** intelligible. That is not to say, of course, that they see in **Y** the possibility that the judge may decline to exercise his duty to render judgment. If that were the issue, Dworkin would have a trivial victory. Rather, the positivists adhere to **Y** in the sense that they deny that the judge has a duty to make render judgment. If that were the issue, Dworkin would have a trivial victory. Rather, the positivists adhere to **Y** in the sense that they deny that the judge has a duty to make any particular decision: he has a duty to decide, but he has discretion in the exercise of this judgment. (5)

For Dworkin, such judgment is always to be exercised on the basis of knowledge of the rights of the parties. Again, the difference between semiotic and logical models casts light on the significance of the difference between Dworkin and the positivists. Dworkin argues that the judge is always under an obligation to act so as to give effect to the pre-existing rights of the parties, and that this obligation must always be exercised upon knowledge of what those rights are. Let **K** represent the judge's knowledge, and (**r**) the legal right of the plaintiff to judgment in his favour. Dworkin's theory may be represented by a semiotic square invested as follows:

A	**K(r)**	'The judge knows that the plaintiff has a right to judgment'
E	**K(-r)**	'The judge knows that the plaintiff has no right to judgment'
O	**-K(r)**	'The judge does not know that the plaintiff has a right to judgment'
I	**-K(-r)**	'The judge does not know that the plaintiff does not have a right to judgment'

Using the same processes as above, starting with either contrary, one can always conclude with the other contrary, and thus end up with a position in which the judge has the necessary knowledge. The contraries are privileged in this sense as the places where operations begin. Here too, the square includes a closure rule, or semiotic constraint, which would not be found in the full, logical version. It is this closure rule which 'chooses' the semic opposite to the exclusion of any 'third possibility'. In the hexagon, we would have the additional points Y and U, of which Y (which stands in triadic opposition to both A and E) is a state of non-knowledge on the part of the judge: he knows neither that the plaintiff has a right to judgment, nor that he lacks such a right. Such a closure rule is assuredly a matter of semiotics, not logic. The legal system conveys the appearance, not least through the way in which judges talk and write, that judges always do know about the rights of the parties. But that is an account of surface legal discourse, and may well represent a semiotic appearance which has little relation to reality. Dworkin is well aware of this situation. He concedes that it would take a judge of superhuman abilities, a Hercules, to demonstrate the rights of the parties in hard cases in a manner which would convince his colleagues to the same degree as they are likely to be convinced in easy cases (1978:105ff.). Knowledge of this kind may only be an ideal, but it is still generative of the obligation of the judge in decision-making: the judge is always under a duty to approach as nearly as he can the standards of a Hercules in giving effect to the pre-existing rights of the parties. Since these rights are structurally determinate (the conclusion at the end of the analysis of the first version of the 'no right answer' thesis, from which we concluded that positivists need not dissent), it follows that Dworkin would assent to formulae in which the presence or absence of pre-existing rights entails the duty of the judge (and not vice versa). As Alexander and Bayles put it (1980:269), Dworkin must hold:

$$'p \supset Oj(q)$$

$$'-p \supset Oj(-q)$$

meaning that it must be the case **either** that Tim has a right, in which event the judge has an obligation to find in his favour, **or** Tim does not have a right, in which event the judge has an obligation not to find in his favour. This assumes the argument regarding knowledge made above. Dworkin would not subscribe to any formula expressed in terms of the judge's lack of knowledge of the rights of the parties, since legal discourse does not conceive of the possibility that the judge may lack any such knowledge.

9.2 INTERPRETATION IN LAW AND LITERATURE

Dworkin has himself appealed to literary analysis as an analogue for legal reasoning. (6) Notwithstanding his explicit comparison of the two areas, his work presents a more remote parallel to the Greimasian syntagmatic level than does MacCormick's theory of institutional fact.

Dworkin introduces his analogy from literary criticism as an argument against the second version of the 'no right answer' thesis (9.1), so as to show **how** a closure rule, reflecting the pre-existing rights of the parties, fills the logical space left by previous institutional action:

> Suppose a group of Dickens scholars proposes to discuss David Copperfield as if David were a real person. They propose to say, for example, that David attended Salem House, that he was industrious, and so forth. They might well develop the following ground rules governing these various assertions.
>
> (1) Any proposition about David may be asserted as 'true' if Dickens said it, or said something else such that it would have been inconsistent had Dickens denied it.
>
> (2) Any proposition may be denied as 'false' if Dickens denied it, or said something else such that it would have been inconsistent had Dickens said it.
>
> The second version of the no-right answer thesis would hold in the literary enterprise, for there would be many propositions about David that the participants would know were neither assertable as true nor deniable as false. Dickens never said that David had a homosexual affair with Steerforth, and it would not have been inconsistent with anything he did say if he had denied it. But he did not deny it, and it would not have been inconsistent with anything he said if he had asserted it. So the participants can neither assert nor deny the proposition, not because they lack sufficient information, but because they have sufficient information to be certain that, under their rules, the proposition is neither true nor false. (1977:73f.)

Positivists holding to the second version of the no-right answer thesis argue similarly, says Dworkin. For them, the ground rules of the legal system say that a legal proposition may be true (or valid) only 'if a sovereign has issued a command of a certain sort, or if officials have adopted rules of a certain form in a certain way, or something of that sort. The same proposition will be deniable as false only if a sovereign has commanded to the contrary, or if officials have adopted a contrary rule, or something of that sort' (1977:74). But if the sovereign has neither commanded that **p**, nor commanded that **-p**, there is a logical space, which can only be filled by an exercise of the judge's discretion. As Alexander and Bayles might formalise the argument (9.1), the ground rules provide for **S(p)** and **S(-p)**, but not for **-S(p v -p)**. Dworkin now seeks to argue that there is no logical space in that latter situation, because **S** does not exhaust the ground rules of the legal system, any more than (1) and (2) above exhaust the ground rules of literary analysis. Literary criticism in fact often takes the form of an exercise with a ground rule of the following kind:

> (3) A further proposition about David is assertable as true (or deniable as false) if that further proposition provides a better (or worse) fit than its negation with propositions already established, because it explains in a more satisfactory way why David was what he was, or said what he said, or did what he did, according to those already established propositions.

Similarly, propositions of law may be asserted or denied in accordance with whether they 'provide a better (or worse) fit with the political theory that provides the best justification for propositions of law already established' (1977:75). Just as the question of what ground rules are adopted by the literary critics is, for Dworkin, a question of fact, so too the question of whether the legal system adopts ground rules such as those typically contemplated by the positivist (such that there is a right answer where **S** but no right answer where **-S**) or ground rules more like (3) above, is a matter of fact. Dworkin claims, inter alia, to present a more accurate version of these facts. The status of his claims is thus comparable to that of the semiotician dealing with narrative: he claims that the communication of meaning in narrative does not flow from the concept of narrative, but rather from the way narrative actually works. One of the disputed facts is, in effect, whether legal systems have adopted closure rules such as will produce a right answer in every case. Dworkin notes that modern positivism differs from 'orthodox positivism' in this respect: 'Orthodox positivism, in each of its forms, claims some sort of conceptual connection between law and the particular act or act (sic) designated by the theory as the distinctive law-creating act' (1977:74). In orthodox positivism (represented, for example, by the jurisprudence of John (not J.L.) Austin) there can thus be no closure rule, since the presence of a law-creating act is a necessary condition, and this condition may not be fulfilled. But modern positivism (that of Hart) has everything turn 'on the question of which ground rules of assertion the participants in the legal practice in fact follow' (1977:74), and it is a feature of the modern debate that Hart and his followers have argued strongly that many of the cr teria proposed by Dworkin for legal adjudication can be 'incorporated' into the positivist rule of recognition, even though they do not involve specific law-creating acts. Nevertheless, the positivist will still deny what Dworkin strongly maintains, namely that Common Law legal systems have actually adopted ground rules of a kind such that the logical space must always turn out to be filled. In part, as Dworkin observes, the difference turns upon what the protagonists are prepared to accept as 'ground rules'.

Let us go back to (3) and consider how (and when) it may assist our literary critics in determining a literary question which is not answered by either (1) or (2). Dworkin uses as an example the question of whether David Copperfield had a homosexual affair with Steerforth. Nothing in the novel tells us explicity that he did, necessarily entails that he did, or even makes it highly probable that he did; nothing in the novel tells us explicitly that he did not, necessarily entails that he did not, or even renders it highly probably that he did not. Nevertheless, this appears to Dworkin to be a question which literary critics are in fact likely to be able to debate in an intelligible manner. Their answers will not be reducible to their personal tastes or whims. 'Participants assert a proposition about David as true (or deny it as false) if that proposition provides a better (or worse) fit than its negation with propositions already established, because it explains in a more satisfactory way why David did what he did, or said what he said, or thought what he thought, according to the established propositions' (1977:77f.). Such criteria of judgment are not self-created (thus generating what Dworkin seeks to deny, namely a case of 'strong discretion',

1978:31-9). Rather, they depend upon a particular form of fact, which Dworkin calls 'facts of narrative consistency, like the fact that the hypothesis that David had a sexual relationship with Steerforth provides a more satisfactory explanation of what he subsequently did and thought than the hypothesis that he did not' (1977:78). Such a hypothesis, generating the 'more satisfactory explanation', can be claimed to be a 'fact' in that it can claim a form of objectivity (9.3); it does not depend upon the personal whims or created standards of the critic. Where, then, do the criteria of the 'more satisfactory explanation' come from ? Dworkin answers thus:

> In the literary exercise, participants are trained to respond to certain questions of a highly specific form which . . cannot be said to be questions about the external world. They are trained to subject their responses to the disciplines of reflection and consistency, and then to make certain assertions that their training authorises them to make on the authority of these responses so disciplined. (1977:80)

There is, of course, a school of literary theory which holds that it is not training which provides authority, but authority which provides training. But we may leave that issue aside, and accept Dworkin's assumptions. What he is saying is that there exist within the literary world conventions of judgment, which may not render a conclusion certain, or even highly probable, but which may be deployed in such a way as to lead to the probability, after sufficient argument, of a consensus as to which solution to the problem is the most likely. The 'right answer' is thus a relative notion: it is the best answer as recognised by the conventional standards of the profession. Everyone participating in the literary game will find that he has some beliefs as to those conventions, which therefore generate views as to the best answer to particular problems. Since the critic does not invent the conventions, but rather assimilates them, his judgment in arriving at a view on such questions represents an exercise of 'weak' discretion (1978:31ff.). Just as these conventions in fact lead in one direction towards the best possible solution, they also indicate in the other direction what solutions are not tolerable at all: 'In some cases the argument will be so strong for a particular proposition, no doubt, that we should say that any participant who did not agree with that proposition was simply incompetent at the exercise' (1977:78).

Dworkin is often credited with holding the view that there is one right answer to every legal problem. We have seen that in his 1977 article, he interprets the notion of 'right answer' in relative terms: the best answer. But he also introduces a further qualification to the claim which his earlier work seemed to make, namely that 'it might nevertheless be sensible to say that there is no right answer to a question of law in certain very special cases' (1977:82). But these 'very special' cases turn out to be rather significant in terms of the distinction between the logical and the discursive levels of legal argument. Dworkin puts the argument thus:

> In certain circumstances, even in the third form of the literary exercise, it might be right for the participants to refuse to assert either that David had some property or that he did not. Suppose the question is raised whether David had type-A blood or not, and there is no reason to think that a boy with that blood type would be more likely to have had the history and character Dickens stipulates than a boy with any other blood type. The proposition that David had type-A blood is not vague; we can say that any historical boy would either have had type-A blood or not, and that there is a right answer to the question whether he did, even though we shall never know. But the assertion conditions of the literary exercise forbids saying that of David; it seems more sensible, given these conditions, to say that though the proposition that he had that blood type is not true, the proposition that he did not is not true either. (1977:82)

Let us use the symbol **L** to indicate the rules of literary criticism, and the symbol **(p)** to mean the proposition that David had type-A blood. Let **L(p)** therefore mean (as representing Dworkin's theory) that there exist literary criteria such that the proposition that David has type-A blood is the best possible answer to the question of whether he had type-A blood or not. Dworkin is now saying that in such a case we may conclude neither that **L(p)** nor **L(-p)**, but rather **-L(p v -p).** Without once again reproducing either the full classical square or the full hexagon of Blanché we can see immediately that these three possibilities represent one of the triadic oppositions within the hexagon (figure 18):

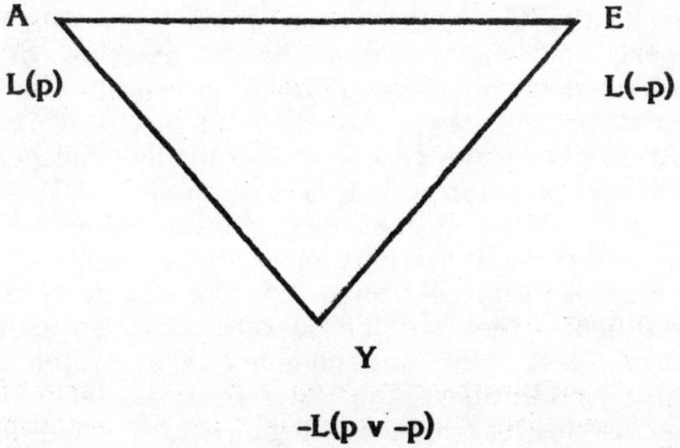

(Figure 18)

Of course, conceived as a point on the logical hexagon, Y need not be considered in any sense as a 'very special case', or in any way different in status from **A** or **E.** But Dworkin provides reasons why **Y** should here be regarded as special, and as not constituting a significant qualification of his thesis. Once again, in neutralising **Y,** Dworkin shows his orientation towards the semiotic, rather than the logical form of the square. He defines the occasions when one might expect **Y** to be manifested as follows:

> The occasions on which the participants would be tempted to say that there was no right answer to some question about David would be a function of two considerations. The first is the length of the novel, or, rather, the density of the information that Dickens does in fact supply. The second is the character of the question. If it is a question about a feature that is randomly distributed throughout a population, so that the fact that a boy had the specific characteristics Dickens described, no matter how dense the description, can have little bearing on the question of

> whether he had the feature in question, then it is more likely that the question will have no right answer. (1977:83)

Similarly, Dworkin argues, in the case of law:

> Once again, the occasions on which this claim might properly be made would be a function of two considerations: the density of the information supplied by the settled law, and the degree to which the question put by the case could be thought independent of whatever information is so supplied. This fact suggests that though these occasions might be frequent in immature legal systems, or in legal systems treating of only a limited range of the conduct of its constituents, they will be so rare as to be exotic in modern, developed, and complex legal systems. In these jurisdictions the intersections and interdependencies of different legal doctrine will be so intense that it will not be possible to maintain the third position against the other two. (1977:83f)

Once again, it is clear that Dworkin ultimately rests his case upon contingent facts of the legal system, as reported in the language of legal argument. That is why his orientation is far closer to the semiotic rather than the logical model. At the same time, we may note the particular kind of facts to which (alone) Dworkin would have us attend. The incidence of these 'very special' cases is a function of the text and of apparently objective, rational standards which might be applied to it: the degree to which the question put by the case could be thought independent of whatever information is so supplied, not the degree to which it is actually considered independent. Dworkin noticeably stops short of attributing the boundaries to the conventions of the interpreters. Impliedly, the criteria of coherence are universal. Both here and in his distinction between principles and policies, Dworkin veers towards a semantic (systemic) rather than a pragmatic (goal-oriented) account of interpretation.

We have seen in this section how closely Dworkin tries to associate the analysis of the discursive level of legal argument with the logic of norms of the legal system. A realist at heart, his preferred conception of the logic of norms (in contrast to that, for example, of the logician Kalinowski) is that manifested by the discursive level of legal argument itself:

> It may be that the supposition that one side may be right and the other wrong is cemented into our habits of thought at a level so deep that we cannot coherently deny that supposition, no matter how sceptical or hard-headed we wish to be in such matters. That would explain our difficulty in stating the theoretical argument in a coherent way. The 'myth' that there is one right answer in a hard case is both recalcitrant and successful. Its recalcitrance and success count as arguments that it is no myth. (1978:290)

'One right answer' is thus a supposition at the deep level of our thinking, which is reflected in various ways at the level of manifestation of legal discourse. The semiotician would have no quarrel with this, though he would want to go further. What he would reject is the inference drawn in the last sentence. For him, effective communication entails no adherence to the truth-claims of the message.

9.3 DEMONSTRABILITY AND THE SEMIOTIC PROCESSES OF LEGAL ARGUMENT

Jurisprudential positivists have long been attracted to natural science models (7), and in this respect Dworkin presents merely a particular variety of positivism. The object of study is to be defined in terms of some empirical criteria, and knowledge about such objects of study must be subject to objective criteria of validation. In other words, the natural science model states both ontological and epistemological criteria for scientific activity. Dworkin's attack on Hart may be read as a claim that both the ontological and the epistemological criteria of legal positivism have been too narrowly drawn. Yet in arguing for broader criteria in both these respects, Dworkin seeks still to adhere to a scientific model: he claims that the judge, even in hard cases, is dealing with a species of 'fact', and that his knowledge of such facts is subject to a form of objective validation. But his epistemology proves more plausible than his ontology.

Dworkin calls the ontological and epistemological presuppositions of the second version of 'no-right-answer' (9.1) the 'demonstrability thesis':

> This thesis states that if a proposition cannot be demonstrated to be true, after all the hard facts that might be relevant to its truth are either known or stipulated, then it cannot be true. By 'hard facts' I mean physical facts and facts about behaviour (including the thoughts and attitudes) of people. By 'demonstrated' I mean backed by arguments such that anyone who understood the language in which the proposition is formed must assent to its truth or stand convicted of irrationality. (1977:76)

This, as we shall see, is precisely the kind of model which Kelsen endorses. **(8)** It is also fully compatible with Searle's conception of 'institutional fact', whereby 'brute facts' are objectively qualified as instances of a particular institution, in the light of the relevant institutional rules (8.2). Just as Searle argues that 'brute facts' are not the only kinds of fact, Dworkin maintains that 'hard facts' are not the only kind of fact to be encountered in the legal system. There could, for example, be 'moral facts', in virtue of which a proposition of law might be true. The proposition that Tom's contract is valid might be true in virtue of a belief that judges have a moral duty to enforce the promises that compose a contract. **(9)** But this takes us one stage further than the analysis of Kelsen or Searle. Here, 'hard facts' (what the participants said or did, including their attitudes to their actions) are interpreted first in the light of the rules of legal institutions, so as to produce the proposition 'that Tom's contract is valid'; thereafter, that particular institutional fact is further interpreted in the light of what we may assume for the purposes of this argument to be moral conventions, in order to judge whether they constitute what Dworkin terms a 'particular moral fact' (that Tom's legally valid contract ought in morality to be enforced by the judge). **(10)**

But Dworkin does not rest his argument upon the existence of such 'moral facts' (1977:77). There do, however, exist in the legal system facts which are in principle susceptible to objective knowledge, and which go beyond conclusive legal qualifications of hard facts.

Dworkin reverts to his literary analogy. The intelligibility of literary criticism depends, he claims, upon the assumption of the existence of 'facts of narrative consistency' (1977:78):

> Participants assert a proposition about David as true (or deny it as false) if that proposition provides a better (or worse) fit than its negation with propositions already established, because it explains in a more satisfactory way why David did what he did, or said what he said, or thought what he thought, according to the established propositions. (1977:77f.)

For example, he suggests, the hypothesis that David had a sexual relationship with Steerforth provides a more satisfactory explanation of what he subsequently did and thought than the hypothesis that he did not.

But what, in reality, are such 'facts of narrative consistency'? Dworkin is fully aware of the obvious empiricist objection. The participants in the literary exercise, he argues, 'do have reasons for preferring one proposition to another, or at least they think they do, and even when they disagree each of them thinks he can distinguish cases when his opponents have genuine reasons on their side from cases when they do not. If they have all made a mistake, and no reasons exist, it is difficult to see why they think they do, and how their exercise can have had the success it has' (1977:79). Again, we observe the level at which Dworkin seeks to justify his argument: it is the level of participation. We cannot discount the fact that the participants think they have reasons. What, however, is the precise significance of the fact that the participants think they have reasons? It is not, as this passage might suggest, that their agreement is evidence of an ontological fact (going beyond that mere agreement), without which the intelligibility of the exercise could not be understood. It is rather that adherence to the belief in narrative consistency is a condition of participation in the debate. (11) It seems, therefore, that Dworkin here accepts a conventional basis for the literary exercise. The conventions are set by the participants, and no-one who participates in the exercise will be allowed to ignore them. These conventions may of their nature fail to render particular judgments demonstrable, but these are the conventions which have been adopted for the exercise in question. No one participant makes up these conventions himself. Rather, he is able to apply them through the training he has received for the purposes of participation: 'Whatever sense statements about narrative consistency may have, they are given that sense by the enterprise that trains participants to make and respond to such statements' (1977:81).

The success of Dworkin's argument does not, however, depend at all upon a broadening of empiricist ontology. Our analysis of Greimasian semiotics shows how the very strictest of positivist views in defining the object of study may be combined with a naturalist epistemology and realist conclusions (6.1-3). The whole burden of Dworkin's critique can properly be couched at the epistemological level, even if we adopt a conventionalist (Searle) rather than a universalist (Kant) version of it. We do not have to reify 'principles' any more than we have to reify 'rules'. Both may be regarded, quite consistently with Dworkin's approach, as part of the conventions adopted by the participants. There is, indeed, an instructive comparison to be drawn here between law and literature. As Michaels puts it: 'Judges cannot decide that contracts are ambiguous in the same way and for the same reasons that literary critics can. But this is not because legal **language** is less tolerant of ambiguity than poetic language is; it is because the institution of the law is less tolerant of ambiguity than the institution of literary criticism is. Judges do not read the same way literary critics do' (1979:33). 'Institutional fact' is inherently no less demonstrable than 'brute fact': everything depends upon the nature of the institution concerned, and of the institutive rules adopted for its recognition.

It is precisely the nature of the interpretive conventions adopted in law that yields for Dworkin both a denial of the demonstrability of the 'right answer' and an affirmation of its objective legal quality. Dworkin's theory of interpretation claims that certain conventions of consistency both exist, and ought to exist, in the legal system. A 'right answer' generated by such conventions of consistency would have the same status as a 'fact of narrative consistency' generated by literary criticism. It will not be 'even in principle demonstrable by ordinary scientific methods. Since no one ever did have just the history and character Dickens said David did, we cannot provide ordinary arguments of probability, even when all the histories of real people are known, that would necessarily convince any rational man either to accept or reject the hypothesis' (1977:78).

We are left with a very plausible and important critique of the positivist viewpoint: the operations of the legal system do not proceed in a uniformly demonstrable fashion. The existence of rules within the legal system may be capable of demonstration; but answers to hard cases also exist within the legal system, even if they cannot be demonstrated, but only be shown to possess the best claims to (conventional) plausibility. The positivist, by contrast, is prepared to assert the legal existence only of that which he can demonstrate. It is this which leads to the positivist opposition of law with discretion: discretion begins where law ends, law ends where discretion begins. In other words, if there is no applicable legal rule, clearly stateable in terms of a rule of recognition, then the judge has a discretion to decide; if the judge has no discretion to decide, that must be because there is a clearly stateable legal rule, demonstrable in terms of the rules of recognition of the system. The fact that Hart agrees that standards other than rules (principles, policies etc.) do play a role within legal argument only supports Dworkin's contention that for the positivists demonstrability is an underlying condition of law. For Hart, while broadly anticipating Dworkin's account of the role which principles actually play in legal argument (12), would view hard cases as ones where the judge has a discretion, guided no doubt by these principles, but where there exists no law until the judge actually makes a decision. (13) Until the time that he makes the decision, the outcome is not demonstrable; once he has made the decision, the outcome is demonstrable. Principles therefore are part of the analysis of discretion, not of law; significantly, legal principles form no part of Hart's (secondary) rules of adjudication. (14) Law and discretion are opposed terms: law must be demonstrable, discretion is the absence of law.

Dworkin concedes that the 'demonstrability thesis' is an argument which 'has not always been recognized or clearly set out in the thoughts of those whom it has influenced' (1977:76). If so, we might well conclude that its influence has been, and continues to be, all the more powerful. At the semi-popular level, the 'objectivity' of the legal system is an essential part of its legitimation; the ideological importance of the appearance of objectivity is manifest. In our culture, the natural sciences have long provided the dominant image of 'objectivity', and it is unsurprising that a system of coercion which requires legitimation should project itself in terms of that image. But the question goes beyond ideology and legitimation. Demonstrability is also important in semiotic terms (e.g. Bastide 1981). It is a concomitant of some sign systems more than others. The arguments of legal theorists regarding the role of demonstrability in the legal system (a claim differently expressed by Kelsen's notion of 'objective meaning') reflect parallel differences regarding the nature of the semiotic system which characterises the law.

In linguistic theory, we encounter at least two semiotic relations for which demonstrability is claimed. First, there is the relation between the **signifiant** and the **signifié** according to the semantics of Saussure. The association of a particular sound-image with a particular mental-image in any particular language is arbitrary; for Saussure, it was the very arbitrariness of the association between the sound-image and the mental-image which produced such demonstrability (1.2). Similar claims are often made in terms of syntactic relations, especially by Chomsky and his followers. For them, indeed, the important distinction between sentences which are grammatically well-formed and sentences which are not grammatically well-formed is based upon, and explicitly justified in terms of, the intuitive judgment of natural speakers of the language. Both Saussure and Chomsky have been concerned almost exclusively with signs viewed from the **linguistic** point of view. **(15)** It is these particular semantic and syntactic relations of linguistic signs for which such demonstrability is claimed. It does not necessarily follow that the comparable syntactic and semantic relations of signs viewed in the **discursive** context will have comparable properties. On these grounds, Pettit criticises the structuralist attempt to extend linguistic methods (1975:47): whereas the effect of a grammatical structure is that it is 'intuitively clear' whether a particular sentence is grammatical or not, the structuralist's narrative structures do not admit of such 'intuitively clear' judgments. **(16)**

The parallels between the jurisprudential debate over demonstrability, and the semiotic issues variously raised in the Chomskian and Saussurian traditions, are not mere analogies. The legal system depends upon the communication of messages between senders and receivers, even if these senders and receivers communicate at a distance, and often in a form such as deliberately to conceal their respective identities. Such communication depends upon signs of some kind. Here, we are concerned with the nature of those signs. Do they operate through the medium of a code, like that of the syntactic structures of a particular natural language, such that sentences are immediately recognised as well-formed or not ? At the semantic level, do they possess the arbitrariness of the linguistic sign, with the result that we can expect the unproblematic communication of meaning to be achieved ?

Most of the jurisprudential theorists considered in this book reply to these questions in the affirmative, even if they fall short of claiming that such demonstrability operates throughout the system of legal communication. Hart is a case in point. He regards the rule of recognition as a master rule specifying 'some feature or features possession of which by a suggested rule is taken as conclusive affirmative indication that it is a rule'. **(17)** Indeed, he describes the functions of secondary rules as a class as specifying 'the ways in which the primary rules may be conclusively ascertained, introduced, eliminated, varied, and the fact of their violation conclusively determined' (1961:92). Here, it is the relationship between one signifying element of the legal system (a primary rule) and another signifying element (the secondary rule) which is taken to 'indicate' that the primary rule properly belongs to the legal system in question. There thus exists a legal syntax in terms of which the proposed primary rule may be regarded as well-formed. The proposed primary rule possesses some signifying element which provides a 'conclusive affirmative indication' (Hart's phrase) to this effect. Hart's theory of interpretation (once the terms of a particular primary rule have been so recognised) suggests that the words used convey, for the most part, an unproblematic meaning (the 'core of settled meaning'), in line with the Saussurian semantic theory.

Yet on closer examination, both the syntactic and the semantic relations in law have special features. Natural languages are learned, for the most part, without formal instruction in grammar; the recognition of sentences as grammatically well-formed equally proceeds spontaneously ('intuitively'), without explicit reference to the rules. But the recognition of a primary rule as belonging to a particular legal system proceeds differently. G/L points out that it is a special feature of the 'grammar of law' that it seeks to be explicit (1976:87f.). Kelsen goes further: it is a peculiarity of an object of legal cognition that it 'can even say something about its own legal meaning': for example, 'The men assembled in Parliament can expressly declare that they are enacting a statute.' Thus, communication in law sometimes includes a 'legal self-interpretation' (1967:3). It is as if an English speaker were to preface his utterance with the words: 'What I am going to say is good English' !

Demonstrability at the semantic level also seems to operate differently in law. Take the case of **Riggs v. Palmer. (18)** No-one doubted that the rules contained in the New York statute were legally well-formed (in terms of the secondary rules of the New York legal system). Nor was there any doubt about the meaning of those words. A beneficiary was qualified to succeed if he was named in the will, and the will had been properly executed. In **Riggs v. Palmer,** a grandson was named in the will. That same grandson had murdered the testator. Nevertheless, the grandson was clearly covered by the words of the statute, which made no exception for such a case. But the New York court held that the maxim that a person ought not to profit from his wrong should be applied here, and denied the right of the grandson to inherit. There are two possible ways of accounting for this. One would be to say that a principle was allowed to override a rule, in a case where the two conflicted. The second, which Dworkin would appear to prefer (1978:77f.), is that we have here a conflict between two principles: the principle that statutes ought normally to be interpreted literally, and the principle that a person ought not to profit from his wrong. In the present case, the latter principle was judged to outweigh the former. Whichever form of analysis one prefers, the conclusion seems to follow that the literal meaning of a legal rule is never safe in the process of judicial interpretation, however demonstrable or 'intuitively clear' that meaning might appear to be. Dworkin, of course, denies that this results from arbitrariness on the part of the judge. On the contrary, it is the result of a conventional rationality which pervades the legal system. The demonstrability which results from the arbitrariness of the linguistic sign is thus subverted by the rationality of the legal semiotic itself. But here, such codes as carry the message of this rationality are not explicit. Whereas the legal system presents the appearance of being based entirely upon explicit codes, the reality is different. Even Dworkin's principles do not necessarily complete an account of the different codes operating within the legal system. On his own account, even the apparently self-evident principle which supports the application of the rule of precedent is the result of tacit social conventions, and may on occasion be subverted. It seems, therefore, that there is no inherent distinction between easy and hard cases, but rather some kind of code which tells us whether the case is to be regarded as easy or hard. **(19)**

When we reach this stage, it seems that we have to distinguish the two functions which Dworkin claims his theory of legal reasoning equally fulfils. We may continue to endorse Dworkin's view as a normative theory, a view of what legal reasoning ought to aspire to be. But we may have to part company with him in his claim that he provides an accurate account of what it actually is. At the very least, Dworkin's account, while constituting a significant advance upon the vision of a legal system in terms of the opposition between law and discretion (above), itself fails to provide a complete account. What he has told us is that the formalist view of law as a set of codes which produce demonstrability is insufficient; in addition, the law operates explicitly with symbols, which require non-demonstrable interpretation. But Dworkin here does no more than to expand the formalist account.

The real realist will wish to go further, and ask whether there exist other codes or symbols (whether demonstrable or non-demonstrable) which also convey messages. This is not the place to consider examples or relevant bodies of theory. But the argument in this section itself raises at least two possible areas for further investigation. The first is the codes through which the legal well-formedness of rules is conveyed. We know what the explicit grammar of the legal system says about this. But we may wonder whether, in practice, the messages are differently conveyed. Many practitioners would affirm such a difference. That, indeed, is part of the common complaint of practitioners (in retrospect) that the legal education they received was too 'academic'. What they are saying is that the codes which they actually use in practice to recognise law are different from the codes which they are taught in law schools. The codes they actually use are far less sophisticated - and perhaps far more demonstrable in their actual operation. They are the codes of practitioners' handbooks, H.M.S.O. imprints, etc. Again, if one asks a practitioner how the distinction between an 'easy' and a 'hard' case is to be recognised, he is likely to give a very different answer from that found in the books. Here, too, there are social codes involved, tacit codes which may well produce greater demonstrability, and which in some cases underlie but in others cut across the symbols in the books.

We may conclude by returning to the notion of arbitrariness. The syntactic codes of the law are not arbitrary in the same sense as are syntactic structures of natural languages. Some languages may put the subject before the verb, others after. One cannot justify the choice, in either direction, on rational grounds. Therefore, once the rule has been learned in a particular natural language, it becomes self-evident, internalised, unproblematic. But the choice of particular syntactic rules in a legal system is far from arbitrary. Far too much turns on it. The choice between defining statute in terms of assent in a bicameral legislature and assent in a unicameral legislature is a question quite open to rational debate, and indeed much ink has been spilled upon it. That is because the question matters: issues of power, ultimately affecting the whole range of human life, depend upon it, in a manner in which they cannot be said to depend upon the choice of whether the subject follows or precedes the verb. That, too, is the reason why the arbitrariness of the linguistic sign does not account sufficiently for the interpretation of words in the law. Too much hangs on the matter. **(20)** When we interpret the words of the law, we are interpreting them with a view to the effect of our interpretation upon the lives of the litigants, and others beyond. Mere arbitrariness, even such as results from a **system** of differences such as is proposed by structural semantics, is not a sufficient basis for decision. That, again, is a very good reason why the academic study of law differs from its interpretation in practice. Exercises in legal semantics, conducted in the law school, are exercises in the meanings of words, phrases, propositions, principles. Exercises in legal semantics conducted in the lawyer's office, or the courtroom, are exercises with the lives of the people involved. One might certainly wish that they would be conducted at the level of Hercules, using explicit if non-demonstrable codes. In practice, they are conducted in part through the use of other implicit codes. These latter social codes may well be non-linguistic, but we may suspect that they resemble linguistic codes more closely than do those of the formalist theories, in that they are, indeed, both unconscious (internalised) and (in more than one sense) arbitrary.

9.4 A CHARACTERISATION OF DWORKINIAN SEMIOTICS

Thus, far, Dworkin's theory of interpretation has been presented merely in terms of that to which it is opposed, and that to which it is compared. It is opposed to a positivist view, which limits the 'legal' to that which is demonstrably legal (9.3); it is compared to literary criticism, in which plausibility is taken to reside in the best possible application of conventionally accepted criteria (9.2). In fact, Dworkin's theory of legal interpretation is far more positive and specific than this might suggest. Consideration of some of its features enables us to attempt a characterisation of Dworkinian semiotics.

First, we have to ask what is the corpus which provides the framework within which questions of interpretation are to be answered. For the literary critic, the corpus is clearly defined, at least in principle. Questions about the relationship between David and Steerforth are to be answered on the basis of 'propositions already established' concerning those characters in the novel **David Copperfield.** The analogue to the novel **David Copperfield** is for Dworkin the whole legal system, which extends over a variety of authoritative texts. The ideal judge ('Hercules' - 1978:105) 'must construct a scheme of abstract and concrete principles that provides a coherent justification for all common law precedents and, so far as these are to be justified on principle, constitutional and statutory provisions as well' (1978:116f.). Dworkin adopts a theory of mistakes (1978:118-23) which allows, and indeed requires, the judge to set aside some authorities as 'mistakes', in so far as they might contribute to the generation of principles and exercise a 'gravitational force' on other decisions. **(21)** The analogy with literary interpretation still holds good here; the literary critic is not required to give equal, or indeed any, significance to everything stated in it.

In operating within his interpretative framework, thus defined, Hercules is bade to employ a methodology which takes account of 'principle' but not 'policy' (1978:113-5). A 'principle' is defined as a 'standard that is to be observed, not because it will advance or secure an economic, political or social situation deemed desirable, but because it is a requirement of justice or fairness or some other dimension of morality'; a 'policy' is 'that kind of standard that sets out a goal to be reached, generally an improvement in some economic, political, or social feature of the community' (1978:22). Principles are propositions that describe the rights of individuals and groups within society; policies, by contrast, advance the collective goals of society (1978:90ff.). There is a major difference between the operation of arguments based on principle and policy arguments. The former carry an inherent demand for consistent application; the latter carry little or any such demand (1978:113f.). The role of judges is to apply the rights of individuals and groups within society as consistently as possible; it is the role of the legislature to adopt policies which will secure collective goals, through measures which may confer benefits or impose burdens on individuals inconsistently. For example, economic considerations may make it desirable to provide subsidies to certain manufacturers but not to others, or to apply them for short periods (thus favouring some) and then to terminate them (thus prejudicing others). It is for the legislature to enact such policies; it is for the administration to administer them. Judges should not be called upon to decide hard cases in the light of such considerations. If the judge is to deploy interpretative techniques such as will allow him to decide hard cases by selecting that proposition which fits best into the overall structure of the legal system, that overall structure must be conceived as a rational, consistent whole.

In interpreting the legal system, the judge is thus looking for evidence of the rights which the legal system is taken to endorse. When Dworkin speaks of using the concept of statutory purpose in statutory interpretation (1978:116), he is not talking about some 'mental state of particular legislators' (which might be taken to underlie the 'communicational model' of Hart, given the latter's conception of 'meaning', 7.1 above), but rather such 'arguments of principle and policy (which) might properly have persuaded the legislature to enact just that statute' (1978:108). Those arguments of principle and policy will not be purely subjective or speculative; they will have been derived through a consideration of the constitution and body of legislation of the community in question, and of the constitutional and political theory which those documents imply; indeed, the draftsmen of the constitution intend that subsequent interpreters work out their own theories of the meaning of the constitution (Schauer 1982:808) - an attempt to marry authorial intention and systemic interpretation through a theory of delegation. When Hercules considers the impact for the future of particular past precedents, he is to view them not in accordance with the individual intentions of their individual authors, but rather within the context of 'all other judicial decisions within his general jurisdiction and, indeed, statutes as well, so far as these must be seen to be generated by principle rather than policy'. The job of Hercules is thus one of rational reconstruction: 'the law may not be a seamless web; but the plaintiff is entitled to ask Hercules to treat it as if it were' (1978:116).

We see from this two notable characteristics of Dworkinian semiotics. First, it is fiercely systemic. The choice of rationale of a particular statute or precedent is to be judged on criteria of 'fit' with other aspects of the system. In the interests of coherence, Dworkin even requires the development of a theory of 'mistakes', through which some features of the legal system may be ignored, precisely because they have come to fit badly, and thus weaken the coherence of the system as a whole. In its emphasis upon system, Dworkinian semiotics may be regarded as the application of a form of structural semantics at the discursive level. However, the system concerned is not one based upon arbitrary associations and differences: on the contrary, it is a system based upon rationalism. It proceeds not by means of arbitrary signs, but by 'indices' or 'symbols' (1.2). The statutes and precedents are not signs of rights; they themselves embody these rights, and are reflections, or evidence, or symptoms of a more comprehensive system of rights. If Hart presents us with a pragmatic theory of interpretation dressed up in the form of semantics (7.2-3), Dworkin provides the converse - a semantic theory, masquerading as pragmatics. The methodology required of Hercules may be reflective and demanding. The evidence for the theory may be taken from the activities of an interventionist American judiciary. But this should not obscure Dworkin's underlying conceptual claims. Rights are pre-existent in the system; they are not created (though they may be discovered) by the judges. The legal system should be viewed synchronically, as a system at a particular point in time, notwithstanding the fact that both principles and policies may have changed in the past, and may yet change again in the future.

This conclusion leads us to pose the same question of appropriateness as has been directed at both Hart and MacCormick. Is this conception of legal semiotics really appropriate to the setting in which it is claimed to operate ? For Dworkin, the setting is undoubtedly that of judicial determination of hard cases. Dworkin claims that his theory is both descriptive and normative, that it provides a reasonably accurate account of the way judges do argue, together with reasons why such parameters of argument are appropriate. On both counts, his view is open to serious challenge. It has, indeed, been argued that Hercules belongs more properly to the Harvard or Yale lecture theatre, rather than the bench of the Supreme Court. (22) MacCormick, in particular, has maintained that 'consequentialist argument' - an evaluation of any proposed ruling in terms of its consequences, and those of others like it, both for the parties and for society as a whole - must rank alongside considerations of consistency and coherence as the 'second- order justifications' employed in the legal system (1978:105ff.). In other words, judicial argument should look outside its own systemic frame of reference, as well as inside; it is extensional in nature, as well as intensional.

CHAPTER TEN

Kelsen and the Semiotics of Legal Acts

(10.1) Conceptions of the Norm: There are notable ambiguities in Kelsen's conception of the norm and its relation to an act of will. Sometimes it appears as a propositional content referring to future action, at other times as the imperatival force of previous acts. A synthetic conception attaches propositional content to acts and imperatival force to the qualification of those acts as norms, but even the propositional content of an act is ultimately denied by Kelsen. **(10.2) Forms of Meaning:** Kelsen distinguishes two forms of meaning, subjective and objective. It seems clear that the latter refers to the force (validity) of an utterance rather than its propositional content. Subjective meaning (including possibility of performance in a relationship of imputation) is a necessary condition of objective meaning and this too appears to be regarded by Kelsen as at least including force as well as propositional content, if not as excluding the latter. **(10.3) Conditions of Meaning:** A condition of 'objective meaning' for Kelsen is the presupposition of a basic norm (**Grundnorm**) authorising the constitution, which he fashions 'by analogy' on Kant's transcendental categories. But the **Grundnorm** is required only if we actually experience the workings of a particular legal system as objective. In his early work, Kelsen also assumes a condition of 'reasonableness' in legal systems, such as to necessitate the postulation of rules to avoid norm-conflicts. But this too came to be regarded as a contingent fact about particular legal systems. **(10.4) Hierarchical Relations within the System:** Kelsen's movement away from a communicational model of law, involving relationships between general and particular legal propositions, is seen in his analysis of legal errata through the doctrine of normative alternatives, wherein formal conditions of validity take priority over material conditions. The same trend is apparent in Kelsen's analysis of interpretation 'outside the frame' of a statute, and in his ultimate rejection of the 'logic of norms', wherein he completely separates norms from legal propositions. **(10.5) Decisions and Doctrine:** Norms for the later Kelsen are the meanings of acts of will directed towards past, known facts. This makes it difficult to explain those norms of competence which still seem required for formal authorisation. An alternative analysis (Oppenheim) sees validity, correctness and enforceability as features of legal sentences. 'Correctness' relates to the cognitive relations betwen sentences, enforceability to the pragmatic quality deriving from statement by a competent authority. Incorrect sentences may still be enforceable. **(10.6) Kelsen and Greimasian Semiotics:** The later Kelsen's conception of the law is understandable in terms of Greimasian semiotics: legal 'recognition' is constitutive of legal meaning. General norms remain 'virtual' until such recognition is accorded to their cognitive implications. But Greimasian semiotics regards any normative relationship between legislator and judge merely as one part of the message legal discourse seeks to convey.

10.1 CONCEPTIONS OF THE NORM

Conceptually, Kelsen's approach to legal theory stands further away from that of semiotics than does that of any other of the theorists considered in this book. The author of the 'Pure Theory' (**Reine Rechtslehre**) is concerned with norms, not facts (1967:70, 75). Nevertheless, Kelsen's conception of the norm is intimately bound up with the relationship between facts and the different kinds of meaning which may be attributed to them. Semiotic relationships are therefore involved in Kelsen's conception of the norm; the legal norm belongs to a particular semiotic universe - that of 'objective meaning' (of a particular type). But Kelsen's statements on the nature of the norm show traces of an internal conflict between the use of two different semiotic models - a 'communicational' model on the one hand, and something resembling a 'speech act' model on the other. (1) The former is best seen in Kelsen's view of the normal workings of the 'hierarchy of norms' (the **Stufenbau** theory, representing the 'dynamic' aspect of law), and is expressed by the conception of the norm as 'a schema of interpretation'; the latter is best reflected in Kelsen's description of 'wrong' legal decisions or 'unconstitutional' statutes, in his late 'irrationalist' phase denying any 'logic of norms', and in the conception of the norm as the 'meaning of an act of will'. The use of semiotic models as analytical tools in exploring these and related aspects of Kelsen's thought assists in identifying the nature of the difficulties in his theory (2); conversely, Kelsen's own difficulties assist in the identification of issues which must be tackled in any developed semiotic theory of law.

Kelsen shows ambivalence between what Harris has called the propositional and imperatival attributes of legal rules in his account of the nature of the norm. (3) This, as Harris points out, would make then indistinguishable from the propositions of legal science, which Kelsen was later to regard as a wholly separate realm (10.5 below). The ambivalence is apparent from the very first pages of **Reine Rechtslehre.** The norm is presented both as the meaning of an act of will and as a schema of interpretation by reference to which such meanings can be attributed:

> The external fact whose objective meaning is a legal or illegal act is always an event that can be perceived by the senses (because it occurs in time and space) and therefore a natural phenomenon determined by causality. However, this event as such, as an element of nature, is not an object of legal cognition. What turns this event into a legal or illegal act is not its physical existence, determined by the laws of causality prevailing in nature, but the objective meaning resulting from its interpretation. The specifically legal meaning of this act is derived from a 'norm' whose content refers to the act; this norm confers legal meaning to the act, so that it may be interpreted according to this norm. (1967:3f., para. 4a)

> 'Norm' is the meaning of an act by which a certain behavior is commanded, permitted, or authorized. (1967:5, para. 4b)

It thus seems as if, for Kelsen, the norm is bi-directional: at one and the same time it is the meaning attributed to an act which took place **before** the attribution of that meaning, and it looks forward to the attribution of meaning to future acts which may be interpreted by reference to it. The same ambiguity is reflected in Kelsen's accounts of the relations between the act and the norm. In **Reine Rechtslehre** he describes the notion of an act of will 'creating' a norm (thus regarding the two as quite distinct entities) as a 'figure of speech' (1967:7), a view repeated in the last phase of his work (1973:217). Nevertheless, he later gives an account of contract which appears to adopt such a distinction:

> The contract as a norm-creating fact, and the norm created by this fact, need to be clearly distinguished . . . One speaks of the conclusion of a contract and means by this the acts which constitute the norm-creating set of facts. And one speaks of the validity of a contract and means by this the norm created by these facts; for only a norm - not an act - can be 'valid'. (1967:260)

Kelsen does not here argue, as one might expect, that the legally valid contract is the objective meaning of the acts constitutive of the contract. Rather he suggests that those acts create a separate norm. The argument is perhaps best explicable in terms of institutional theory (8.1): a valid legal norm represented by the consequential rules of an institution is created by acts themselves qualified as legal in terms of the relevant institutive rules.

We may characterise these two conceptions of the norm as emphasising, respectively, 'propositional' and 'imperatival' features, 'propositional' where the norm is presented as a 'schema of interpretation', 'imperatival' where it is presented as the meaning of an act of will. The former involves communicational functions, particularly as they appear between different levels of the legal hierarchy; the latter involves a characterisation of the particular force of an utterance, rather than its propositional content. The different semiotic functions of the two models are reflected in the contexts in which Kelsen uses them.

The Norm as a Schema of Interpretation

According to this conception, Kelsen presents the norm as the means by which a particular kind of meaning is attributed to acts in the external world. To this extent, they are comparable to Searle's institutional rules, by virtue of which a particular institutional meaning may be given to 'brute facts'. As Kelsen puts it:

> The norm functions as a scheme of interpretation . . the qualification of a certain act as the execution of the death penalty rather than as murder - a qualification that cannot be perceived by the senses - results from a thinking process: from the confrontation of this act with the criminal code and the code of criminal procedure. That the mentioned exchange of letters between merchants constitutes legally a contract, results exclusively from the fact that such an exchange conforms with conditions defined in the civil code. That a document is objectively **as well** as subjectively a valid testament results from the fact that it conforms to conditions stipulated by this code. That an assembly of people is a parliament, and that the meaning of their act is a statute, results from the conformity of all these facts with the norms laid down in the constitution. That means, that the contents of actual happenings agree with a norm accepted as valid. (1967:4)

Norms then, not only represent legal meanings; they are also constitutive of legal meanings. **(4)**

The norm thus appears to have the semiotic properties of external reference and direction to an addressee. When the constitution lays down norms in conformity with which acts in a legislative assembly may have the objective meaning of a statute, those norms refer to events which are to take place in the future, in the outside world, and the norms are directed to people who may perform such acts (or judge them), since by 'norm' we mean 'that something **ought** to be or **ought** to happen, especially that a human being ought to behave in a specific way' (1967:4). Because, according to this conception, the confrontation of an act with the norm which will constitute its schema of interpretation is, as Kelsen puts it, a 'thinking process' (5), it follows that any thinking person may form such a judgment, and that the correctness of such a judgment will depend only upon the correctness of the thought. Even the person at whose behaviour the act of will is directed may normally be capable of that thinking process. Therefore, the person whose behaviour is governed by a norm is in a position to know whether his action will be legal or not. In these early pages of **Reine Rechtslehre,** 'subsumption' is, in effect, the instrument of objectivity, and objectivity - meaning the availability of objective knowledge of the law - is in theory available to all:

> If the 'ought' is also the objective meaning of the act, the behavior at which the act is directed is regarded as something that **ought** to be not only from the point of view of the individual who has performed the act, but also from the point of view of the individual at whose behavior the act is directed, and of a third individual not involved in the relation between the two . . then the 'ought' as the objective meaning of an act, is a valid **norm** binding upon the addressee, that is, the individual at whom it is directed. The ought which is the subjective meaning of an act of will is also the objective meaning of this act, if this act has been invested with this meaning, if it has been authorized by a norm, which therefore has the character of a 'higher' norm. (1967:7f.)

Legal norms, in the formulation of **Reine Rechtslehre,** refer to human behaviour (1967:12). The act of will of which they are the meaning must be directed towards the regulation of behaviour which is human. Since human behaviour necessarily occurs in space and time, legal norms must refer to the spatial and temporal dimensions of human acts, even if those dimensions are unlimited. Moreover, it is not every kind of human behaviour for which a norm may provide a schema of interpretation. If there is a relationship of automatic compliance, or conversely of impossibility of compliance, between the norm and the behaviour, then the relationship of obligation or imputation cannot arise, and the act of will cannot be interpreted as a law. Kelsen gives 'a norm prescribing that one ought to die' as an example of the former, and a norm 'that one ought not to die' as an example of the latter; both are, in the universe of normative discourse, 'meaningless' (1960:181).

In short, this conception of the norm involves a proposition as to what people in the future ought to do, and provides a means subsequently to judge the objective legal quality of those acts. (6)

The Norm as the Meaning of an Act of Will

It is difficult to reconcile this first conception of the norm with Kelsen's identification of the norm with the 'meaning of an act of will' and his remark that the notion of creation of a norm is figurative. The tension becomes all the more acute in Kelsen's later work, in which a firm wedge is driven between the roles of cognition (legal science) and volition (norms) (10.5, below). Can the norm simultaneously be the meaning of an act of volition and the thinking process by which a particular meaning is attributed to that act ?

Troper has pointed to Kelsen's theory of interpretation as a reflection of this tension. For Kelsen, interpretation consists in establishing the meaning of the norm to be applied. But this, Troper suggests, totally contradicts Kelsen's own definition of the norm. The norm is the meaning of an act of volition. If interpretation is the determination of the meaning of something, then a norm cannot be the object of interpretation. It is absurd to suppose that one could determine the meaning of a meaning (1981:521).

The only alternative, according to Troper, is to make use of Kelsen's distinction between **Rechtsnorm** and **Rechtssatz.** If the norm itself cannot be the object of interpretation, then it must be the **Rechtssatz,** the linguistic proposition which expresses the norm, which is the object of interpretation. When this linguistic proposition is not clear, then we have a problem of the meaning of the norm which it is the function of interpretation to resolve: what exactly is the meaning of the words which express the norm ? (7) But Troper is not satisfied with this account. Kelsen, he says, still wrongly claims that the function of interpretation is to determine the meaning of the norm, but on his own account interpretation is concerned only with determining the meaning of the linguistic proposition which expresses the norm. In other words, the object of interpretation is not a norm, but only a text (1981:521).

I believe that the later Kelsen would have accepted Troper's criticism. Increasingly, he appears to have embraced the view that the norm and the linguistic proposition are different worlds of experience, even though the latter claims (for ideological reasons, as Kelsen comes near to suggesting on the last page of the second edition of **Reine Rechtslehre**) to express the former. On this understanding, interpretation belongs to the world of legal propositions, that is to the science of law, or legal doctrine. It may also impinge psychologically upon the activities of the law-applying organs whose acts will have the meaning of legal norms. But the attribution of that objective meaning to those acts does not depend upon the cognitive activities of the law-applying organ.

A Synthetic Conception of the Norm

There are indications that Kelsen was aware of the tension between his various formulations. He expresses the view that it is the act of will itself - and not some separate norm created by it - which prescribes future behaviour:

> 'Norm' is the meaning of an act by which a certain behavior is commanded, permitted or authorized. The norm, as the specific meaning of an act directed toward the behavior of someone else, is to be carefully differentiated from the act of will whose meaning the norm is . . (1967:5)

The behaviour is commanded, etc., by the **act**; the norm is the meaning of that act. In an article published in 1960, this formulation is combined with the view that creation of a norm by an act of will is figurative:

> That a norm is the meaning of an act of will intentionally directed to the behavior of another (or many others) is expressed figuratively by saying that a norm is 'created' or 'posited' through an act of will. (1960:180)

Yet here too, Kelsen slips on the very next page back into the conventional shorthand which describes the norm itself, rather than the act of which it is the meaning, as directing behaviour:

> To say that a norm 'refers' to actual behavior is to say that the norm can be applied to actual behavior, that actual behavior can be confronted with it, that this behavior can be interpreted according to it and judged as conforming to or departing from it. (1960:181)

On this account, the norm has the properties of a proposition only in so far as it is the meaning of an act which has the qualities of a proposition. It is the act of will itself which is viewed as having the semiotic properties of external reference and direction to an addressee. The act of will is the act communicating the will of the addressor that the addressee should behave in a certain manner. Even if expressed by gesture instead of speech (1967:7), it is, in a very real sense, a speech act - an act of will which communicates a message. Such a speech act has the meaning of a legal norm if created in conformity with another 'higher' (another expression which, as Kelsen occasionally reminds us (1967:221), is used metaphorically) norm. Even in **Reine Rechtslehre,** the norm is not itself viewed as a proposition, but rather as the meaning of an act which has a propositional content. It is because that act has such a propositional content that the norm may then be used as a schema of interpretation for further acts. And that relationship, as we have seen from a passage already quoted, is accepted by Kelsen in **Reine Rechtslehre** as cognitive: the qualification of a certain act as the execution of the death penalty rather than as a murder . . . 'results from a thinking process: from the confrontation of this act with the criminal code and the code of criminal procedure' (1967:4).

One ambiguity does, however, remain. For the most part, Kelsen speaks as if the norm is the meaning of the **total** act of will, that is, of the combined effect of the will and its propositional content, as interpreted by reference to the higher norm. But there is a passage where he appears to distinguish between the act of will and its propositional content, and to ascribe the term 'norm' only to the latter:

> The norm, as the specific meaning of an act directed toward the behavior of someone else, is to be carefully differentiated from the act of will whose meaning the norm is: the norm is an **ought,** but the act of will is an

> **is.** Hence the situation constituted by such an act must be described by the statement: The one individual wills that the other individual ought to behave in a certain way. The first part of this sentence refers to an **is,** the existing fact of the first individual's act of volition; the second part to an **ought,** to a norm as the meaning of that act. **(8)**

But perhaps Kelsen is only saying here that the propositional content of the act of will becomes a norm in so far as that act of will is qualified as authorised under the terms of the higher norm.

We might summarise this 'synthetic' view by distinguishing between the ontological status of the norm and its semiotic function. **(9)** Ontologically, the norm has no existence separate from that of the act of will, of which it is a particular meaning. At the same time, that meaning functions to communicate messages regarding future behaviour. One might compare the arm movements of a traffic policeman. Those movements have a certain meaning in terms of the semiotic code he employs; he is not creating some ontologically independent entity. Yet at the same time, those actions - assuming that they are performed in a communicative context - serve to address instructions regarding the movement of traffic to road users. We might also distinguish the semantic content of the movements from their illocutionary force. Despite persistent ambiguities, it seems best to regard Kelsen's description of a norm as the 'meaning' of an act of will as denoting its illocutionary force (objective meaning) as an act recognised as legally valid.

Later, however, Kelsen clearly rejected any such semiotic synthesis:

> Indeed, the 'addressing' of a norm to a person means nothing more than that the **behaviour** of a person, a piece of human behaviour, is obligated. It is not the person as such, in the totality of his existence and behaviour, that the norm relates to, but rather a particular piece of human behaviour. The norm is 'addressed to a person', in that it posits as obligatory some piece of behaviour on the part of **one** person, or a determinate or indeterminate number of persons. To be the 'addressee' of a norm is only a way of saying

> that the behaviour decreed in the norm to be obligatory is human behaviour, the behaviour of a person. (1973:221)

The meaning of an act of will cannot be a **proposition that** behaviour is legally qualified in a certain manner: 'Norms . . are merely meanings; but they are not the meanings of acts of thought, nor are they thoughts, therefore, but are rather the meanings of acts of will' (1973:225). In short: 'Obligation, the norm, is the meaning of an act of will' (1973:217).

Kelsen now appears to deny that the meaning of his act of will can itself be a legal proposition (which in turn can fulfil a communicative function). No such proposition is therefore 'addressed' to people whose behaviour appears to be governed by the general norm (the meaning of the act of will in question). Whereas Kelsen had earlier linked the notions of 'subjective meaning' and 'objective meaning', which would allow him to admit the communicative function as part of the subjective intention of the act of utterance, he now appears to discount entirely the subjective meaning of the act. (**10**)

10.2 FORMS OF MEANING

'Meaning' (**Sinn**) is clearly important to Kelsen. It plays a role in each of his different conceptions of the norm, sometimes identified with the norm (the imperatival conception), sometimes functioning as the product of the interaction between the act and the norm (the propositional conception). But the term 'meaning' is notoriously polysemic, and we need to examine further in exactly what sense Kelsen uses it.

The opening sections of **Reine Rechtslehre** show the centrality for Kelsen of the distinction between 'subjective meaning' and 'objective meaning'. It is the latter which is equated with 'legal meaning' and also frequently with 'validity'. But even 'subjective meaning', as here used by Kelsen, is used with reference to pragmatic rather than semantic characteristics of the act in question. This is what Oppenheim calls 'official quality'. (**11**) Kelsen seeks to distinguish between such official quality as people may think an act has, whether rightly or wrongly ('subjective meaning') and that official quality which it actually has, according to the legal system ('objective meaning'). We see this from Kelsen's own example:

> Somebody makes some dispositions, stating in writing what is to happen to his belongings when he dies. The subjective meaning of this act is a testament. Objectively, however, it is not, because some legal formalities were not observed. (1967:3)

Thus, by the 'subjective meaning' of the writing, Kelsen appears not to refer to a semantic analysis (of whatever kind) of its words, but rather to the view taken by the writer (and perhaps others) as to the status in law of that document. **(12)** But the writer's opinion is not conclusive of such status; the written act also has an objective meaning, which may or may not agree with the subjective meaning, namely whether or not it really is a valid testament in law.

There is, however, another dimension to Kelsen's understanding of 'subjective meaning'. Nothing can have even the subjective meaning of a legal act unless it can be construed as a norm, and this in turn requires the presence of the relationship of imputation. Anything which does not involve that relationship would be 'meaningless' as a norm; this is why statements directing behaviour which is physically either inevitable or impossible cannot be norms (10.1). It is in this same context that Kelsen argues that a minimum of effectiveness is also a condition of the validity of a legal norm. **(13)**

It is this view that we do not attribute the meaning of a norm to an act of will which prescribes something which is not minimally effective, which seems to underlie Kelsen's position in the classical Pure Theory on expressly conflicting norms. If a statute concurrently obliges the subject to do **x** and not to do **x**, then the act of will which produced that statute must be regarded as meaningless in the normative sense, since it is impossible for the subject to give effect to incompatible prescriptions. If a statute contains clauses which cannot be interpreted as compatible,

> then the legislator creates something meaningless; we then have a meaningless act of norm creation and therefore no act at all whose subjective meaning can be interpreted as its objective meaning; no objectively valid legal norm is present, although the act has been

> posited according to the basic norm. The basic norm does not bestow the objective meaning of a valid norm upon every act, but only upon an act that has a meaning - the subjective meaning that individuals ought to behave in a certain way. The act must be meaningful in this normative sense. If the act has a different meaning (such as the meaning of an assertion, for example of a theory propounded in a statute) or no meaning at all (for example, if a statute contains nonsensical words or prescriptions incompatible with each other), then no subjective meaning is present that can be interpreted as objective meaning; no act is present whose subjective meaning is capable of being legitimized by the basic norm. (1967:207)

Later Kelsen was to resile from this viewpoint. By implication, each prescription within the statute was to be treated as a separate act of will, and objective meaning required only that the act of will should come from a competent authority. The fact that the two norms, taken in combination, might place the subject in a position of legal dilemma was no longer regarded as relevant to the meaning of the act as legal. It might, of course, represent a cogent criticism of the law, but that was a different matter. Kelsen seems not, however, to have abandoned the other conditions of subjective meaning. In particular, he seems in his later work still to maintain that the impossible law is not a law, and that a minimum of effectiveness is necessary for the attribution of legal meaning. Here, one may have to qualify the conventional view of Kelsen. Such sociological factors as possibility of implementation or minimum of effectiveness do enter into his conception of legal validity, but through the route of his assumptions regarding 'subjective meaning'.

These two dimensions of legal meaning - the necessity of a relationship of imputation on the one hand, objective legal validity on the other - may when taken together help to resolve one level of contradiction in Kelsen's text. Sometimes he speaks of legal validity or objective meaning as a characteristic of acts or facts **(14)**; elsewhere, he says that 'only a norm' - not an act - can be 'valid'. **(15)** These views are compatible if we say that Kelsen requires the agent to view his act as creating a relationship of imputation, so that his act has the subjective meaning of a norm, before that norm can be given the 'objective meaning' of legal validity. To say this, of course, implies once again that the act whose meaning is a norm has a forward projection (as creating the relationship of imputation), even if this relationship is not given propositional form. But such an analysis hardly answers all the questions. It is not entirely clear why the need for a relationship of imputation is assigned to the level of subjective meaning; certainly, it seems to survive in the later Kelsen, despite the increasing radicalisation of his exclusion of 'impure' phenomena, such as the attitudes of the participants.

'Meaning' for Kelsen is thus the question of whether an act or a norm belongs to a particular universe of discourse, in this case legal discourse. Objective legal meaning is a form of institutional meaning, but it is conferred not in accordance with the views of the participants but according to objective criteria, even though these objective criteria appear, in the later Kelsen at least, as no more than the fact of decision by a competent legal organ. The act of a footballer in kicking the ball into the net may have the subjective meaning of a 'goal', in that the player understands his act as having that significance under the rules of the game of football. If the referee so rules, the act also has the objective meaning of a goal; if he whistles for off-side, the subjective meaning of the act does not correspond to its objective meaning.

10.3 CONDITIONS OF MEANING

If an act or norm is to belong to the universe of legal meaning, certain conditions must be fulfilled. The universe of legal discourse is a universe of norms, and therefore any acts which are regarded as legal must function within relationships of imputation; since the legal universe is 'objective', the conditions for the existence of such objectivity must also be satisfied. Kelsen takes the view that the validity of a norm can be derived only from another norm, and not from a fact. Hence, behind the constitution, there must stand a **Grundnorm** or basic norm, which provides the basis (**Grund**) of the validity of the norms of the constitution. The **Grundnorm** is therefore a condition of 'objective meaning'.

The nature of this condition has been the subject of

much debate, and Kelsen himself changed his opinion about it. In **Reine Rechtslehre,** the **Grundnorm** appears as a condition of our actual thinking about the legal system, a condition without which it would not be possible for us to think in the way we do. It is by virtue only of the **Grundnorm** that legal science is able to interpret acts as having the objective meaning of legal validity. As Kelsen puts it: 'It merely makes conscious what most legal scientists do, at least unconsciously, when they understand the mentioned facts not as causally determined, but instead interpret their subjective meaning as objectively valid norms, that is, as a normative legal order, without basing the validity of this order upon a higher, meta-legal norm, that is, upon a norm enacted by an authority superior to the legal authority; in other words, when they consider as law exclusively positive law. The theory of the basic norm is merely the result of an analysis of the procedure which a positivistic science of law has always applied.' **(16)** Kelsen's affinity here to Kant has been the subject of some discussion. **(17)** Indeed Kelsen himself explicitly makes the comparison:

> Insofar as only the presupposition of the basic norm makes it possible to interpret the subjective meaning of the constitution-creating act (and of the acts established according to the constitution) as their objective meaning, that is, as objectively valid legal norms, the basic norm as represented by the science of law may be characterized as the transcendental-logical condition of this interpretation, if it is possible to use by analogy a concept of Kant's epistemology. Kant asks: 'How is it possible to interpret without a metaphysical hypothesis, the facts perceived by our senses, in the laws of nature formulated by natural science ?' In the same way, the Pure Theory of Law asks: 'How is it possible to interpret without recourse to meta-legal authorities, like God or nature, the subjective meaning of certain facts as a system of objectively valid legal norms describable in rules of law ?' The epistemological answer of the Pure Theory of Law is: 'By presupposing the basic norm that one ought to behave as the constitution prescribes, that is, one ought to behave in accordance with the subjective meaning of the constitution-creating act of will -

> according to the prescriptions of the authority creating the constitution.' The function of this basic norm is to found the objective validity of a positive legal order, that is, to interpret the **subjective** meaning of the acts of human beings by which the norms of an effective coercive order are created, as their objective meaning. (1967:202)

It should be stressed that Kelsen sees the function of the **Grundnorm** in terms of the understanding of **our actual legal experience.** It is, therefore, tied to our experience of particular systems of positive law. If a particular society has rules of conduct which are not experienced as having an objective dimension of legality beyond their subjective meaning, then there is no need in such a system to presuppose a **Grundnorm.** Or, more accurately, such a **Grundnorm** is **not** presupposed in the legal thinking of that particular society:

> The fact that the basic norm of a positive legal system **may** but **need not** be presupposed means: the relevant interhuman relationships may be, but need not be, interpreted as 'normative,' that is, as obligations, authorizations, rights, etc., constituted by objectively valid norms. It means further: they can be interpreted without such presupposition (i.e. without the basic norm) as power relations (i.e., relations between commanding and obeying or disobeying human beings) - in other words, they can be interpreted sociologically, not juristically. **(18)**

It is the contingent nature of the **Grundnorm** which distinguishes it from the Kantian categories, and leads Kelsen to describe it as constructed by way of analogy. The **Grundnorm** is not a universal legal category, but is related to particular legal systems. Kelsen stresses:

> To understand the nature of the basic norm it must be kept in mind that it refers directly to a specific constitution, actually established by custom or statutory creation, by and large effective, and indirectly to the coercive order created according to this constitution and by and large effective; the basic norm thereby furnishes the reason for the validity of

> this constitution and of the coercive order created in accordance with it . . only if this basic norm, referring to a specific constitution, is presupposed, that is, only if it is presupposed that one ought to behave according to this specific constitution - only then can the subjective meaning of a constitution-creating act and of the acts created according to this constitution be interpreted as their objective meaning, that is, as objectively valid legal norms, and the relationships established by these norms as legal relations. (1967:201)

To put Kelsen's view in semiotic terms, we may say that the **Grundnorm** represents a condition of the existence of the language system within which coercive orders are qualified as objectively legal. If we do not use that coercive language system, we have no need to presuppose the **Grundnorm.**

Yet even in **Reine Rechtslehre,** Kelsen shows some self-doubt on the status of the **Grundnorm.** He concedes that there is a certain parallel between the **Grundnorm** and a theory of natural law, which makes the difference between them 'relative rather than absolute' (1967:219). This is because the **Grundnorm,** according to the classical theory, 'is not a positive but a presupposed norm, hence not a norm of the positive law whose validity is founded on the basic norm; and according to the natural-law doctrine, the validity of positive law likewise rests on a norm that is not a norm of positive law and functions as a value standard of this law' (1967:219). In this passage, Kelsen goes on to identify the difference between the **Grundnorm** and natural law in terms of the function of natural law as providing an external standard by which the very validity of positive law may be assessed. However, at the conceptual level, there remains the difference that natural law presupposes a fact of which human beings could have **no possible experience** (viz., the will of God to behave in a certain way), while the **Grundnorm** is the presupposition of a norm of which we do have actual (albeit indirect) experience, in our daily operation of the legal system.

Also significant is Kelsen's description, in the classical Pure Theory, of the nature of the **Grundnorm:**

> Since this basic norm cannot be the meaning of an act of will; and since this norm (rather: the statement

> about it) is logically indispensable for the foundation of the objective validity of positive legal norms, it can only be the meaning of an act of thinking: the science of law can state no more than: the subjective meaning of the acts by which legal norms are created can be interpreted as their objective meaning only if we presuppose in our juristic thinking the norm: 'One ought to obey the prescriptions of the historically first constitution.' (1967:204).

The passage perhaps raises more questions than it answers. It is not entirely clear whether the 'act of thinking' is that which can be understood only in terms of the **Grundnorm,** or whether the **Grundnorm** is the meaning of an act of thinking. Probably, it is both. More significant, perhaps, for the later development of Kelsen's thought is he distinction which he interjects between the **Grundnorm** itself and 'the statement about it'. Even at the level of the **Grundnorm,** Kelsen is already feeling his way towards the distinction between **Rechtsnorm** and **Rechtssatz.** And in this context, there is special reason for concern. For if the **Grundnorm** is, indeed, specific to a particular legal system, it must refer to the constitution of that legal system. But how can it 'refer' to something outside itself, if it does not possess the extensional properties of a linguistic proposition ? But if it does possess that referential function, can it be only a 'norm' (the meaning of some earlier act), which is conceptually distinct from a linguistic proposition which expresses it ? This, rather than the conventional criticisms of the **Grundnorm,** may well be the point at which the whole system breaks down. **(19)**

Legal meaning also involves the existence of relationships of imputation, according to which people are subjected to obligations to behave in a certain manner. That, too, generates conditions of legal meaning for Kelsen, at least in his early work. In a paper of 1913, he maintained that two contradictory norms could not exist within the same normative system: they 'cannot be valid alongside one another **if the system is to be reasonable** and if the individual subject to the norm is to be able to comply in turn with each of them without thereby violating some other norm of the same system.' **(20)** Since norms themselves contain liability to coercive orders, there must be a rule against contradiction, since otherwise the individual subject would not be able to avoid such coercive orders by any human choice open to him. This assumes, as Kelsen says, a condition of 'reasonableness' in the system, meaning that a legal system must allow its subjects the opportunity to avoid coercive orders. At this stage, Kelsen regards law as a **system of meaning:** 'since the cognition of law, like any cognition, seeks to understand its subject as a meaningful whole and to describe it in non-contradictory statements, it starts from the assumption that conflicts of norms within the normative order which is the object of this cognition can and must be solved by interpretation'. **(21)**

Later, Kelsen was to abandon this particular condition. **(22)** The nature of the system to which law belonged was now viewed in much reduced terms. It was not a cognitive system, but rather a set of individual decisions, linked together only by the fact that they belong to a common system of authorisation. What Kelsen previously regarded as a condition of all normative cognition **(Rechtserkenntnis),** without which no act of will could be meaningful **(sinnvoll),** now becomes a contingent condition, which may or may not be incorporated by particular legal systems. But how, then, are we to distinguish between legal systems which have adopted this additional condition, and those which have not, in the absence of a positive norm stating that condition ? Kelsen's answer would have to be phenomenological. Just as a unified legal system is experienced as such, so too a unified legal system (unified, as becomes apparent from Kelsen's last work, on the basis of norms of competence alone), with the now-additional condition of normative consistency, must be experienced as such.

10.4 HIERARCHICAL RELATIONS WITHIN THE SYSTEM

The character of Kelsen's semiotic presuppositions comes most sharply into focus in the context of the relations between legislator and judge. The legislator typically addresses general norms to the judge; the judge typically addresses norms to other officials concerning a particular individual ('individual norms'). One might expect that if the judge adopts an impossible interpretation of the law, or misapplies it, his act is objectively invalid; conversely, that where he correctly applies it, his individual norm is valid by virtue of its conformity to the general norm which he is applying. But any such expectations require a communicational model of the functioning of the legal system, one which claims that norms have a propositional content. Kelsen increasingly moves away from any such view.

Legal Errata

If a court, even a court of first instance, makes a decision, and thus creates an individual norm, which legal doctrine would regard as in conflict with a general legal norm (whether a statute or precedent), that decision for Kelsen 'is not null according to positive law, even if it is regarded as "unlawful" by the court authorized to decide the question. The norm is merely annullable, that is, it can be invalidated by a procedure determined by the legal order' (1967:268). Doctrine may perhaps **predict** that an appeal court will overturn the decision, but that prediction lacks the force of law. Until and unless the court's decision is overturned, that decision has the objective meaning of legal validity, since it was made by a court endowed with competence by a higher norm. What, then, is the nature of this competence ? Both here and in relation to the 'unconstitutional' statute, Kelsen offers a theory of normative alternatives: the courts 'are authorized by the legal order to create either an individual norm whose content is predetermined by the general norm **or** an individual norm whose content is not predetermined, but to be determined by the organs themselves' (1967:269); similarly, since a statute remains valid until such time as it is declared unconstitutional, 'the meaning of the constitution regulating legislation is not that valid statutes may come into being only in the way directly stipulated by the constitution, but also in a way determined by the legislative organ itself' (1967:273).

The doctrine of normative alternatives is presented by Kelsen as a way of accounting for different forms of authorization of legal norms. Kelsen points out that it is a peculiarity of law that it regulates its own creation. 'This can be done by a norm determining merely the procedure by which another norm is to be created. But it can be done also by a norm determining, to a certain extent, the content of the norm to be created' (1967:221). The qualification 'to a certain extent' reflects Kelsen's view that every application of law also involve some degree of law creation (1967:236,

244f.), since the general norm does not contemplate the particularities (of person, etc.) which are included in the individual norm. In another sense, however, Kelsen gives priority to 'formal' over 'material' law in the process of application. For while he claims a 'systematic connection between the so-called formal and so-called material law (that is, between the determination of the delict and the sanction on the one hand and the determination of the law-applying organ and his procedure on the other)' (1967:231), he goes on to argue that 'determining the organ is the minimum that must be accomplished in the relation between higher and lower norm' (1967:235). A higher norm may thus determine the organ, procedure and content of the lower norm to be created (1967:235), as in a rule describing a norm of criminal law, which he formulates as: 'If an organ, whose nomination is determined by a general legal norm, has ascertained, in a procedure determined by a general legal norm, that facts are present to which a general legal norm attaches a certain sanction, then this organ ought to order a sanction determined in the earlier-mentioned legal norm, in a procedure determined by a general legal norm' (1967:231). But it is equally possible that the higher norm may determine only the organ, 'that is, the individual, who is to create the lower norm, while leaving both the procedure and the content of the norm to be created to the discretion of this organ' (1967:235). Yet even in that latter case, 'still the higher norm is applied in the creation of the lower one' (ibid). Kelsen takes this argument to its logical conclusion. 'This higher norm, the norm that determined the organ, is applied in every act of the organ. In Plato's ideal state, in which judges may decide all cases entirely at their discretion, unhampered by any general norms issued by a legislator, every decision is, nevertheless, an application of the general norm that determines under what conditions an individual is authorized to act as a judge. Only on the basis of this norm he can be considered as a judge of the ideal state; only then can his decision, as having been reached within the ideal state, be attributed to this state' (ibid).

It is in this context that we must view Kelsen's discussion of 'wrong' legal decisions. The defect in the lower norm consists in its failure to comply with what is a contingent element - normally one of content - in the higher norm. The higher norm has sought to determine the lower in respect of content and procedure as well as competence.

The lower norm has been created by such a competent organ, but in breach of a condition of procedure or content specified by a higher norm. Had the higher norm sought to determine only the organ, then the lower norm created by that organ would necessarily have been an application of the higher norm, even though there were no material conditions to be fulfilled. But since here there were, contingently, material conditions to be fulfilled, does the failure of the lower norm to fulfil them deprive it of validity ?

Commentators have sought either to reject Kelsen's theory of normative alternatives **(23)** or to draw its teeth by suggesting that the two alternatives do not have the same status within the legal system. Paulson takes the latter path (1980:192). He cites Kelsen's view that the constitution prefers the path of material to that of merely formal authorization (1967:274f.), as shown by the institution of judicial review and the possibility of legal sanctions against the officials who participate in an unconstitutional act. But this is a truly extraordinary argument. It is astonishing to find Kelsen himself suggesting that the constitution can 'give preference' to one path over another. That, in Kelsen's own terms, is a matter of legal politics, of values, not of the objective meaning of acts of will. After all, the mere existence of judicial review could lead just as much to the invalidation of constitutional statutes, or the overturning of correct legal decisions, as the contrary.

Notwithstanding any preference which participants in the legal system may infer from the constitution, and which may serve as motives for their actions in relation to it, the fact remains that legal errata are understood as just as legally valid as correct decisions. Correct decisions conform to both formal and material authorising conditions; errata conform only to formal authorising conditions, but nevertheless are just as valid as correct decisions. What, then, is the function of material authorising norms ? Kelsen was later to grasp this nettle; conformity to material authorising norms was a matter of 'justification', not validity. **(24)**

Interpretation

What is the position of a judge when faced with the task of interpreting a statute whose words are ambiguous ? The ambiguity of the words presents a cognitive (or semantic) problem. The very judgment that the words of the statute are ambiguous implies that more than a single interpretation is possible. Kelsen categorises as 'cognitive interpretation' the process of ascertaining the list of **possible** interpretations of the statute. He is clearly of the view that those possibilities will be limited, although he does not express any particular semantic theory of the processes involved. He does refer to the statute as constituting a 'frame' (**der Rahmen**). 'In all these cases, the law to be applied constitutes only a frame within which several applications are possible, whereby every act is legal that stays within the frame' (1967:351). Clearly, it is implicit that any interpretation which goes outside the frame is no longer legal. The law-applying organ will thereby have exceeded its competence, which is limited by the cognitive frame of the statute.

Kelsen maintained this position right from his first article on interpretation (1934:9-17) up to and including the second edition of **Reine Rechtslehre.** A synoptic table compiled by Losano (1981:95) allows us to trace the literary history. Looking back from the second edition of **Reine Rechtslehre,** we see that the main body of the chapter on interpretation, being para.45 and its sub-paragraphs (a) - (e), all correspond to material first published as early as the 1934 article. However, paras.46-47 contain new material, and provide a vital pointer to the last phase of Kelsen's thought.

Even here, as Losano points out (1981:98), Kelsen reaffirms the general character of the relation between will and cognition:

> If not only the interpretation of the statutes by courts or administrative authorities, but the interpretation of law in general by law-applying organs is to be characterized, the following may be said: In the application of law by a legal organ, the cognitive interpretation of the law to be applied is combined with an act of will by which the law-applying organ chooses between the possibilities shown by cognitive interpretation. (**25**)

But almost immediately he goes on to add:

> Here it is to be noted: By way of authentic

> interpretation (that is, interpretation of a norm by the law-applying organ) not only one of the possibilities may be realized that have been shown by the cognitive interpretation of the norm to be applied; but also a norm may be created which lies entirely outside the frame of a norm to be applied. (1967:354)

In these two last sections of the second edition of **Reine Rechtslehre,** Kelsen is particularly concerned to distinguish between interpretation by the science of law, which can only be 'cognitive' and never 'authentic', and interpretation as an act of will of the competent law-applying organ, designated 'authentic' interpretation. The titles of the sections are significant: 'Interpretation as an Act of Cognition or Will' (para.46), 'Interpretation by the Science of Law' (para.47). Kelsen seems to be working towards a complete antithesis between the two categories, so that cognition is as irrelevant to authentic interpretation as will is to cognitive interpretation.

Not a few Kelsenian scholars are unhappy with the radical attitudes of the later Kelsen. As regards interpretation 'outside the frame of the norm to be applied', Losano has mounted a two-fold critique (1981:100-3), designed to reduce the impact of this addition to the second edition of **Reine Rechtslehre,** and to render it more compatible with the 'classical' Pure Theory. On the one hand, he makes a terminological objection: if the norm enunciated by the judge really is outside the frame of possible meanings of the norm to be applied, then we cannot speak of 'interpretation' (whether 'authentic' or of any other kind). But this is only a terminological objection. As we have seen, Kelsen distinguishes within this very section between application of law (where the norm does remain within the frame of the norm applied), and creation of law, where it does not. Beyond that, however, Losano seeks to identify 'authentic interpretation' with the **function** of judicial interpretation (viz., application in particular cases, or adjudication), and 'scientific interpretation' with the **procedure** of interpretation (whether by the judge or anyone else). He thus concludes that scientific interpretation remains a precondition of authentic interpretation, since the judge (if he is interpreting at all) must first use scientific interpretation in order to identify the frame of the superior norm being interpreted, before choosing (as Kelsen would insist, on non-legal grounds) the particular interpretation to adopt.

I find myself in agreement with the first part of this distinction, but not the second. Losano rightly argues that an act of will is the characteristic element of authentic interpretation, and that since every will must be directed to some end, Kelsen must mean by 'authentic interpretation' not the logical mechanism by which the general norm is analysed, but rather the purpose which the legal organ seeks to pursue with its act of will (1981:101). So far, so good. He then goes on to argue that since knowledge of the meanings of a norm - independent of the purposes for which they may be used - is for Kelsen the characteristic element in scientific interpretation, Kelsen must mean by 'scientific interpretation' the process by which one comes to know the possible meanings of a legal norm, and thus the nature and structure of all (including judicial) legal reasoning. This does not seem to me to follow. In para.47 of the second edition of **Reine Rechtslehre**, Kelsen does not in fact describe cognitive interpretation (here identified with 'jurisprudential', i.e. doctrinal, interpretation) as a procedure of the judge, but nevertheless recognises that it may have a function. Specifically, 'a writer who in his commentary extols a specific interpretation among many possible ones as the only 'correct' one, does not render a function of legal science, but of legal politics. He seeks to influence legislation' (1967:356). Losano may object that such 'scientific interpretation' is not merely the ascertainment of the 'frame' of the higher norm, but the choice within that frame. Indeed, Kelsen does give the impression that ascertainment of the frame is a neutral, objective matter, and that it is only the choice within the frame which involves non-legal criteria, and which is political in character. But even granting this rather naive linguistic approach, it is difficult to see how Kelsen's view of creation of law outside the frame of the norm to be applied can accommodate scientific interpretation as a necessary stage in its own procedure.

In the end, Losano concludes that Kelsen's view can only be accepted in a sociological sense: judges may in fact create law outside the frame of the statute, but according to legal theory they must remain within it (assuming it to be cognitively applicable). If the judge goes outside the frame, then, according to Losano, he does not apply a legal norm, but rather has recourse to an extra-legal norm (1981:103). But this, I would suggest, is not a viable interpretation of Kelsen's intentions. We may accept the terminological objection to the use here of the word 'interpretation', but at the same time maintain that the decision of the judge going outside the frame of the statute would still be regarded by Kelsen as based on a higher legal norm. Just as a judge charged with determining the constitutionality of a statute may (i.e. has the competence to) determine that issue either within the semantic framework of the constitution itself or, alternatively, outside that framework and through other criteria of his own, so too may the judge, in applying any higher norm, choose either to remain within the semantic framework of that higher norm, or go outside it. Kelsen comes to the view that no satisfactory account of our legal system, as we experience it, can be given unless we assume the existence of norms of competence which give judges such alternatives.

Right Decisions

Just as important, and even more illuminating for the ultimate phase of Kelsen's thought, is his analysis of the 'right' decision, the case where a lower norm is created apparently in accordance with the material conditions laid down by a higher norm. This is the everyday case where a judge straightforwardly 'applies' an unambiguous statute. What, we may wonder, could be less problematic ? **(26)** As late as the second edition of **Reine Rechtslehre,** Kelsen maintained the view that the higher norm thus 'determines' the content of the lower norm (1967:235). 'The act by which the individual norm of judicial decision is created is usually predetermined, as has been said, by general norms of formal and material law' (1967:242); the judge may depart from the material content of the higher norm (only) where the legal order explicitly authorizes him to do so. **(27)** In the last phase of his thought, Kelsen rejected any logical relationship between a general norm and an individual norm which might be subsumed under it. Such relationships could exist only as between propositions (which might be true or false), but not between norms (which could only be valid or invalid). Adopting a radical differentiation of **Rechtsnorm** and **Rechtssatz,** he even withdrew his earlier claim of an 'indirect' logical relationship between norms, whether in terms of contradiction or inference (material subsumption):

> The error of believing that the two principles in question (the law of non-contradiction and the rule of inference) are applicable to legal norms is thus partly due to the fact that legal norms and statements about them are not kept clearly separate . . . it emerges from the foregoing that the two most important logical principles, the law of non-contradiction and the rule of inference, are applicable to the relations between norms of a positive legal system neither directly nor indirectly - as I still supposed, however, in my **Reine Rechtslehre** (2nd edn, 1960). **(28)**

On the relation between general and individual norms, he stated categorically: 'There can be no normative syllogism having a general norm as its premise and an individual norm as its conclusion' (1973:243), and in an essay of 1968 extended this view into a general denial of the practical syllogism. For Kelsen now maintained that an 'imperative is valid as a norm only if it is posited as the meaning of a real act of will' (1973:257f.); an imperative directed to an individual could not be valid merely as the logical entailment of a general imperative. As Paulson has put it, 'what is critical for Kelsen is not subsumability but the act of putative subsumption' (1975:781). Kelsen shows no reluctance to proclaim the practical implications of this view for the general workings of the legal system, in direct contradiction to what has been described above as the 'commonsense' view of the relation between legislation and judicial decison. He asks us to consider the relation between the general norm 'All thieves are to be punished' and the individual norm 'Smith the thief is to be punished'. There can be a logical rule of inference between the two **Rechtssätze** having that content, but not between the two **Rechtsnormen:**

> The same applies to the rule of **inference.** Nobody denies that from the truth of the statement: 'The general norm "All thieves are to be punished" is observed', i.e., from the truth of 'All thieves are punished', it follows logically that such statements as 'The individual norm "Smith the thief is to be punished" is observed', and 'Smith the thief is punished' are true. So far as the applicability of the logical rule of

> inference to legal norms is concerned, the question is whether, from the validity of a general norm such as 'All thieves should be punished', the validity of an individual norm such as 'Smith the thief should be punished' follows logically in just the same way as it follows from the truth of the general statement 'All men are mortal' that the individual statement 'Socrates is mortal' is true. And this question must receive a negative answer, so far as it relates to **positive** norms, which are all that can be dealt with in legal science, as a science of positive law. **(29)**
>
> The individual norm whose validity is in question, viz. 'Smith the thief should be punished, i.e., sent to prison', can only rank as a positive norm if it is positive through an act of will of the competent judge. No norm without an authority which posits it, i.e., no norm without an act of will, of which this norm is the meaning . . The individual norm 'Smith the thief should be sent to prison' can only be the meaning of an act of will, and such an **act of will** cannot be arrived at by way of a logical inference, i.e., by a **thinking** process. If it is true that all men are mortal, it can only be true that Socrates is mortal and not that he is immortal. But even if the general norm holds, that 'All thieves should be sent to prison', it is still possible - as shown - for the individual norm to hold, that 'Smith the thief should **not** be sent to prison' . .
>
> The individual norm 'Smith the thief should be sent to prison' could be implicit in the general norm 'All thieves should be sent to prison' only if the act of will whose meaning is the individual norm were implicit in the act of will whose meaning is the general norm. But . . only the court, which has established that Smith has stolen a horse from the farmer, can will that he should be sent to prison as a thief. And the judge is a different man from the legislator. His act of will cannot be implicit in the act of will of another man. (1973:240-2)

In the course of this important argument, not all of which has here been reproduced, Kelsen offers a number of reasons to deny the relationship of inference between the general and the individual norm. He contemplates, in effect, three different situations. First, the individual norm may never in fact be posited: Smith the thief may not be caught, he may not be convicted, etc. Since the **norm** (unlike the proposition) that 'Smith the thief ought to be imprisoned' can come into existence only as the meaning of an act of will of the competent authority, here the judge, it follows that in such a case no such individual norm is ever created. Secondly, Kelsen contemplates the case where the judge may, for whatever reason, pronounce a contrary norm, that Smith, even though legally found guilty of theft, ought **not** to be imprisoned. The reasons for that latter individual norm are irrelevant, for Kelsen's purposes. The judge may be authorised to exercise a discretion to override the law, or he may not be so authorised. He may have made a mistake or he may have decided to judge the case not in accordance with the general norm (an application of the theory of 'normative alternatives'). Whatever the reason, the result is the same: the individual norm which we might have expected to be inferred from the general norm fails to be created. Most important, however, from the conceptual point of view, is the third possible situation. Suppose that the judge does find Smith guilty and does sentence him to a term of imprisonment in accordance with the general norm. Even there, Kelsen now insists, the validity of that individual norm in no way depends upon the logical relation of inference. It rests solely upon the status of the act of will of the judge. In the last part of the passage quoted above, Kelsen is making a most important point: the legal system does not consist in abstract propositions, but in the acts of will of men, to which, in appropriate circumstances, the objective meaning of legal validity can be attached. There can be no causality in the exercise of such acts of will, nor can they be constrained by logical relations. If the semantic content of the act of will of the judge happens to bear a relationship of inference to the semantic content of the act of will of the legislator, that is solely because the judge willed it to be so. The act of will of one man cannot be implicit in the act of will of another. (**30**)

Kelsen proceeds to state his view as to what actually is the relationship between a general norm and an individual norm which 'applies' the general norm:

What **can** be said of the relation between the general

> norm 'All thieves should be sent to prison', and the individual norm 'Smith the thief should be sent to prison', is this: **if** the general norm holds, that all thieves should be sent to prison, **and if** the competent court has established that Smith is a thief, **and if** the said court has posited an act whose subjective meaning is that Smith should be sent to prison, then the meaning of the **court's act** is in accordance with the general norm which it has to apply and the validity of the individual norm forming the meaning of this act can be **justified** by the validity of the general norm. **(31)**

When Kelsen says that in this case 'the validity of the individual norm . . can be **justified** by the validity of the general norm', he seems, once again, to be referring back to the theory of normative alternatives. Here the judge's choice to base validity on a material authorising norm enables him to justify his norm by reference to that material authorising norm, even though his individual norm would be valid in the absence of such justification. Kelsen goes on to stress that no particular motivation is required of the judge. The relationship here in issue exists whenever the judge chooses to do that which is in fact in accordance with the general norm, even if he does so for some quite extraneous reason: 'The "motives" he has in positing the individual norm which accords with the general one, are irrelevant' (1973:260). This complements the irrelevance of the motives of the judge who posits a norm **not** in accordance with the general norm.

The radical character of the later Kelsen is fully recognised by the editor of this collection, Ota Weinberger, who in a recent paper has contrasted the 'classical conception' of the Pure Theory with 'Kelsen's later irrationalism concerning norms' (1981). He recognises that Kelsen derives these conclusions from the distinction he draws between **Rechtsnormen** and **Rechtssätze.** But he advances a semiotic argument against this distinction:

> It is important to distinguish between the meaning of a sentence and the pragmatic function which it fulfills in a given situation. If a law-creating organ utters a norm-sentence, this use of the sentence **may** fulfill the pragmatic function of legislation. The sentence itself

> bears a message which is to be grasped by the receiver (and addressee of the norm or any other person). The meaning of the sentence should be identical for the sender and the receiver of the message. The consequence class of the message should also be identical on both sides of the channel. The pair of the two notions 'legal norm' and 'legal sentence' is based on a misconception of the character of communication and led to Kelsen's erroneous rejecton of normative entailment. (32)

By criticising Kelsen in these terms, Weinberger directs our attention to the fact that Kelsen has abandoned a communicational model of legal semiotics. In effect, Weinberger argues as follows. The higher legal organ creates a norm; the lower organ recognises that norm and creates a new one. The lower organ can 'recognise' what the higher organ creates, in that the higher organ 'utters a norm-sentence', that is, a normative proposition which has both a pragmatic function (for example, the particular illocutionary force of legislative validity) **and** semantic content. It can possess such semantic content, because it is a normative **proposition.** (33) As a proposition with semantic content, it may be analysed in terms of the theory of communication. The semantic content is the sender's message, and must be grasped (recognised) by the receiver with the same semantic content. As a proposition, the message may carry logical entailments. Since the receiver recognises the same proposition as the sender emits, the logical entailments recognised by the receiver must be the same as those intended by the sender. Thus, if the legislator emits a norm-sentence with the semantic content 'All thieves should be imprisoned', then the judge, the receiver of this message, must recognise that it is a logical entailment of that norm-sentence that 'Smith the thief should be imprisoned'. Weinberger seems prepared to accept Kelsen's insistence that 'Smith the thief should be imprisoned' becomes a norm of positive law only when a norm-sentence to that effect is emitted by the judge, that is, when the judge creates that norm by positing it. But Weinberger sees that latter act of creation as authorised only by virtue of the judge's recognition of the higher norm, and since the higher norm is a proposition which includes its own logical entailments, the judge in recognising it also recognises that the logical entailments are part of the communicated message. He thus accepts a rule of inference as between norms, since on the one hand he identifies norms with normative propositions (which the later Kelsen rejects) and on the other hand appears to reject Kelsen's theory of normative alternatives, thus seeing normative entailment from the higher to the lower norm as the **only** route to normative validity. (34)

For the late Kelsen, communication of the content of norms is now a matter quite separate from legal validity. Such communication is relevant to justification - we might say, to the level of legal rhetoric or legitimation. Along with the process of interpretation, it is part of the sociology of law, not the science of positive law. Legal norms are now viewed solely as the meanings attached to past acts of will, not propositions by which future acts of will may be interpreted (10.1). They are things we do with words, their illocutionary force being determined by formal authorisation.

10.5 DECISIONS AND DOCTRINE

Such logical relations as Kelsen's 'inference' must belong to legal doctrine, the study of the inter-relationship of legal propositions (**Rechtssätze**); what Kelsen calls 'objective meaning' (or validity) belongs to the sphere of authorised legal decisions (**Rechtsnormen**). (35) Just as a logical inference cannot generate a valid norm, so too by his act of will the judge does not create true legal propositions. The latter is the function of legal science, in describing the effect of the actions of the judge - in other words, in describing, in propositional terms (the only route open to legal science, which does not have the authority to create norms) the norms of positive law. What the competent legal organ does is to transform a situation in terms of the legal meaning of the behaviour comprised in it. However, the organ can transform only that to which it directs its will, and it cannot direct its will to circumstances which it does not know (1973:242). Kelsen argues that the individual norm 'Smith the thief should be sent to prison' cannot be implicit in the general norm 'All thieves should be sent to prison', because 'The legislator who wills that all thieves should be sent to prison cannot already will that Smith, who has stolen a horse from the farmer, should be sent to prison, since he cannot know that a person called Smith will exist and steal the farmer's horse' (1973:242). This is the converse of Kelsen's rejection of the idea that the act of will has a propositional content. A propositional content allows the act to serve as a schema of interpretation of future acts. Now, Kelsen requires the act of will to be directed towards acts which have already taken place, and which are thereby known. In other words, the object of the act of will must itself be cognizable through positivist criteria. Hence, the norm is now entirely retrospective, rather than bi-directional. Subsumption no longer belongs to positive law, but only to descriptive statements about it - the domain of legal doctrine.

But Kelsen fails to apply this analysis to the subsumptive relationship which generates the competence of the legal organ. He still seeks to maintain the objective quality of legal validity, albeit now basing this entirely upon formal rather than material authorisation. Comparing the command of a court with the command of a highway robber, he observes:

> But the subjective meaning of an act of command is only its objective meaning as well, and thus a binding norm, if the act is authorised by a norm presupposed as valid. (1973:244)

It is the act that has to be authorised, not its propositional content. Kelsen himself goes on to show that the relationship between a general, statutory norm and an individual, judicial norm can generate justification of the individual norm 'not in a normative but in a theoretical syllogism, since neither the major premise nor the conclusion are norms, but rather statements, and **statements,** moreover, **about the validity of norms'** (1973:245). How, then, is actual legal validity generated ? Is it, quite simply, 'presupposed', or does it derive from a norm by which the court gains its competence ? Kelsen's view on this matter is not entirely clear, but it would seem difficult for him to argue that even formal authorisation, deriving from norms of competence, can be generated by acts of will as he now defines them. Suppose that a constitution empowers the legislator to appoint judges. Applying Kelsen's own analysis of general and individual norms regarding theft, we would have to argue that the constitutional norm is a general norm, and that the act of will of the legislator appointing **X** or **Y** as judge cannot be implicit in it. The constitutional norm may serve as a justification for the statutory norm, but that justification operates in the sphere of statements about norms, not norms themselves. We cannot therefore use the constitutional norm to explain how the act of will of the legislator appointing **X** or **Y** as judge is legally valid. The norm is no longer functioning as a 'schema of interpretation'. Shall we, then, say quite simply that the legal validity of these acts is 'presupposed', and that such a presupposition is lacking in the case of the command of the gunman ? But if so, in what sense is legal validity a matter of 'objective' meaning ? Is not Kelsen re-writing the **Grundnorm**, his basic presupposition, in something like the form: 'Regard as legally valid the acts of will of all organs which are conventionally regarded as legally competent ?'

Kelsen does not appear to deal with this objection. Rather, he seems to assume that the competence of the judge can be conferred by an authorising norm, without involving the relationship of subsumption, or converting the norm into a normative proposition. But even if this were possible, difficult problems would arise. Is the competence of the judge truly unlimited, subject only to the contingency of reversal on appeal ? If there are limitations upon it, how are they to be conceived and defined ? Can the judge pass a sentence in excess of the maximum prescribed by the law ? It seems to follow from Kelsen's views that such a sentence would be legally valid, until and unless reversed, the virtual inevitability of such reversal counting only as a sociological prediction. Can the judge then invent new criminal offences ? Can he exceed the jurisdiction of the court in which he currently sits ? Can he 'find' facts for which no evidence has been led, given that the 'finding' of facts is regarded as the process of constituting those facts at law (1967:240-2) ?

The endpoint of Kelsen's development appears to be the complete separation of two spheres of legal discourse: the discourse of competent legal authorities, expressed through their acts of will, and the discourse of statements about law, expressed through such cognitive operations as subsumption. The former no longer depends upon the latter. The norm, Kelsen maintains, cannot function in both spheres. It 'cannot contain both an imperative, i.e., prescriptive, **and** an indicative, i.e., descriptive factor. For prescription is the meaning of an act of will, while description is that of an act of thought. Willing and thinking are two essentially different functions, and there can therefore be no thinking immanent in willing' (1973:230).

The last phase of Kelsen's thought raises questions whose importance are no less diminished by the difficulty of Kelsen's own answers. The requirements of positivity in effect force Kelsen to abandon any notion of objective meaning in terms of material authorisation, or at least to locate it in a cognitive sphere quite separate from that to which he assigns the idea of 'legal validity'. But even the basis of this validity is thrown into doubt by Kelsen's own analysis: no satisfactory account is given of the source of validity of the competence of the legal organ, once the norm is redefined in strictly positivist terms, and the relationship of subsumption is thereby destroyed. **(36)**

There is a school of legal semiotics which accepts much of the Kelsenian argument, without falling into these difficulties. Brief reference may here be made to the work of Felix Oppenheim, writing in the tradition of Carnap, and more recently that of Kalinowski and other logicians of the Polish school. Oppenheim sets out to describe law as 'a class of **sentences,** constituting a **language** which expresses the legal rules, decisions, commands of that community at that moment' (1944:142). Those sentences may be either imperative or declarative, but that distinction is a pragmatic one, depending upon the persons who utter the sentences and the purposes for which they are uttered. **(37)** This is the nature of the distinction between legal decisions and legal doctrine: the two are not conceived as belonging to different conceptual universes, of will on the one hand and thought on the other.

Being sentences of a language, laws can be analysed in terms of their syntactic, semantic or pragmatic properties. Oppenheim identifies the syntactic properties of statements in terms of their 'correctness'. The question here is whether they are (to use the Chomskian analogy) grammatically well-formed, and this judgment results from the application of other sentences which lay down the criteria of correctness (in terms of procedure and perhaps content). The second dimension is the truth of statements of law. Some sentences of law assert facts (with reference to the outside world); thus, 'semantical features determine the truth conditions of those sentences . . which assert facts' (1944:152). Furthermore, 'in order to find out whether the sentences . . have **official quality** we have to study their relationship to authorities which have stated them, i.e. their pragmatical properties' (ibid). Oppenheim proceeds to construct a notion of legal validity drawing upon all three dimensions: 'if . . a sentence . . is at the same time correct, not false (i.e., either true or imperative), and competently stated, we call it a **valid** sentence . .' (1944:153). We should note that Oppenheim's conception of syntactics, which generate the property of legal sentences as 'correct', includes relationships of semantic logic, such as would fall within Kelsen's notion of subsumption, and thus relate to the cognitive sphere. Thus, for Oppenheim, cognitive correctness forms one of the conditions of legal validity. What, then, does he make of the problem which seems to have forced Kelsen down the route towards 'irrationalism' ? What of incorrect (and thus, in Oppenheim's terms, non-valid) judgments of courts, or unconstitutional statutes ? These, he tells us, are enforceable statements of law, even though they are invalid: there exist 'non-valid laws and decisions which it is not possible to annul, because they have been enacted by authorities whose statements are final and cannot be reversed by any other power' (1944:154f). Official statement, the pragmatic criterion, is thus the sole condition of enforceability, irrespective of the truth or falsity of the sentence, or its correctness: in short, independent of its validity. **(38)**

10.6 KELSEN AND GREIMASIAN SEMIOTICS

Already in **Reine Rechtslehre,** Kelsen's doctrine of legal **errata** was based upon an important semiotic consideration. As Paulson puts it:

> Even if the individual norm does not conform to the material authorising norm, it remains a part of the law unless and until it is successfully challenged in the courts or - one might add parenthetically - formally abrogated. When opportunities for challenge have passed, the norm may become firmly ensconced in the legal system in spite of its lack of material authorisation. That is, although the norm was defective, the defect or error was not shown in a

> legally prescribed way while it was still possible to do so. And there is nothing surprising in this. The phenomenon of firmly ensconced individual norms, some of them in fact produced in error, is well known in private law from the doctrine of **res judicata.** (1980:184)

For the positivist, it is not possible to rely on a supposition that a legal decision is erroneous; any such error must be **shown** to be erroneous in a legally recognised procedure. In short, the error of the former legal decison is only established, indeed it is only constituted, when a further legally identifiable decision is made. We might say that the error counts only once it is 'verified'. For G/L **'vérification juridique'** is an essential part of the semiotic process itself. Without it, the legal grammar is not complete.

Ultimately, Kelsen was to arrive at the same view. He was to regard verification as necessary not merely in the (apparently) exceptional case when judicial error or the unconstitutionality of a statute was alleged, but in every case. In other words, verification became necessary for Kelsen as a constitutive process in the attribution of legality to any act, whether it was **prima facie** (that is, cognitively) correct or not. This is another way of expressing the fact that the norm came to be regarded no longer as a 'schema of interpretation', with a bi-directional quality, but only as the meaning of an earlier act of will, necessarily applied retrospectively.

The relationship between a general, statutory norm and a particular, judicial decision invites interesting comparison between the theories of Kelsen and G/L. We have seen that Kelsen ultimately moved to the view that a general norm could contain no normative implications in relation to particular cases which might be subsumed under it, if the knowledge of the facts of those particular cases was not within the cognizance of the person whose act of will had the meaning of the general norm (10.4 above). The general norm thus became, for Kelsen, no more than that - a general norm, without normative connection to other acts of will in the legal system. One way of expressing this (not one which would have appealed to the later Kelsen) would be that the general norm is an incomplete message; it represents only part of that which is necessary to determine particular cases. G/L take a rather similar view, as we have seen from their account of **production juridique** through legislation and **vérification juridique** (through judicial decision). The function of **production juridique** is only to take a term from non-legal discourse, and through using it in a statute to incorporate it within the referential level of law - as having the **potentiality** of legal meaning (2.2). Such meaning remains potential until such time as the judge uses that term in the course of adjudication, by giving it an actual legal meaning (and thereby confirming its status as part of the legal universe). Carrion-Wam takes this argument for the insufficiency of legislation as an act of legal communication one stage further. For him, the addressee (receiver) of the legal message sent by the legislator is not the judge but the ultimate subject to whom the permission/prohibition/requirement applies, and the judge is merely an intermediary (5.2). Only when the judge applies the legislative message can one say that there is a real 'sender' (the legislator) and 'receiver' (the subject). Before that stage, the sender of the message is a mere 'linguistic construction' while the receiver is 'an empty space, an eventuality that will be realised and defined . . .' only when the judicial discourse is itself communicated to him (1983:33-4).

Despite this similarity, there remain important differences. For Kelsen, the general norm and the individual norm are both complete entities, being the objective meanings (respectively) of the act of will of the legislator and the act of will of the judge. The fact that they do not directly interconnect does not destroy the semiotic function of the system, but rather reflects important aspects of it. For G/L, on the other hand, **production juridique** and **vérification juridique** are elements in a single structure, the production of legal meaning. From the semiotic point of view, they are interdependent.

Does this mean that G/L, after all, are able to achieve what Kelsen cannot, namely the rehabilitation of material authorisation ? That is neither their object, nor the effect of their argument. The relationship between the legislator and the judge, both conceived as semiotic objects, involves neither subsumption nor authorisation. The relationship between the two is not conceived in hierarchical terms nor is 'objective meaning' the result. If there is a notion of objectivity, that is part of the message which semiotics seeks to explain.

PART FOUR

Conclusions

CHAPTER ELEVEN

Pragmatics, Validity and the Unity of the Legal System

(11.1) Syntactics, Semantics and Pragmatics: the Attack on Formalism: Legal positivism and structural linguistics have been attacked as displaying the same formalist neglect of historical and pragmatic features. Greimasian semiotics seeks to incorporate pragmatics on the basis of its own, very different methodological presuppositions. **(11.2) Legal Validity:** Jurisprudential theories adopt a range of approaches to legal validity, which may be characterised as syntactic, semantic or pragmatic. Hart seeks uneasily to compromise between syntactic and pragmatic approaches. 'Logical semiotics' are more compatible with formalist accounts of the legal system; discursive semiotics regards legal validity simply as part of the message which is communicated. **(11.3) The Unity of the Legal System:** Semiotic considerations support the distinction between meaning, interpretation and adjudication. The peculiar involvement of pragmatic factors in adjudication has been stressed in both Scandinavian realism and 'Polish logic'. Separate consideration of the contexts of legislation, doctrine and adjudication assist in resolving tensions perceived in the legal philosophies of Hart and MacCormick, and serves to locate the relevance of Dworkinian semiotics. But the 'legal system' involves the interaction of discursive processes which extend far beyond these three activities traditionally privileged by legal philosophy.

11.1 SYNTACTICS, SEMANTICS AND PRAGMATICS: THE ATTACK ON FORMALISM

Both legal positivism and structural semiotics have attracted anti-formalist criticisms, the former from realists of various descriptions, the latter often in the name of pragmatic conceptions of language (1.1). Peter Goodrich (1984a) has recently mounted an integrated attack upon both legal and linguistic formalism: legal positivism is seen as itself endorsing a formalist conception of language system, while structural semiotics, like legal positivism, seeks a false reification of its subject-matter. In particular, Goodrich suggests that the work of Greimas 'represents the apotheosis of positivism in the addition of a further layer of descriptive metalanguage superimposed upon the dominant belief in the univocality of legal language' (1984a:183). The manner in which Goodrich poses the problem is indeed valuable. But his survey necessarily neglects significant nuances of the traditions he attacks. In particular, legal positivism is by no means monolithic in its endorsement of formalism. **(1)** It is worth re-examining both traditions in the light of this question, to ascertain how far they seek to, and succeed in, integrating the concerns of pragmatics.

In his account of legal language, if not of the legal system, Hart presents us with a theory of legal pragmatics, dressed up in semantic clothing. The tension is one which has recently attracted some attention from philosophers. **(2)** On the one hand, he speaks of open texture as if it were an inherent property of language, rather than a function of language use; and he endorses the dominance, within legal language, of the 'core of undisputed meaning' - a phrase pregnant in its connotations, notwithstanding the interpretation I have suggested of it in 7.2 above. On the other hand, there is the denial of any 'right answer' to a legally controversial problem (1961:128), - a phrase echoed by Sampson (expressing a pragmatic approach to semantics) when he argues that it is as meaningless to speak of the 'right answer' to a question regarding the meaning of a word as it is to a question about what is fashionable in dress (1980a:51).

The relation between semantics and pragmatics does present itself with one peculiarity in the case of law, as was argued above in distinguishing between 'meaning' and 'interpretation' (7.2). The problems regarding the use of the language of law which Hart discusses are no ordinary problems of the meaning of words, or even of the range of application of general terms. The words are to be interpreted at a distance - in terms of person, time and place. Difficulties of interpretation arise when new situations occur, ones which were not present to the mind of the original author. And they arise in contexts when much hangs upon the decision. Small wonder that in these circumstances there is objection to the tyranny of pre-determined meanings. The case of non-contentious legal interpretation is fundamentally no different. There is a 'core of undisputed meaning' precisely because the meaning has not been disputed.

Dworkin's position is the converse. His really is a semantic theory, masquerading as pragmatics. While the evidence for his argument is taken mainly from the judgments of the American courts, and in particular the Supreme Court with its then-interventionist, quasi-radical image, Dworkin's theory is one of pre-determined legal meanings, which form a consistent system. It has much in common with the Saussurian approach, stressing intensionality ('principles') rather than extensionality ('policies'). Coherence with the system is valued above such exercise of discretion as may take into account the particular circumstances which have given rise to the need to apply the rule. Just as Hart's pragmatics uses language which creates the semiotic appearance of semantics, so too Dworkin's semantics, by using the evidence of American judicial interventionism, presents the appearance of pragmatics. And a number of commentators (not including Hart) have been deceived.

In terms of the distinction formulated in 7.2 above, Dworkin presents a theory of 'meaning', Hart a theory of 'interpretation'. Dworkin's orientation is intensional, Hart's extensional. Dworkin's approach is basically onomasiological, looking for the underlying concepts and working from there to appropriate formulations; Hart's is semasiological, starting from rule formulations and examining what interpretation should be given to them in particular contexts. (3) The two approaches are complementary. But the precise manner of their integration awaits a systematic solution. MacCormick (1978) may be thought to have attempted just this, in according to Dworkin's 'rights' and 'principles' a merely presumptive status, subject to possible overriding by (pragmatically conceived) 'consequentialist' argument.

That kind of accommodation is not difficult for legal positivism to make. After all, the basic claim of legal positivism is that law is a matter of human choice, not natural determination (1.3). One application of the theory of incorporation is that human beings in society may choose to adopt a system of rational coherence, but may equally impose limits upon the degree to which they will be bound by it. Legal positivism encounters no problem in moving towards classical pragmatics. Language is taken to 'refer' to the outside world, and to serve the goals of those who use it. The historical links between twentieth-century positivism and the tradition of J.L. Austin (4) are hardly surprising. For speech act theory goes one step further towards implementation of the pragmatic philosophy. Words now do not merely refer to the outside world; they may also act in the outside world. And legal words are a prime example of language with a performative character - performing, of course, the goals of their users. (5)

The corresponding move, whereby structural linguistics seeks to accommodate pragmatics within its own conceptual framework, faces greater theoretical obstacles. Nevertheless, a great deal of effort has been directed in recent years by members of the Greimasian school to achieving precisely this. (6) The focus of their attention has been upon the account given of the act of enunciation in the discourse itself. An early example is found in G/L's account of the legislative utterance recorded in the 1966 Loi (5.1), and Carrion-Wam conceives of 'juridical pragmatics' in much the same way, as operating within the discourse. The 'act of enunciation' may itself be analysed in terms of Greimasian narrative grammar. The act involves senders and receivers, subjects and objects, the transference of modal values. In this way, the concerns of a truth-conditional version of semantics can be accommodated within the discursive conception of 'verediction', and those of rhetorical analysis within the discursive account of 'persuasion' - both involving the transference of particular combinations of modal values. Greimasian semiotics thus claims to be able to incorporate and refine not only the speech act tradition but also the New Rhetoric (and indeed the newer rhetoric) and the theory of argumentation. (7) Thus whereas Goodrich (1984a) sees 'sociolinguistics, social discourse, law as social discourse' as 'alternative approaches', preferable to the (formalist) dominant paradigm of legal science and legal semiotics, the Greimasian school claims to be able to give a superior account of just these pragmatic phenomena.

It is worth pausing to consider the theoretical basis for the Greimasian claim. For many would, with Goodrich, see the rival socio-linguistic, rhetorical and critical approaches as much more satisfying, in that they grapple with the details of the ('surface') discourse, and seek to relate it to the ('real') outside world. **(8)** Why should the Greimasian school not see such approaches as compatible and complementary ? The answer is provided in recent papers by Greimas and Landowski (1983). Traditional pragmatics is seen as violating two methodological postulates of semiotics. First, it adopts a 'realist' view of the outside world, as opposed to one constructed in our language and discourse (Landowski 1983:llf.). That is why Greimasian semiotics rejects both the notion of 'referent' adopted in the Peircian school and any truth-conditional version of semantics. **(9)** Second, Greimasian semiotics rejects psychologism, and with it any account of either 'context' or non-discursive interaction which might lead to a 'psycho-social-stylistics' (Greimas 1983:7). Both of these restrictions are attributable to a methodological positivism which insists on confining the object of study to that communicational process which we can lay on the table for examination (6.1). It is semiotics which here claims to be the really 'critical' science. Greimas observes that pragmatics claims to have discovered the indirect and 'dodging' character of discourse. But European linguistics, well before the **Mythologies** of Barthes, has long seen in language not a cloak, somewhat modulated by the value attached to truth, of the reality of things, but rather a tissue of lies and an apparatus of social manipulation (1983:7).

The philosophical scepticism inherent in this approach might appear to prevent any accommodation with logical semiotics or logical semantics, insofar as they employ notions of truth-conditions. But the relationship with linguistic pragmatics in the tradition of Wittgenstein, Austin and Searle appears more complicated. One aspect of the approach of this school gains unqualified approval from Greimas: in its analysis of presuppositions and conversational implicatures, pragmatics has not confined itself to the surface linguistic level, but has helped to identify the existence of a deeper level of signification (1983:6f.). But in its use of the vague notion of 'context', and its association of the 'force' of an utterance with psychological conditions of the participants, it violates the methodological postulates noted above. This, of course, implies an important challenge which Greimasian semiotics is only now beginning to recognise and face. Can an account of pragmatics be provided which views it as part of a constructed system of communication (as opposed to a 'real outside world') and which does not rely upon presumed psychological states in the participants (themselves only mediated through language) ? To do so, the Parisian school has to make one vital move. It must view inter-personal communication (whether by language or behaviour) as itself a discourse, wherein messages are communicated regarding the psychological states of the participants. It insists on doing so by applying narrative grammar to this discourse, rather than confine its attention to surface phenomena, such as occurs in traditional stylistics or conversational analysis. (10) Thus Bastide gives the following account of the notion of the 'reliability' of the addresser: 'it is common that an actor playing the part of an Addresser will try to secure an agreement from the Addressee by displaying his own reliability, or by denying the reliability of other possible Addressers. This would be a second-order communication pattern, where the object could be called 'reliability' (that of the Addresser, in producing the first message object, and that of the Addressee, in making good use of it). A corresponding practice of the Addressee will meet this second Object.'

There is one point at which this difference in theoretical orientation between Greimasian semiotics and traditional pragmatics is of the greatest importance to contemporary legal philosophy. A major plank in Hart's jurisprudence is the idea that a 'rule' has to be distinguished from a mere 'regularity of behaviour' in terms of the 'internal point of view' (1961:86-8). The participants in a rule-governed activity possess a 'critical reflective attitude' to the relevant behaviour-patterns (1961:55). If this 'internal point of view' is a purely psychological phenomenon, rather than an attitude (comparable to 'reliability' in the last paragraph) which is communicated in discourse, then Greimasian semiotics can take no account of it, and is likely to dismiss it as part of the myth which the discourse of legal philosophy itself seeks to communicate. The elaboration of an alternative account of a social 'rule' must count as one of the most important contemporary tasks of semiotics. **(11)**

In the next two sections, two parallel issues, the concept of legal validity and the postulate of the unity of the legal system, are considered in the light of these different semiotic and pragmatic orientations.

11.2 LEGAL 'VALIDITY'

The notion of legal validity represents the claim to legitimation of legal processes made from within the legal system. Assuming the legitimacy of the legal system as a whole, 'validity' is a qualification of individual phenomena as belonging to the legal system, and thus as being correct in its terms. The need for such a notion is evident. Law involves the application of coercion against the individual; such force requires justification; justification lies at the level of the restriction of the exercise of such power to the organs established by society for that purpose and to circumstances sufficiently clearly defined as to allow the individual to choose his course of action accordingly. The need for such tests of membership as are represented by criteria of validity thus rests upon a moral and political philosophy, according to which coercion is justified only if it is regulated in ways which allow the subjects of the system to choose their actions in relation to it.

But how is the notion of validity to be analysed ? We may note, first of all, a number of straightforward approaches, wherein we find a seemingly simple correlation between jurisprudential positivism, naturalism and realism on the one hand and syntactic, semantic and pragmatic approaches to semiotics on the other. Positivist legal philosophy is characterised by its emphasis upon the recognition of a proposition as legal in terms of its form, while naturalist views seek to characterise legal material in terms of their content. Thus it would not be totally misleading to suggest that positivism identifies law in terms of a syntactic theory, while naturalism seeks to identify it in terms of its semantics. **(12)** By contrast, realist approaches tend to reject both positivism and naturalism as falsely claiming to identify law in terms of some inherent quality, instead of in terms of its use within society - a view which stresses the pragmatic aspects of law.

But the matter turns out on closer examination to be more complicated. Recall the argument of G/L regarding **production juridique** (2.2, 5.1). They maintain that the legal lexicon is constituted by 'naming in legislation', so that a term which previously had the semic characteristic of **asémanticité juridique** will now have that of **sémanticité juridique.** We might characterise such a view as 'positivist' in the sense that it appears to require satisfaction of a test of pedigree (relating to the form of the normative proposition) for the purposes of legal recognition. (G/L conceive this as a semantic process, in that it relates to the constitution of a word which will bear meaning in the special language of law.) But for G/L, it is not the act of naming - an event in the outside world - which is constitutive of **sémanticité juridique,** nor is the effect of **production juridique** a pragmatic one, in the sense that it bears directly upon the relationship between the user and the text. What G/L observe is the use of the term in the legislative text itself, from which they infer the message which the text passes to its receiver (the latter, too, being constructed by the text itself).

Similar questions need to be asked when we consider apparently 'pragmatic' accounts of normativity. Raz seeks to place Hart at least partly in the speech-act tradition, in giving the following account of 'internal statements' (which he regards as 'fraught with difficulties'):

> The law is for Hart an immensely complex social practice or set of practices. In part the meaning of legal statements can be given a truth-conditional analysis. Legal statements are true if and only if certain relations obtain between them and the complex legal practices. But it would be wrong to say that legal statements are just statements about the existence of those practices. The truth-conditional analysis does not exhaust the meaning of legal statements. To understand them one must also understand their standard uses and what they express. Their typical use is to provide guidance by criticizing, commending, demanding, advising, approving, etc., and they express acceptance by the speaker of standards of behaviour towards conformity with which the statement is used to guide its addressee.

> This view of legal statements is meant to accommodate both their social-factual and their normative aspects. The factual aspect is captured by a truth conditional analysis. The normative one is accounted for by an explanation of the illocutionary force of the statements, and by the fact that they express not only the speaker's beliefs but also his practical attitude, his willingness to be guided by certain standards. (1981:448)

We see here a very significant tension. Such a separation of the legal correctness of statements (in terms of social practices which determine conclusively, through rules of recognition, when such a statement is correct), and their illocutionary force (as normative, and expressing the speaker's internal beliefs and attitudes) can generate only a formalist version of pragmatics, since fulfilment of the truth-conditions is itself a necessary (if not a sufficient) condition of the illocutionary force of the statement. **(13)** We may recall Oppenheim's clearer conception of the inter-relationships (10.5), according to which both 'syntactic' tests of 'correctness' and 'pragmatic' criteria of 'official quality' need to be satisfied in order to generate legal 'validity'. It is only the later Kelsen, on this analysis, who ultimately defines legal validity in exclusively pragmatic terms. MacCormick seeks to resolve Hart's dilemma in a different way. He adopts a formalist conception of validity, tying it to strict criteria of recognition (a 'syntactic' approach) while conceding that there exist aspects or parts of the legal system which cannot be described in such terms. We have no such criteria for the identification of 'legal principles', nor therefore can we maintain a 'distinction between valid and invalid principles of law' (1973:28).

One possible diagnosis of Hart's dilemma would be to say that he is torn between two different approaches to the semiotics of legal validity, the one a 'logical' approach compatible with the Peircian tradition, the other a 'discursive' approach more akin to that of Greimas. According to the former, represented here by Oppenheim, 'validity' is a way of describing certain relationships between elements within the language of law (its syntactic, semantic and pragmatic dimensions), and thus properly belongs to the 'meta-language' of law. It is only within this meta-language that a rule can be generated such as states the criteria of validity in terms of syntactic, semantic and pragmatic features. The logical approach thus regards the notion of 'validity' as belonging to a hierarchically separate level from the phenomena to which it may be applied. **(14)** By contrast, discursive semiotics sees 'validity' as part of the message of the text itself (3.3), and seeks to analyse the way in which that message is conveyed. 'Validity' is thus a particular semantic investment of modal attributes sent by the legislator to the semiotic object concerned (in G/L's text, the SC). 'Validity' would be regarded as part of the 'valorisation of what is communicated', contained within the discourse itself (Bastide). Here as elsewhere, it need hardly be emphasised, the semiotician implies no endorsement of the truth-claims of the message he describes.

11.3 THE UNITY OF THE LEGAL SYSTEM

Much of the argument advanced in this book, albeit in the context of the exegesis of some very different authors, leads us to doubt a major tenet of legal positivism, the unity of the legal system. The argument has taken different forms in different contexts. We can now review and develop the issues.

In discussing the Hartian notion of a 'core of settled meaning', I distinguished what I called the 'question of meaning' from the 'question of interpretation'. **(15)** The former was a question of the meaning of words, a linguistic question calling for a linguistic equivalent; the latter was a question of application to a determinate and separate proposition. That distinction needs to be refined, and applied to different legal contexts. If we find a correlation between such contexts and different semiotic features (including the activities involved in the questions of meaning and interpretation), we may be justified in concluding that the law consists not in a single semiotic system, but in several. And if we accept the methodological premises of Greimasian semiotics, it will follow that we must abandon the postulate of the unity of law, and view it as a set of interacting semiotic systems, the nature of whose interaction requires observation and study, and cannot be presupposed in advance.

Kalinowski provides a convenient starting point when he distinguishes three activities which belong to the life of the law: the statement (édiction), study and application of legal norms - broadly corresponding, at least in some jurisdictions, to legislation, doctrine and 'jurisprudence'. If we are confronted with the text of a statute, and asked what it means, then we are asked a 'question of meaning', relating to what has been stated in the first of Kalinowski's three activities. The question relates to the characteristic use of the words in the language-community concerned, on the assumption of minimal contextual clues. The question may thus be answered on the basis of the syntax and semantics of that language. **(16)** The characteristic use of the words will here represent the 'core' of their meaning, and it is the object of the question to elicit this core. Given the assumption that people normally mean what they say, we can further assume that it was this core meaning which 'the legislator' intended to communicate to his audience.

Since, however, the addressee of legislation is rarely asked to answer such a 'question of meaning', the legislation does indeed remain (as G/L put it) **virtuel** until it is applied. And when it is applied, the legislative message is likely to be used in a way which could not have been fully anticipated by its author. To say this is, in part, to reformulate in semiotic terms the argument of Kelsen (10.4) that an individual norm (generated by an act of will) cannot be presupposed in a general norm (also generated by an act of will). For the legislator cannot anticipate the value of 'Y' in the future 'question of interpretation', which takes the form 'Is Y to be subsumed within (the legislative) X ?'.

In advancing this argument, I have in mind not only the context of the activity of judicial decision-making, but also that of the study of law. It is, of course, possible (and perhaps more desirable than is generally acknowledged) to present students with a legislative text, and ask them simply 'what does it mean ?'. But the study of law, other than at a very basic level, does not proceed in this way. Rather, it poses questions of interpretation to the legislative text: 'Would situation Y be covered by legislative text X ?' where situation Y will typically be formulated within the 'penumbra' of the meaning of X - in other words, as a 'hard case'. If the Y chosen for study is within the 'core' of X, then this is merely a different way of asking 'the question of meaning', or rather teaching the answer to it.

Although judicial application of statute may appear to take the same form as its study, both involving 'the question of interpretation', there are in reality important differences. The study of law involves merely the relationship between propositions, whether that relationship be conceived in purely doctrinal terms, or be extended to include the values or socio-economic implications of the decision. But the judge knows that there will be real consequences in life of his decision whether Y is subsumed within X or not. (17) The context of his deciding 'the question of interpretation' is not academic, it is the lives of the litigants. Nor is it only the consequences of deciding one way or another which vary as between the lecture theatre and the courtroom. The manner in which the facts present themselves - the very constitution of Y - will also vary. In the context of study, Y is indeed a proposition, its various components constructed and limited to serve the didactic purpose concerned. But in the context of the courtroom, Y is a proposition abstracted from the facts of life, and the very act of abstraction (in order to constitute Y) itself involves crucial decision-making processes. These processes, too, cannot in reality be separated from pragmatic considerations: the effect in law of constructing the facts in one way or another. That is just one reason why it is difficult to label cases, in advance, as either 'easy' or 'hard'.

Such a distinction between doctrinal interpretation and judicial application is hardly new. Alf Ross rightly associated it with the relative incidence of 'cognitive' (including semantic) and 'pragmatic' considerations:

> Our starting point must be that the task of the judge is a problem of practical action. He has to reach a decision whether the exercise of force shall be put into effect against the defendant (the accused party) or not. Knowledge of various things (the facts of the case, the substance of the rules of law, etc.) plays, of course, a part in this decision, and to that extent the administration of justice is based on cognitive processes. But this does not alter the fact that the administration of justice, even though its course is prepared by cognitive processes, is in its very nature and definitively a decision, an act of volition . . . pragmatic factors in the administration of justice are considerations based on an evaluation of the practical reasonableness of the result judged in relation to certain presupposed fundamental evaluations. The

> pragmatic factors are hereby placed in contrast to the purely linguistic. Their influence is felt in a far higher degree than is generally assumed. (1958:136, 145)

We have also had occasion to note Kelsen's ultimate insistence on a radical differentiation between legal doctrine and legal norms (10.5); at the end of the second edition of **Reine Rechtslehre** he observes that the claim to the existence of a single right answer to a question of interpretation is a fiction, which may have 'political advantage', but which cannot be admitted into the scientific study of law (1967:355f.). Polish jurists have also devoted their attention to the semiotic differences between these different legal activities. Wroblewski notes that it is a peculiarity of legal (judicial) interpretation, by contrast to other ways of understanding linguistic expressions, that there exists on the judge a normative duty to decide the case, and therefore a duty to fix a meaning for the legal norm in question even when it is not possible to determine the question 'with purely linguistic tools of syntactical and semantic analysis' (1963:408f). **(18)** Like Ross, he stresses the insufficiency of linguistic analysis, even when 'the question of meaning' can thus be satisfactorily answered:

> A legal norm has some meaning within that kind of rules governing legal language, but the meaning may not be sufficient for the purpose of deciding a concrete case. It may not be sufficiently clear in respect of that case for many reasons, from its vagueness to the feeling that the norm taken in its immediate meaning may lead to an unjust or purposeless decision. (1963:409)

Wroblewski goes on to note the involvement of three types of interpretative directives governing the resolution of difficult problems of interpretation. He calls them linguistic, systemic and functional. One way of expressing the difference between judicial and doctrinal interpretation is the inevitable presence of such functional directives in the former, but not the latter. That is why Dworkin, who of the jurists here considered maintains in the strongest form the postulate of the unity of the legal system, errs. An academic Hercules might be confined to directives of principle (systemic considerations); a judicial Hercules cannot avoid, even if he chooses to ignore, policy (functional) considerations. **(19)** Kalinowski draws a fundamental distinction between the language of law (in which legal rules are stated) and the language of jurists, and further distinguishes both from the logic of norms. **(20)**

In the light of this argument, it is possible to resolve tensions which have been observed in the legal philosophy of both Hart and MacCormick. When Hart puts forward his rule of recognition as providing a 'conclusive affirmative indication' of the legal status of a primary rule, he may be viewed as claiming the sufficiency of a syntactic rule for the purposes of establishing the illocutionary force of the utterance at the level of discourse; similarly, any claim to the semantic sufficiency of the 'core' in Hart's theory should be read as referring to the 'meaning' of legal norms, and not to the process of their interpretation. For such purely linguistic objectives, a truth-conditional version of semantics may, indeed, suffice. But when we move to judicial interpretation, any determination of a case on the basis of linguistic criteria alone represents a decision on the part of the judge so to decide it, to the exclusion of systemic or pragmatic considerations.

We may resolve MacCormick's (related) problem in a similar way (8.2). The working of legal institutions and legal concepts is presented by MacCormick as a cognitive convenience, for the purposes of the exposition of the law (8.3). But that argument assumes the definability of the concepts and institutions, in terms of necessary and sufficient conditions, not merely 'ordinarily necessary' and 'presumptively sufficient' conditions. Doctrine cannot develop in the latter way, on MacCormick's own account, since those factors which render the conditions merely 'ordinarily' necessary and 'presumptively' sufficient are factors which become apparent in the course of adjudication, from consideration of the consequences of a proposed decision. MacCormick, like Hart, assumes that the context makes no difference to the interpretative processes involved: there is one law, and one mode of legal interpretation. In reality, it is quite different. Such correspondence as may exist between the 'meaning' of a statute, its doctrinal interpretation, and its judicial application is a purely contingent fact, whose relative incidence in different legal systems invites study, but which, on the basis of the arguments here presented, cannot be taken as a postulate. It is, as the Greimasian school would insist, part of the message which legal texts (in their various ways) convey. And judged by the present state of mainstream Anglophone jurisprudence, that message has been all too effectively communicated.

These three contexts fall far short of exhausting the semiotic systems whose inter-relationship makes up what we call the legal system. The fact that these are the three contexts which receive predominant jurisprudential attention is itself significant. Studies of lawyer-client interaction and of out-of-court settlement **(21)** are marginalised, as belonging to the sociology of law. The unity of the legal system is again presupposed. It is the same law which is involved in these situations, even though it is here studied 'in action' rather than 'in the books'. Still more significant is the neglected area of non-contentious law (non-contentious only because it has not been contested). The following kind of argument is presupposed. If the law is not contested, that must be because it is clear. If it is clear, it must be understood. Thus the absence of contest is taken as evidence of adequate communication of the law; the message received by the citizen is taken to be the same as that addressed by the lawgiver. **(22)** But this semiotic argument in favour of the unity of the legal system neglects the processes of translation inevitably involved. Quite apart from distortions of content, a change in form in which the law is transmitted necessarily affects the overall message. Such differences of linguistic form may be perceived even within the organs of public administration. Sourioux and Lerat compare a (legislative) **arrêté** with an administrative circular on the same subject. The **arrêté** is seen by them as an example of normative style, as evidenced **inter alia** by the restriction of the modalities used in it to the categories of the 'logic of norms'; the circular, by comparison, is less restricted in its linguistic range, and more personal in its modes of address (use of first and second person forms). The **arrêté** is public and impersonal; the circular has the characteristics of a document 'd'ordre interne' (1976:103-6). A great deal more change is involved as the law is translated in both written and oral discourse, for the 'benefit' of the ordinary citizen. **(23)** To these various arguments, none of which are new to jurisprudence, Greimasian semiotics brings a further consideration, which derives directly from its definition of the object of study. Rejecting (along with some versions of legal realism) any reification of 'law' or 'normativity' (other than as the particular semantic investment of modal values transferred in a discourse), Greimasian semiotics has to adopt a non-traditional definition of the object of study. As we have seen, it defines that object of study in terms of the discourse itself - not even the genre of legal discourse (legislative, doctrinal, jurisprudential) but the particular discourse under consideration (e.g. the 1966 Loi). Thus, when we consider the 'life-history' of 'a law', we have not one object of study, but several - each one corresponding to a particular discursive object (a piece of legislation, a circular, a judgment, a newspaper report, an interview, a textbook, even a unit of interactive behaviour). It is to the characteristics of the members of this set of discourses, their inter-relationships and their specificity (if any) as a set, that attention is directed in the final chapter.

CHAPTER TWELVE

Towards a Semiotic Model of Law

(12.1) Semiotic Variables within the Legal System: In order to understand both the nature of the differences between the various activities which occur within the legal system, and the manner in which they interact, it is necessary to note the variations between them in terms of semiotic characteristics. Such variables include the nature of the audience, the directness of communication, the strength of presuppositions regarding coherence, and the structure and processes of semiosis. **(12.2) Towards the Construction of a Semiotic Model of Law:** The Peircian and Saussurian traditions of semiotics generate different views of the inter-relationship of different semiotic systems within law, in accordance with the underlying differences regarding the status and nature of the 'referent', and of the minimal units of legal signification. The 'logical' school points towards an hierarchical account of the inter-relationhips, while the 'discursive' school stresses the syntagmatic relations within the communicational process itself. The Saussurian tradition does not resist historical views of the ideological penetration of natural into legal language. But it suggests that rhetorical techniques may themselves be accommodated within structural semiotics. **(12.3) The Specificity of Law:** Despite claims that the specificity of law resides only at the pragmatic level, both syntactic and deep semantic features of legal discourse stand out as peculiar to it. Legal discourse claims to regulate its own creation, and to practice self-interpretation. Monosemicity and restricted connotations are characteristic claims of legal discourse. The capacity to create 'inferior' semiotic objects, the special claims of the legal **acteur**, and the relation of 'recognition' to 'competence' also emerge from the Greimasian analysis as contributing to the specific appearance of law.

12.1 SEMIOTIC VARIABLES WITHIN THE LEGAL SYSTEM

The analysis of legislation, doctrine and adjudication in terms of the categories of syntactics, semantics and pragmatics (11.3) represents only one of the variables to be encountered once we examine the semiotic characteristics of different aspects of the legal system. Such variables call for systematic analysis, both in order to grasp the variety of semiotic activities which comprise the legal system, and as a prelude to any attempt to construct a model of their inter-relationship. In this section, I attempt such a preliminary survey, not confining myself to the problematics of Greimasian semiotics, but including some basic concerns of the sociology of communication.

Audience

Greimas uses the phrase **groupes sémiotiques** to refer to groups whose members possess in common a competence to send and receive a certain type of discourse (1976:53). Within the legal system, a great variety of such groups exist, each characterised by its own set of semiotic features. For this purpose, even the differentiation between legislative, doctrinal and judicial functions proves too broad; within each of them, distinct **groupes sémiotiques** may be discerned, each with its own objectives, texts, and processes of semiosis. (1) But this threefold division of legal activities may serve as a convenient starting point.

What is the audience for legislative discourse ? 'The community,' one may think. That, assuredly, is the message which legislative discourse conveys, by stating no express restriction of the audience, but rather implying, through an enactment formula which mentions the representatives of the whole community, that it is to the whole community that it is addressed. But a moment's thought is sufficient to convince us of the unreality of that view. A jurist might be more tempted to identify the judiciary as the audience for legislation: it is the judiciary which is charged with enforcing it. But once again, the answer smacks of unreality. Judges are called upon to 'apply' legislation only when things go wrong. When they do go wrong, the judge will 'refer' to the relevant statute. The statute book, for the judge, is a reference work, to be consulted (only) as and when the occasion demands. The same is broadly true of the practitioner, even though the circumstances in which he may be called upon to refer to the legislation may not be restricted to 'contentious' business. In reality, there is a much more significant audience for legislation, a **groupe sémiotique** whose involvement in the legal process is given a remarkably low profile in most jurisprudential literature (Hart is a partial exception): the administration. (2) Legislation is not self-fulfilling. But at the same time it need not remain 'virtual' until such time as it is applied by the judge (as G/L appear to imply). Almost every piece of legislation is directed towards a section of the bureaucracy, which will be charged to put it into action, and not merely to refer to it when matters go wrong. In this sense, the real audience for taxation statutes is the Inland Revenue Department, not the judge who may on occasion be required to adjudicate an individual tax matter, or even the citizen whose affairs will be regulated by (a very small proportion of) the tax legislation. Again, pace Holmes, criminal statutes have as their primary audience neither the criminal, nor his lawyer, nor the man in the street. (3) When the law of theft is changed by statute (as has occurred twice in England in the last twenty years), no circular drops through the letterbox. (That will not avail the citizen when he finds himself charged with a criminal offence, since ignorance of the law is no defence - a maxim or rule which itself powerfully communicates the myth of a unified legal system.) The real audience of criminal statutes is, once again, a particular section of the administration, the police and the prosecuting agencies. They really must read the whole statute, and adjust their everyday behaviour to it (that, at least, is the message), since it is the administration of that part of the law which is the everyday concern of that agency. Of course, in suggesting that the real audience for legislation is a section of the administration, I do not imply that it is the whole of that section of the administration, from its most senior to its most junior levels. Within each agency, there will exist specialist organs charged with the task of communicating the legislative message throughout the agency in the most appropriate manner. Not infrequently, the section of the administration charged with the activation of legislation will itself be given power to complete or supplement or detail the legislative message by the drafting of 'secondary legislation'. It is hardly accidental that we use this term 'secondary legislation', to refer to supplementary law-creation by the administration, not the judiciary.

What is the audience of judicial discourse ? A recent study by Paterson (1982) of the judicial activities of the Law Lords (the ultimate appellate court in Great Britain), based upon interviews and observation, suggests a relatively restricted **groupe sémiotique:** fellow Law Lords and that senior section of the Bar with which the judges interact in the course of the hearings. In other words, the primary audience of the senior appellate court is the senior ranks of the legal profession itself. The speeches are not written for the edification of law teachers or law students (despite the frequent entertainment they provide for both), even less for the general public. **(4)** When we ask about the audience of the inferior judiciary, we are similarly forced towards a restrictive conclusion. High Court decisions are rarely reported, but they are discussed amongst judges of equal rank at table. Magisterial decisions are discussed, if at all, amongst fellow magistrates.

Similarly, with doctrinal writing. The primary audience of doctrinal writing is juristic, the legal academic community. This is the primary audience of scholarly articles and monographs. For the most part, didactic literature, written for students, is clearly distinguishable.

The pattern which emerges from all this is striking, if hardly surprising. The primary audience for most genres of legal discourse is a group whose interests and composition is remarkably similar to that of the authors of the literature in question. There is no single genre of legal literature which serves to unify the legal system; on the contrary, these several genres not only exemplify but fortify the separateness of the various semiotic systems at work within 'the law'.

The character and interests of the particular audience necessarily affect, inter alia, the nature of the message it communicates. The primary audience of legislation is the administration; its message is about action, not system or justification. The primary audience of the judiciary is the senior Bar and fellow-judges, trained to persuade; the message of their discourse is primarily justificatory. (5) The primary audience of doctrine is academic; its message concentrates on systemic considerations. The legislative discourse is thus a discourse of norms; the judicial, a discourse of rhetoric; the doctrinal, a discourse of concepts.

Simi ar analyses may be constructed for other semiotic groups involved in the legal system. There is the discourse amongst practitioners (a discourse of status and profit ?). Amongst the non-lawyer subjects of the law, there are also distinct semiotic groups. For some, the law is a discourse of manipulation, negotiation, strategy, while for others it is a discourse of fate. (6)

Inter-Personal or Distanced Communication

It was consideration of the legal system as a communication process that caused Olivecrona to doubt that law could be conceived in terms of commands (which imply direct address) and to conclude that law consists of imperatives without an addressee (1971:219). But one is not bound to conclude that the imperatives lack an addressee. Rather, it is a case of communication at a distance, with no personal interaction between the sender and receiver of the message. Viewed in this way, the relationship between legislature and citizen would need to be analysed as an example of mass communication, along with 'the media' and works of fiction. Yet even here, the analogy breaks down. Legislation, as it reaches the general public, is filtered through numerous communicative agencies; it is not a direct communication, such as connects 'Fleet Street' to the breakfast table.

If one abandons the myth of unity, and looks separately at the various semiotic groups operative within the law, one finds that there is a far greater degree of inter-personal communication involved than the popular conception would suggest. Once again, the myth is part of the message which legal discourses (in their various ways) seek to convey. The image of mass communication, from a collective, impersonal legislature to a collective, undifferentiated public, itself serves to suggest that form of objectivity which is associated with lack of personal involvement. (7)

Conclusions

The presence or absence of direct communication in the various semiotic systems of law has two important implications. In direct, inter-personal communication, the receiver of the message is in the best possible position to judge both the intention of the sender and his sincerity. As for the content of the message, Carzo suggests that there exists in law no direct equivalent to the capacity of the sender of the message, in inter-personal communication, to judge whether his intended meaning has been correctly received. Instead, Carzo suggests, some structural 'feedback' device is required, in order to ensure at least some minimal correspondence between meaning and interpretation. He notes that where the sender anticipates difficulties of decodification of his message by the receiver, he may adopt the technique of sending a second, or even contemporary interpretative message, as in a ministerial circular accompanying a set of regulations (1981:78f.). We may add that messages in one form of legal discourse may serve, secondarily, as feedback devices in relation to a different legal discourse. The publication of judgments is not designed primarily to assure Parliament that the legislative message has been properly understood by the judges, but it can serve this function, as may be seen from those occasions when Parliament legislates to reverse what it sees as erroneous statutory interpretation by the judges.

Inter-personal communication also involves the satisfaction of sincerity conditions. In a different context, Eco gives the following example:

> If I ask someone what time it is and if he answers /6:15/, my interpretation of this expression can conclude that (provided there are not other co-textual clues and provided the speaker is not a notorious liar or a psychotic subject) the speaker positively said that it is 45 minutes to 7 and that he intended to say so. (1984:3)

Eco uses this example to argue that there can be circumstances in which words have a univocal meaning. If I am to conclude that the respondent meant that it really was 45 minutes to 7, it is necessary not only that his words be capable of bearing that meaning, but also that I should believe in his sincerity in uttering them. My belief in his sincerity results not from the content of the communication but from its inter-personal dimension, the fact that I asked him a question and he responded to my face. A parallel question to that relating to 'feedback' thus arises. Insofar as legal communication operates at a distance, what structures are provided for the satisfaction of sincerity conditions ? Once again, it seems, there is a gap between the image communicated of the law, and the underlying realities. The image is one of a system whose sincerity is pre-supposed, beyond question. The criteria, at most, consists of the 'official quality' (Oppenheim) of the source of the message. If it is printed by HMSO, and purports to be a statute, it is a statute. (The Clerk of Parliament, after all, must have certified the Parliamentary Roll.) In reality, sincerity conditions are fulfilled in those inter-personal communications which take place in the much smaller semiotic groups (very commonly peer groups) described above.

Semiotic structures and processes

In relation to each semiotic group within law, we have to ask what semiotic structures and processes it uses. Does it use binary oppositions, for example, or multi-member sets, in a relationship of hyponymy ? We have seen reason to believe that the former semiotic structure characterises judicial argument, while the latter is more appropriate to legal doctrine, and the overall classification of the legal universe.

In asking about semiotic processes (1.2), we are posing a problem increasingly viewed in cognitive terms. What cognitive processes are involved in the receipt and recognition of the signals which convey the message ? 'Recognition' may be a notion more central to linguistics than to law. (8) But Hart has placed it in the forefront of contemporary legal philosophy, through the weight and character he attaches to his 'rule of recognition'. For he sees it as conveying meaning - that of the illocutionary force (as legal) of the utterance - in a particular way. It is an 'identifying mark', a 'authoritative mark' for the 'conclusive identification of the primary rules of obligation' (1961:92f.). Such a notion of a 'mark' which conclusively conveys the meaning assigned to it in a particular code evokes the process of semiosis of the linguistic sign, as conceived by Saussure. In terms of Mounin's distinction

(1.2), it is a 'sign' rather than a 'symbol', being more akin to the process by which a Frenchman decodifies the meaning of the word 'sang' than that by which he understands the cultural significance of the Parthenon. This, indeed, is the source of the 'demonstrability thesis' which Dworkin rightly attacks: to put his criticism at its weakest, the legal system contains a variety of semiotic processes, only some of which operate in this way. Others are closer to Mounin's symbols, in that they require conscious knowledge and interpretation of a whole system of cultural signals.

MacCormick is quite ready to concede the variety of semiotic processes which operate within law, while denying that any such concession invalidates the claims of legal positivism. Leaving that latter issue to one side, we may note some distinctions which he himself observes. He notes that the recognition of instances of a particular legal institution may not always proceed in the same way (1973:10f.). It may not simply be the application of defined criteria to a fact situation, such that conformity or lack of conformity to those criteria indicates conclusively the presence or absence of the instance of the legal institution. That may occur where the institution itself is defined by statute. But where it is a 'common law' institution, where no particular set of words has the force of a legislative definition, the criteria for the existence of an instance of the institution may not be as 'clearly stateable' as in the statutory example. It is in this context, for MacCormick, that the criteria may be less than conclusive:

> Yet when we see, as I have tried to show, how the necessary flexibility of the law depends upon the elaboration and acceptance of arguments from policy and from principle, we see at the same time why the concept of law cannot be tied down to being simply an institutional concept in the philosophical sense, covering simply the criteria of validity and the rules valid in terms of them. We have neither criteria of validity for legal principles, nor therefore a distinction between valid and invalid principles of law. (1973:28)

Thus for MacCormick there are different semiotic processes involved in the recognition of different types of law, and the recognition of fact situations as 'instances' of particular legal categories (once the latter are established).

Recognition of instances of legal institutions is taken by MacCormick to be more comparable to the recognition of statutory rather than common law rules, in other words to operate more with signs than symbols. (9)

A full examination of the range of semiotic structures and processes involved in the law would be of considerable interest. How is the legal message conveyed, for example, in the lawyer-client interview ? Does the lawyer seek to explain the law, or rather project a message of his own reliability as an instrument of it ? If the latter, by what semiotic processes is this achieved - verbal, visual, behavioural, etc. ? How is the law conveyed to the general public through the media or the administration ? Above all, perhaps, how is it that apparently incompatible messages are effectively conveyed to the general public regarding the law: that it is precise and known, that lack of knowledge of it is no excuse, yet at the very same time that really it is the lawyer's business, and not that of John Citizen ?

Coherence

The degree of coherence expected within a particular kind of legal discourse is another important variable. Kelsen recognised this in his ultimate position on conflicting norms (10.4-5). In judicial discourse, conflicting norms may co-exist, but in legal doctrine, composed of propositions about legal norms, conflicting norms cannot co-exist. Kelsen argues for this distinction on the grounds that propositions make truth-claims while norms do not. A better way of putting this, from the semiotic point of view, would be to say either that each individual norm represents a separate discourse, whereas legal doctrine represents a single, systemic discourse (in which coherence is expected), or to say that judicial discourse, if regarded as a single entity, has a lower expectation of coherence than does legal doctrine.

This is not to suggest that coherence is an inherent quality of any kind of discourse; rather, it is a contingent fact about the interpretative conventions of the semiotic group concerned. As Sbisà and Fabbri put it: 'it could even be affirmed that coherence, as such, does not exist, and that there are simply different degrees in the amount of co-operative work required from the partner/hearer if he is willing to take the text as a coherent one and, correspondingly, different degrees in the partner's willingness to co-operate.' (10)

In Chapter 9, some of the processes by which different strengths of claim to coherence may be communicated were observed. The denial of 'logical space' is made in the discourse by the placing of deontic oppositional categories within the framework of a semiotic, rather than a logical square. This has the effect of denying the 'third possibility' (9.1). But in assessing Dworkin's argument, it was suggested that his analysis and that of the positivists which he opposes relate to different types of discourse. The positivist account is concerned essentially with the logic of norms, and their 'scientific' representation. Dworkin, by contrast, claims to provide an account of legal argument. And even legal argument, as has been observed, may have different semiotic characteristics in the didactic discourse of academe, and the pragmatic discourse of the court.

Some apparent correlations

Can we correlate such variables as the structure and process of semiosis with those of audience and communicational context ? One way of posing this question would be to ask whose needs are best served by each particular structure or process. Who needs immediacy of perception ? Whose interest is served by symbolic interpretation ?

It was suggested earlier (2.5) that a pure semantics (rid of indeterminacy, by being reduced to a purely formal language) would be in the interests neither of communication to the public nor adjudication by judges. With the development of formal, logical representations of law, whether computer-assisted or not, the means will be available to ensure that 'meaning' (as understood by Hart, in the sense of authorial intention) can be communicated to any receiver competent to decode that formal language. Yet assuredly our judges, and not only our judges, would resist the imposition on them of such a system. For them, like MacCormick, linguistic indeterminacy is indeed a resource; it does not represent a 'crisis in communication', as Hart would have it. But for the jurist, interested in legal doctrine, the formalisation of law is a benefit: a tool towards its systemic analysis. It is the jurist, not the practitioner, the judge or the sociologist of law, who has seen fit to develop deontic logic.

Equally significant, and somewhat less obvious, may be

a further correlation, suggested indirectly by J.L. Austin. He argued that the illocutionary act ('which has a certain force in saying something') is conventional, whereas the perlocutionary act ('which is the achieving of certain effects by saying something') is not: 'A judge should be able to decide, by hearing what was said, what locutionary and illocutionary acts were performed, but not what perlocutionary acts were achieved' (1975:121f.). Not everyone would accept the non-conventionality of the means of producing perlocutionary effects. Nevertheless, the type of point Austin makes deserves more systematic consideration. Is there a difference between the manner of recognition of the illocutionary force of a legal utterance, its perlocutionary effects and indeed its propositional content? And do any such distinctions correlate with audiences and communicational contexts?

One may hazard the suggestion that a distinction between the semiotic characteristics of illocutionary force and propositional content may assist in resolving some of the conflicts observed in jurisprudential positivism. When Hart advances the rule of recognition as an 'authoritative mark' of the status of a primary rule, he is talking precisely of the illocutionary force of that rule; he says nothing, thereby, about the communication of its propositional content. (11) When discussing the communication of the propositional content of legal utterances, Hart makes no further use of the idea of rules of recognition, but falls back upon the semantic categories of 'core' and 'penumbra', with the results discussed above. It is this same distinction between force and content which underlies the difficulties of Kelsen in resolving the relations between formal and material authorisation. Material authorisation requires satisfaction of tests relating to propositional content, even for the purposes of establishing the illocutionary force of a legal utterance. But Kelsen, as we have seen, ultimately abandoned that view.

Sbisà and Fabbri label the 'necessary conditions' conception of illocutionary force as the M1 model of pragmatics, wherein 'attention focuses on the linguistic form of the speech act, failing to consider the latter in terms of a theory of actions' (1980:3). They argue, instead, for a different model (M2), wherein they 'consider the hearer as an active participant':

> The neutral, passive (in principle, objective) recognition of the speaker's communicative intention turns into the more problematic process of attributing a communicative intention to the speaker and taking him to be responsible for it. (1980:4)

This is not to deny the presence in M2 of 'force-indicating devices'; rather, it attributes to the receiver a far more active process in interpreting the meaning and effect of the force-indicating device. According to this viewpoint, therefore, 'trying to formulate a complete list of necessary and sufficient conditions for the performance of an illocutionary act is here pointless' (1980:4). We have seen just this tension between different models of pragmatics apparent in MacCormick's institutional theory, where he seeks to build, effectively, an M2 model on the basis of Searle's M1 foundations. In reality, we may suspect, the difference between the two models may reflect different levels of analysis, comparable to the distinctions between 'Langue' and 'Parole' or that between 'pure' and 'descriptive' semantics. The distinction also correlates with that between 'meaning' and 'interpretation', as that distinction has been used in this book. **(12)**

Yet even so, there appear to be differences, at the level of real interaction, between communication of illocutionary force within a legal system and communication of its propositional content - the former operating largely through 'signs', the latter through 'symbols'. Why should this be so ? The answer must surely take account of different audiences and communicational contexts. In general, it may be suggested, there is less scope for interactive negotiation of illocutionary force than there is in the case of propositional content. When the legislature passes a statute on theft, it thereby indicates conclusively to all possible audiences that the activity of stealing is subject to legal regulation. It does not thereby indicate in the same conclusive manner how the activity of stealing should thus be regulated. Propositional content can more readily be negotiated than illocutionary force. One reason why it can be more readily negotiated is the fact that propositional content is far more likely to be the subject-matter of interactive communication. Another may be that illocutionary force depends not upon the interpretation of words, but upon choices between modalities which are overtly structured in our discourse as binary oppositions (and which thus reflect very directly the constraints of the semiotic square): the 'statute' is either 'valid' or 'invalid'.

This is not to say that all propositional content may be negotiated, that the semiotic process involved is always that of the interpretation of symbols. It depends very much on the audience and communicational context concerned. The motorist cannot 'negotiate' the meaning of the traffic lights. They are there as 'authoritative marks' of the content of the behaviour which is legally required in that situation. The reason is obvious. At the other extreme, lawyers are uniquely privileged in the 'competence' (power to say) accorded them to negotiate the propositional content of the law applicable to their clients. They can negotiate that law amongst themselves, or with the judge, in that they can argue for one interpretation of the law or another. (That is not to say that they have competence to argue for any interpretation, even one completely 'outside the frame'. But such constraints as may operate on them derive not from the language of the law but from conventions relating to proper 'professional' behaviour.) Indeed, the lawyer is privileged even to negotiate the effect of a clear criminal law on his client, however much the English legal system, at least, seeks to deny or conceal the process of 'plea bargaining'. (13)

Viewed in this light, the problem of 'discretion' assumes an even more important role than that which it presently plays in jurisprudential analysis of judicial reasoning. The presence of the discretion of some draws its significance from the absence of the discretion of others. We need to know far more clearly the contours of those semiotic groups to whom a competence to negotiate the propositional content of the law is accorded. Those are the groups to whom a competence is given to treat the signals of the law as 'symbols' rather than 'signs'.

Eco (1984) has recently argued that such semiotic oppositions as 'sign' and 'symbol' should be viewed as differences of degree, rather than of kind. (14) His argument is of interest to both the psychologist and the philosopher, in that he sees the operation of a cognitive, inferential process in the interpretation of all signals, both those conventionally regarded as 'signs' and as 'symbols'. (15) The effect of adopting such a continuum (16), and of stressing the common cognitive processes involved along it, does not, however, lead Eco to reject the possibility that a single meaning is to be attributed to a certain text in some circumstances. 'Many texts have undoubtedly many possible senses, but it is still possible to decide **which one** has to be selected if one approaches the text in the light of a given topic, as well as it is possible to tell of certain texts **how many** isotopies they display' (1984:3). Disambiguation is here achieved from within the text, by what Eco elsewhere calls 'co-text' (as distinguished from 'context').

From the point of view of the semiotic analysis of legal systems, it makes no significant difference whether we regard these distinctions as ones of degree or of kind. We are still left with distinct semiotic groups, with distinct purposes, communicational contexts, processes and structures of semiosis. The image of the unitary legal system remains part of the message, not the reality.

The traditional classification of jurisprudential theories, as positivist, naturalist or realist, is associated with the variables discussed in this section. These different approaches to legal theory select or emphasise or privilege one particular form of legal discourse above others. Positivism privileges those forms of legal discourse in which 'recognition' is primarily a 'syntactic' process, involving 'signs' rather than 'symbols', and leading to conclusions regarding what Chomsky calls 'well-formedness'. Naturalist theories are concerned with the semantic relations between propositions, thus with the recognition of 'meaning' through symbols. Realist theories are directed to the recognition of the expressive or affective 'force' of their subject-matter, that is the (pragmatic) relations between discourse and its users, especially those involved in the process of interpretation. (17) The semiotic processes by which such 'force' is conveyed are here more varied: the 'discourse' itself is essentially interpersonal, rather than textual. From correlations such as these, we could construct models of jurisprudential theory, each one characterised by the semiotic features which it emphasises in the legal discourse to which it attends. Such an endeavour assists in understanding the jurisprudential theories of individual writers - not because any one of them is likely to fall exclusively within one of the models, but because the models will assist in identifying the particular mixture or synthesis favoured by the writer concerned. For example, if we take Hart's theory not as it presently stands, but in its strongest possible reconstructed version (the strategy which Hart himself adopts in relation to the 'command' theory), it emerges that he favours a syntactic account of 'recognition' and a pragmatic account of 'interpretation', but attaches the qualification 'validity' primarily to the former. More significant still, semiotic analysis may assist in the comparative analysis of legal systems, by attending to the incidence of semiotic variables found within them. (18)

12.2 TOWARDS THE CONSTRUCTION OF A SEMIOTIC MODEL OF LAW

We may not be able to reduce law to a single semiotic system. But we can characterise the various semiotic systems which claim to be legal, and we can analyse their inter-relationship. Such an endeavour would refine and advance Hart's programme in the following respect. It would endorse his rejection of the search for a definition of 'law'. It would attend, rather, to questions of variety and inter-relationship. But it would conduct its investigation not at the level of the different linguistic uses of 'law', conceived as a concept, but rather at that of the discursive products and practices of different semiotic groups.

Any such attempt to build up an overall semiotic model of law must necessarily take positions on some basic theoretical issues: the status and identity of the 'referent', and the minimal units of signification. Very different results will be obtained, depending upon the choices made on these issues.

The issue of the referent is perhaps best encapsulated in the observation of Kalinowski (1976:11), noted above (4.3), that whereas semiotics is concerned with syntactics, semantics and pragmatics, logic (or, we may add, logical semiotics associated with truth-conditional semantics) is concerned with relations between states of being and propositions about them. This takes us back to fundamental issues in the conceptual structure of semiotics (1.2). For if we adhere to the Peircian tradition, which in its triadic structure of signification incorporates a relationship between discourse and the outside world, we will necessarily construct a different model from one based upon the Saussurian dualist conception. In short, the Peircian tradition is apt to generate hierarchical models, premised upon the existence of independent levels of reality (outside world and signification) and the relationships between them, whereas discursive semiotics incorporates the outside world in terms of the claims made by the text, and sees such dimensions as the content of the message and its logical structure in terms of different levels of signification of a single discourse. (19)

The Peircian tradition of semiotics thus faces a further problem, which does not trouble discursive semiotics. Having admitted the 'referent' as an object of the outside world, which plays an integral part in the structure of signification, it has to identify the referent of any particular significatory process. Legal positivism, whose underlying semiotics are overwhelmingly 'extensional' in this sense, has to face that problem with respect to the referent of the concept 'law'. The variety of answers implied to this question is all too rarely appreciated. For example, John Austin conceived 'law' to refer to empirical behaviour patterns. (20) For Hart, on the other hand, the referent of the word 'law' is a psychological concept, something which actually exists in people's minds, and to which they implicitly refer in their uses of the term (as a linguistic concept). We then have to ask other, parallel questions. If the referent of 'law' is a psychological concept, is the same to be said of 'rule'? An affirmative answer might be indicated by Hart's emphasis upon the 'internal point of view' as distinguishing rule-governed behaviour from merely convergent behaviour (11.1). But Harris has seen reason to conclude that for Hart 'a positive legal rule is to be equated with a "rule-situation", that is, with a social situation in which a certain pattern of behaviour is regarded as a standard' (1979:24f., 52ff.). This is not the place to enter upon the merits of Harris's exegesis. Suffice it to observe that the adoption of a Peircian version of semiotics in legal philosophy may well entail (especially on Hart's account) the identification of not just one referent, but of many. It follows that any postulate of the unity of the legal system must provide a satisfactory account also of the inter-relationship of such referents.

A reflection of this problem is found in the differing views which are taken of the relationship between a rule and its formulation. (21) Most lawyers would regard as unproblematic the proposition that different rule formulations may refer to a single rule. That implies a view of the referent in line with that of Peircian semiotics. But the matter has not proved uncontroversial in philosophy. Hanson (1977:43f.) notes that different views of the relation between rules and their linguistic expressions have been taken, on the basis of different presuppositions in the philosophy of language. Thus Ganz (1971:26-37) identifies rules with linguistic entities (inscriptions), while Black (1963) takes a rule to be that which is expressed by a rule-formulation. According to the latter view, different rule-formulations may express the same rule, since the rule is a non-linguistic entity, to which the formulation refers. Ganz, by contrast, takes a view more akin to that of Saussurian semiotics, implying the independence of each rule-formulation. Greimasian semiotics would certainly be more in sympathy with the latter view. What, then, would it say in response to the claim that legal experience shows that different rule-formulations do indeed refer to one single rule ? The answer would be that such a relation of 'reference' is part of the message which the discourse (here successfully) conveys. We are not thereby committed to the truth of that claim. We are, however, interested in analysing how it is successfully communicated.

Whether we adopt the presuppositions of Peircian or Saussurian semiotics, one further question needs to be answered. What are the minimal units of signification ? But here too, differences in conception of the referent are necessarily reflected.

We have seen that Greimasian semiotics gives a straightforward answer to this question. Legal discourse is simply discourse with a particular content, a particular 'semantic investment'. If discourse in general is modelled upon semantic relations within the sentence, as Greimasian semiotics claims, then the minimal units of legal discourse are those same minimal units of discourse in general, **actants** and **fonctions,** which are modelled respectively upon nominal phrases and their predicates (3.2-3). The simplicity of this model is perhaps hidden from view by G/L's talk of a 'legal grammar' (5.1) and of the process of **production juridique** as constituting lexemes as part of a particular semantic universe. But the 'legal grammar' which they analyse is itself part of the message of the text; it does not represent any mechanism, separate from that of narrative grammar, by which the text itself is produced. Indeed, we have seen how the 'legal grammar' is itself conveyed as a message through the same inter-relations of **actants** and

fonctions which characterise both discourse in general, and a particular discourse (the content of the 1966 Loi). **Production juridique** is constitutive of a separate semantic universe in the sense that it establishes the lexemes of a particular discursive practice, that of a particular discursive group (those involved in legislative discourse). If one then asks: 'what makes this particular discourse "legal" ?', the answer must lie quite simply in the semantic investment of the message (the force of the modalities which it claims to transmit) and the effectiveness which it possesses in communicating those claims.

A different model is necessary for those who associate legal discourse with an external referent, whether that be a social situation in the outside world, or indeed a logical structure. An example of the latter approach is to be encountered in work on the computerisation of legal discourse, an activity which assumes that the non-formalised language of a legal discourse (one which contains semiotic constraints or presuppositions, as shown in the present analysis of Dworkin) can be reduced to a formalised language. **(22)** Depending upon the nature of the formalisation, this may entail the claim that legal discourse really 'has' a logical structure different from that of the semiotic logic exposed in Greimasian analysis. Bourcier provides an example of such a hierarchical model of legal semiotics. She argues that legal discourse is a 'referential discourse' in the sense that its expressions permit the speaker to indicate one or more particular objects of the (legal) universe of discourse. These objects of discourse are definitions, norms, sanctions and the like, as identified (sometimes explicitly) by particular utterances of the legal system, as in cross-references to articles of codes and statutes (1979:16). Law has its own conceptual structure, based on a particular cognitive and logical organisation of the language which it uses. Legal concepts are quite distinct from the language in which they may be expressed; frequently they remain implicit (1979:17-19). On this kind of account, the minimal units of legal discourse may be regarded as specific to law, and not as mere semantic investments of the minimal units of discursive structures in general. On Bourcier's argument, the legal concept stands as a strong candidate to be regarded as the minimal unit of a non-linguistic legal semiotic.

In the analytical tradition, associated with the

pragmatic rather than the logical analysis of legal language, we encounter claims to the effect that 'legal language' can indeed be distinguished as a sub-group of the natural language to which it belongs. Engisch, for example, distinguishes 'normative' from 'descriptive' concepts. The latter refer 'to real or seemingly real objects, objects that are fundamentally perceptible or in some other way open to experience: 'man', 'death', 'cohabitation', 'darkness', 'red', 'velocity', 'intention'. Such concepts remain descriptive, notwithstanding the fact that they may have acquired 'as juridical concepts, a particular message, which can be perfectly distinguished from the meaning of the corresponding biological, theological or physical concepts'. He further distinguishes 'normative juridical concepts' as pointing 'to data that are not immediately perceptible or open to experience, but only come to be imagined and understood in connection with the world of the norms'. He gives as examples the concept that something 'belongs' to another person (which logically presupposes a sense of property as a normative complex), 'matrimony', 'relationship by marriage', 'under age'. Although such 'normative' concepts do not 'point to' empirical or ordinarily experiential data (as do 'descriptive' concepts), they can be defined in terms of the latter. Engisch points to a further, narrower conception of 'normative' concepts, being those which involve an evaluation, and cannot be defined in purely descriptive terms - for example, the qualification of behaviour as 'dishonest', 'unjust', 'indecent', etc. **(23)**

Unfortunately, this analysis does not take us far enough to reach what might be called the minimal units of **legal** signification. Engisch claims, and succeeds, only in identifying types of **normative** concepts, and their relationship to the descriptive concepts of ordinary language. This, I believe, is the issue which underlies a criticism by Martino of Scarpelli's view of legal language. **(24)** With signs which designate things, property and relations of pure fact, or at least ones not qualified by norms and values, Scarpelli contrasts **concetti qualificatori,** concepts which serve to qualify things, property and relations according to norms or values, such as 'subjective right', 'legal person' or 'legal transaction'. **(25)** One characteristic of **concetti qualificatori** according to Scarpelli is their insusceptibility to lexical definition: they cannot (pace Engisch) be reduced to factual language, but rather require to be defined in normative terms, following the form: 'if . . . then . . . ' In this way, technical legal terms serve to affirm the application of a normative conclusion to a hypothetical (legally defined) set of facts. Martino (1975:55) objects. Legal terminology cannot in itself affirm any normative conclusion; such a conclusion comes only from the use of such terminology within a legal utterance. This argument is in the spirit of Kelsenian jurisprudence: normativity exists only within the structure of a norm, and a particular legal term can represent, at best, only part of a norm. In this sense, no particular class of terminology can itself be truly regarded as 'normative' (not even such modalities as 'prohibited, permitted, required'). For Martino, the minimal unit of legal signification is a norm. It is only when a full norm is uttered that 'normative concepts' (such as those of either Engisch or Scarpelli) can be regarded as legal. We have here a very direct application of basic positivist tenets to legal language itself. No terms, even normative ones, can be inherently legal (cf. 1.1). They become legal only when they are incorporated. They can be incorporated only by being stated in that syntactic form which a legal system recognises as constituting a well-formed legal utterance.

Thus far, our discussion of the minimal units of legal signification has taken as its implied context the written texts of legislative, judicial and doctrinal discourse. But these represent only some of the semiotic activities which make up the law (11.3, 12.1). Minimal units must also be sought for the semiotic processes of legal interaction which do not use the written medium. Here too, positions have to be taken on the status and identity of the referent. The concept of 'moves' in conversational analysis represents one attempt to tackle this question. But there are forms of legal behaviour which involve no language at all. The driver observes, or does not observe, the traffic light. Conte suggests, but does not elaborate, the notion of a 'praxeme', modelled on 'phoneme', in the sense of a 'unit of practice' (1984b at 1.1). If we are prepared to extend the notion of discourse to include sequences of behaviour, there is no reason why Greimasian narratology cannot be used here too. The only difference is that here the behaviour is 'real' rather than 'fictional'.

When we come to consider the structure of an overall semiotic model of law, we see the importance of the different semiotic presuppositions here outlined. The Peircian tradition generates hierarchical models, while the Saussurian tradition as represented by Greimas sees the relationship between different discourses as residing on the same level. In the Peircian tradition, for example, it would be possible to regard the discourse of legal texts (whether legislative, judicial or doctrinal) as referring to an object, law, which has, at a 'deep' level, a structure describable in logical terms. The effect of this could be to equate deep structure with pure or logical semantics ('meaning'), and surface structure with pragmatics ('interpretation') or rhetoric. This is the relationship for which Katz argues: 'I shall try to show that, on this thesis, surface structural phenomena receive a coherent, general interpretation in terms of the central concept of rhetorical significance in much the same way that deep structural phenomena receive a coherent, general interpretation in terms of the central concept of logical or cognitive meaning' (1972:420). Similar models underlie many conceptions of the relationship between legal language and law. Bourcier, noted above, provides just one example. We may recall also Kelsen's strict differentiation of the linguistic expression of a norm from the norm itself - clearly necessary when a norm, for Kelsen, has a required logical structure, incorporating the relationship of imputation. Since what we actually read in the texts is the linguistic expression, this being taken to refer to something which does not appear in the texts themselves, the former is regarded as the 'surface', the latter as the 'deep' level. The most advanced attempt to develop such a model thus far is that of Kalinowski (SJ), who seeks to integrate pragmatics (whatever the identity of the user) into such a scheme by the construction of metalinguistic statements (X states A, X interprets norm A, X applies norm A), where norm A, the object of the metalinguistic statement, is itself a linguistic statement.

Greimasian semiotics would see such relationships quite differently. Rhetoric, justification, is not a particular level of the text, nor is it to be regarded in pragmatic terms, as a particular perlocutionary effect. It is part of the message of the text itself, and the whole apparatus of narrative grammar, with its syntagmatic and paradigmatic levels, is to be applied to it. The message is conveyed through the transference of modal values, with their particular semantic investments. What rhetorical analysis might regard as a stylistic device designed to persuade (in opposition to the 'content' of the text) might thus appear as a particular mode of transfer of a 'making-to-believe'. Such a rhetorical or justificatory text certainly has its 'deep' structure, according to Greimasian analysis. But that deep structure is the structure of signification of the rhetoric itself, not a separate logical level to which the rhetoric imperfectly refers. Suppose, then, that we adopt the distinctions which Kalinowski, developing the work of earlier Polish jurists, proposes - between legal language (as exemplified by legislative texts), the language of jurists (including, for these purposes, judges) and the logic of norms. Hierarchical presentation of the relations between these languages might have the language of jurists refer to the language of law which itself refers to the language of norms. Greimasian semiotics would see each one as a separate discourse, with its own surface and deep levels, which **claims** a relationship to the others both expressly and impliedly, in the content of the messages it contains. But despite such claims, there exists no ontological relationship between these various discourses. In the 1966 Loi, G/L see the relationship between legislator and SC in syntagmatic terms: the legislator sends messages of a certain kind (modal values) to the SC, which invests it with its competence. When a judge writes a judgment, he may not refer explicitly to the statute (if that it be) which gives him his competence. But nevertheless, the discourse of the judge **claims** that the judge acts as subject, in that he is the receiver of the appropriate modal competence in a different discourse.

The construction of an overall semiotic model of law also requires consideration of the relationship between 'legal' and 'natural' language. We have seen formal arguments constructed for the autonomy of the legal lexicon (2.6). Such arguments may be differently formulated in terms of the choices made by particular semiotic groups as to the structure of the semantic system used in their particular discourse, 'choice' here being understood in the broad structuralist sense (1.3). Such an argument could be applied not only to legislative discourse, but also to judicial and juristic. There is no contradiction between arguments for the formal autonomy of particular legal languages and the claim that historically much of the semantic investment of the legal lexicon is derived from the natural language, including the ideological connotations which the latter bears. Thus we find Carrion-Wam, in particular, advancing such a view (5.2), while affirming G/L's theory of legal grammar, including the production within it of the legal lexicon. The transference of general social values into the legal system, through the use of ordinary language, has been widely observed. (**26**) Baldinger (1980:46) quotes an example from the judgment of a Frankfurt Labour Court, called upon to determine the meaning of 'employee' in the absence of a formal legal definition. The Court commented: 'A logical determination of the concept is not possible because into the concept "employee" a typical and real social evaluation is condensed.' But it would be wrong to view such a transference of values as an inevitable causal effect of the use of natural language, a kind of **damnosa hereditas.** Whatever the judge in the Frankfurt Labour Court may say or think, it is his choice - or at least that of the semiotic group to which he belongs, and by which he is constrained - to accept that social evaluation, since he/it has the power to refuse to do so (5.2).

It is a characteristic of some types of legal discourse, particularly judicial and doctrinal, that they purport to provide an account of their own production. They provide solutions to legal problems, while at the same time claiming to show the process by which those solutions have been produced. Here, modern critical approaches, particularly sensitive to rhetorical figures, come into their own. The work of Goodrich is a good example. By this means, the falsity of the text's account of the production of its own meaning is shown. The text presents a restricted agenda of explicit arguments directed towards the conclusion (the restrictions varying from author to author, as may be seen by comparing Dworkin and MacCormick). The rhetorical devices within it may be conceived by the author as the means by which he seeks to solicit the assent of his audience. But by the same token, provided he identifies with that audience, these will be the very rhetorical factors which have influenced him, a member of the same semiotic group.

There are, of course, wider issues of the relationship of history and structure involved here. It may be argued that even if a structural analysis assists in revealing the rhetorical devices and ideological stance of a discourse, it does not advance the search for the historical factors which determine the production of that discourse in the first place. History is one thing, structure another. Marxists, in particular, accuse structuralists of avoiding the really important issue. **(27)** But the problem faced by the Marxist historian is that he claims that **his** discourse stands somehow outside history and outside discursive analysis itself. The semiotician can observe the truth-claims made in historical discourse as in any other discourse, and can describe the manner in which they are communicated. The validity of the truth-claims of that discourse lie beyond his competence. But he will be inclined to accord no greater status to the claims of 'scientific' history than to those of 'objective' legal validity.

12.3 THE SPECIFICITY OF LAW

In the course of this book, various indications have emerged of the specificity of law, notwithstanding the view of Greimasian semiotics that legal discourse is only one particular semantic investment of discourse in general, and that the same narrative grammar applies to it. Nor does the rejection of the postulate of the unity of the legal system (11.3) negate the possibility that we may identify features of that set of semiotic systems which make up 'the law' as specific to it. **(28)**

Kalinowski regards the specificity of legal semiotics as residing primarily at the pragmatic level (SJ). It is neither the syntax nor semantics of legal statements which make them special, but rather the particular 'force' which is attributable to them. It should be noted that this is a quite different claim from that which identifies the specificity of law with its characteristic modal operators, the deontic relationships of prescription, prohibition, permission, etc. **(29)** The Greimasian analysis, however, indicates other possible candidates for specificity, located at both the surface and deep levels. Specificity is located at the level of the claims made by the discourse, not its structure: legal discourse at most represents a 'secondary semiotic system' (1.2). The law claims to regulate its own creation; the grammar of law, as G/L observed, is special in that it seeks to be explicit (1976:87f.). Kelsen, incidentally, goes even further. Not only does law regulate its own creation (1967:221); objects of legal cognition are peculiar in that they can even say something about their own legal meaning, as where parliament expressly declares that it is enacting a statute, thus giving a 'legal self-interpretation' to its own utterance (1967:3). It is rather as if an English speaker were to preface his utterance with the words: 'What I am going to say is good English' !

This power to regulate its own meaning is well illustrated by comparing semantic change in legal and natural language. As Carzo has observed (1981:88), semantic change is institutionally controlled in legal language, but not in natural language. Thus, whereas semantic change in natural language normally occurs as a matter of gradual drift, semantic change in an institutionalised setting may occur overnight, at a quite identifiable moment in time. The meaning of any term used in the law may be changed overnight by legislation or precedent. In a different context, Sampson considers the change in the meaning of the English word 'gay' from an adjective descriptive of a general joyful, carefree state of mind to an increasingly restricted use to designate a homosexual. He notes that once the new meaning becomes institutionalised, it is also likely to become more rigid: 'now that the new sense of **gay** has led to incorporation of the word into the title of formal institutions such as the Gay Liberation Movement, it may be that the sense has become relatively rigid - such an institution is likely to equip itself with articles of association defining the meaning of **gay**, which turns the word into a technical term like **atom.** But during the transitional period the implications of a given use of the word must surely have been very fluid, indeterminate, unpinnable-down' (1980a:59f.). At the same time, we must note that this characteristic may not hold true equally for all types of legal discourse. Dworkin himself has pointed to an important variation; 'rules' may be changed overnight, but 'principles' alter gradually. Principles, he tells us, may be eroded, but rules have to be torpedoed (1978:40).

Aspects of the semantic structure of law have also been held forth as manifesting the specificity of law, irrespective of the manner of their production. Baldinger points to a particular problem encountered by jurists. They should be pitied, he says, because they have to draw precise borders, although using ordinary language (2.5). 'From the viewpoint of language theory, this is impossible; yet, juridically, punishment, and even the alternative **guilty-innocent** depends on such a limiting of reality . . . for jurists, the borders of meanings are more decisive than the centre of meanings, while in ordinary language, the centre is more important than the edges' (1980:42f.). Of course, jurists are not the only specialist users of the natural language who have to use imprecise tools for more precise ends. However, the specificity of the juristic problem becomes more marked in one particular form of legal discourse, where the result of a seemingly semantic problem will materially affect the lives of the litigants. That is why Wroblewski sees the specificity of legal language as residing in the particularly high degree of choice available to the judge through the strategies of legal interpretation (1963:414f.). Nevertheless, the incidence of monosemicity does appear, on the evidence (2.4), to be relatively higher in legal discourse than one would expect in the ordinary language (although this may be a characteristic of 'scientific' discourse in general). What may be more significant is the image of monosemicity which is communicated by some types of legal discourse to some types of legal audience, accompanied by the appearance of 'restricted connotations' (G/L 1976:85), the deprivation of words of their ordinary language connotations when transformed into legal discourse.

I turn, in conclusion, to three features which appear from the Greimasian analysis of the 1966 Loi in terms of narrative grammar. First, we find the generation within the discourse of 'inferior semiotic objects'. Not only does the law constitute the legislator and the judge as semiotic objects, capable of producing and communicating meaning; it also enables those semiotic objects to constitute further, apparently inferior, semiotic objects such as the **société commerciale,** which in turn can construct and communicate legal meaning. Traditional legal analysis comes close to a recognition of this special characteristic, when it speaks of artificial legal personality.

One might suggest that the specificity of law lies, in this regard, in the fact that such semiotic objects as the **société commerciale** are made to appear as **inferior** semiotic objects, dependent upon the superior semiotic objects of the legislator and judge. This may be taken to be but one reflection of the fact that hierarchy is part of the specific appearance of the legal semiotic. Hierarchy thus joins such notions as 'objective meaning' and 'norm' as Kelsenian concepts which, from the semiotic viewpoint, represent the appearance of law as a system of communication. The semiotic reality would be that the legislator, the judge and the **société commerciale** are equivalent expressions of a metalanguage which admits of the construction of semiotic objects by a combination of **énoncés qualificatifs** and **énoncés fonctionnels** (3.2, 4).

A second notable feature of legal discourse was observed in considering the status of the SC as an **acteur** (the particular semantic investment of an **actant**) in the narrative grammar (3.2), especially when we juxtapose this view with the institutional theory of MacCormick (8.1-2), according to which the SC would stand as a 'legal institution', the instances of which would only be found outside the text, in real life (or at least, in other texts). We do not have to adopt an extensional concept of discourse to recognise that the legal institution 'SC' makes claims in relation to phenomena outside the legislative text, which the character in a novel, also found at the level of manifestation, does not. We might adapt to this context Hart's formulation of the difference between a 'sign' and a 'signal', the former being associated with the external, the latter with the internal point of view (1961:87f.). Hart distinguished a 'sign that' something will happen from a 'signal for' it to happen. The legal **acteur** may be regarded, in this sense, as a 'signal for' something to happen, rather than a sign that it will or has happened. The Greimasian analysis, however, would insist that this 'signal for' is to be understood as a semiotic phenomenon, a part of the message which the text conveys, rather than a psychological phenomenon associated with the mind of the receiver.

My last suggestion also derives from comparison of the Greimasian syntagmatic level with MacCormick's institutional theory. I noted in the latter context (8.1) that, in law, 'recognition' or 'verediction' appears to be directed to the 'competence' syntagm of the narrative algorithm, rather than to 'performance'. That was based upon the argument that MacCormick's institutive/terminative rules represent 'competence', while the consequential rules manifest 'performance'. The focus of interest of legal discourse is in those 'states' in which things may legally exist, rather than with the actions which may transform them from one legal state to another. The latter are the conditions of the former, but interest is directed primarily to the state of legal existence (in doctrinal discourse, 8.3) or the consequences thereof. By contrast, ordinary discourse, and indeed narrative discourse, is more interested in human action, rather than with the states which may result from it. That is why performance presupposes competence in the narrative discourse (30), whereas competence entails performance in the legal syntagm. One might illustrate this distance between ordinary discourse and legal discourse in terms of one of MacCormick's own examples, the Edinburgh commuter paying his fare on the bus. The passenger gets on, tenders his money and says 'Waverley' (the railway station). The driver takes the money and says 'thanks'. The competence of the passenger to pay that money is presupposed, and what the driver recognises by his response is the act of paying, as a personal relation. A juristic interpretation would be different. The performance is 'the state of being entitled to ride on the bus to the station', and when the driver acknowledges the fact of payment, he is acknowledging the satisfaction of necessary conditions of the entitlement of the passenger to travel to the station. The act of payment here forms part of competence, not performance; the latter is the state of entitlement which has been successfully achieved - and, indeed, recognised at the narrative level by the driver's 'thank you'.

Notes

Chapter 1: Mapping the Issues

1 See, e.g., Kennedy (1979) and the recent symposium in the **Stanford Law Review** 36/1-2 (1984).
2 See Burton and Carlen (1979), Hutchinson (forthcoming), Heller (1984).
3 See literature cited below, ch. 7, n. 36.
4 Positivism here means the claim to the existence of an autonomous system, whatever the origins of that system. It is thus no criticism to point out that both linguistic positivists like Saussure and legal positivists like Hart view language and law as essentially social phenomena. Sampson (1980:43-8) has an interesting discussion of the background to Saussure's view, in terms of the dispute between Durkheim and Tarde as to the nature of 'social facts'. He claims that Saussure reflects to some degree the Durkheimian view that social facts (including laws) are ideas in the 'collective mind' of society.
5 The application of linguistic methods in structuralist semiotics is not confined to units of language larger than the individual sentence, but extends to non-linguistic systems. The pioneering work in this area was the application by Lévi-Strauss of methods inspired by the analyses of phonology by Jakobson to the study of anthropological data, notably kinship systems.
6 See also Eco 1984:4, arguing for the mutuality of interest of semiotics and the philosophy of language. For an account of the range of linguistic theories, in terms of the historical / diachronic v. systemic / syntagmatic oppositions, and with attention to differences relating to the conception of the subject and referent, see Heller 1984:133-55.
7 On the speech act theory in relation to semiotics, see also Eco 1984:12f., Harrison 1979:166f. See Kevelson

(1982a) on legal speech acts in the light of Peircian semiotics.

8 Perrott also seeks to compare Hart's relationship of primary and secondary rules to the operation of Chomsky's deep structures. For an earlier, very different discussion of the linguistic presuppositions of Chomsky and Hart, see Anon (1967).

9 Patte in Calloud 1976:x-xi, with reference to Benveniste 1974:215-238.

10 Kalinowski 1980:347 argues similarly against Kelsen's conception of the 'meaning of an act of will'. Similar issues are reflected in the distinction between 'sign' and 'signal' and in the difference between Arnaud and Mounin on the 'meaning' of the French Civil Code (both discussed below).

11 The most direct attempt to apply Peircian semiotics to law is to be found in the work of Roberta Kevelson; see Bibliogaphy. In 1982b and 1985, she considers the influence of Peirce on American Legal Realism, and on the legal sociology of Gény.

12 On the three Peircean categories, see e.g., Eco 1976:68ff.; Hervey 1982:26-9.

13 This is the terminology of Ogden and Richards (1923), adopted for the purpose of analysing the language of law by Williams (1945:73). For the identification of 'object' with 'referent', see Hervey 1982:28. Eco 1976:59f. provides a useful discussion of the relationship between Peirce, Ogden and Richards, and Frege (**Zeichen, Sinn, Bedeutung**). See further Jori (1985), s.v. 'Semiotica' and 'Referente'.

14 For the argument that Peirce required a psychological state only on the part of the receiver of the sign, and not on the part of its emitter, see Eco 1976:15f.

15 Searle 1983:79ff., esp. 98-100.

16 While anticipating the development of a general theory of semiotics, Saussure restricted his own concerns to language. His analysis is based upon semantics, the study of the meaning of **words.** Hence, the conventional translation 'sound-image'. As it might be applied outside linguistics, the **signifié** does not, of course, have to take the form of sound. See further Jori, n.13 above.

17 At 1966:123, Saussure notes that while the syntagms occur in discourse, the associative relations are outside discourse, being associated in memory, so that each word 'unconsciously calls to mind a host of other words.' Eco 1976:14f. describes Saussure as 'leaving it (the **signifié**) half way between a mental image, a concept and a psychological reality'. On this issue as debated in the philosophy of language see Lyons

1977:109-14, who seeks to distinguish the psychological process of concept formation from the involvement of such concepts in the semiotic processes of everyday communication. On Lyons' 'compromise' conception of the referent, see Greimas and Courtés 1982:260.

18 For a useful classification of philosophies of language, distinguishing 'referential' and different forms of 'intensional' approaches, and their relation to the theory of legal semantics, see Moore (1981).

19 1982:260. For adoption of this viewpoint for the purposes of legal semiotics, see Carrion-Wam (1979:84f., 1982-3:162f.,171 and 1985). See also Eco 1976:60.

20 Eco describes the aim of his most recent book as 'to show that these notions are not incompatible' (1984:1). Aspects of his solution are considered in section 12.1 below.

21 Williams, extracted in Lloyd (1979:63).

22 Cf. Barthes (1967:35-8), opposing 'sign' as 'an unmotivated and exact relation' to 'symbol' as 'an analogical and inexact relation'. Ogden and Richards, invoked by Williams (1945:73), distinguish exclusively in terms of nature and convention: a symbol is a particular species of sign, 'a conventional sign: it is a sign that is consciously designed to stand for something.' On the classifications of signs, see further Jori (1985), s.v. 'Segno'.

23 Cf. Prieto, who defined an 'index' as an observable fact which provides information on other non-observable facts. But that observable fact is not generated for the purpose of communication, and serves functions other than communication.

24 But Eco 1984:8f., 18ff., now stresses the semiotic commonality between such phenomena, in terms of inferential processes.

25 However, insofar as the 'signal' involves a natural referent, it is excluded from the Saussurian concept of the sign: Greimas and Courtés 1982:298.

26 See Eco 1976:12 on Barthes and Kristeva. See also Eco 1984:166ff. on the history of the notion of 'code'.

27 For further uses of structural analysis by Arnaud, see the Bibliography. For criticism of Lévi-Straussian methodology in this context, see Carzo (1976). Arnaud (1973) provoked a number of useful reviews and review articles: Brutti (1975), Morin (1973), Sbriccoli (1973) and Losano (1970) on earlier work of Arnaud. A wider-ranging appreciation of his work is provided by Carrion-Wam (1982-3, 1985). For other applications of structuralism to law, many of them inspired by Lévi-Strauss, see Brimo (1978, 1978a), Dauchy (1981, 1982 -

with particular reference to Deleuze), Ghezzi (1966), Gil (1973), Hauriou (1971), Hermann (1975), Jackson (1979, 1979a, 1979b, 1980, 1980a, 1980b, 1980c, 1980d, 1981), Lacambra (1973), Lamsdorff-Galagane (1969), Miaille (1976 - a critical viewpoint), Pernia Hermann (1977), Robertshaw (1975, 1980, 1981, 1985 and forthcoming), Watkin (1980), Watkins (1970). French legal anthropology has also sought to take account of Levi-Strauss: Le Roy (1978, 1981, 1984), Rouland (1984, 1984a); but see also Snyder (1981).

28 On the arbitrariness of the linguistic sign, see Barthes 1967:35-8; on the system of differences, see Utaker 1974:92.

29 Comparison may be made with Sperber's conception of symbolism (1975). Eco seeks to reduce the difference by viewing the process of semiosis as involving an inference rather than an equivalence. Nevertheless, he distinguishes 'symbols' as 'cases of textual production that do not rely on a preestablished portion of the encyclopedia but invent and propose for the first time a new interpretive connection' (1984:2 and ch.4).

30 Cf. Culler 1975:19, commenting on Mounin 1970:14: 'Mounin's view seems to rest on a very questionable theory of language and stands condemned by the conclusions that it forces up on him: literature is not a system of signs because one cannot speak of encoding and decoding by fixed codes.'

31 Greimas 1966:30f.; Eco 1976:8f., 16: 'a signification system is an autonomous semiotic construct that has an abstract mode of existence independent of any possible communicative act it makes possible. On the contrary . . . **every act of communication to or between human beings** - or any other intelligent biological or mechanical apparatus - **pre-supposes a signification system as its necessary condition**' (at 9). See further Jori (1985), s.v. 'Comunicazione' and 'Significato'.

32 Eco 1976:18. In the context of law, cf. the remarks of A. Carcaterra 1979:112.

33 Cf. Eco 1976:55; Hervey 1982:134-6.

34 Barthes is by no means a typical structuralist (if there is such a thing). For some peculiarities see Hervey (1982:137-9), whose chapter 5, together with Sturrock's essay on Barthes in Sturrock (1979), constitute probably the best English introductions to the subject. See now also Culler (1983).

35 As applicable to law, see especially the bibliography of Danet (1980); Crystal and Davy (1969), Danet (1984, 1984a), Kurzon (1984), Mellinkoff (1963), O'Barr (1982).

36 For accounts of legal language in the Saussurian tradition, see also van den Bergh and Broekman (1979) and Warat (1976). Attention has not been confined to written texts. See also the dramaturgical analysis of legal procedures by Carlen (1976).

37 From this generalisation, the involvement of legal philosophers in the development of deontic logic forms an exception, to the extent that that logic has been built upon the tradition of inferential semantics (Frege, Carnap); this approach is best exemplified today in the work of Georges Kalinowski. For bibliography, see di Bernardo (1977).

38 1978:235, quoted in Harris 1981:627. See also Olivecrona 1962:169f., 1971:223, 261f.

39 1962:177. Cf. Williams: 'for lawyers language has a special interest because it is the greatest instrument of social control' (1945:71).

40 1962:175, criticised by Harris 1981:628f., though to my mind the points of distinction he makes are more apparent than real.

41 Cf. Goodrich 1983a:258, on parallel issues.

42 As witness, for example, the title of Jameson's book **The Prison-House of Language** (1972).

43 The division of semiotics into syntactics, semantics and pragmatics was proposed by Morris (1938:35), adapting a classification of Peirce, between pure grammar, logic and pure rhetoric. On the relation of the latter to the medieval trivium, see Kretzmann 1967:395. I am indebted for this reference to M. Kalinowski. See also Kalinowski's remarks at 1965:5, associating also Carnap, Church and Reichenbach with this approach.

44 See, e.g., Sampson 1980a:56ff. But even Sampson is able to give limited endorsement to the Saussurian notion of a synchronic language-state (1980:48).

45 1980:224. We may note that Olivecrona took support from Malinowski's account of the Trobriand language of magic (1971:254).

46 See also Leech 1974:71. Searle, the foremost modern representative of the speech act tradition, describes 'language as use' as a slogan rather than a philosophy (1969:146). See also the compromise sought by Lyons (1981:168), noted below; and Hart's endorsement of such a position (7.2 below).

47 E.g. Calame (1982), Greimas and Landowski (1983); see further section 11.1 below. Other signs of convergence between Parisian semantic and pragmatic approaches may be found in the work of Ducrot (1972), Parret (1983) and, for legal applications, Bourcier (1982).

48 Cf. Harrison 1979:166f., quoting Searle 1969:17. On the intentional paradigm in legal interpretation, see Schauer 1982:804f.

49 E.g. Bastide, noting that while the author of a story may know from the beginning where he is going to lead the discourse, he may still 'be suspected of not knowing the micro-universe of values the semiotician credits him with communicating in his discourse.'

50 See Ahonen 1983:19-28, who seeks to build up a model by combining this tradition with the work of Giddens (1979). See also his remarks on legal theory, particularly at 59f. This issue is central to Heller's discussion of structuralism as a mode of critique (1984).

Chapter 2: Structural Semantics and Legal Language

1 The Groupe belongs to the Ecole des Hautes Etudes en Sciences Sociales (Université de Paris), and is affiliated to the C.N.R.S. as part of the Institut National de la Langue Française.

2 Hawkes (1977) provides a useful introduction to European structuralism, with some reference also to the semiotics of Peirce. An instructive study with greater concentration on literature, and on the comparison with hermeneutics, is McKnight (1978).

3 One consequence of this is the exclusion of any truth-conditions semantics.

4 Following the definition of Morris 1938:6, 'the formal relations of signs to one another' (see further Lyons 1977:114f.).

5 Lyons 1977:240f.

6 See also Utaker 1974:73, 81f. on Jakobson's distinctions between polar, privative, logical and qualitative types of opposition.

7 Mounin 1965:20, quoted in Baldinger 1980:70f.n.4; Lyons 1977:317.

8 Ducrot and Todorov 1979:265. Lerat 1983:33 doubts that semes are necessarily 'minimal' units.

9 Differences of degree may also be analysed in oppositional terms, using more v. less. See Utaker 1974:82.

10 See further Lerat 1983:35.

11 Coseriu in Baldinger 1980:37; Lyons 1977:305ff.

12 See further in section 8.2, below, esp. n.22, and note 4 to ch.7.

13 For other studies of French legal language, see Legault (1979), Mimin (1978).

14 See, e.g., Guilbert, quoted in Sourioux and Lerat

1976:35.

15 In fact, the example may well be disputed: the written document might well be regarded as an early form of legally recognised manifestation of will. The authors' other example, **accession**, is more convincing: on the one hand it refers to the mode of property acquisition derived from the Roman **accessio**; on the other, to the act by which a State declares its adherence to an international treaty.

16 See also Sampson's illuminating remarks on the institutionalisation of the changed meaning of the English word 'gay' (1980a:59f.).

17 See Greimas and Courtés 1982:29f.

18 Greimas 1966:44f.; Calloud 1976:38; Ducrot and Todorov 1979:266; for a sceptical view, see Lerat 1983:51f.

19 This issue is taken up further below, sections 7.2-3, 11.3, 12.1.

20 1980:42. See also Martino (1977:8), who distinguishes between the open texture and necessary indeterminacy of the language of norms and the semantic determinacy of the content of the law. Here, it is the logic of norms (cf. Kalinowski) which is distinguished from the indeterminacy of legal language.

21 **Riggs v. Palmer**, as discussed in contemporary jurisprudence; see section 9.3 below.

22 See further G/L 1976:83-5. They argue that there also exists within law a referential discourse, which presents itself as an account of the social world itself, but which may be no more than an elaboration of ideology. The legislative discourse, by contrast, is made up of performative and normative utterances. The background appears to be the distinction between **Loi** and **Doctrine**, or in Kelsenian legal philosophical terms **Rechtsnorm** and **Rechtssatz.** Both types of legal discourse may make claims regarding social and economic realities, and may play their part in them. But for the purposes of semantic analysis, G/L maintain, it is the two discursive levels themselves which are the sole realities, and it is their mutual dependence and relations which constitute a structural question whose elucidation takes us some way to define the specificity of legal discourse as such.

23 Thomas 1974:110, approving Carcaterra.

24 Thomas 1974:118. This in turn raises the question of the nature of relations within such 'classemes'. Do they reflect simply the semantic logic of the natural language, or a particular semantic logic of a legal language (Bourcier 1976:117), or do they refer to a non-linguistic 'logic of norms' (Kalinowski 1972) ?

25 1974:12. See also Carzo 1981:76-8, 87, on Scarpelli, Bobbio and Tarello.

26 Murphy and Rawlings 1981-82:623ff.

27 Who now even in the civilian tradition threatens to supersede the **bonus paterfamilias:** see Sourioux and Lerat 1976:68.

28 Thomas 1974:115, on the moral vocabulary of Justinianic law.

29 The choice need not take the form of selection from within what is on offer in the natural language. As Thomas observes (1974:118), the meaning of a term in the legal lexicon may differ from that in the ordinary language by the addition as well as the subtraction of semes.

Chapter 3: The Syntagmatic Level of Legal Discourse

1 Much use has been made in recent American legal writing of the literary analogue. See the symposium in the **Texas Law Review** (1982); that in the **Rutgers Law Review** (1976) is concerned mostly with legal themes in literature, rather than in literary theory. Dworkin's contribution is discussed in chapter 9 below. The American literature betrays hardly any knowledge of continental narratology, and is more related to interpretation theory (and the 'New Criticism') than to semiotics. It shares few of the Greimasian claims outlined in this paragraph.

2 But G/L are not alone. See also Bourcier (1978).

3 'Deep structures' have entered the vocabulary of American legal scholarship - Kingson (1976, 1977), Ginsburg (1977) - but the relationship between its use here and in either continental structuralism or Chomskian linguistics is loose.

4 This distinction has not gone without criticism. See Chatman 1972:61 for Todorov; Culler 1975:85,95 and 1975a:127; Lodge 1981:18f.

5 The results should therefore be regarded as hypotheses inviting verification in relation to the rest of the text. Cf. the approach of Bastide, forthcoming.

6 Jameson 1972:125; Galland 1973:39.

7 Greimas 1966:180; Calloud 1976:28.

8 See Greimas and Courtés 1982:20f. ('Auxiliant') and 141 ('Helper'). The role of the subject's capacity ('competence') in the narrative syntagm is discussed in section 3.4.

9 Galland 1973:39; Calloud 1976:29-32.

10 See further Calloud 1976:33f.

11 Calloud 1976:26; Greimas and Courtés 1982:5f.

12 I owe it to Paolo Fabbri that these categories derive from grammatical analysis. But the argument is somewhat evocative also of Rousseau's analysis of the relationship between the individual and the collectivity in the general will: **Du Contrat Social** I, 6-7; II, 3. See further section 4.2 for the 'logical' level reflected in these oppositions.

13 'Implication' is one of the operations within the 'semiotic square', discussed further in sections 4.2-3 below.

14 See Greimas 1966:193f., listing Propp's 31 functions; see also Galland 1973:38; McKnight 1978:156.

15 Hawkes 1977:93; cf. Calloud 1976:17f.

16 1976:106, cf. section 3.1 above. The 'logic' underlying this model is discussed in the context of the 'semiotic square', chapter 4 below.

17 See further McKnight 1978:201; Galland 1973:42.

18 1979:62f. The terminological distinction between 'manipulation' and 'competence' is not used by G/L, who combine these notions within 'contract'.

19 The classification of these syntagms has given rise to dispute. The following sequence of syntagms is taken as characterising narrative: contractual syntagm, disjunctional syntagm, performancial syntagm (Calloud 1976:25-8). The contractual syntagm clearly corresponds to the first phase of the algorithm: the process by which the contract is established, or as Calloud more recently puts it - 'manipulation'. The 'performancial syntagm' is taken to cover all three of the former 'tests' of Propp, thus (in different forms) competence, performance and recognition. The intermediate stage of a 'disjunctional' syntagm, covering movements such as arrival and departures and displacements of various kinds, might appear redundant, and has been so argued by Culler (1975:213f.). Indeed, it seems to overlap with both contract and performance, on Greimas' own account: the opening of the story can be represented as the establishment of a contractual conjunctive relation between the sender and receiver-subjects, followed by a spatial disjunction between the two **actants**; the end of the story will be marked, on the contrary, by a spatial conjunction and a final transfer of values, instituting a new contract by a new distribution of values (1970:182, quoted by Bremond 1972:366f.).

20 McKnight 1978:201; cf. Galland 1973:47.

21 1979:64; stated in more anthropomorphic terms at 1976:28.

Chapter 4: The Paradigmatic Level of Legal Discourse

1 See Greimas 1970:136ff.; Galland 1973:43f. The application of the square to semic categories, rather than to propositions, is a modern development. See further section 4.3 at nn. 14-15 below.

2 Cf. Bastide, forthcoming. Lyons 1977:272 touches on the same point in noting that not all contraries are dichotomously opposed to each other. On the conventionality of oppositions like black v. white, cf. Kevelson 1977:83.

3 Greimas 1970:163; Bremond 1972:364.

4 Greimas and Rastier 1968:89. Cf. Bastide, forthcoming, describing the semiotic square as 'a convenient means of summarizing, in an organized model, the semes and figures found during analysis, and which allows, in certain cases, for the prediction of missing semes or figures'.

5 Greimas 1968:86f.; McKnight 1978:169.

6 1966:1975f.; Hawkes 1977:93f. Perhaps the best account of the reasoning here involved is provided by Ricoeur 1981:283f. See also McKnight 1978:175f. on the use of the semiotic square in order to formalise the semiotic relations involved in the transference of objects of value at the syntagmatic level of the narrative grammar.

7 This appears to be one instance where Utaker (1974:83-5) is correct in arguing that the Greimasian contradictory is a Hegelian (privative) rather than a logical opposition. Cf. de Libera 1976a:53f.; aliter Kalinowski 1981:5. See also Nef 1976:14f., Ricoeur 1980:31.

8 This is one point of distinction between the European and American semiotic traditions, with the latter remaining closer to logic, including the propositional logic of the school of Carnap. Cf. Landowski 1981:126; Kalinowski 1965:5. The work of Kalinowski is of particular interest in this connection, since he reflects the more strictly logical approach of both the American and Viennese (Carnap) tradition, while at the same time entering into dialogue with the Parisian school of Greimas.

9 There is an element of harmonisation in this exposition of G/L 108f.; on the face of it, 'legitimate social interests' (bottom left) are regarded as subject to a system of legislative prescriptions and prohibitions at 108, but belong to a vast area of unregulated behaviour at 109.

10 1968:88; he also claims such a relationship with the Klein group in mathematics and the Piaget group in

psychology, on which see Nef 1976:9-11, Ricoeur 1980:30.

11 Blanché 1966:22ff.; Gardies 1972:53ff.; de Libera 1976:28ff.

12 Cf. Kalinowski, 1972a:166, Theorems 25 and 27:
$$(25)\ A \supset -O;\ (27)\ -A \supset O.$$

13 Kalinowski's T2, 1972a:165, given that we start with the axiom that E is the contrary of A, such that the truth of A entails the falsity of E.

14 Blanché 1966:30; Bousquet 1977:65; Ricoeur 1980:30, discussed further below.

15 I am indebted to a conversation with Paolo Fabbri for saving me from error on this point.

16 A combination of the formal version in Bousquet 1977:66 with the invested version in Galland 1973:44, 1976:24 (here corrected), which appears in a note added by the editors of **Etudes Théologiques et Religieuses,** where they claim, inter alia, that oppositions like black vs. white represented the material out of which even Aristotle constructed his logical square, citing **Categories** 6:6a17.

17 1966:50f.; see also Bousquet 1977:66.

18 E.g. Chabrol 1967:207-9, Bremond (1972), Bousquet (1977), Ricoeur (1980), Kalinowski (1981).

19 Additionally, it must be said that their use of terminology is not always the same. In particular, Greimas appears to use 'conjunction' and 'disjunction' in a broader sense than Blanché: 'disjunction' is applied to the relationship between both contraries and contradictories by Greimas (1968:88), whereas it is used by Blanché only in the context of the relationship between the contraries and the compound term. We also encounter some difficulties in the use of 'contraries' and 'negation' (see also Ricoeur 1980:8, 30). Greimas himself seems to endorse just this kind of distinction, when he writes that logic is phrastic and operates only by substitutions, whereas he is concerned with discursive semiotics, whose statements possess a positional signification (1976a:91f., cf. Ricoeur 1980:6).

20 On the distinction between presupposition and implication in semantics, see Lerat 1983:83f.

21 In this context, I use the term 'semiotician' in opposition to 'logician' for the sake of convenience. M. Kalinowski rightly draws my attention to the fact that Carnap and the tradition descended from him use the term 'semiotic' in a quite different sense, to refer to metalogic.

22 See also Kalinowski 1972a:167.

23 I have here adopted 'manipulation', following the terminology of Calloud; Greimas here speaks more

generally of 'factitive modalities'. See, however, the entry on 'manipulation' in Greimas and Courtés 1982:184-6, as well as those on 'modality' (193-5) and 'factitiveness' at 115f. For an analytical account of combined modalities, called 'enunciati deontici iterati', see Mazzarese (1982).

24 Traditionally, logicians have used the term 'modality' to refer to such (aletheic) conceptions. That terminology is preserved in Gardies (1972), who considers the relations between 'norms' (deontic modalities) and 'modalities' (aletheic) in Chapter II.

25 Indeed, Greimas defines 'modalisation' in very broad terms: 'a modification of the predicate by the subject', 1976a:90.

26 Particularly that of Kalinowski, supra note 22.

27 The former being described as **'modalités virtualisantes'**, the latter as **'modalités actualisantes'**.

28 Here, the analysis in terms of the semiotic square runs parallel to that of classical logic. See Gardies (1972), as in note 24 above. For a recent discussion of the apparent isomorphism of the aletheic and deontic quadrats, see Mazzarese (1982).

29 This special semantic endowment is, however, irrelevant from the viewpoint of either logic or semiotics. For the latter, it would exist on the same level as any other semantic investment of **faire.** If viewed in this light, we have to conclude that 'power' is indeed inter-definable with 'duty', being merely a special case of 'permission'. On this point, we have seen that Greimas adheres to such inter-definability. **'Permissivité'** first appears in his analysis in position I of a square where A is **'prescription'** (1976a:97): it is the nominalisation of the sub-contrary **'ne pas devoir ne pas faire'**, in a relation of deixis with **devoir faire.** But for Greimas, if not for Kalinowski, it is possible to reverse such a deixis, so that **permissivité** becomes a contrary. If we substitute **faire** for the first Greimasian exercise in superimposition (1976a:101), we see that by taking **'permissivité'** and superimposing that in the form **pouvoir faire** upon the original square based upon **devoir faire,** a relation of complementarity is produced. Greimas defines such a relation of complementarity as that which characterises two terms which occupy the same taxic position; it is a relation which may be interpreted as the possibility of inscribing those two terms in the same modal programme (1976a:102). It seems, therefore, that 'power' and 'duty' are inter-definable for the semiotician. See Greimas 1976a:100; Bastide, forthcoming.

30 This, in fact, is the level at which such a distinction is made by ohfeld 1919:50f.; Hart 1961:27ff.; Ross 1968:135. See also Dias 1976:64. Later commentators have indeed sought to present Hohfeld's scheme in the form of a logical square (Dias 1976:35, on Williams). What Hohfeld called 'opposites' are in logical terms contradictories; what Williams called 'contradictories' have some (but not many) of the logical attributes of contraries. Hohfeld also introduces 'correlatives', as representing the inter-personal dimension. Comparison of the theorems formulated by Kalinowski to represent the operations within the square (1972a) will readily show how far short of this logical model the Hohfeldian scheme falls. If, for example, we present the square in the form most likely to generate contraries at points A and E, by investing A as 'right' and E as 'duty', although we can generatee T25, T28, T29 and T32, we cannot generate T26, T27, T30 or T31. The square cannot work, since it seeks to combine incompatible axes: right v. no-right and duty v. privilege relate to modal values in the same person; the other axes, Hohfeld's 'correlatives' and Williams' 'contradictories', are inter-personal. In order to formalise the underlying logical or semiotic structures in the form of a square, one would have to detach and treat separately these various axes. This shows that the principal function of Hohfeld's scheme, as indeed he proclaimed, was to produce linguistic equipment which would distinguish the various relations we actually use in legal discourse, rather than to attempt analysis of their underlying structure. I am indebted to Neil MacCormick for comments which have helped me to clarify my view on this point.

Chapter 5: The 'Legal Grammar'

1 Which G/L themselves would deny, since 'narrative' is regarded as a level rather than a genre of discourse.

2 This question is pursued more systematically elsewhere: see chs. 11 and 12 below.

3 It lies beyond the scope of this book to consider the general philosophical parentage of the Greimasian approach. Suffice it to say that the phenomenology of Husserl would play a prominent part in such a reconstruction. The full development of a semiotic approach to legal philosophy should not neglect the direct influence of phenomenology on Jurisprudence, on which see Schiff (1982) and literature there cited, especially Amselek (1964, 1973), Poulantzas (1964) and

Friedmann (1973). See also Harrison 1979:166 on the affinity of phenomenology (esp. Ricoeur) to speech act analysis, based on their common assimilation of meaning to action; cf. Bloor 1983:8f. on the origins of the conception of meaning as a mental act.

4 G/L appear to come closest to an account of the legal status of the legislator where they refer to the existence of a 'metalanguage' as a means of testing the validity of the grammar, but the testing they have in mind is in relation to the internal coherence of the concepts and rules, and the conformity of its utterances with the canonical forms of legal utterance established by that grammar (1976:91).

5 The SC stands as 'receiver' to two distinct 'senders' (110f.), the other being the totality of partial wills of all the participants in the common enterprise (3.2, 4.2 above).

6 1976:91. It is not clear whether, by use of the term 'envisage', G/L mean to imply that this procedure of verification is impliedly present in the legislative discourse (such as the 1966 Loi) itself.

7 English quotations are taken from Carrion-Wam (1985) and forthcoming. Some of this material first appeared in Carrion-Wam (1976-7, 1979).

8 Cf. Carzo 1983:67f.

9 1967:354. See further section 10.4 below.

Chapter 6: Preliminary Conclusions for Legal Theory

1 Hart is hardly an exception to this, when one takes account of the central role given in his theory to acceptance of the secondary rules by officialdom.

2 If the main issue between positivism and natural law is conceived in these terms, then the debate initiated by Ronald Dworkin may be regarded as a purely local difficulty within positivism, relating only to the definition of the required 'institutional means' by which law is to be recognised. Dworkin defines those means more broadly than Hart, so that the tests do not give rise to such 'clearly demonstrable' results as Hart both requires and expects. Significantly, MacCormick sees demonstrability as an inessential tenet of positivism. Like Dworkin, he is able to see cognitive processes as part of the 'institutional means' for the recognition of law.

3 It is not quite clear whether G/L are using the term 'metalanguage' purely metaphorically, and, if not, whether the legislative discourse is regarded as a 'metalanguage' for the discussion of issues in judicial

discourse, or whether they here refer to the (sometimes unstated) **'énoncés qualificatifs'** which institute the legislator and the judge themselves.

4 'Semiotics is in principle the discipline studying everything which can be used in order to lie' - Eco 1976:7.

5 Cf. Bastide, forthcoming.

6 The nature and sources of Kelsen's concept of 'objectivity' are much discussed. A forthcoming book by Dr. K. Lee contains a valuable discussion. See also chapter 10, esp. 10.2, below.

7 I am assuming, for the purposes of this argument, that 'objectivity' is a form of truth-claim regarding the validity of a norm within a particular normative system. On this problem, see Kalinowski 1980:351-4, responding to the argument advanced by Kelsen that norms, not being facts, cannot be true or false.

8 Kelsen goes furthest in this direction, though Hart is not too far behind. The latter sought to explain the normative character of 'social rules' (of which legal rules are a species), thus distinguishing them from mere commands backed by threats from the sovereign power (John Austin's nineteenth century version). It is, perhaps, not surprising that twentieth century positivists have felt more impelled to attend to questions of 'authority' (e.g. Raz 1979), 'legitimacy' and 'validity' than their nineteenth century predecessors. Like the father of modern positivism, Thomas Hobbes, they lived in times which brought home the possibilities of abuse of sovereign power.

9 Echoes, here, of a 'behaviourist' approach.

10 The collection of that title by Nef and others (1976) has attracted considerable attention in France.

11 This does not necessarily imply an 'innateness hypothesis', such as that attributed to Chomsky, which supposes that the basic structures must be represented physically within the genetic endowment. Semioticians have been far less concerned with this issue than Chomsky and his critics.

12 1976:94. See also Greimas 1976a:95, noted in 4.4 above, on universals in modalities. This orientation is not, however, shared by all members of the school. See Bastide, forthcoming, distancing herself from the search for universal categories, but nevertheless hoping that semiotic research will develop a list of the most commonly encountered isotopies. For discussions of the character of structuralist naturalism, and its use in legal philosophy in opposition to positivism, see Brimo 1978:197-223, placing structuralism within 'le courant rationaliste', Brimo (1978a), Jackson (1979,

1982).

13 The study of 'mentalités' in France still reflects Durkheimian 'collective representations'.

14 Such an opposition is suggested by G. Carcaterra (1984:23), arguing that culture is the place of expression of the semiotic acts which are norms, and that normativism therefore makes law into a cultural product, and the complete antithesis of nature.

15 Kalinowski himself, while adopting a quite different conception of 'sémiotique juridique', makes a threefold distinction between the logic of norms, legal semiotics, and legal reasoning (1965). Comparison of the respective formalisations of these three may be expected to form an important instrument for the further development of jurisprudence, more productive than some of the slogans sometimes taken to represent the opposing viewpoints of logic and rhetoric.

16 This latter correlation is pursued particularly in chapters 7 and 8 below, in relation to Hart and MacCormick.

17 Even a professed 'agnostic' like Harris can construct a history of the development of the logical structures of legal science in terms of Lévi-Straussian binary oppositions. For example, the binary opposition inside/outside comes to be attached to abstract normative propositions, which are 'assumed by modern legal science either to be inside or outside a particular system of law', and thus to explain 'the principle of exclusion' (1981:39). A structuralist would be unlikely to use Lévi-Straussian binary oppositions in order to construct the kind of historical account which Harris proposes; nevertheless, binary oppositions would certainly enter into any account of what makes legal science, conceived as a synchronic system, appear as meaningful.

18 On Kelsen's approach to Kantian methodology, see section 10.3 below. This is not the place to try to disentangle the Kantian and Husserlian threads in the Greimasian theory.

19 In this respect, Bremond perhaps stands closer to Ricoeur than the Barthesian view would suggest, in so far as narrative is conceived by Bremond as the series of choices to be made by the narrator at each point in the story, from amongst the various ways of continuing the story on the basis of what has already been told up to that point (McKnight 1978:180).

20 1966:211ff.; McKnight 1978:194.

21 For further criticisms of the 'anthropomorphic' level, and of the relationship between the logical and anthropomorphic levels, see Bremond 1972:369-74;

McKnight 1978:179; Ricoeur 1980:20.

22 Patte in Calloud 1976:x-xi on Benveniste 1974:215-38. For a defence of the methodological restriction to the text, see Calloud 1976:9f.

23 In this context, Arnaud's study of the French Civil Code (1973) deserves particular attention. He is concerned with underlying socio-economic realities, and seeks to elicit them through a 'deep structural' analysis of the text of the Code, inspired by the methods of Lévi-Strauss. However, he does not exclude reference to the social context of the Code for the purposes of this analysis. On Arnaud's method, see also Carrion-Wam (1985).

24 The issue, here, is that between Structuralism and Marxism. See, e.g., Viet (1965), Mounin (1967), Lefebure (1971), Marc-Lipiansky (1973), Glucksmann (1974), Polacek (1976, 1976a), Schaff (1978), Sumner (1979).

25 Of the Realists, Ross (1958, 1968) most closely approaches this orientation. While denying positivist ontological claims, he has made a major contribution to the development of deontic logic, with which in their different ways both American and European semiotics are closely concerned.

26 Particularly associated with Hägerström, Olivecrona and Ross. The approach to legal language is here directed more than in Greimasian semiotics to its function in producing psychological effects in the audience (thus generating the feeling of obligation). See especially Olivecrona (1971).

27 See Finch 1979:186f., quoting Gray: 'the courts put life into the dead words of the statute', and Gray's approval of Bishop Hoadly: 'Nay, whoever hath an absolute authority to interpret any written or spoken laws, it is he who is truly the law-giver to all intents and purposes, and not the person who first wrote or spoke them.'

28 This is argued in sections 10.4-5 below, and see 10.6 for further comparison of G/L with Kelsen.

29 For evidence of judicial awareness of the dissimulation of law, see Lord Radcliffe, quoted by Paterson (1982:140f.): 'If judges prefer the formula - for that is what it is - that they merely declare the law and do not make it, they do no more than show themselves wise men in practice. Their analysis may be weak, but their perception of the nature of the law is sound. Men's respect for it will be the greater, the more imperceptible its development' (1961:39.)

30 G/L give the code of table manners as an example. It may be noted that Kelsen concludes his discussion of

the relation between an act and its meaning in law with a paragraph drawing attention to the ability of the legal system to define the performative character of its own written or spoken acts (1967:3).

31 A view supported by the empirical study of Sourioux and Lerat; see section 2.4 above.

32 See further section 7.2 below for Hart's views. On 'easy cases' as involving the use of deduction, see MacCormick (1978:ch.II).

33 E.g. Ross 1958:151-5.

Chapter 7: Hart and the Semiotics of Legal Rules

1 Other, diverse examples of Witggensteinian influence on legal theory may be found in Ackerman (1977, 1980), Beck, Körner (1981), Pitkin (1972) and Probert (1972).

2 (1953), 1961:234. See more recently Hacker (1969); on the history of definition, Eco 1984:ch.2.

3 Cf. Horovitz 1972:155; Moore 1981:249ff. Harrison (1979:166) approves Searle (1969:17): 'A theory of language is part of a theory of action simply because speaking is a rule-governed form of behavior.'

4 See further Baker (1977), who points particularly to the tension between Hart's acceptance of a truth-conditions conception of meaning on the one hand, and the notion of the peculiar 'defeasibility' of legal concepts on the other. At the same time, Baker points to the 'decreasing influence' of J.L. Austin, in relation to Hart's gradual movement away from emphasis upon speech acts in favour of emphasis upon the 'internal point of view', together with the quiet disappearance of the notion of defeasibility (1977:29,42). See also Horovitz 1972:149-56; Moore 1981:237-9.

5 1952:62. The emphasis (original) of 'but recognising it without necessarily responding in these ways' opposes words to Holloway's conception of (all) signs, which Hart earlier expressed thus: 'Any object or event may be a sign and will be one if by virtue of its regular connection with something else it elicits regularly from some individual a response which "on the simplest level" might be just behaving on the occurrence of the sign as one would on the occurrence of the thing signified' (1952:60). Hart argues for the distinction between words and signs from the example of a 'natural sign' (cloud as an indicant of rain). But this is only one particular type of sign, what Peirce called an 'index' (1.2 above).

6 See also Strawson 1964:445f. on Grice, from which it

could be argued that Grice does not in fact go as far as Hart, but anticipates Strawson's own refinement. Neither Grice nor Strawson make any reference to Hart's earlier treatment. Hart however acknowledges assistance from Grice at the vital point of his argument, 1952:61.

7 1971:8f., on which see also Harrison 1979:186. On Austin, see further Strawson 1964:459; Harrison 1979:168.

8 This, in effect, is argued by Moore (1981:248) when he stresses the 'obvious irreducibility of the meaning of a sentence to any set of intentions of one particular speaker when he utters it on a particular occasion. The meaning of a sentence is a function of the conventions of its language, and, while those conventions may be a function of the intentions with which a **people** speaks, these conventions cannot be a function of the intentions of one speaker alone. A speaker cannot literally arrogate to himself Humpty Dumpty's power to "make words mean what he pleases" (although he can mean what he pleases by them).' Moore concludes his discussion of Grice with the observation that 'utterance-meaning is not a function of speaker's-meaning (Grice's first claim) even though speaker's-meaning is a function of the speaker's intentions (Grice's second claim)' (1981:252). This is precisely what Hart neglects in his remarks of 1952, as noted in the text above.

9 A leading member of the functionalist school in European semiotics. See further section 1.2 above.

10 The modern discussion commences with Strawson (1950).

11 1953:5. Se also Fuller's criticism of Hart's 'pointer theory', discussed by Moore 1981:274ff.

12 This tension is parallel to that identified by Baker (1977) (truth-conditions and defeasibility). See also Moore 1981:237-9.

13 E.g. Jori (1979), esp. 161-75.

14 Or perhaps the often unstated social context is always involved in principle in the standard uses of the relevant expressions, but can remain unstated when such standard use is assumed to be correlated to a social context which is itself (viewed as) standard ?

15 1961:10. Presumably, this use of 'sign' is not to be understood in terms of the opposition between 'word' and 'sign' in note 5 above.

16 For a different type of approach to this same problem, see Jackson (1984) - an argument for different spheres for formalism and realism which is taken up in terms of semiotics in chapters 11 and 12 below.

17 On the **noyau sémique** see section 2.5 above. Here as elsewhere, Hart's observations on legal language should be viewed in part as responding to those of Williams. The latter (1945:191) had already remarked that 'the words we use, though they have a central core of meaning that is relatively fixed, are of doubtful application to a considerable number of marginal cases.' See also Ross 1958:114. Hart himself identifies Waismann's 'Porosität' (cf. 'open texture') as the source of inspiration, 1961:249, 1983:274f. See also Jori (1985), s.v. 'Significato' (s.1), on Waismann. German jurisprudence had been familiar with the core/periphery image rather earlier. Heck 1919:173 had distinguished the conceptual nucleus of an indeterminate concept (Begriffskern) from its conceptual periphery. See Baldinger 1980:55, quoting Engisch (1964).

18 1983:7f., where Hart concedes the error of treating 'the indeterminacy of legal rules as if this were always a purely linguistic matter . . . in fact . . the question whether a rule applies or does not apply to some particular situation of fact is not the same as the question whether according to the settled conventions of language this is determined or left open by the words of that rule.' See also Williams' denial of the sufficiency of linguistic analysis for judicial purposes - 1945:181-4, 301. On the distinction between 'meaning' and instances of application, see more recently Schauer 1982:806.

19 For a broader attack on such definitions, and an account of the history of the matter, see Eco 1984:ch.2.

20 Twining and Miers (1982:206) are thus not entirely correct in opposing to the Hartian formulation the Wittgensteinian concept of 'family resemblance'. But whether Hart's method is a genuine reflection of that of Wittgenstein can itself be debated. For discussion of the notion of 'paradigms' (used by Hart), and for comparison of Wittgenstein and Putnam, see Moore 1981:195, 205f., 281-92.

21 1961:123. Cf. Abraham 1981:773f.

22 Hart 1961:131f. Such claims to the dominance of the 'core' have been criticised from a variety of viewpoints as unreliable assumptions. See Williams 1945:179, 181; Goodrich 1983a:263f.

23 Cf. 1961:124 on the incidence of 'open texture'.

24 1967:271; Moore 1981:15; and see now Hart 1983:8 (also reprinting the 1967 essay). See also Anon, 1967:860ff.

25 Cf., now, Eco 1984:22: 'One cannot think of the sign

without seeing it in some way characterised by its contextual destiny, but at the same time it is difficult to explain why a certain speech act is understood unless the nature of the signs which it contextualises is explained.' See also Eco 1976:95.

26 See also the criticism of Hart in Horovitz 1972:176-82.

27 Cf. Anon, 1967:857.

28 1958:606, now reprinted at 1983:63.

29 Here Hart's philosophy of meaning connects with the strong understanding of 'communication' proposed by Mounin, 1.2 above.

30 Hacker 1977:7 regards such statements as survivals of a truth-conditions conception of meaning, now 'relegated to presuppositions of assertion' in **The Concept of Law.** It is not at all clear what Hart here means by 'necessary conditions'. In formal terms, a new situation must manifest all the conditions stated in the general rule, if the general rule is to apply. But that begs the question of how the terms of the general rule are to be interpreted, in the context of adjudicating on the particular situation.

31 Cf. Ross 1958:120.

32 Engisch too pays special attention to the relation between determinacy and the revisability of judgments. See Baldinger 1980:58-61.

33 It is on these grounds, incidentally, that Summers (1961:490-2) has argued that symbolic logic is of little assistance to lawyers in resolving questions of interpretation; see Tammelo 1964:359.

34 See 1983:6f., where Hart claims never to have held the view that the judge may legislate **de novo** when the rules run out.

35 To describe Hart's approach as 'hermeneutic' (Hacker 1977:12ff., MacCormick 1981:28ff.) is surely misleading on this account alone. Meaning for Hart is that which the author intends (and shows he intends) to convey, not what the receiver attributes to the utterance.

36 For the latter approach, see Betti (1955, 1978), Haba (1972, 1978, 1979), Lieber (1880), McIntosh (1982), Strömholm (1978).

Chapter 8: MacCormick and the Semiotics of Legal Doctrine

1 For the logical analysis of the two groups, we may usefully invoke Conte's distinction between ontic and deontic eidetico-constitutive rules (1983:47f. at 1.2.1). The institutive/terminative rules are 'ontic', comparable to Searle's 'A checkmate is made when the

king is attacked in such a way that no move will leave it unattacked'; the consequential rules are 'deontic', comparable to 'Castling is not permitted if the king is in check.'

2 Cf. Calloud 1979:59f.

3 For a Lévi-Straussian interpretation, see Harris (1981), duscussed at n.17 to ch.6, above. For discussion of Kelsen's norm structure in the light of both Lévi-Strauss and deontic logic, see Lacambra (1973). Goodrich too appears to view the Pure Theory as structuralist (1983a:254). MacCormick is himself less convinced of the determinacy of legal institutions; for discussion, see section 8.2 below.

4 For MacCormick's distinction between the existence of an institution and instances of that institution, see 1973:7-9. On the ontological problem which MacCormick recognises, see 8.2 below. Comparison may be made with Pollastro's discussion of constitutive rules in terms of the Peircian distinction between 'types' and 'tokens' - 1983:235ff.

5 Nor would it be entirely farfetched to regard the specification of necessary circumstances on the one hand, or invalidating circumstances on the other, in terms of the actantial roles of helper/opponent. The parallel becomes even closer, given the more recent modalisation of this actantial role by Greimas; see section 3.2, esp. n.7, above.

6 1961:77-96. Hart distinguishes between the two classes in two different ways. Broadly, 'primary' rules are rules about behaviour, while 'secondary' rules are rules about other rules. But Hart seeks also to correlate this distinction with another, identifying primary rules with 'duty-imposing' rules and secondary rules with 'power-conferring' rules.

7 A similar account of the common significatory structure of public law and private law acts is provided by Kelsen 1967:2-4; see further, sections 8.2 and 10.1 below.

8 In arriving at this analysis, I owe much to an exchange of views with Landowski. In my first draft, I had taken the view that by **vérification juridique** G/L meant verification by the judge of the claims of the legislator that the rules which he provides are legal. That is a view which I still maintain to be tenable, in terms of the overall Greimasian conceptual framework. Landowski conceded that their text could be read in this sense, but indicated that the authors intended to refer to the legal qualification of acts by the judge in the course of the 'application' of the law. At the same time, Landowski rightly objected to my initial view,

that the SC in the text should be viewed as an **actant** in relation to **acteurs** which were the instances of that legal institution to be found in life. He convinced me that even the SC in the text should be viewed as an **acteur** (though performing an actantial role). But acceptance of his view on this latter point seems to me to strengthen my original reading on the former, and thus also to the argument now presented in the text.

9 The distinction between law and literature may be less than absolute, even in this regard. Note the observations of Greimas at 1976a:100.

10 On silence as a sign in legal discourse, see A. Carcaterra 1979:97f.; Carzo 1983:65.

11 For MacCormick's view of legal institutions as lacking purposes see 1973:29f. One distinction is made by Greimas between those syntagms of the narrative algorithm which, according to the argument here presented in the text, do appear most prominently in the legal discourse, and those which do not. 'Manipulation' and 'verediction', unlike 'competence' and 'performance', are said to be 'translative' relations, with a 'cognitive' role (1976a:95f). Factitive modalisation is a cognitive activity which seeks to stimulate some bodily activity; verediction is a cognitive operation (ex post facto) which takes the form of knowledge about objects in the world. Neither of these characteristics, we may note, should make them any the less relevant to the study of law.

12 This line of argument has been particularly influential in the analytical school of legal philosophy in Italy, led by Bobbio and Scarpelli. On the contribution of Bobbio, see also Guastini (1978); see further n.4 to ch.11. Most recently, Pintore (1983) pays considerable attention to the work of MacCormick, and relates it (at 769) to the work of G. Carcaterra (1974) on 'norma costitutiva' and later Italian literature. The logician Amadeo Conte has inspired valuable analyses of the differences to be encountered within the broad class of 'constitutive rules': see the Bibliography s.v. Conte; see also Pollastro (1983) and for comparison of Searle and G. Carcaterra, Mazzarese (1982) and Guastini (1983).

13 1969:50; the term 'brute facts' goes back at least to an article of Anscombe of 1958, as cited by Searle.

14 1967:3f. Cf. Carcaterra 1984:5f. on the principle of normativity.

15 1973:4, citing Searle 1969:50–3; 8.1 above.

16 Kelsen too would probably accede to these two empirical conditions.

17 Or impossible laws, on which see also Daube (1967).
18 MacCormick's empirical conditions should be understood against the background of Searle's 'propositional content conditions', according to which the illocutionary force of speech acts depends in part on satisfaction of sincerity conditions which include aspects of the conventional propositional content of the particular speech act; see Searle 1969:59. I am indebted to Dr. M. Sbisà for drawing my attention to this point.
19 1973:9, a striking parallel to G/L's view of **production juridique**, 2.2 above.
20 See further section 10.3 below. A similar question may be asked regarding the ontological and epistemological bases of Greimasian semiotic constraints, particularly when claims are made for their universality. But on this question I go no further in this book than the remarks in section 6.2 above.
21 The argument has to be viewed as in the context of the opening salvos of Dworkin's attack on Hart (considered further in Chapter 9, below). MacCormick explicitly addresses this issue at 1973:28-30.
22 1949:172ff. Although one may state necessary positive conditions of legal terms, no definition will capture the range of possible negative conditions which provide defences to their applicability. Excellent discussions of the issues involved may be found in Horovitz 1972:149-56 and Baker (1977). See further ch.7, note 4.
23 See also Searle 1969:55 for recognition of a similar tension.
24 (1980). For further discussion, see section 11.1 below.
25 To similar effect is the argument of Martino (1975:55) against Scarpelli, that the latter's 'concetti qualificatori' cannot be normative in isolation from a normative utterance.
26 Ross would not dissent from this view of the function of systematic legal concepts.
27 See further section 12.1 below, esp. note 9, on the implications for this argument of legal informatics.
28 1944:39-42; 1981:100-6.
29 I have, myself, offered a different, but not incompatible, view of the significance of this phenomenon, in terms of the place of the form in the development of (explicit) classification, taken as one measure of the cognitive development of the legal system (1980a:363f). The issue may be taken to represent, in microcosm, the differences between historical and formalist approaches. Daube's view exemplifies the use of classification as an active force

in development; my cognitive developmental interpretation complements this view by suggesting that the classification reflects a particular systemic state of affairs. Ross's analysis must similarly be taken as a necessary element in the analysis of technical legal terminology, but not as a complete account of it.

30 See further Jackson (1984d).

Chapter 9: Dworkin and the Semiotics of Legal Argument

1 Dworkin here means 'contrary', in contrast to 'logical negation', which is his term for 'contradictory'.

2 On these grounds, the carrification of liable v. exempt is a deviant square, akin to reality v. appearance, and unlike the carrifications of deontic logic (the squares on 'duty' and 'power') discussed in 4.4 above.

3 Cf. Alexander and Bayles 1980:271.

4 Cf. Bankowski and Maher 1981:4f.

5 A further reflection of this difference in orientation is to be found in MacCormick's accusation that Dworkin offends against 'the law of excluded middle', when he opposes 'strong' and 'weak' discretion (in his sense) as exclusive alternatives (1978:249f.). For MacCormick, discretion is neither strong nor weak but (in his sense) 'limited'.

6 The theme has become a popular one. See Abraham (1979), Papke (1980), Schauer 1982:829f., and various symposia, especially that in the **Texas Law Review** 60/3 (1982). The development of interpretation theory in the United States (e.g. Fiss (1982)) increasingly invites comparison with those of continental Europe, e.g. Esser (1954) in Germany; the 1969 symposium on 'Logique Judiciaire' in France, and see Mahillon (1978).

7 This theme is explored in a forthcoming book by Dr. K. Lee.

8 10.2 below. Hart 1983:141 maintains that 'all variants of English positivist jurisprudence subscribe to this view', that 'though the law may be at points incomplete or indeterminate, so far as it is determinate there are means of demonstrating what it is by reference to a legal system's criteria of validity or its basic provisions concerning the sources of law.' Scottish positivist jurisprudence, in the person of Neil MacCormick, does not however appear to subscribe to the need for such demonstrability. See section 7.2 above.

9 Dworkin is not necessarily here claiming the existence of inherent moral qualities, such as would sustain a

notion of 'moral fact' independent of the morality established by convention. He is aware that 'the demonstrability thesis seems to depend upon an answer to the question of what there is.' MacCormick agrees that the controversy depends on different views of what exists when people disagree on the answer to a hard case (1978:247n.26). For Dworkin's degree of self-identification with natural law, see Dworkin (1982a).

10 In this passage (1977:77), Dworkin uses the term 'moral fact' with reference to both the moral criteria by which particular facts may be judged, and the qualification of such facts as moral (a 'particular moral fact') once they have been so judged. The use of such language seems to make unnecessary ontological claims. When Searle and MacCormick speak of 'institutional fact', they refer only to brute facts qualified in the light of institutional rules. They do not refer to the institutions themselves as 'facts'. MacCormick, as we have seen, expresses some of the difficulty in accounting for the ontological status of such institutions: 8.2 above.

11 Dworkin 1977:79, where there is a notable shift from 'facts of narrative consistency' to 'beliefs of narrative consistency' (not even: 'beliefs in the fact of narrative consistency').

12 Hart 1983:7, 137-41.

13 See, particularly, Hart 1958:606; Jackson 1982:158.

14 1961:94. These are described by Hart as 'secondary rules empowering individuals to make authoritative determinations of the question whether, on a particular occasion, a primary rule has been broken.' Of course, by 'authoritative determinations', Hart here means 'determinations made by authority', not 'demonstrable determinations'. But in identifying the primary rule itself, the judge must make use of rules of recognition, which specify criteria which will provide 'a conclusive affirmative indication' of the status of a suggested rule (1961:92). Hart appears less committed to the 'demonstrability' of rules emanating from judicial decision (1961:95), but here he has in mind only the difficulties in ascertaining the **ratio decidendi** of a case. He is not interested in what further may be inferred from particular decisions, since anything further does not have the authority of a precedent.

15 I.e. in units not exceeding a sentence. See section 1.3 above.

16 It is on such grounds too that the French linguist and semiologist Georges Mounin takes objection to the

suggested parallel between law and language. See further, section 1.2 above.

17 1961:92; cf. Dworkin 1978:40f.

18 115 N.Y. 506, 22 N.E.188 (1889), discussed by Dworkin at 1978:23ff. Compare the English case re **Re Sigsworth** [1935] Ch.89, on which see Williams 1982:109f.

19 Cf., e.g., Moore 1981:199. Such a conclusion appears to command increasing support also in semiotics and linguistics. See Eco 1984:34-9, arguing for a 'semiosic continuum' of strong and weak codes, and holding that 'inference' (rather than equivalence) is involved in the decoding of every linguistic sign. Comparing Peirce, he maintains that 'the fact that perception takes place without effort does not invalidate its inferential mechanism' (at 35).

20 Cf. Moore 1981:277, opposing two linguistic considerations, those which stem from the purposes of the rules, or 'more general considerations of fairness and justice'. Moore here seeks to refine the views of Fuller, and rightly gives **Riggs v. Palmer** as an example.

21 At 1978:326f., Dworkin goes further, in allowing the judge occasionally to deny even the 'enactment force' of a precedent, when it conflicts with the political morality of the legal system or the rights which the legal system confers. Here, in deference to legal form, Dworkin suggests that the judge should not say that he is denying the force of precedent, but rather should 'lie' and misreport the existing state of the law.

22 Guest (1979); Jackson (1984).

Chapter 10: Kelsen and the Semiotics of Legal Acts

1 See further Mazzarese 1982:410 for a logical analysis of this issue. She considers two possible ways of accounting for deontic metalanguage: as hierarchical (as in the **Stufenbau** theory) or as included in the language of constitutive rules.

2 Broadly, we can say that Kelsen moved from a communicational model towards a speech act version. This movement occurs most prominently just after the publication of Hart's **Concept of Law**, in which the latter endorses a communicational model (7.3 above) and appears finally to abandon his former 'ascriptive' view, characterised by the feature of 'defeasibility'. But my object in the text is not historical. Greater consistency in Kelsen could be achieved by periodisation of his work, as indicated in one context

by Paulson (1983). But it is questionable whether Kelsen was fully consistent on these questions at any stage in his writings. In this chapter, I am particularly indebted to Stanley Paulson for his published work, his (as yet) unpublished seminar papers in London and (twice) in Liverpool, and for critical comments and correspondence on both this and an earlier version of this chapter. He will still disagree with much that is here written, but our disagreements may turn out to be productive. See further Jackson (1984c).

3 1981b:33. Harris points out that in **General Theory of Law and State** Kelsen had advanced a purely propositional account of the norm, as 'the expression of the idea . . that an individual ought to behave in a certain way', and had denied that legal norms were necessarily created by acts of will (at 33-6). Paulson has also highlighted the difficulties in constructing a coherent view of Kelsen's conception of the norm: see 1975:773-5, 1978:225-7, 1982:163f. See also Lachmayer (1985) for a critical view of Kelsen's conception of a norm as a **'Deutung'**, rendered 'interpretative projection'.

4 Cf. G. Carcaterra 1984:12f.

5 See also Raz 1981:449, 454 on Kelsen's cognitivist interpretation of legal discourse.

6 For a strong affirmation of the notion that a norm must be a proposition, if there is to be a principle of normativity, by virtue of which it is reference by a norm to facts which renders those norms legal, see Carcaterra 1984:6f. But a norm cannot be any kind of proposition. The principle of normativity also entails for Carcaterra the principle of historicity, which insists that norms are functions of historical facts (1984:17f.).

7 Kelsen 1979:221 n.1, quoted in French translation by Troper 1981:521.

8 1967:5. Carcaterra 1984:59 points to a related ambiguity concerning the very status of the categories 'is' and 'ought'. Kelsen oscillates between regarding them as distinct worlds and distinct modes of thought.

9 Dr. Lee, in her forthcoming work, expresses a similar view in terms of the ontological and epistemological status of the norm.

10 See 10.2 below on 1967:207, where the presence of a subjective meaning of the act of norm creation is presented as a necessary condition of the existence also of objective meaning.

11 See further 10.5 below.

12 Cf. Paulson 1975:776, citing Kelsen's example of the gunman and the tax collector in 1966:6. Kelsen's text

appears not to refer to the semantic content of the testament. Much of the problem identified in 10.1 resides in Kelsen's lack of sensitivity to the distinction between 'propositional content' and 'force'.

13 1967:11. In his later period, too, he repeats the view that 'a norm loses its validity . . if the norm is in fact no longer followed' (1973:217). Thus, desuetude becomes a non-contingent part of a legal order, not by virtue of the hierarchy of norms, but as flowing from the very notion of legal meaning; see further Harari (1974).

14 E.g. 1967:3f., quoted in 10.1 above. See also 1967:207, where even the **Grundnorm** is said to bestow the objective meaning of a valid norm upon acts. See also 1967:218, quoted in 10.3 below, according to which it is 'relevant interhuman relationships' which may be interpreted as 'objectively valid norms'.

15 1967:260, quoted in 10.1 above. See also 1967:221.

16 1967:204f. See also Raz 1981:452.

17 E.g. Bjarup 1981:7; Steiner (1981); Wilson (1981); Paulson 1983:13f.; Goodrich 1983a:253. See, however, Bulygin (1980) and the forthcoming work of Dr. Lee. Paulson draws my attention also to Ebenstein (1945).

18 1967:218, cf. 1960:185.

19 Kelsen never satisfactorily resolved this question. He did abandon the view that the **Grundnorm**, as the presupposition of the legal validity of **norms**, could be an epistemological presupposition - an act of thinking. He ultimately applied the theory of fictions of Vaihinger, and converted the **Grundnorm** into a fictitious act of will (see, recently, Raz 1981:452f.; Stewart 1981:14; Bjarup 1981:23f.,27). But then he was faced with the problem of relating this **Grundnorm** to the system of legal doctrine, that of **Rechtssätze**.

20 Paulson's translation in Paulson 1983:7; emphasis in the original.

21 1967:206. In order to avoid contradictory norms, Kelsen sought for a considerable period to 'presuppose' rules to resolve such conflicts, such as the **lex posterior**; see Paulson (1983). Such rules are required as epistemological presuppositions, in order to explain the workings of a legal system experienced as reasonable, in just the same way as the **Grundnorm** has to be presupposed in order to explain our experience of objective legal validity. There is an interesting passage in 1973:236f., where Kelsen even in his later phase describes the **lex posterior** as 'posited by the legal authority, or presupposed as valid'. Here, Kelsen seems to have in mind a psychological presupposition by the legislator, rather than an epistemological

presupposition.

22 At 1967:205f. he argued that conflict between norms did not itself involve 'a logical contradiction' but nevertheless maintained that two legal norms could contradict each other 'indirectly', since an 'assertion describing a normative order by saying that a certain norm is valid according to that order' could be true or false. Later, Kelsen changed his mind, and claimed that mutually conflicting norms could both be valid, even though contradictory statements could not (1973:235, 252 n.8). The individual subject is now pulled in conflicting directions, and is presumably liable to a coercive order whatever he chooses to do. Reasonableness is no longer a condition of meaning of the system, even though imputation still is. In the case of contradictory norms, the individual subject must still exercise an act of will, even though he is now restricted to a choice of which norm to violate. For criticism of Kelsen's ultimate view on contradictory norms, see Kalinowski 1980:354f. See further section 10.4, s.v. 'Right Decisions'.

23 Harris 1979:86; Troper 1981:527.

24 1973:243, quoted below at n.31.

25 1967:354. See also Ross 1958:136 on the combination of cognition and volition in judicial interpretation.

26 Even in the second edition of **Reine Rechtslehre** (1967:244f.), Kelsen insists that such an application of the law is creative in character, even while invoking again the image of the cognitive 'frame'.

27 1967:244. This relationship has been described by Harris (1977:356f.) in terms of the logical relation of 'subsumption'.

28 1973:246. See further Harris 1977:356 and Paulson 1981:806 on the rather odd continuation of this passage. On Kelsen's earlier view, see Paulson 1975:783f.

29 The use of this particular example suggests that Kelsen might have had in mind the contrary argument of Oppenheim 1944:148. Against Kelsen's view, see Kalinowski 1980:356.

30 Paulson 1982a:162 notes that in 1979:193n. Kelsen quotes Dewey 1924:22: 'No concrete proposition, that is to say, one with material dated in time and space, follows from any general statements or any connections between them.'

31 1973: 243, emphasis in original. For criticism of this argument, see Kalinowski 1980:360.

32 1981:6, cf. 1977:19-40.

33 A 'norm-sentence', in Schramm's translation of Weinberger's 1981 article.

34 On the problem of whether formal authorisation itself involves the logical operation of subsumption, see Weinberger 1981:10f.; Troper 1981:527; and Harris's solution in terms of authorisation from the institutional roles of the agents, rather than from a specific norm or rule - 1977:358f., 1979:87f. See further section 10.5 below.

35 Paulson 1982a:161 on Kelsen 1979:201 notes that inference may still obtain between norms of different degrees of generality, if not between general and individual norms. But this must be read as a relationship between **Rechtssätze** of different levels of generality.

36 Cf. Paulson 1975:781f.

37 Cf. Lee, forthcoming: 'it is possible to maintain that a similar distinction exists between a sentence containing an "ought" and the use of it on a particular occasion to make a prescription. Up to a point, Kelsen does recognise the distinction himself - he maintains that the sentence "thieves ought to be imprisoned", occurring in a criminal law text book is not a prescription itself but a descriptive statement with "ought" as its cognitive object . . . but he fails to explore it further in this context . . . If he were to press the distinction, he might have realised (1) that its typical illocutionary force is that of a prescription when the context is one of law-making, but it loses this force if the context is one of codifying or theorising about the law, and acquires a descriptive illocutionary force. And if the sentence were uttered in a context of testing a microphone, then it has neither a prescriptive nor a descriptive illocutionary force; (2) that sentential meaning is both a question of syntactical rules and semantical rules, none of which appears to be matters open to the individual language user like the judge to fiddle about with as his whims dictate . . .' See also Moore 1981:162, referring to a similar response by Hart to the realists.

38 Cf. Nino 1978:364f. On Oppenheim, see further Carrion-Wam 1982-3:129-38 and (1985).

Chapter 11: Pragmatics, Validity and the Unity of the Legal System

1 For the placing of Hart, Kelsen and Dworkin on a continuum of formalism, see Jackson (1984).

2 Hacker 1977:6f.; Baker 1977:42.

3 For the terms 'onomasiological' and 'semasiological', see Baldinger (1980).

4 I refer here not only to Hart and MacCormick, whose relations with Austin and Searle respectively have been touched upon in Chapters 7 and 8, but also the analytical tradition as found on the continent, and particularly in Italy, notably by Bobbio and Scarpelli. The work of Tarello, G. Carcaterra and Jori, representing the next generation of Italian legal philosophers, also stands predominantly in the analytical tradition, although in varying degrees they increasingly draw also upon structural linguistics. Particularly noteworthy, in this regard, are the articles contributed by Jori to the forthcoming encyclopedia, **Strumenti del sapere contemporaneo,** s.v. 'Semiotica', 'Segno', 'Comunicazione', 'Significato', 'Sistema e Discorso', 'Referente'. See also note 12 to ch.8.

5 In the general philosophy of language, some recent work of M. Sbisà indicates an increasing sympathy for aspects of structural linguistics from within the analytical tradition. For the approach of logical semiotics towards the formalisation of legal pragmatics, see Kalinowski's forthcoming revision of his 'sémiotique juridique', applying the work of Martin and Montague.

6 For a bibliographical orientation, see Landowski (1982), particularly at 12f., on work (especially that of Parret) directed towards the construction of a 'pragma-sémiotique', and for the association of analytical pragmatics with the 'American' semiotic tradition (descended from Peirce, Morris and Wittgenstein: at 1982:9f.). For comparison of Wittgenstein and structural linguistics, see Pettit (1972).

7 See Landowski's bibliographical survey at 1982:12-19, significantly covering also the claims of logical semiotics, in the Peircian tradition. It is along these lines that Greimasian semiotics will take its stance vis-à-vis the school of Perelman, the more recent and critical accounts of rhetoric as in the work of the Brussels Saint-Louis group (van de Kerchove, Ost, Lenoble), Goodrich and Schreckenberger, adjudicative theories such as those of Dworkin and MacCormick, and logical approaches to semiotics as represented by the Polish school (Ziembinski, Wroblewski and, in France, Kalinowski). In the recent work of the logician Amadeo Conte we find eclectic use of notions from both Peircian and Saussurian semiotics: see 1984a:2.2.3.2, using the Peircian opposition between type and token, cf. 1983:52 (at 1.2.2.3); and his use of Hjelmslev's syntagmatic/paradigmatic distinction at

1983:54-6 (1.3), and also in (1984a) and (1984b). For references, see the entries in the bibliography under the authors here named.

8 For a survey and bibliography, see Goodrich (1984a). Particular reference may be made to Atkinson and Drew (1979) for conversational analysis; see also Wilkinson (1981). The use of discourse analysis in the spirit of critical legal studies is variously reflected in Carlen (1976), Delgado Ocando, and Burton and Carlen (1979).

9 See now the attempt of Eco 1984:44f. to reformulate the radical dualism of expression plane and content plane of Hjelmslev in the light of Peirce's semiotics.

10 See generally Landowski in Greimas and Landowski (1983); Fabbri and Landowski (1983). Sbisà and Fabbri 1980:15f. note that in their preferred (M2) model of pragmatics, based on interaction, the notion of context is problematic. 'Who is then to decide, if not the participants themselves, by which description the participants are to refer to the situation in which they are acting ?' But the 'moves' of Goffman's analysis, though preferred in Sbisà and Fabbri to the Austinian model of speech acts, would themselves be viewed in narrative terms by the Greimasian school.

11 Hart's 'internal point of view' represents an uneasy compromise between a strictly syntactic and a pragmatic account of legal philosophy. See further Goodrich 1983a:258-61 for an analysis of Hart's notion of acceptance.

12 Perrott (1980) has suggested a parallel between Chomskian syntactic structures and Hart's union of primary and secondary rules. But he does so not in the spirit of positivism, but in order to suggest, from the analogy, that our genetic endowment may include legal (as well as linguistic and musical) 'deep structures'. A full examination of this argument will appear elsewhere.

13 Thus it would be compatible, at best, with Sbisà and Fabbri's 'M1' model, not 'M2'. Note, at the same time, that Austin himself took 'truth' to be contextually-relative: 'what is judged true in a school book may not be so judged in a work of historical research' (1975:143f.).

14 The logician Conte, by contrast, is closer to discursive semiotics when he distinguishes 'eidetico-constitutive rules' from 'anankastic constitutive rules', the former constituting the meaning of the phenomena to which they refer, the latter constituting the 'validity' of that which they concern (1984a at 3.3.1). See also his pupil, Mazzarese (1982), as discussed in note 1 to ch.10.

15 Section 7.2. Comparison may be made with Ross's distinction (1958:117) between 'interpretation by meaning' and 'interpretation by reference'.

16 'Semantics' as understood by structural semantics; according to the classification of Morris, the question would be entirely one of syntactics.

17 Interpretation theory increasingly recognises, as Abraham 1981:782 points out in a similar context, that interpretive strategies are a function of particular audiences, their cultures, purposes and professional needs.

18 Recall the formulations of Dworkin's discursive presuppositions, in 9.1 above.

19 A different argument for the insufficiency of linguistic interpretation is advanced by Moore (1981:277f., 293f.) on the basis, inter alia, of general considerations of fairness and justice. At one level, such considerations can and should count as 'systemic' considerations, such as would be relevant also for doctrinal or didactic interpretation, but at another level, that of justice to the parties in their particular circumstances, it relates specifically to judicial interpretation. Dworkin seeks to establish a society's conception of justice as a systemic consideration.

20 Kalinowski (1965), and his revision of the section in that book on 'la sémiotique juridique', which I have had the benefit of reading in typescript.

21 For the former, see Dingwall and Lewis (1983); on the latter, Ross (1970).

22 See Arnaud 1981:397ff., on various sources of distortion and blocking of the transmission of the message.

23 Interesting work is being done on the linguistic analysis of attempts to simplify legal language. See the works of the Charrows, cited in the Bibliography. The campaigners (largely in the United States) are not always fully aware of the semiotic implications of their activities.

Chapter 12: Towards a Semiotic Model of Law

1 For discussion of the status of constitutional language as a special discourse, see Schauer 1982:779-803.

2 On administrative discourse, from the viewpoint of Greimasian semiotics, see Landowski (1974). See also Twining and Miers 1982:302, 316, on the need to determine who is the primary audience when deciding what drafting will best secure intelligibility.

3 For a recent discussion of Holmes on the point of view

of the 'bad man' and his practitioner, see Wilcox (1981).

4 See esp. 1982:9-11 for previous research and for the Law Lords' own perceptions; ch.2 generally for Paterson's own inferences.

5 Cf. Murray 1982:850f. on the use of analogy.

6 See Perrin (1981) on the strategies of the state, the judges and the litigants in divorce proceedings, inspired in part by earlier work of Arnaud (1974, 1979).

7 Kelsen, we may recall, in revising his view of the relationship between general and individual norms, moved away from a 'communicational' model.

8 Cf. Goodrich 1983b:258f.

9 See further 1973:22ff., 28f. The point has been developed at length by MacCormick in his work on legal reasoning, where the distinction represented here in my text as one between 'sign' and 'symbol' is discussed in terms of the relative incidence of deductive and non-deductive justification (1978). In other respects, MacCormick is less sensitive to the variety of semiotic processes involved in the law. His account of legal concepts (8.3) is one which assumes that the operational needs of the lawyer and the legal writer are equivalent (more broadly, that they represent a single 'semiotic group'). But in reality, we may doubt any such equivalence (11.3), other than as a matter of temporary convenience. Such temporary convenience is, indeed, to be found in the history of Scots Law, where the economics of law publishing in a small jurisdiction have forced practitioners and students towards a single market. But as information technology becomes cheaper and more widely accessible, we may find a very real demonstration of the differences between doctrinal and practitioner writing, which are more commonplace elsewhere.

We may well be approaching a period when legal practitioners no longer need the legal writer at all. What they need is the legal information technologist, who can take them as quickly as possible to the very specific issue which is the subject of their immediate practical concern. For this purpose, the classificatory processes involved in simplifying 'institutive' and 'consequential' rules (8.2) may be both time-consuming and potentially dangerous. The law student may have the time to work out a problem, and the intellectual process involved is, in his context, both beneficial and without risk to the outside world. The practitioner frequently has less time, and his misjudgments involve far greater risk. What he therefore needs is a system which will communicate to him a very specific answer to his particular problem, in the minimum of time and with the least risk of error. Two developments in legal technology point in this direction, and both take away from the lawyer the onus of himself operating the classificatory system. The one is the use of legal information retrieval systems, particularly by the use of 'search and locate' techniques such as 'keywords in combination'. Here, the lawyer is directed towards the most relevant primary source material, through the mechanical search for particular words, and without his having to restrict the material through a preliminary exercise in classification. Thus, a legal practitioner researching a problem by traditional methods will first select the cases he wishes to read - by reference, in part, to the classificatory concepts under which that case is indexed in the reports. That may well exclude relevant material. By using a search for keywords in combination through the whole text of a whole corpus of cases, he may well encounter relevant material which was not indexed under that concept which the practitioner thought would be most relevant. Again, algorithmic programs are being written for the solution of standard legal problems. Here, the practitioner saves time and avoids the risk of working out the problem himself through the use of the classificatory techniques required by the institutional representation of the law. In principle, we may expect information technology to advance from the level of the discursive representation of the law, as represented by the law reports (which the practitioner still has to interpret) to the level of the logic of the norms themselves, with particular reference to the full range of combination of variables which exist within them. At that stage, programming must surely take a form far closer to my set (4) to (11), as discussed in section 8.3 above, rather than to either MacCormick's (1) and (2) or his interpretation of Ross in terms of (3). Under such a system, the legal practitioner would be able to key in either a plus sign or minus sign (yes or no) in terms of each of the variables which his program will tell him to be relevant. The computer will then search the program until it finds the formula whose variables are compatible with those of the conditions interrogated by the practitioner, and which gives the solution for the particular problem in which he is interested. Studies of legal informatics relevant to a semiotic analysis of law include Bergeron (1977), Bourcier (1979), Catala (1978), Edwards and Barker (1975), Martino (1978, 1979, 1982).

10 1980:14. They compare the concept of conversational implicatures, as used by Grice and others.
11 Cf. Raz 1981:448, noted in section 11.2 above.
12 Note Searle's own recognition of the difficulties, at 1969:54f.
13 See Baldwin and McConville (1977).
14 In my preliminary study of the relationship of structuralism and law (1979), and also in some more recent articles (1982, 1984), I have argued more generally for the model of continua rather than opposites.
15 He takes support from Peirce for his conception of the inferential nature of the sign: 'Peirce was aware of the fact that perception is always presumptive evidence, a source of potential semiosis. The fact that perception takes place without effort does not invalidate its inferential mechanism (see **C.P.** 5.266-68).' (1984:35)
16 Eco uses a legal example in relation to this continuum. 'At first glance, correlational codes seem to obey the equivalence model, whereas institutional codes seem to obey the inferential one. The difference is not, however, so clear-cut. For instance, the Roman law (as opposed to the Anglo-Saxon common law, which is rather a body of examples endowed with instructional or implicative power) looks like a system of correlations: the Italian Codice Penale (penal law code) does not say explicitly that murder is bad and does not forbid it as such, but rather, correlates various forms of homicide with various forms of punishment. On the other hand, the Italian Codice Civile (civil law code) is a set of directions as to how one should act, and at the same time a set of sanctions correlated with violations of the norm' (1984:165f). On this account, we may understand in semiotic terms the difficulty encountered in 19th-century positivism, in seeking to reduce all law to the model of criminal law commands.
17 See also Winner and Winner (1976:183) on Pjatigorskij, for whom syntactics relate to the manner in which the text is 'intuitively felt' as distinct from other texts; semantics to the understandability of a text, as not containing insurmountable difficulties hindering its comprehension, and pragmatics to the 'necessary means of conscious transmission of communication' by the author to other individuals.
18 See Kevelson (1982). Two examples may be taken from the Greimasian approach: (1) the nature of the subject, as revealed by the choice of modal values transferred to him (1976a:105); (2) the typology of possible SC's revealed by different relations of 'possessor' and 'thing

possessed' (1976:101f.).

19 For Kalinowski (SJ), semantics cannot be conceived exclusively in terms of relations to the outside world; the relations of expressions to their **significata** must be considered before the relation of those expressions to their **designata**.

20 For a strong argument for Austin's empiricism, see Morrison (1982).

21 On this distinction, see Twining and Miers 1982:136-40.

22 See note 9 above.

23 Engisch (1964), translated in Baldinger 1980:56-8.

24 Martino 1975:50ff., esp.55, on Scarpelli (1959).

25 A third, distinguishable class of terms belongs to the 'metalanguage' of law, being terms by which norms and normative utterances may be described.

26 See, e.g., Cain 1983:111.

27 See literature cited n.24 to ch.6, above. Althusser is the central figure in attempts to resolve this problem.

28 See also Arnaud 1981:398ff., section 3.3.2. An interesting argument **against** the specificity of legal argument is advanced by Moerman (1973), comparing the 'practical logic' of natural conversation.

29 E.g. Carrion-Wam, 'Semiotic Research'. A. Carcaterra (1979:109) sees such deontic operators as 'legal primitives', but this does not necessarily imply their specificity to law.

30 Bastide, forthcoming; see 8.1.

References

Anon (1967), 'Jurisprudence and the Nature of Language: Contrasting Views of Hart and Chomsky', **Washington Law Review** 42, 847-72.

Abraham K. (1979), 'Statutory Interpretation and Literary Theory', **Rutgers Law Review** 32, 676-94.

Abraham K. (1981), 'Three Fallacies of Interpretation: A Comment', **Arizona Law Review** 23, 771-83.

Ackerman B.A. (1977), 'The Structure of Subchapter C: An Anthropological Comment', **Yale Law Journal** 87, 436-46.

Ackerman B.A. (1980), 'Four Questions for Legal Theory', **Nomos** (1980), 351-75.

Ackerman B.A. (1977), **Private Property and the Constitution,** New Haven and London, Yale U.P.

Ahonen P. (1983), **Public Policy Evaluation as Discourse,** Helsinki, The Finnish Political Science Association.

Alexander L. & Bayles M. (1980), 'Hercules or Proteus ? The Many Theses of Ronald Dworkin', **Social Theory and Practice** 5, 267-303.

Amselek P. (1964), **Méthode phénomenologique et théorie du droit,** Paris, L.G.D.J.

Amselek P. (1973), 'The Phenomenological Description of Law', in **Phenomenology and the Social Sciences,** ed. M. Natanson, Evanston, Northwestern University Press.

Amselek P. (1978), 'Avons-nous besoin de l'idée de droit naturel ?', **Archives de Philosophie du Droit** 23, 343-53.

Arnaud A.-J. (1968), 'Structuralisme et droit', **Archives de Philosophie du Droit** 13, 283-301.

Arnaud A.J. (1970), 'Nouvelles de structuralisme', **Archives de Philosophie du Droit** 15, 466-71.

Arnaud A.-J. (1973), **Essai d'analyse structurale du Code**

Civil Français, Paris, L.G.D.J.
Arnaud A.-J. (1974), 'Autopsie d'un juge', **Archives de Philosophie du Droit** 19, 197-228.
Arnaud A.-J. (1977), 'Une méthode d'analyse structurale en histoire du droit', **Ius Commune**, Sonderhefte 6 (**Vorstudien zur Rechtsgeschichte**, ed. J.M. Scholte), Frankfurt-a-Main, Klostermann.
Arnaud A.-J. (1979), 'Du bon usage du discours juridique', **Langages** 53, 117-24.
Arnaud A.-J. (1979a), 'Le droit français des biens entre jeu et providence', **Archives de Philosophie du Droit** 24, 213-34.
Arnaud A.-J. (1981), **Critique de la raison juridique. 1. Où va la Sociologie du Droit ?**, Paris, L.G.D.J.
Arnaud A.-J. (1982), 'Le concept de 'raison juridique' comme mode de dépassement de l'opposition traditionelle entre l'être et le devoir-être', CETEL 18, 24-36.
Arnaud A.-J. (1982a), 'Crise contemporaine de nos sociétés, crise du droit et réflexion juridique', CETEL 18.
Arnaud A.J. (1985), 'Fact as Law', in Carzo and Jackson (1985).
Atkinson J.M. & Drew P. (1979), **Order in Court**, London, MacMillan, 1979 (Oxford Socio-Legal Studies).
Austin J.L. (1975), **How To Do Things With Words**, 2nd ed. by J.O. Urmson & M. Sbisà, Oxford, The Clarendon Press.
Baker G.P. (1977), 'Defeasibility and Meaning', in **Law, Morality and Society**, ed. Hacker & Raz, Oxford, The Clarendon Press, 26-57 (Hart Festschrift).
Baldinger K. (1980), **Semantic Theory**, ed. R. Wright, Oxford, Blackwell.
Baldwin J. and M. McConville (1977), **Negotiated Justice**, London, Martin Robertson.
Bankowski Z.K. & G. Maher (1981), 'Ordinary Language and Judicial Discretion', **Rechtstheorie** 12, 1-8.
Barthes R. (1967), **Elements of Semiology**, trld. Lavers and Smith, London, Jonathan Cape.
Barthes R. (1977), **Image, Music, Text**, trld. S. Heath, London, Fontana/Collins.
Bastide F. (1981), **La démonstration**, Paris, Groupe de Recherches sémio-linguistiques (**Documents** III no.28).
Bastide F., 'The Semiotic Analysis of Discourse', forthcoming.
Beck A., 'The Games Analogy: Rules and Principles',

References

Semiotica, special issue on legal semiotics, forthcoming.
Benveniste E. (1974), **Problèmes de Linguistique Générale II,** Paris, Gallimard.
Bergeron V. (1977), **Words, Computers and Communication in Law,** Ottawa, Les Editions de l'Université d'Ottawa.
Bergh G.C.J.J. & J.M. Broekman (1979), **Recht en Tal,** Deventer, Kluwer.
Bernstein B. (1971-7), **Class, Codes and Control,** London, Routledge & Kegan Paul, 3 vols.
Betti E. (1955), **Teoria generale dell'interpretazione,** Milan, Giuffrè, 2 vols.
Betti (as subject) (1978), 'Emilio Betti e la scienza giuridica del Novecento',**Quaderni fiorentini** 7, 1-452.
Bjarup B. (1981), 'Hans Kelsen's Theory of Law and Philosophy of Justice', ALSP Conference Paper, Edinburgh, 1981, forthcoming in Tur and Twining (1985).
Black M. (1963), 'The Analysis of Rules', in **Models and Metaphors,** ed. Black, Ithaca, Cornell U.P.
Blanché R. (1966), **Les Structures Intellectuelles,** Paris, J. Vrin.
Bloor D. (1983), **Wittgenstein. A Social Theory of Knowledge,** London, MacMillan.
Bobbio N. (1950), 'Scienza del diritto e analisi del linguaggio', **Rivista trimestrale di diritto e procedura civile** 4, 342-67.
Bobbio N. (1955), 'Sul raggionamento dei giuristi', **Rivista di Diritto Civile** 1, 3-13.
Bourcier D. (1976), 'Argumentation et définition en droit, ou Les grenouilles sont-elles des poissons ?', **Langages** 42, 115-22.
Bourcier D. (1978), 'Gendarmes et Oedipes. Le Procès des narrations. Notes sur le système narrative du droit', **La Narration Nouvelle** 4, 139-49.
Bourcier D. (1979), 'Information et Signification en Droit', **Langages** 53, 9-32.
Bourcier D. (1982), 'The Judge's Discourse: Research on the Modelization of Reasoning in Law', in **Artificial Intelligence and Legal Information Systems,** ed. C. Ciampi, Amsterdam, I.103-16.
Bousquet F. (1977), 'Carré logique et carré sémiotique', in **L'Ancien Testament. Approches et Lectures,** ed. A. Vanel, Paris, Editions Beauchesnes, 63-72 (Le Point Théologique, 24).
Bremond C. (1972), 'Le modèle constitutionel de A.J.

Greimas', **Semiotica** 5 (1972), 362-382, reprinted in **Logique du récit,** Paris, Editions du Seuil, 1973, 81-102.
Brimo A. (1978), **Les grands courants de la philosophie du droit et de l'état,** Paris, Pedone, 3rd ed.
Brimo A. (1978a), 'Structuralisme et rationalisation du droit', **Archives de Philosophie du Droit** 23, 189-211.
Broekman J. (1975), 'A Structuralist Approach to the Philosophy of Law', **Proceedings of the American Catholic Philosophical Association** 49, 37-48.
Brown C.H. (1974), **Wittgensteinian Linguistics,** The Hague, Mouton (Approaches to Semiotics, Paperback Series 12).
Brutti M. (1975), 'Alcuni usi del concetto di strutture nella conoscenza giuridica', **Quaderni fiorentini per la storia del pensiero giuridico moderno** 3/4, 763-99.
Bulygin E. (1980), 'Kant y la Filosofia del Derecho Contemporaneo', **Archivos Latinoamericanos de metodologia y filosofia del derecho** 1, 59-68.
Burton F. & Carlen P. (1979), **Official Discourse,** London, Routledge & Kegan Paul.
Cain M. (1983), 'The General Practice Lawyer and the Client: Towards a Radical Conception', in **The Sociology of the Professions: Lawyers, Doctors and Others,** ed. R. Dingwall & P. Lewis, London, MacMillan, 106-30.
Calame C. (1982), 'Enonciation: véracité ou convention littéraire', **Actes Sémiotiques - Documents** IV, 34, Paris, Groupe de Recherches Sémio-Linguistiques, E.H.E.S.S. - C.N.R.S.
Calloud J. (1976), **Structural Analysis of Narrative,** Philadelphia & Missoula, Fortress Press & Scholars Press.
Calloud J. (1979), 'A Few Comments on Structural Semiotics: A Brief Review of Method and Some Explanations of Procedures', **Semeia** 15, 51-83.
Carcaterra A. (1968), **Struttura del linguaggio-precettivo,** Bari, Cacucci.
Carcaterra A. (1970), **Dolus Bonus/Dolus Malus,** Napoli, Jovene.
Carcaterra A. (1972), **Semantica del linguaggio giuridico-precettivo romano,** Bari, Cacucci.
Carcaterra A. (1979), 'Per una semiotica dei testi legislativi', **Quaderni Latinoamericana** III-IV, 93-122.
Carcaterra G. (1974), **Le norme costitutive,** Milan, Giuffrè.
Carcaterra G. (1979), **La forza costitutiva delle norme,** Roma, Bulzoni.
Carcaterra G. (1984), **Il principio di normatività,** Roma,

Bulzoni.
Carlen P. (1976), **Magistrates' Justice**, London, Martin Robertson.
Carrion-Wam R. (1976-7), 'Elementos de sémiotica juridica', **Annuario: Istituto de derecho comparado** 261-320, Faculdad de Derecho, Universidad de Carabobo.
Carrion-Wam R. (1979), 'Preliminares de una semiotica juridica', **Revista de ciencias sociales** 15, 67-119.
Carrion-Wam R. (1982-3), 'Panorama de la Semiotica Juridica', **Investigaciones Semioticas** (IS) 2/3, 116-90.
Carrion-Wam R. (1985), 'Semiotica Juridica', in Carzo and Jackson (1985) (translation of 1982-3).
Carrion-Wam R., 'Semiotic Research on Law in Venezuela', to appear in **The Semiotic Sphere**, ed. T.A. Sebeok and J. Umiber-Sebeok, New York, Plenum, forthcoming.
Carrion-Wam R., 'La Produccion de la sentencia', **Festschrift Cossio**, forthcoming.
Carzo D. (1976), 'Codici normativi e comunicazione sociale. Una prospettiva di ricerca', **Sociologia del diritto**, 335-62.
Carzo D. (1981), **I Segni del Potere**, Milan, Giuffrè.
Carzo D. (1983), 'Discorso giuridico e 'codice' normativo. Primi appunti per una grammatica giuridica', **Sociologia della Comunicazione** 2/3, 65-70.
Carzo D. and B.S. Jackson, eds. (1985), **Semiotics, Law and Social Science**, Reggio and Rome, Casa del libro editrice, in association with **The Liverpool Law Review.**
Catala P. (1978), 'L'Informatique et la rationalité du droit', **Archives de Philosophie du Droit** 23, 295-321.
Chabrol C. (1967), 'Structures intéllectuelles', in **L'Ancien Testament - Approches et Lectures**, ed. Vanel, Informations sur les sciences sociales, 205-9.
Chatman S. (1972), 'On the Formalistic-Structuralist Theory of Character', **Journal of Literary Semantics** 1, 57-79.
Charrow V., J.A. Crandall & R.P. Charrow (1982), 'Characteristics and Functions of Legal Language', in **Foundations of Communication**, ed. R. Posner, Berlin, Walter de Gruyter, 175-90.
Charrow V.R. (1982), 'Linguistic Theory and the Study of Legal and Bureaucratic Language', in **Exceptional Language and Linguistics**, London, Academic Press.
Charrow R.P. & V.R. (1979), 'Making Legal Language Understandable: A Psycholinguistic Study of Jury Instructions', **Columbia Law Review** 79/7, 1306-74.
Combet G. (1981), 'Cinq ans après', **Le Bulletin** 17, 32-5,

Paris, Groupe de Recherches Sémio-Linguistiques, E.H.E.S.S. - C.N.R.S.

Conte A.G. (1981), 'Konstitutive Regeln und Deontik', **Ethics, Foundations, Problems and Applications,** Vienna, Holder-Pichler-Tempsky, 82-6.

Conte A.G. (1983), 'Paradigmi d'analisi della regola in Wittgenstein', in **Wittgenstein. Momenti di una critica del sapere,** ed. R. Egidi, Napoli, Guida Editori, 37-82.

Conte A.G. (1984), 'Idealtypen für eine Theorie der konstitutiven Regeln', **Proceedings of the 11th World Congress on Philosophy of Law and Social Philosophy,** Berlin, Dunker & Humboldt, III, 1-12.

Conte A.G. (1984a), 'Phénoménologie du langage déontique', **Les fondements de la pensée normative,** ed. G. Kalinowski, Roma, Università Gregoriana Editrice.

Conte A.G. (1984b), 'Semiotica delle regole costitutive', paper delivered to the Third Congress of the International Association for Semiotic Studies, Palermo, 1984.

Crystal D. & D. Davy (1969), **Investigating English Style,** London, Longmans (ch.8: 'The Language of Legal Documents').

Culler J. (1975), **Structuralist Poetics,** London, Routledge & Kegan Paul.

Culler J. (1975a), 'Defining Narrative Units', in **Style and Structure in Literature,** ed. R. Fowler, Oxford, Blackwell, 123-142.

Culler J. (1983), **Barthes,** London, Fontana Paperbacks.

Danet B. (1980), 'Language in Legal Process', **Law and Society Review** 14, 445-564.

Danet B. ed. (1984), 'Studies of Legal Discourse', Special Issue of **Text** 4-1/3.

Danet B. (1984a), 'The Magic Flute: A Prosodic analysis of binomial expressions in legal Hebrew', **Text** 4-1/3, 143-72.

Daube D. (1944), 'Some Forms of Old Testament Legislation', **Proceedings of the Oxford Society of Historical Theology,** 36-46.

Daube D. (1967), 'Greek and Roman Reflections on Impossible Laws', **Natural Law Forum** 12, 1-84.

Daube D. (1981), **Ancient Jewish Law,** Leiden, E.J. Brill.

Dauchy P. (1981), 'Une conception objective du lien d'obligation: les apports du structuralisme à la théorie du contrat', **Archives de Philosophie du Droit** 26, 269-80.

Dauchy P. (1982), 'L'Oubli et le fondement du droit', **Archives de Philosophie du Droit** 27, 245-50.

References

Delgado-Ocando J.M. (1973), **Normas, Lenguaje y Verdad,** Centro de estudios de filosofia del derecho LUZ, Maracaibo.

Delgado-Ocando J.M. (1975), **Consideraciones sobre los elementos semioticos del derecho,** Centro de estudios de filosofia del derecho LUZ, Maracaibo (Cuaderno de trabajo, 9).

Delgado-Ocando J.M. (1977), **Textos para un analisis semiotico de la ilicitud,** Centro de estudios de filosofia del derecho, Universidad del Zulia, Maracaibo.

de Libera A. (1976), 'La sémiotique d'Aristote', in Nef (1976), 28-48.

de Libera A. (1976a), 'Note sur 'On Binary Opposition' d'Arild Utaker', in Nef (1976), 49-55.

Dewey J. (1924), 'Logical Method and Law', **Cornell Law Quarterly** 10, 17-27.

Dias R.W.M. (1976), **Jurisprudence,** 4th ed., London, Butterworths.

di Bernardo G., ed. (1977), **Logica, Deontica e Semantica,** Bologna, Il Mulino, with bibliogaphy by Di Bernardo & A.G. Conte at 349-447.

Dingwall R. & P. Lewis, eds. (1983), **Sociology of the Professions: Lawyers, Doctors and Others,** London, MacMillan.

Ducrot O. (1972), **Dire et ne pas dire,** Paris, Hermann.

Ducrot O. & Todorov T. (1979), **Encyclopedic Dictionary of the Sciences of Language,** trld. C. Porter, Oxford, Blackwell, Baltimore, Johns Hopkins U.P.

Dworkin R. (1977). 'No Right Answer ?', in **Law, Morality and Society,** ed. P.M.S. Hacker & J.Raz, Oxford, Clarendon Press, 58-84.

Dworkin R. (1978), **Taking Rights Seriously,** London, Duckworths.

Dworkin R. (1982), 'Law as Interpretation', **Texas Law Review** 60/3, 527-50.

Dworkin R. (1982a), 'Natural Law Revisited', **University of Florida Law Review** 34, 165-88.

Ebenstein W. (1945), **The Pure Theory of Law,** Madison, University of Wisconsin Press.

Eco U. (1976), **A Theory of Semiotics,** University of Indiana Press.

Eco U. (1984), **Semiotics and the Philosophy of Language,** London, MacMillan.

Edwards T.H. & J.P. Barber (1975), 'A Computer Method for

Legal Drafting Using Propositional Logic', **Texas Law Review** 53, 965-1004.
Engisch K. (1964), **Einführung in das juristische Denken,** Stuttgart, 3rd ed.
Esser J. (1954), 'Interpretation im Recht', **Studium Generale** 7, 372-9.
Fabbri P. & E. Landowski (1983), 'Explorations stratégiques', **Actes Sémiotiques - Bulletin** VI, 25, esp. Landowski at 5-17 (Groupe de Recherches Sémio-linguistiques, E.H.E.S.S.-C.N.R.S.)
Finch J. D. (1979), **Introduction to Legal Theory,** London, Sweet & Maxwell, 3rd ed.
Fiss O.M. (1982), 'Objectivity and Interpretation', **Stanford Law Review** 34/4, 739-63.
Fletcher G.P. (1976), 'The Metamorphosis of Larceny', **Harvard Law Review** 89, 469-530.
Fletcher G.P. (1978), **Rethinking Criminal Law,** Boston & Toronto, Little, Brown & Co.
Galland C. (1973), 'Introduction à la méthode de A.J. Greimas', **Etudes de théologie religieuse** 48, 35-48, translated in **The New Testament and Structuralism,** ed. A.M. Johnson, Pennsylvania, The Pickwick Press, 1976, 1-21 (Pittsburgh Theological Monograph Series, 11).
Ganz J.S. (1971), **Rules. A Systematic Study,** The Hague, Mouton.
Gardies J.-L. (1972), **Essai sur les fondements a priori de la rationalité morale et juridique,** Paris, L.G.D.J.
Ghezzi G. (1966), 'A proposito di 'strutturalismo' e di metodo dell' indagine giuridica', **Rivista trimestrale di Diritto e Procedura Civile** 20, 1411-27.
Giddens A. (1979), **Central Problems in Social Theory: Action, Structure and Contradiction in Social Analysis,** Berkeley, University of California Press.
Gil A. Hernandez (1973), **Estructuralismo y Derecho,** Madrid, Alianza Editorial.
Ginsburg M.D. (1977), 'Deep Structure of Taxation', **Yale Law Journal** 86/4, 798-806.
Giuliani A. (1970), 'La norma retorica e la logica del linguaggio normativo', **Rivista internazionale di filosofia del diritto** 47, 374-90.
Goodrich P. (1983), 'The Antinomies of Legal Theory: An Introductory Survey', **Legal Studies** 3/1, 1-20.
Goodrich P. (1983a), 'The Rise of Legal Formalism, or the Defence of Legal Faith', **Legal Studies** 3/3, 248-66.

Goodrich P. (1984), 'Rhetoric as Jurisprudence', **Oxford Journal of Legal Studies** 4/1, 88-122.
Goodrich P. (1984a), 'Law and Language: An Historical and Critical Introduction', **Journal of Law and Society** 11/2, 173-206.
Goodrich P. (1984b), 'The Role of Linguistics in Legal Analysis', **Modern Law Review** 46, 523-34.
Goodrich P. (1985), 'Language, Text and Sign in the History of Legal Doctrine', in Carzo and Jackson (1985).
Greimas A.J. (1966), **Sémantique Structurale**, Paris, Librairie Larouse.
Greimas A.J. & Rastier R. (1968), 'The Interaction of Semiotic Constraints', **Yale French Studies** 41, 86-105.
Greimas A.J. (1969), 'Eléments d'une grammaire narrative', reprinted in Greimas (1970).
Greimas A.J. (1970), **Du Sens**, Paris, Editions du Seuil.
Greimas A.J. (1971), 'Narrative Grammar: Units and Levels', **Modern Language Notes** 86, 793-806.
Greimas A.J. (1976), **Sémiotique et Sciences Sociales**, Paris, Editions du Seuil, 1976 ('Analyse sémiotique d'un discours juridique', with E. Landowski, at 79-128 = 'G/L').
Greimas A.J. (1976a), 'Pour une théorie des modalités', **Langages** 43, 90-107.
Greimas A.J. (1976b), 'Entretiens avec A.J. Greimas sur les structures élémentaires de la signification', in Nef (1976), 18-26.
Greimas A.J. (1981), 'Contre-Note', in **Le Carré Sémiotique**, ed. E. Landowski, 42-46 (**Le Bulletin du Groupe de Recherches Sémio-linguistiques**, no.17, Mars 1981).
Greimas A.J. & J. Courtés (1982), **Semiotics and Language. An Analytical Dictionary**, trld. L.Crist et al, Bloomington, Indiana University Press.
Greimas A.J. & E. Landowski (1983), 'Pragmatique et Sémiotique', **Actes Sémiotiques - Bulletin** V, 50, Paris, Groupe de Recherches Sémio-Linguistiques, E.H.E.S.S. - C.N.R.S.
Grice P. (1957), 'Meaning', **Philosophical Review** 66, 377-88.
Guastini R. (1978), 'Norberto Bobbio: analisi del linguaggio e teoria formale del diritto', **Materiali per una storia della cultura giuridica** VIII/1, 293-356; IX/2, 523-41.
Guastini R. (1983), 'Teorie delle regole costitutive', **Rivista internazionale di filosofia del diritto** 60/4, 548-64.
Guastini R. (1983a), 'Cognitivismo ludico e regole costitutive', **La teoria generale del diritto. Problemi e**

tendenze attuali. Studi dedicati a Norberto Bobbio, ed. U. Scarpelli, Milan, Comunità, 153-76.

Guest S. (1979), 'Legal Education and Legal Theory', **Current Legal Problems**, 179-97.

Guiraud P. (1971), **Le sémiologie**, Paris, P.U.F.

Haba E.P. (1972), 'Ciencia Juridica: QUE 'ciencia' ?', Universidad de Costa Rica, Faculdad de Derecho.

Haba E.P. (1978), 'Lo Racional y lo Razonable', **Revista de Filosofia, Universidad de Costa Rica** XVI/43, 1-32.

Haba E.P. (1979), 'Apuntes sobre el lenguaje juridico (II): El problema de la precision', **Rivista de ciencias juridicas** 38, 225-317.

Hacker P.M. (1969), 'Definition in Jurisprudence', **The Philosophical Quarterly** 19, 343-7.

Hacker P.M.S. (1977), 'Hart's Philosophy of Law', in **Law, Morality and Society**, ed. G.P. Baker and J. Raz, Oxford, O.U.P., 1-25.

Hanson B. (1977), **Application of Rules in New Situations, A Hermeneutical Study**, Lund, C.W.K. Gleerup.

Harari A. (1974), 'Desuetude', in **Studies in Jewish Legal History in Honour of David Daube**, ed. B.S. Jackson, London, Jewish Chronicle Publications, 101-13 (parallel edition: **Journal of Jewish Studies** 25).

Harris J.W. (1977), 'Kelsen's Concept of Authority', **The Cambridge Law Journal** 36/2, 353-63.

Harris J.W. (1979), **Law and Legal Science**, Oxford, The Clarendon Press.

Harris J.W. (1980), **Legal Philosophies**, London, Butterworths.

Harris J.W. (1981), 'A Structuralist Theory of Law: An Agnostic View', in **Sociological Approaches to Law**, ed. A. Podgorecki and C.J. Whelan, London, Croom Helm, 33-43.

Harris J.W. (1981a), 'Olivecrona on Law and Language - The Search for Legal Culture', **Tidsskrift for Rettsvitenskap** 94, 625-46.

Harris J.W. (1981b), 'Kelsen's Labyrinth of Norms - A Reply', ALSP Conference Paper, Edinburgh, 1981.

Hart H.L.A. (1949), 'The Ascription of Responsibility and Rights', **Proceedings of the Aristotelian Society** 49, 171-94.

Hart H.L.A. (1952), 'Signs and Words', **Philosophical Quarterly** 2 (1952), 59-62 (review of J. Holloway, **Language and Intelligence**).

Hart H.L.A. (1953), **Definition and Theory in Jurisprudence,**

Oxford, The Clarendon Press, reprinted in **The Law Quarterly Review** 70 (1954), 37-60, and Hart 1983:21-48.

Hart H.L.A. (1958), 'Positivism and the Separation of Law and Morals', **Harvard Law Review** 71, 593-629, reprinted in Hart 1983:49-87.

Hart H.L.A. (1961), **The Concept of Law,** Oxford, The Clarendon Press.

Hart H.L.A. (1967), 'Problems of the Philosophy of Law', **Encyclopedia of Philosophy,** London, MacMillan, VI. 264-76, reprinted in Hart 1983:88-119.

Hart H.L.A. (1983), **Essays in Jurisprudence and Philosophy,** Oxford, The Clarendon Press.

Hauriou A. (1971), 'Recherches sur une problématique et une méthodologie applicables à l'analyse des institutions politiques', **Revue de droit public et de la science politique** 87, 305-52.

Hawkes T. (1977), **Structuralism and Semiotics,** Berkeley and Los Angeles, University of California Press.

Heck P. von (1919), **Gesetzesauslegung und interessenjurisprudenz,** Tübingen, J.C.B. Mohr.

Heller T.C. (1984), 'Structuralism and Critique', **Stanford Law Review** 36/1-2, 127-98.

Hermann D. (1975), 'A Structuralist Approach to Legal Reasoning', **Southern California Law Review** 48, 1131-94.

Hervey S. (1982), **Semiotic Perspectives,** London, George Allen & Unwin.

Hohfeld W.N. (1919), **Fundamental Legal Conceptions as applied in Judicial Reasoning,** New Haven and London, Yale University Press.

Horovitz J. (1972), **Law and Logic, A Critical Account of Legal Argument,** Wien and New York, Springer Verlag.

Hutchinson A.C., 'From Cultural Construction to Historical Deconstruction', **Yale Law Journal,** forthcoming.

Jackson B.S. (1975), **Essays in Jewish and Comparative Legal History,** Leiden, E.J. Brill.

Jackson B.S. (1979), **Structuralism and Legal Theory,** Liverpool, Liverpool Polytechnic Press, Occasional Paper 20.

Jackson B.S. (1979a), 'Towards an Integrated Approach to Criminal Law: Fletcher's Rethinking Criminal Law', **The Criminal Law Review,** 621-9.

Jackson B.S. (1979b), 'The Concept of Religious Law in Judaism', **Aufstieg und Niedergang der römischen Welt,** Berlin, W. de Gruyter, 33-52.

Jackson B.S. (1980), 'Towards a Structuralist Theory of Law', **The Liverpool Law Review** 2, 5-30.

Jackson B.S. (1980a), 'Historical Aspects of Legal Drafting in the Light of Modern Theories of Cognitive Development', **International Journal of Law and Psychiatry** 3, 349-69.

Jackson B.S. (1980b), 'History, Dogmatics and **Halakhah**', in **Jewish Law in Legal History and the Modern World**, ed. B.S. Jackson, Leiden, E.J. Brill, 1-26.

Jackson B.S. (1980c), 'Modern Research in Jewish Law: Some Theoretical Issues', in **Modern Research in Jewish Law**, ed. Jackson, Leiden, Brill, 136-57.

Jackson B.S. (1981), 'On the Problem of Roman Influence on the Halakah and Normative Self-Definition in Judaism', in **Jewish and Christian Self-Definition**, ed. E.P. Sanders, London, SCM Press, II, 157-203, 357-79.

Jackson B.S. (1982), 'Structuralisme et 'sources du droit'', **Archives de Philosophie du Droit** 27, 147-60.

Jackson B.S. (1982a), 'Legal Drafting in the Ancient Near East in the Light of Modern Theories of Cognitive Development', **Mélanges à la mémoire de Marcel-Henri Prévost**, Paris, PUF, 49-66.

Jackson B.S. (1984), 'On the Tyranny of the Law', **Israel Law Review** 18/3-4, 327-47.

Jackson B.S. (1984a), 'Structuralism and the Notion of Religious Law', **Investigaciones Semioticas** 2/3 (1982-83), 1-43.

Jackson B.S. (1984b), 'The Ceremonial and the Judicial: Biblical Law as Sign and Symbol', **Journal for the Study of the Old Testament** 30, 25-50.

Jackson B.S. (1984c), 'Kelsen between Formalism and Realism', forthcoming.

Jackson B.S. (1984d), 'A Semiotic Approach to Biblical Law', paper delivered at the Third International Congress of The Jewish Law Association, to be published in the conference proceedings.

Jackson B.S. (1985), 'Dworkin on Discretion: Some Semiotic Perspectives', in Carzo and Jackson (1985).

Jakobson R. (1953), 'Results of the Conference of Anthropologists and Linguists', **International Journal of American Linguistics**, Memoir 8, Baltimore, Waverly Press, 11-21.

Jameson F. (1972), **The Prison-House of Language: A Critical Account of Structuralism and Russian**

Formalism, Princeton and London, Princeton University Press.

Jori M. (1979), 'Hart e l'analisi del linguaggio', **Materiali per una storia della cultura giuridica** IX/1, 161-228.

Jori M. (1979a), 'Definizioni e livelli di discorso giuridico', in **Definizioni Giuridiche e Ideologie**, ed. A. Belvedere, M. Jori & L. Lantella, Milan, Giuffrè, 483-530.

Jori M. (1980), **Il formalismo giuridico**, Milan, Giuffrè.

Jori M. (1985), Articles on 'Comunicazione', 'Referente', 'Segno', Semiotica', 'Significato' and 'Sistema e Discorso', **Strumenti del sapere contemporanea**, Turin, Unione Tipografico-Editrice Torinese (UTET).

Kalinowski G. (1959), 'Y a-t-il une logique juridique ?', **Logique et Analyse** 2, 48-53.

Kalinowski G. (1959a), 'Interprétation juridique et logique des propositions normatives', **Logique et Analyse** 2, 128-42.

Kalinowski G. (1964), 'Le Syllogisme d'Application du Droit', **Archives de Philosophie du Droit** 9, 273-85.

Kalinowski G. (1965), **Introduction à la logique juridique**, Paris, Presses Universitaires de France.

Kalinowski G. (1969), 'La logique des lacunes en droit', **Archives de Philosophie du Droit** 14, 353-62.

Kalinowski G. (1970), 'Le Raisonnement juridique et la logique juridique', **Logique et Analyse** 13, 3-62.

Kalinowski G. (1972), **La logique des normes**, Paris, Presses Universitaires de France.

Kalinowski G. (1972a), 'L'Axiomatisation et la formalisation de la théorie hexagonale de l'opposition de M.R. Blanché (Système B)', **Les Etudes Philosophiques** (1967), 201-9; reprinted with corrections in **Etudes de logique déontique I (1953-1969)**, Paris, L.G.D.J., 1972, 161-7.

Kalinowski G. (1972b), 'La sémantique et la pragmatique', **Archives de Philosophie** 35, 177-93.

Kalinowski G. (1972c), 'Philosophie et logique de l'interprétation en droit', **Archives de Philosophie du Droit** 17, 39-49.

Kalinowski G. (1973), 'Norms and Logic', **American Journal of Jurisprudence** 18, 165-97.

Kalinowski G. (1976), 'Un aperçu élémentaire des modalités déontiques', **Langages** 43, 10-18.

Kalinowski G. (1980), 'Une mise en question de la logique des normes', **Archives de Philosophie du Droit** 25, 345-65.

Kalinowski G. (1980a), 'Loi juridique et loi logique.

Contribution à la sémantique de la loi juridique', **Archives de Philosophie du Droit** 25, 123-36.
Kalinowski G. (1981), 'Carré sémiotique et carré logique', **Le Bulletin du Groupe de Recherches Sémio-Linguistiques (EHESS),** 17 (Mars 1981), 5-9 (**Le Carré Sémiotique,** ed. E. Landowski).
Kalinowski G. (S.J.), **La sémiotique juridique,** revised version, to appear in Spanish translation, Universidad de Carabobo, Venezuela, forthcoming.
Katz J.J. (1972), **Semantic Theory,** New York, Harper & Row.
Kelsen H. (1934), 'Zur Theorie der Interpretation', **Revue Internationale de la Théorie du Droit,** 9-17.
Kelsen H. (1945), **General Theory of Law and State,** trld. A. Wedberg, Harvard University Press.
Kelsen H. (1960), 'On the Basis of Legal Validity', trld. S. Paulson, **American Journal of Jurisprudence** 26 (1981), 178-89.
Kelsen H. (1966), 'On the Pure Theory of Law', **Israel Law Review** 1, 1-10.
Kelsen H. (1967), **The Pure Theory of Law,** trld. M. Knight, Berkeley & Los Angeles, University of California Press.
Kelsen H. (1973), **Essays in Legal and Moral Philosophy,** ed. O. Weinberger, Dordrecht, D. Reidel.
Kelsen H. (1979), **Allgemeine Theorie der Normen,** Vienna, Manzsche- und Universitätsbuchhandlung, 1979.
Kennedy D. (1979), 'The Structure of Blackstone's Commentaries', **Buffalo Law Review** 28/2, 205-382.
Kevelson R. (1977), **Inlaws/Outlaws: A Semiotics of Legal Systems,** Bloomington: Center for Language and Semiotic Studies, Peter de Ridder Press.
Kevelson R. (1981), 'Semiotics and Structures of Law', **Semiotica** 35, 183-92.
Kevelson R. (1982), 'Comparative Legal Cultures and Semiotics: An Introduction', **American Journal of Semiotics** 1/4, 63-84.
Kevelson R. (1982a), 'Language and Legal Speech Acts: Decisions', in **Linguistics and the Professions,** ed. R.J. Di Pietro, New Jersey, Ablex, 121-31.
Kevelson R. (1982b), 'Peirce as a Catalyst in Modern Legal Science: Consequences', in **Semiotics 1980,** ed. M. Hertzfeld and M.D. Lenhart, New York, Plenum, 241-54 (Proceedings of the Fifth Annual Meeting of the Semiotic Society of America).

References

Kevelson R. (1985), 'Toward a Global Perspective on Legal Semiotics', in Carzo and Jackson (1985).

Kevelson R., 'Interpretation, Freedom and Dawnings of Authority in the Law', **Semiotica,** special issue on legal semiotics, forthcoming.

Kingson C. (1976), 'Deep Structure of Taxation - Dividend Distributors', **Yale Law Journal** 85/7, 861-913.

Kingson C. (1977), 'Deep Structure of Taxation - A Reply', **Yale Law Journal** 86/4, 806-8.

Körner S. (1981), 'Uber sprachspiele und rechtliche Institutionen', **Ethics, Foundations, Problems and Applications,** Wien, Holder-Pichler-Tempsky, 480-91.

Kretzmann N. (1967), 'History of Semantics', **Encyclopedia of Philosophy,** New York, Free Press and MacMillan, VII, 358b-406a.

Kurzon D. (1984), 'Themes, hyperthemes and the discourse structure of British legal texts', **Text** 4-1/3, 31-55.

Lacambra L.L. (1973), 'Variaciones sobre estructuralismo juridico', **Anuario de Derecho Internacional Hispano-Luso Americano** 4, 629-41.

Lachmayer F. (1985), 'Norm and Interpretative Projection', in Carzo and Jackson (1985).

Lamsdorff-Galagane V. (1969), **Estructuralismo en la filosofia del derecho?,** Santiago de Compostela, Porto y Cia.

Landowski E. (1974), 'Le Langage Administratif', in **L'Administration,** ed. J. Sallois, Paris, Hachette, 358-89.

Landowski E. (1978), 'Towards a Semiotics of Scholarly Discourse', **Structuralist Review** 1, 84-91.

Landowski E. (1981), 'Etudes textuelles juridiques et politiques en France de 1975 à 1978', in **La Recherche en Sciences Humaines. Humanités, 1979-1980,** Paris, Editions du CNRS, 124-8 (with G. Kalinowski).

Landowski E. (1982 and 1984), 'Bibliographie Sémiotique', **Actes Sémiotiques-Bulletin** V,22 and VII,29, Paris, Groupe de Recherches Sémio-linguistiques, E.H.E.S.S. - C.N.R.S.

Leech G. (1974), **Semantics,** Harmondsworth, Penguin Books.

Lefebure H. (1971), **Au-delà du structuralisme,** Paris, Anthropos.

Legault G.A. (1979), 'Fonctions et structure du langage juridique', **Meta** 24/1, 18-25.

Lenoble J. & F. Ost (1981), **Droit, Mythe et Raison,** Bruxelles, Presses Universitaires des Facultés Universitaires Saint-Louis.

Lepschy G.C. (1970), **A Survey of Structural Linguistics,** London, Faber & Faber; 2nd ed. 1982, Deutsch.
Lerat P. (1983), **Sémantique Descriptive,** Paris, Hachette.
Le Roy E. (1978), 'Pour une anthropologie du droit', **Revue interdisciplinaire des études juridiques** 1, 71-100.
Le Roy E. (1981), 'Démarche systémique et analyse matricielle des rapports de l'homme à la terre en Afrique Noire', **Bulletin de Liaison de l'Equippe de Recherche en Anthropologie Juridique** 3, 75-94 (Université de Paris I - Panthéon - Sorbonne).
Le Roy E. (1984), 'Legal Paradigm and Legal Discourse: The Case of the Laws of French-speaking Black Africa', **International Journal of the Sociology of Law** 12, 1-22.
Lévi-Strauss C. (1968), **Structural Anthropology,** trld. Jacobson & Schoepf, London, Penguin Books.
Lieber F. (1880), **Legal and Political Hermeneutics,** St. Louis, F.H. Thomas & Co., 3rd ed.
Lloyd D. (1979), **Introduction to Jurisprudence,** London, Stevens & Co., 4th ed.
Logique (1969), **La logique judiciaire,** Travaux et Recherches de la Faculté de Droit et des Sciences Economiques de Paris, Paris, P.U.F.
Losano M. (1970), 'Strutturalismo e scienza giuridica contemporanea', in **Strutturalismo e scienze umane,** ed. R. Boudon, Turin, Einaudi, 183-97.
Losano M. (1981), **Forma e realtà in Kelsen,** Milan, Edizioni di comunità, 1981.
Lyons J. (1977), **Semantics,** Cambridge, Cambridge University Press, 2 vols.
Lyons J. (1981), **Language and Linguistics, An Introduction,** Cambridge etc., Cambridge University Press.
MacCormick D.N. (1973), **Law as Institutional Fact,** Edinburgh, University of Edinburgh Press, reprinted in **The Law Quarterly Review** 90 (1974), 102-29.
MacCormick D.N. (1978), **Legal Reasoning and Legal Theory,** Oxford, The Clarendon Press.
MacCormick N. (1981), **H.L.A. Hart,** London, Edward Arnold.
Mackaay E. (1979), 'Les notions floues en droit ou l'économie de l'imprécision', **Langages** 53, 33-50.
Mahillon P. (1978), 'Postface: Le role du juge dans l'interprétation', in van de Kerchove (1978), 565-78.
Malinowski B. (1923), 'The Problem of Meaning in Primitive Languages', Supplement to Ogden & Richards (1923).

Marc-Lipiansky M. (1973), **Le Structuralisme de Lévi-Strauss,** Paris, Payot.
Martino A.A. (1975), **Le Definizioni Legislativi,** Turin, Giapichelli.
Martino A.A. (1977), 'Le progettazione legislativa nell'ordinamento inquinato', **Studi parlamentari e di politica costituzionale** 10/38, 1-21.
Martino A.A. (1978), 'La formalizzazione dei sistemi normativi', in **L'informatica giuridica al servizio del Paese,** Roma, Palazzo dei Congressi (conference paper).
Martino A.A. (1979), 'Proceso Cognitivo y Modelizacion del Razonamiento Juridico', **Représentations des Connaissances et Raisonnement dans les Sciences de l'Homme,** ed. M. Borillo, Rocquencourt, Institut National de Recherche en Informatique et en Automatique, 488-99.
Martino A.A., ed. (1982), **Deontic Logic, Computational Linguistics and Legal Information Systems,** Amsterdam, New York, Oxford, North-Holland Publishing Company.
Mazzarese T. (1982), 'Metanorme e linguaggio deontico: un'analisi logica', **Materiali per una storia della cultura giuridica** XII/2, 409-45.
McIntosh S.C.R. (1982), 'Legal Hermeneutics: A Philosophical Critique', **Oklahoma Law Review** 35, 1-72.
McKnight E.V. (1978), **Meaning in Texts,** Philadelphia, Fortress Press.
Mellinkoff D. (1963), **The Language of the Law,** Boston, Little Brown.
Miaille M. (1976), **Une Introduction Critique au Droit,** Paris, Maspero.
Michaels W.B. (1979), 'Against Formalism. The Autonomous Text in Legal and Literary Interpretation', **Poetics Today** 1/1-2, 23-34.
Mimin P. (1978), **Le Style des Jugements,** Paris, Librairies Techniques.
Moerman M. (1973), 'The Use of Precedent in Natural Conversation: a Study in Practical Legal Reasoning', **Semiotica** 9, 193-218.
Moore M.S. (1981), 'The Semantics of Judging', **Southern California Law Review** 54/2, 151-294.
Morin J. (1977), 'Jurists Confront Society', **Canadian Journal of Political Science** 10/2, 426-7 (review of Arnaud 1973).
Morris C.W. (1938), 'Foundations of the Theory of Signs', **International Encyclopedia of Unified Science,** University

of Chicago Press, I, 1-59.
Morris C.W. (1971), **Writings on the General Theory of Signs,** The Hague and Paris, Mouton.
Morrison W.L. (1982), **John Austin,** Edward Arnold, Modern Jurists.
Mounin G. (1965), 'Essai sur la structuration du lexique de l'habitation', **Cahiers Lexiques** 6, 9-24.
Mounin G. (1967), 'Linguistique, structuralisme et marxisme', **La Nouvelle Critique** 7, 19-24.
Mounin G. (1970), **Introduction a la Sémiologie,** Paris, Editions du Minuit.
Mounin G. (1973), 'Postface', in Arnaud (1973).
Mounin G. (1974), 'La linguistique comme science auxiliaire dans les disciplines juridiques', **Archives de Philosophie du Droit** 19, 7-16.
Murphy W.T. & R.W. Rawlings (1981), 'After the Ancien Regime: The Writing of Judgments in the House of Lords 1979/80', **Modern Law Review** 44/6, 617-57; 45/1 (1982), 334-61.
Murray J.R. (1982), 'The Role of Analogy in Legal Reasoning', **UCLA Law Review** 29/4, 833-71.
Nef F. et al (1976), **Structures élémentaires de la signification,** Bruxelles, Editions Complexe.
Nida E.A. (1979), **Componential Analysis of Meaning. An Introduction to Semantic Structures,** The Hague, Mouton, 1979 (Approaches to Semiotics, 57).
Nino C.S. (1978), 'Some Confusions around Kelsen's Concept of Validity', **Archiv für Rechts- und Sozialphilosophie,** 357-77.
O'Barr W. (1982), **Linguistic Evidence - Language, Power and Strategy in the Courtroom,** New York, Academic Press.
Ogden C.J. & I.A. Richards (1923), **The Meaning of 'Meaning',** London, Kegan Paul.
Olivecrona K. (1962), 'Legal Language and Reality', **Essays in Honor of Roscoe Pound,** Westport Conn., Greenwood Press, 151-91.
Olivecrona K. (1971), **Law as Fact,** London, Stevens & Co., 2nd ed.
Olivecrona K. (1978), 'Bentham's Veil of Mystery', **Current Legal Problems** 31, 227-37.
Oppenheim F. (1944), 'Outline of a Logical Analysis of Law', **Philosophy of Science** 11, 142-60.
Ost F. (1978), 'L'Interprétation logique et systématique et le postulat de rationalité du législateur', in **L'Interprétation**

en Droit, ed. van de Kerchove, 97-184.
Palmer F.R. (1981), **Semantics,** Cambridge, Cambridge U.P., 2nd ed.
Papke D.R. (1980), 'Law and Literature: A Comment and Bibliography of Secondary Works', **Law Library Journal** 73, 421-37.
Parret H. (1983), **Semiotics and Pragmatics,** Amsterdam/Philadelphia, John Benjamins Publishing Company.
Paterson A.A. (1982), **The Law Lords,** London, MacMillan and SSRC.
Paulson S. (1975), 'Constraints on Legal Norms: Kelsen's View in the **Essays**', **University of Chicago Law Review** 42/4, 768-86.
Paulson S. (1978), Review of Walter, **Der Aufbau der Rechtsordnung, American Journal of Jurisprudence** 23, 224-32.
Paulson S. (1980), 'Material and Formal Authorisation in Kelsen's Pure Theory', **The Cambridge Law Journal** 39/1, 172-93.
Paulson S. (1981), 'Kelsen's Labyrinth of Norms', ALSP Conference Paper, Edinburgh 1981.
Paulson S. (1981a), 'Subsumption, Derogation and Noncontradiction in "Legal Science"', **The University of Chicago Law Review** 48/3, 802-18 (Review of Harris 1979).
Paulson S. (1981b), Review of C.Moench, **Verfassungswidriges Gesetz und Normenkontrolle, Columbia Journal of Transnational Law** 20/2, 391-99.
Paulson S. (1982), 'Stellt die 'Allgemeine Theorie der Normen' einen Bruch in Kelsens Lehre dar', **Die Reine Rechtslehre in wissenschaftlicher Diskussion,** Wien, Mazsche Verlags- und Universitätsbuchhandlung (Schriftenreihe des Hans-Kelsen Institutes, Bd. 71), 122-41.
Paulson S. (1982a), Reviews of Opalek, **Uberlegungen zu Hans Kelsens 'Allgemeine Theorie der Normen'** and Behrend, **Untersuchungen zur Stufenbaulehre Adolf Merkls und Hans Kelsen, American Journal of Jurisprudence** 27, 159-65.
Paulson S. (1983), 'On the Status of the **Lex Posterior** Derogating Rule', **The Liverpool Law Review** V/1, 5-18.
Perelman C. (1960), 'Logique formelle, logique juridique', **Logique et Analyse** 3, 226-30.

Perelman C. (1960-71), **Etudes de logique déontique,** Bruxelles, Bruylant, 4 vols.
Perelman C. (1963), **The Idea of Justice and the Problem of Argument,** trld. J. Petrie, London, Routledge & Kegan Paul.
Perelman C. (1966). 'Raisonnement juridique et logique judiciaire', **Archives de Philosophie du Droit** 11, 1-23.
Perelman C. (1967-8), 'Droit, logique et argumentation', **Revue de l'Université de Bruxelles** 20, 387-98.
Perelman C. (1968), **Le Problème des lacunes en droit,** Bruxelles, Bruylant.
Perelman C. & L. Olbrechts-Tyteca (1971), **The New Rhetoric,** trld. Weaver & Wilkinson, South Bend, Ind., University of Notre Dame Press.
Pernia Hermann P. (1977), **Sobre las posibilidades de un estudio semiologico del codigo civil Argentino,** Centro de estudios de filosofia del derecho, Universidad del Zulia.
Perrin J.-F. (1981), 'Hypothèses pour une analyse de contenu sur les décisions judiciaires de divorce', **CETEL** no.15.
Perrott D. (1980), 'Has Law a Deep Structure ? - The Origin of Fundamental Duties', in **Fundamental Duties,** ed. Lasok et al, Oxford & New York, Pergamon Press, 1-15.
Pettit P. (1972), 'Wittgenstein and the Case for Structuralism', **Journal of the British Society for Phenomenology** 3, 46-57.
Pettit P. (1975), **The Concept of Structuralism,** Dublin, Gill and Macmillan, 1975, reprinted Berkeley and Los Angeles, University of California Press, 1977.
Pintore A. (1982-3), 'Il concetto di persona giuridica nell'indirizzo filosofico analitico', **Quaderni fiorentini per la storia del pensiero giuridico moderno** 11/12, 721-76.
Pitkin H.F. (1972), **Wittgenstein and Justice,** Berkeley & Los Angeles, University of California Press.
Polacek A. (1976), **Systeme und Structuren,** Kiel.
Polacek A. (1976a), 'Marxistischer Aktivismus und der historische Prozess. Erganzungsglosse zur strukturalistischen Forschungsmethode', **Quaderni di storia** 4, 143-55.
Pollastro P. (1983), 'Fenomenologia delle regole costitutive', **Materiali per una storia della cultura giuridica** 13/1, 233-62.
Poulantzas N.A. (1965), **Nature des Choses et Droit,** Paris, L.G.D.J.
Probert W. (1972), **Law, Language and Communication,**

Springfield Illinois, Charles C. Thomas.
Radcliffe Lord (1961), **The Law and its Compass**, London, Faber and Faber.
Raz J. (1979), **The Authority of Law**, Oxford, Clarendon Press.
Raz J. (1981), 'The Purity of the Pure Theory', **Revue Internationale de Philosophie** 35/138, 441-59.
Ricoeur P. (1980), 'La grammaire narrative de Greimas', **Documents de Recherche du Groupe de Recherches Sémio-linguistiques**, E.H.E.S.S., 15.
Ricoeur P. (1981), **Hermeneutics and the Human Sciences**, ed. & trld. J.B. Thompson, Cambridge & Paris, Cambridge University Press & Maison des Sciences de l'Homme.
Robertshaw P. (1975), 'Unreasonableness and Judicial Control of Administrative Discretion: The Geology of the Chertsey Caravans Case', **Public Law**, 113-36.
Robertshaw P. (1980), 'Structuralism and Law: Some Comments', **The Liverpool Law Review** 2, 31-43.
Robertshaw P. (1981), 'Judicial Politics within the State', **International Journal of the Sociology of Law** 9, 201-24.
Robertshaw P. (1985), 'Semantic and Linguistic Aspects of Sex Discrimination Decisions - Dichotomised Woman', in Carzo and Jackson (1985).
Robertshaw P., 'Hierarchies, Metaphors and Judicial Decisions', **Semiotica**, Special issue on Legal Semiotics, forthcoming.
Ross A. (1957), 'Tu-Tu', **Harvard Law Review** 70, 812-25.
Ross A. (1958), **On Law and Justice**, London, Stevens.
Ross A. (1958a), 'Definition in Legal Language', **Logique et Analyse** 3-4, 139-49.
Ross A. (1968), **Directives and Norms**, London, Routledge & Kegan Paul.
Ross H.L. (1970), **Settled Out of Court**, Chicago, Aldine Publishing Co.
Rouland, N. (1984), 'Horizons pour l'anthropologie juridique', **Revue de la Recherche Juridique**, 339-76.
Rouland N. (1984a), 'Persistances et Invariances: Structure, Histoire, Droit', in **L'Anthropologie juridique francophone**, special issue of the **Journal of Legal Pluralism**, forthcoming.
Rutgers (1976), 'Law and Literature: A Symposium', **Rutgers Law Review** 29, 223-317.
Sampson G. (1980), **Schools of Linguistics**, London etc., Hutchinson.

Sampson G. (1980a), **Making Sense**, Oxford, Oxford U.P.
Saussure F. de (1966), **Course in General Linguistics**, trld. Baskin, London, Peter Owen (from 1916 French edition).
Sbisà M. (1980), 'Per una metodologia nella soggettività: domande post-Wittgensteiniane', **Scienze umane** 6, 153-79.
Sbisà M. & P. Fabbri (1980), 'Models (?) for a Pragmatic Analysis', Working Papers and Pre-Publications, Centro Internazionale di Semiotica e di Linguistica, Urbino, Ser. A, no. 91, slightly revised and reprinted in **Journal of Pragmatics** 4 (1981).
Sbisà M. (1982), 'Atti, effetti, ad affetti', **Grazer Linguistische Studien** 17/18, 198-219.
Sbisà M. (1983), 'Actes de Langage et (Acte d)' Enonciation', **Langages** 70, 99-106.
Sbisà M. (1983a), 'Gli atti illocutori: classificarli ?', **Comunicare nella vita quotidiana**, Bologna, Il Mulino, 49-75.
Sbriccoli M. (1973), 'Strutturalismo e storia del diritto privato', **Politica del Diritto** 4, 551-62 (review of Arnaud 1973).
Scarpelli U. (1948), 'Scienza del diritto e analisi del linguaggio', **Rivista di diritto commerciale** 46, 212-18.
Scarpelli U. (1958), 'La définition en Droit', **Logique et Analyse** 34, 127-38.
Scarpelli U. (1959), **Contributo alla semantica del linguaggio normativo**, Turin, Accademia delle scienze.
Scarpelli U. (1969), **Semantica, Morale, Diritto**, Turin, Giappichelli.
Scarpelli U. (1980), 'Teoria formale o teoria strutturale del diritto. Per la dissoluzione della metafora formalistica', **Studi in onore di Cesare Grassetti**, Milan, Giuffrè, III. 169-76.
Schaff A. (1978), **Structuralism and Marxism**, London, Pergamon Press.
Schauer F. (1982), 'An Essay on Constitutional Language', **UCLA Law Review** 29/4, 797-832.
Schiff D.N. (1982), 'Phenomenology and Jurisprudence', **The Liverpool Law Review** IV/1, 5-18.
Schreckenberger W. (1978), **Rhetorische Semiotik**, Munchen, Verlag Karl Alber.
Searle J. (1969), **Speech Acts**, Cambridge, Cambridge University Press.
Searle J.R. ed. (1971), **The Philosophy of Language**, Oxford,

Oxford University Press.

Searle J.R. (1983), **Intentionality,** Cambridge, Cambridge University Press.

Snyder F.G. (1981), 'Anthropology, Dispute Processes and Law: A Critical Introduction', **British Journal of Law and Society** 8/2, 141-80.

Sourioux J.-L. & Lerat P. (1976), **Le Langage du Droit,** Paris, P.U.F.

Sperber D. (1975), **Rethinking Symbolism,** Cambridge, Cambridge University Press.

Steiner H. (1981), 'Alida Wilson's 'Is Kelsen really a Kantian': A Comment', ALSP Conference Paper, Edinburgh 1981, forthcoming in Tur and Twining (1985).

Stewart I. (1981), 'Kelsen and the Exegetical Tradition in Jurisprudence', ALSP Conference Paper, Edinburgh, 1981, forthcoming in Tur and Twining (1985).

Strawson P.F. (1950), 'On Referring', **Mind** 59, 320-44.

Strawson P.F. (1964), 'Intention and Convention in Speech Acts', **The Philosophical Review** 73/4, 439-60.

Strömholm S. (1978), 'Legal Hermeneutics - Notes on the Early Modern Development', **Scandinavian Studies in Law,** 215-41.

Sturrock J. ed. (1979), **Structuralism and Since,** Oxford, Oxford University Press.

Sumner C. (1979), **Reading Ideologies,** London, Academic Press.

Tammelo I. (1964), 'Law, Logic and Human Communication', **Archiv für Rechts- und Sozialphilosophie** 50, 331-66.

Tarello G. (1970), 'Logica simbolica e diritto', **Rivista trimestrale di diritto e procedura civile** 24/1, 261-71.

Tarello G. (1972), 'I ragionamenti dei giuristi tra teoria logica e teoria dell'argumentazione', **Rivista trimestrale di diritto e procedura civile** 24, 394-437.

Tarello G. (1974), 'Code Civil e Regola del gioco burghese', **Sociologia del Diritto,** 143-8 (review of Arnaud 1973).

Tarello G. (1974a), **Diritto, Enunciati, Usi,** Bologna, Società Editrice il Mulino (Saggi 135).

Tarello G. (1980), **L'Interpretazione della legge,** Milan, Giuffrè.

Texas Law Review (1982), Symposium on Law and Literature, **Texas Law Review** 60/3, 373-586.

Thomas Y. (1974), 'Le langage du droit romain. Problèmes et Méthodes', **Archives de Philosophie du Droit** 19, 103-25.

Troper M. (1981), 'Kelsen, La Théorie de l'Interprétation et la Structure de l'Ordre Juridique', **Revue internationale de philosophie** 35, 518-29.

Tur R.H.S. and W.L. Twining eds. (1985), **Essays on Kelsen,** Oxford, Oxford University Press.

Tushnet M. (1983), 'Following the Rules Laid Down: A Critique of Interpretivism and Neutral Principles', **Harvard Law Review** 96/4, 781-827.

Twining W. & Miers D. (1982), **How To Do Things With Rules,** 2nd ed., London, Weidenfeld & Nicolson.

Utaker A. (1974), 'On the Binary Opposition', **Linguistics,** 73-93.

van de Kerchove M. (1978), **L'Interprétation en Droit,** Bruxelles, Facultés Universitaires Saint-Louis.

van de Kerchove M. & F. Ost (1978), 'Possibilités et Limites d'une Science du Droit', **Revue interdisciplinaire des études juridiques** 1, 1-39.

Viet J. (1965), **Les méthodes structuralistes dans les sciences sociales,** Paris & La Haye, Editions Mouton.

Villey M. (1974), 'Préface', Symposium on 'Le Langage du Droit', **Archives de Philosophie du Droit** 19, 1-5.

Vissert' Hooft H. Ph. (1982), 'On Legal Reasoning and the Concept of Practical Reason', **Rechtstheorie** 13, 269-84.

Waismann F. (1945), 'Verifiability', **Proceedings of the Aristotelian Society,** Suppl. Vol. XIX, 119-50.

Waismann F. (1965), **The Principles of Linguistic Philosophy,** ed. R. Harre, London, Macmillan.

Warat L. (1972), **Semiotica y derecho,** Buenos Aires, Eikon.

Warat L. (1976), **El Derecho y su Lenguaje,** Buenos Aires, Cooperadora de Derecho y Ciencias Sociales.

Watkin T.G. (1980), **The Nature of Law,** Amsterdam and Oxford, North-Holland Publishing Co.

Watkins C. (1970), 'Studies in Indo-European Legal Language, Institutions and Mythology', in **Indo-European and Indo-Europeans,** ed. G. Cardona, Philadelphia, University of Pennsylvania Press, 334-45.

Weinberger O. (1981), 'Logic and the Pure Theory of Law', ALSP Conference Paper, Edinburgh, 1981, forthcoming in Tur and Twining (1985).

Wilcox W.H. (1981), 'Taking a Good Look at the Bad Man's Point of View', **Cornell Law Review** 66, 1058-73.

Wilkinson P. (1981), 'A Case for the Conversational Analysis of Courtroom Interaction: some interactional dimensions of legal procedures', Oxford, Centre for Socio-Legal

Studies.

Williams G.L. (1945-46), 'Language in the Law', **The Law Quarterly Review** 61:71-86, 179-95, 293-303, 384-406; 62: 387-406.

Williams G. (1982), **Learning the Law,** London, Stevens and Sons.

Wilson A. (1981), 'Is Kelsen really a Kantian?', ALSP Conference Paper, Edinburgh 1981, forthcoming in Tur and Twining (1985).

Winner I.P. and T.G. Winner (1976), 'Semiotics of Cultural Texts', **Semiotica** 18, 101-56.

Wroblewski J. (1960), 'The Relativity of Juridical Concepts', **Oesterreichische Zeitschrift für offentliches Recht** 10, 269-82.

Wroblewski J. (1960a), 'Semantics as Applied to Legal Interpretation', **Abstracts of Contributed Papers,** 1st International Congress for Logic, Methodology and Philosophy of Science, Stanford University, 144-5.

Wroblewski J. (1963), 'Semantic Basis of the Theory of Legal Interpretation', **Logique et Analyse** 21-24, 379-416.

Wroblewski J. (1964), 'The Problem of the Meaning of the Legal Norm', **Oesterreichische Zeitschrift für offentliches Recht** 3, 253-60.

Wroblewski J. (1966), 'Normativity of Legal Science', **Logique et Analyse** 33, 60-77.

Wroblewski J. (1969), 'Legal Reasoning in Legal Interpretation', **Logique et Analyse** 45, 3-31.

Wroblewski J. (1971), 'Legal Decision and its Justification', **Logique et Analyse,** 409-19.

Wroblewski J. (1974), 'Legal Syllogism and Rationality of Judicial Decision', **Rechtstheorie** 5, 33-46.

Ziembinski Z. (1962), 'Le caractère sémantique des normes juridiques', **Logique et Analyse** 5, 54-65.

Ziembinski Z. (1969), 'Lawyers' Reasonings based on the Instrumental Nexus of Legal Norms', **Logique et Analyse** 12, 112-20.

Ziembinski Z. (1970), 'Norms of Competence and Norms of Conduct', **Archivium Iuridicum** III, 21-30.

Ziembinski Z. (1974), 'Le langage du droit et le langage juridique. Les critères de leur discernement', **Archives de Philosophie du Droit** 19, 25-31.

Ziembinski Z. (1982), 'Semiotical Plane and Sociological Plane of the Theory of Law in Poland', **Rechtstheorie** 13, 443-51.